Advertising
& Promotion

This book is dedicated to
Dulciebella Caitlin

Sara Miller McCune founded SAGE Publishing in 1965 to support the dissemination of usable knowledge and educate a global community. SAGE publishes more than 1000 journals and over 800 new books each year, spanning a wide range of subject areas. Our growing selection of library products includes archives, data, case studies and video. SAGE remains majority owned by our founder and after her lifetime will become owned by a charitable trust that secures the company's continued independence.

Los Angeles | London | New Delhi | Singapore | Washington DC | Melbourne

4th Edition

Los Angeles | London | New Delhi
Singapore | Washington DC | Melbourne

Los Angeles | London | New Delhi
Singapore | Washington DC | Melbourne

SAGE Publications Ltd
1 Oliver's Yard
55 City Road
London EC1Y 1SP

SAGE Publications Inc.
2455 Teller Road
Thousand Oaks, California 91320

SAGE Publications India Pvt Ltd
B 1/I 1 Mohan Cooperative Industrial Area
Mathura Road
New Delhi 110 044

SAGE Publications Asia-Pacific Pte Ltd
3 Church Street
#10-04 Samsung Hub
Singapore 049483

Editor: Matthew Waters
Editorial assistant: Jasleen Kaur
Production editor: Sarah Cooke
Copyeditor: Gemma Marren
Proofreader: Audrey Scriven
Indexer: Silvia Benvenuto
Marketing manager: Alison Borg
Cover design: Francis Kenney
Typeset by: C&M Digitals (P) Ltd, Chennai, India
Printed in the UK

First published 2005
Second edition published 2010
Third edition published 2015
Fourth edition published 2018

Library of Congress Control Number: 2017955134

British Library Cataloguing in Publication data

A catalogue record for this book is available from the British Library

ISBN 978-1-47399-798-1
ISBN 978-1-47399-799-8 (pbk)

At SAGE we take sustainability seriously. Most of our products are printed in the UK using FSC papers and boards. When we print overseas we ensure sustainable papers are used as measured by the PREPS grading system. We undertake an annual audit to monitor our sustainability.

CONTENTS

LIST OF PHOTOS

ABOUT THE AUTHORS

Chris Hackley was the first Chair in Marketing to be appointed at Royal Holloway University of London, in 2004. Prior to that he was head of the Marketing subject group at the University of Birmingham, UK. His PhD from Strathclyde University (AACSB), Scotland, focused on the creative development process in top advertising agencies. He teaches and researches in advertising, marketing, and consumer cultural policy. Chris has published his work in some 200 books, research articles, features, reports, conference papers and presentations. He has consulted on UK alcohol policy with the UK government Cabinet Office and the Department of Health, and with commercial organisations such as ITV, Sky Media, Channel 4 TV, New Media Group and the Huffington Post on topics including **product placement** and native advertising. Professor Hackley is a regular contributor to print and broadcast media on marketing and consumer policy topics with more than 100 media appearances and mentions. He has been interviewed on alcohol policy and media policy for BBC TV, ITV, BBC Radio 4 and Channel 4 TV, and his joint research has been mentioned in most UK national newspapers, and also in some overseas publications such as the *Melbourne Age*, *Harvard Business Review* and *The Times of India*.

Rungpaka Amy Hackley is Lecturer in Marketing at Queen Mary, University of London. Prior to that she was Lecturer in Marketing at Durham University, and before that, she lectured in marketing at the University of Surrey. Dr Hackley's teaching and research focus on advertising, branding, marketing and consumer culture theory research. Her PhD entailed a cross-cultural study of young consumers' experiences of TV product placement, and her first publication from her PhD research was the only UK paper cited by the ITV companies in their response to the UK government's first consultation on UK TV product placement regulation. She also holds a first degree in Mass Communication and a Master's in Marketing. Dr Hackley has presented her research at international conferences in Asia, North America, Australasia, Europe and the UK, and her work has been published in journals such as the *International Journal of Advertising*, *Journal of Business Research*, *Journal of Marketing Management*, *Marketing Theory*, *Asian Journal of Business* and *Proceedings of the Association for Consumer Research*, among others.

PREFACE

We are grateful to the many students, teachers, researchers and practitioners who have contributed in different ways to make this text a successful resource for courses worldwide since it was first published. The fourth edition continues the main themes of the first three. At the time the first edition was published, in 2005, the writing already seemed to be on the wall for advertising and advertising agencies. As digital media changed the world of marketing, and everything else, advertising agencies had to adapt or die. They are adapting, albeit in a business environment that now sees them competing head-on with media agencies, brand consultancies and multi-functional media content producers, all of whom want to eat the advertising agencies' breakfast by taking their core business. Digital is rapidly becoming the largest category of adspend worldwide and agencies are recruiting new skill sets from across the cultural and communication industries to adapt the creative advertising development process to multi-platform, multi-media executions. Agencies are also building strategic skills in the orchestration of campaigns that utilise multiple marketing communication specialists hired in for the job. Amidst all these strategic changes, the guiding theme of the book remains the same. This is the conviction that the foundational skills of creative advertising development continue to lie at the core of the best work in advertising and promotional communication, and across the connected marketing communication disciplines.

A second major theme also continues in the fourth edition, and this is that distinctions between the advertising and promotional disciplines are blurring in the era of convergence. New, hybrid promotional techniques are emerging that further extend advertising's logic across the promotional mix. The book therefore takes a thoroughly inclusive perspective on advertising to include any form of promotional communication whatsoever, reflecting the broadening scope and cross-disciplinary ethos of advertising work and practices. It does not include personal selling and merchandising, and therefore is not a book on marketing communications. It focuses on mediated communications, those typically construed by consumers as having a promotional motive, even if that motive may be very subtle.

One of the intentions of the book was and remains to bring out the creative/account planning perspective more strongly than is typical in managerial advertising and marketing communications texts that approach the topic from a client/account management position. In addition, it offers a broader intellectual treatment of the subject that attempts to bridge the divide between the managerially oriented texts and the socio-culturally oriented texts. In pursuing this aim the text draws on research perspectives from anthropological and sociological consumer culture research, and from media, cultural and sociological studies, as well as from management perspectives and cognitive science. The fourth edition retains this synthesis and is selectively updated with examples, new writing in each chapter to elaborate on particular themes, and new references to cutting-edge research. It aims to be a comprehensive introduction to advertising promotion for students of advertising and promotion, of marketing and all forms of marketing communication.

This text is designed as a comprehensive introduction to the subject for students of advertising and promotion, marketing, communication and management at advanced undergraduate, postgraduate and MBA levels. Publishing moves too slowly, and advertising and marketing practice too quickly, for any textbook in the area to be fully contemporary. However, the text does include numerous references to books and research papers and links to case examples so that students can follow their own lines of interest to investigate particular topics more deeply. The fourth edition is selectively updated throughout the text to include more research perspectives and an updated and broadened range of references and case examples.

Chris Hackley and Rungpaka Amy Hackley, Oxfordshire, 2017.

ONLINE RESOURCES

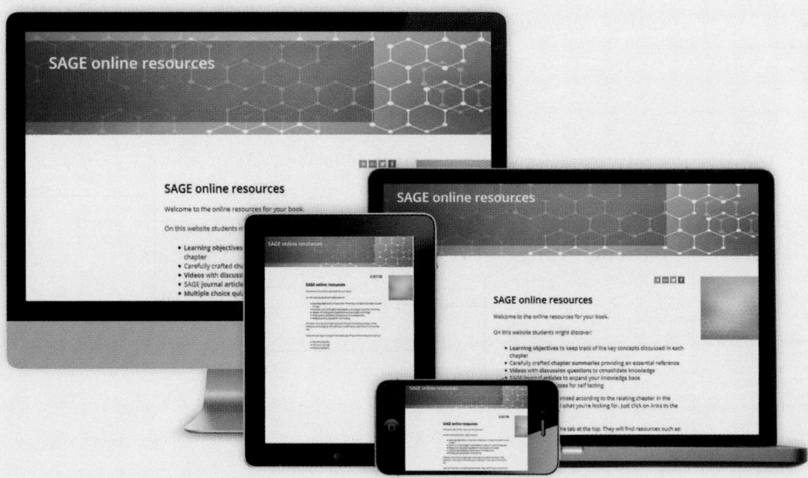

This Fourth Edition of *Advertising and Promotion* is supported by a wealth of online resources for both students and lecturers to aid study and support teaching, which are available at https://study.sagepub.com/hackley4e

FOR LECTURERS

- **Discuss** chapter by chapter examples using the **PowerPoint slides** prepared by the authors.
- **Explore** the book further with this chapter-by-chapter **Tutor Guide** that also includes exciting additional materials for teaching.

FOR STUDENTS

- Watch over 35 videos aligned with the aims of each chapter. They will help you grasp concepts quickly, digest content according to your learning style, and contextualise topics in practical, real-world examples for you to apply to coursework and exams. Each video comes with critical thinking questions to help you extend your knowledge of a topic.
- Support your reading with some extra knowledge and free open access to SAGE Journals Online. The authors have selected the articles that will help you engage with the relevant research and discussions in *Advertising and Promotion*, Fourth Edition.

- Don't just read, watch! Author Chris Hackley provides links to some of the most exciting and innovative ads and real-world examples discussed in the coming pages.
- Surf the net through these links to find relevant websites and helpful links to the industry and different agencies. Remember to reference them in assignments!

ADVERTISING AND PROMOTION UNDER CONVERGENCE

CHAPTER OUTLINE

Chapter 1 sets the scene for the fourth edition by noting the key themes of the book. It opens by outlining continuing changes taking place in the advertising environment, especially the convergence of media channels via the internet, the rise in importance of digital media for advertising, and the consequent changes in media funding models. As a result of these changes, advertising practices are also changing, with a shift in emphasis from traditional broadcast 'spot' and print display advertising towards brand storytelling, branded 'content', 'native' advertising and other forms of hybrid promotional communication designed for sharing on social media. The chapter discusses some of the major challenges facing the industry in the convergence era.

KEY CHAPTER CONTENT

Why study advertising and promotion?

The changing media landscape for advertising and promotion

The challenges posed by digital media for the advertising agency model

The blurring boundaries between advertising and promotional techniques

Studying advertising: consumer, managerial and societal perspectives

Advertising and brand symbolism

Want a primer? Go to https://study.sagepub.com/hackley4e and watch...

***Advertising and Society* to learn**
How to define advertising
How promotion differs from advertising

***Implicit Advertising* to learn**
What place advertising occupies in the new media landscape
What is shaping the media landscape
The techniques agencies and brands use to stay relevant

***Implicit Advertising (2)* to learn**
Additional techniques to exploit the area in between advertising and promotion

... to tackle the video questions at the end of the chapter.

WHY STUDY ADVERTISING AND PROMOTION?

The point of departure for this book is the advertising agency and its practices in creating the kinds of promotional communication that have become closely identified with brand marketing and consumer culture under late capitalism. In this chapter, we emphasise the uncertainty that the future holds for the agency model, but we maintain that the advertising agency remains an important institution for several reasons. Since they began as space-brokers selling classified advertising in the (then) new printed publications some 200 years ago, advertising agencies have been behind much of what passes for marketing practice today. Market research, branding, opinion polling, strategic planning and, arguably, public relations (PR) were formalised into disciplines and developed within advertising agencies. Advertising agencies worked hand-in-hand with media owners, manufacturers and other producers to develop today's promotional culture. During the post-war period, ad agencies in the UK and USA developed ever more persuasive techniques that transformed the realm of consumption (Ogilvy, 1963, 1983; Fletcher, 2008; Griffiths and Follows, 2016). They did not do so in a one-sided application of corporate power, but with the fascinated acquiescence of consumers whom the ad agencies learned to understand (Hackley, 2002). Meanwhile, the various marketing professions bureaucratised as markets grew and they developed their own professional bodies, techniques of expertise, professional examinations and career pathways. Some disciplines that had begun in ad agencies, such as media planning and buying, opinion polling and market and consumer research, were hived off to become independent businesses. Eventually, many sub-disciplinary fields of marketing and promotional communication emerged, each with their own special skill sets, agencies and career paths, such as direct mail and direct response, digital marketing, PR, packaging, sponsorship, out of home (OOH) advertising, brand consulting and more. Today, under media convergence we are seeing the circle turn and advertising agencies are once again under pressure to offer an inclusive set of skills and knowledge to brand clients who demand fully integrated campaigns across multiple media channels (Jenkins, 2008).

We do not wish to overplay the role of advertising agencies in marketing – their influence has been greatly diluted as the marketing professions have expanded in the West during the past 100 years. However, they remain a key focal point for exploring the core skills, techniques and roles of advertising and promotional communication in brand marketing. A focus on the work of advertising agencies enables us to examine not only what advertising and promotion produces and why, but also how it is produced. This is important. The working practices of advertising have been neglected both by managerial writers, who focus on the intended ends of promotional campaigns, and by cultural sociologies of advertising, which tend to focus on the outputs, the finished ads (Cronin, 2004). This book is written primarily for students on advertising and marketing-related educational courses, many of whom might have an interest in the persuasive strategies and creative techniques of advertising and promotion, but it is also written for those with a more general interest in the topic and hence it draws on a wider range of cross-disciplinary concepts and literature than is found in some managerially oriented texts.

This chapter begins with some comments about the ways in which the changing media environment under convergence are influencing changes in the practices, techniques and organisational priorities for advertising and promotion. It then goes on to introduce the three perspectives of the book. These are the managerial perspective, the consumer perspective, and the socio-cultural perspective. Advertising and promotional communication constitute a set of managerial techniques and practices designed to manage demand for brands of all kinds. It, and they, frame the contemporary consumer experience to an extent which, according to some, places the advanced economic regions of the world within a thoroughgoing promotional culture (Wernick, 1991; Davis, 2013). The three perspectives allow us to critically examine the topic from the point of view, firstly, of management who have to rationalise and justify communication strategies within organisations. In the book, we ask questions such as what discursive resources do they draw on to do this, and are some techniques more effective than others? Secondly, we take the perspective of the consumer who has always been more closely implicated in consumption practices and strategies than some theorists would allow, but now are deeply involved as production and consumption merge via the internet (Toffler, 1980) in a thoroughgoing participative economy (Jenkins, 2008). Consumers are active in co-creating consumption practices (Thompson et al., 1989; Xie et al., 2008; Pongsakornrungsilp and Schroeder, 2011; Seregina and Weijo, 2017). We do not simply passively receive advertising and promotional communication but we use it to negotiate a sense of location within the multiple branded identities offered to us by advertising (O'Donohoe, 1994; Ritson and Elliott, 1999). Astute brands and their advertising agencies do not simplistically impose their vision of the world upon consumers (Gabriel and Lang, 2008; Zwick et al., 2008). Rather, they tap into and develop and/or exploit consumer cultural myths and ideologies as Holt and Cameron (2010) demonstrate with their case analyses of Coca-Cola, Harley Davidson and many other iconic brands. Consumers can and do resist and re-frame the ideas of consumption that are presented to them in advertising by creating, in effect, consumption **sub-cultures** (Schouten and McAlexander, 1995; Kozinets, 2002; Hackley et al., 2015). Consumers are not dupes – and advertising effects are more complex than often presumed.

With these three perspectives in mind, the book aims to bring in creative and account planning perspectives that are typically excluded from both the socio-cultural work on advertising and the managerial 'marketing communications' texts, in order to re-frame the idea of a managerial treatment of the discipline.

THE CHANGING MEDIA LANDSCAPE FOR ADVERTISING AND PROMOTION

Advertising is undergoing a time of change and disruption as the industry tries to respond to new media funding models and changing patterns of media consumption. Digital is rapidly becoming the biggest category of adspend globally and advertising agencies are thinking laterally as never before to place their creative stamp on new forms of media content that add value for clients, and to retain their hard-earned position as the creative hubs of the marketing industry (Katz, 2016). The variety of creative solutions that agencies are expected to offer is greater than ever before as clients demand cross-media campaigns in many promotional genres. Social media marketing, especially, is a priority. Many brand clients expect advertising and media agencies to be able to extend creative campaigns across social media with a huge variety of media content including video, blogs, viral, advergames and more (Ashley and Tuten, 2015; Armstrong et al., 2016). As a result, agencies are hiring a wider range of creative expertise including animators, bloggers, scriptwriters, comedy teams, digital creatives and planners, film producers, app designers and model builders, in addition to the traditional two-person creative team with their skills in word-craft and visualisation. Advertising remains an exciting profession for the very dedicated but there are enormous challenges facing practitioners.

One of the key drivers of these changes is the evolution in media funding models. The somewhat mythologised creative revolution that emerged around Bill Bernbach and New York agency DDB in the 1960s occurred in the context of a traditional media-funding model. In Bernbach's day, paid-for advertising generated the revenue to fund media channels. The spot advertising paid for television or radio shows, while the classified and display advertising paid for print publications, with a small contribution from the cover charge. As circulation and viewing figures grew, so did advertising revenue. This funding model set the parameters for advertising, since advertisements had to fit particular genre conditions in order to be suitably differentiated from the editorial content in traditional media vehicles such as newspapers and commercial television or radio shows (Cook, 2001). Back in those days, the advertising agencies earned revenue from commission on the media space they bought, before their media buying departments were hived off as separate businesses. In the West, and especially in Madison Avenue, the epicentre of American advertising, the agencies grew fat on this system and the clients paid handsomely for what were seen as great creative ideas that could motivate and inspire the newly affluent consumers of the post-war period.

Today, the traditional media-funding model is no longer the natural order of things. In fact, the world of old media has been turned on its head by digital communications technology. Advertising agencies no longer earn commission on media that they buy (with their client's money). Today, advertising work is usually billed as a professional service, by the hour. The reason is that mass media has been disrupted by digital communication technology. Media consumption now often occurs via a mobile screen since consumers can access information, news, entertainment and retail choices via a smartphone or other internet-enabled mobile device (Grainge and Thompson, 2015). What is more, consumers are by no means a passive audience to the circus of brand marketing: we share, copy, discuss and critique the content we access on social media, and user-generated content (UGC) has become an important factor in advertising strategies (Berthon et al., 2008; Brodie et al., 2013). Media brands such as newspapers and TV and radio channels are struggling to generate sufficient funding through traditional spot and feature advertising sales. They have to seek new revenue streams by digitising their content, and we will discuss examples of how they are doing this throughout the book. For brand advertisers, buying traditional advertising remains as expensive as ever, but the audience reach is not what it was as

PHOTO 1 VW Bug

Image Courtesy of the Advertising Archives

Doyle Dane Bernbach of Madison Avenue, New York, produced what is regarded by some as the greatest print advertising campaign of all time when they took on the Volkswagen brief for their new Beetle model. It was the late 1950s and the American public were used to big cars. They were not used to buying cars from Germans. The People's Car was not an easy sell, but Bill Bernbach sold it using irony and self-deprecation in creative ways not seen before in American advertising. Bernbach was credited with starting a creative revolution in advertising that lasted for some twenty years.

sales of print publications, along with real-time TV and radio audiences, shrink under the huge magnitude of consumer choice in on-demand services and free-to-access online media.

Advertising agencies, then, along with brand consultants, media agencies and other emerging players, are renegotiating their relationships with the promotional industries by re-defining the practices of advertising. Hybrid forms of promotional communication that combine elements of sponsorship, advertising, advertorial, brand placement, celebrity endorsement and more are being brought within the scope of advertising campaigns, and advertising agencies are trying to broaden their skill sets to compose and orchestrate strategic campaigns that contain many elements. In addition to the 'spot' advertisement that is shared on social media, perhaps in cut-down or re-edited versions, a campaign might include brand-sponsored blogs, sponsored Facebook posts, tweets or Instagram posts, viral memes and videos, broadcasts on YouTube Channels, sponsored video blogs, sponsored sporting or entertainment and activation pop-up events, a **native advertising** feature article, or any of the many emerging forms of promotional communication. Digital promotion on social media is often linked with retail, payment and delivery by a click or two (Pantano et al., 2016; Srinivasan et al., 2016).

Spot advertising during commercial breaks on television or radio, classified and full-colour advertising spreads in press publications, OOH and cinema advertising all retain their high profile, audience reach and dramatic impact. But they are now ineluctably part of integrated, multi-media campaigns. The advertising landscape is becoming pitted with many new media vehicles as digital technology reduces start-up costs for print, internet and broadcast media. There are more magazines, television and radio channels than ever before, especially in digital formats. But the audience reach of each individual mass media vehicle has shrunk and this trend is evident all over the world as TV viewing figures and hard-copy newspaper sales plummet. These new media vehicles are not funded by the traditional model, social networking websites being the most striking example. Their business model has been to build 'traffic', that is, to elicit millions of users, without conventional advertising, and then to try to devise forms of paid-for promotion that fit the ways their users consume the service. So, for example, you have the use of algorithms that monitor Facebook users' patterns of use and target individualised promotions into their newsfeed, known as programmatic advertising. Successful bloggers who generate sufficient viewer traffic can sell advertising on their sites, as can YouTube channel owners (see Chapter 5 case study). Other digital media brands, especially news brands, are creating sponsored content that is 'native' to the page: called native advertising, it takes the conventional 'advertorial' and makes it even less easily distinguished from editorial. We will discuss all these techniques later in the book, especially in Chapter 7.

THE FRAGMENTATION OF MEDIA AUDIENCES

Media audiences are 'fragmenting' across the vastly increased choice of media outlets and platforms. Mass media cannot compete with the potential audience reach of digital media brands as viewing, listener and readership figures for traditional television, print and radio fall. For example, in the UK and the USA, some iconic newspapers established for over 100 years may cease to exist in the not-too-distant future as advertising revenue falls to unsustainable levels because of the drop in hard copy sales. Underlying the reduction in advertising revenue for traditional media, fewer consumers are paying for print media and more consumers are viewing and interacting with free-to-access media content on mobile phones, PCs, laptops and other wireless devices such as netbooks, iPads and e-book readers. What is more, even when we do encounter ads in our media consumption, we can avoid them with ad-blocking software or simply by watching on-demand video or box sets (Kelly et al., 2010).

Equally problematic for conventional advertising, the internet offers massive potential audience reach for cheaply made and easily targeted 'viral' videos and other promotional content, which cost nothing to place on video sharing websites such as YouTube but can generate great reach in 'earned' media, that is, media space that is generated because of social media sharing and is free of charge to the brand. Mass media advertising remains important for generating profile and accessing particular groups, but a large proportion of under-35s in developed economies access all their news, information and entertainment via the internet. They rarely watch live TV or buy paper publications and, therefore, they are not in the habit of regularly watching traditional spot or reading display advertising (Bassiouni and Hackley, 2014, 2016; Williams, 2016). Millennial media consumption habits are permanent – this generation will never consume media the way their parents did. The prospects for traditional mass media brands are alarming.

All these changes mean that what we understand by 'advertising' as a genre of communication is changing, and this has as yet uncertain implications for the advertising industry. Advertising has always been a fluid industry in which creative 'hot shops' and talented individuals could thrive, but the core organisational actors in the advertising environment have consistently been the major 'full-service' advertising agencies. Over nearly 200 years, since the development of mass consumption print publications in the Western world, advertising agencies have proved to be the most flexible and astute of organisational forms in adding skills and techniques to retain their central place in an evolving media environment (Lears, 1994; Nixon, 2003; McDonald and Scott, 2007). They are well used to having to explain exactly what it is they do to add value, and why the client ought to pay for that. But can they deal with the challenges of new media and the digital revolution? What will the top advertising agencies look like in 20 years? Will they still exist? Will they be hybrid media/advertising/promotion/digital agencies? Will there be fewer big agencies but hundreds of teams of specialists all working under in-house brand managers or specialist brand consultants? Will agencies re-organise to re-focus around creative, digital and integrated media planning, and strip away layers of account management? We are already seeing many of these changes come to pass. Or, on the other hand, will the big agencies expand to embrace a wider range of skills, including scriptwriters, animators, bloggers, novelists, film directors, PR and events specialists, digital creatives and more, to become all-purpose, multi-media branded content creators?

SNAPSHOT 1.1

Convergence and visual social media

In marketing, visual images are immensely powerful (Schroeder, 2002; Campbell, 2013). The truism that a picture is worth 1,000 words is borne out by the huge popularity of Instagram, Pinterest, Tumblr and many other visual social media platforms. Viral videos, infographics and other visualisations that capture a theme, meme or sentiment can be hugely powerful for advertisers. Visual imagery that is shared on social media can help advertisers in two ways. Firstly, it might incorporate the brand and act as a pseudo advertisement. For example, the 'selfie that broke Twitter' tweeted by Ellen DeGeneres at the 2013 Oscars was in effect a visual ad for the Samsung smartphone, even though the phone was not seen in the selfie. Secondly, images attract likes, shares and views that give access to a wide audience for algorithm-driven wrap-around and programmatic ads.

ADVERTISING AND BROADCAST 'MEDIA CONVERGENCE'

The convergence era is with us and, for many consumers, television, print media and radio are all accessed from one internet-enabled device (Jenkins, 2008; Meikle and Young, 2011). What convergence means is up for discussion, but, simplistically, we can take as a starting point the technological developments, and the associated economic changes, that are enabling all media to be accessed on one device and viewed via a touch-sensitive screen (Grainge and Thompson, 2015). As smartphones become cheaper and more ubiquitous, the way that many populations of the world access media is changing profoundly. The dynamics of this change are partly driven by the desire of consumers to keep up with the latest communication technologies and the huge popularity of smartphones is generating vast revenues for providers to invest in the next generation of devices (McLuhan, 1964). This is changing the dynamics of the media landscape as more specialist digital media brands emerge to devise new ways of reaching these consumers with advertising and promotional communication on digital content. As devices get more functionality and wifi availability increases, mobile advertising is becoming the new frontier for brands.

The economic impetus behind broadcast media convergence comes, then, on the one hand, from the shrinking audiences for traditional mass media, and, on the other, the vast potential for digital content to reach tens or hundreds of millions and even billions of viewers worldwide. The internet is a potent force in media and advertising because of its potentially vast audience reach and its capacity for targeting, instant response and audience measurement. Another aspect of convergence is genre confusion, where distinct media idioms seem to merge into each other. TV news, for example, once so austere and clipped with po-faced presenters speaking woodenly to avoid emotionalising the news, is now very showbusinessy indeed with star presenters, stories chosen and edited for dramatic effect, cutting-edge computer-aided graphics and pacey editing. Newsreaders, along with people from almost any other walk of life, can become celebrities through media exposure and subsequently many or most of these 'celetoids' become embroiled in marketing initiatives as brand endorsers, advertisers and spokespeople (Hesmondhalgh, 2005; Rojek, 2012). The circulation of brands and celebrity within media has accelerated as entertainment becomes an imperative for all media brands. News is sensationalised and showbusiness gossip has become news. There is a mutual need driving the coalescence of entertainment, marketing and advertising on digital media (Wolf, 2003; Hackley and Tiwsakul, 2006; Sayre, 2007). Traditional mass media brands need to find ways to access the huge audience traffic of the internet, while digital media brands sometimes need to tap into some of the impact available to traditional platforms media brands. Audiences respond to celebrity news, so media brands produce more celebrities to try to generate the viewing figures they need (Hackley and Hackley, 2015).

The implications of convergence for advertisers are profound, but there are still many obstacles to be overcome. These include the lack of common software and hardware platforms to carry video, text and audio on all mobile devices, and the fact that consumers don't really like receiving advertisements on mobile and on social media platforms. To get around the latter issue, hybrid forms of non-interruptive advertising and promotion are emerging that are integrated into the editorial media content, such as sponsored content, brand placement and brand-produced video, blogs and information.

THE CHALLENGES FOR ADVERTISING AGENCIES

The above scenario, then, could eventually result in an advertising environment quite different from any that has gone before. In the movie *Minority Report*, actor Tom Cruise walks past advertising hoardings in the street that are equipped with facial recognition software and they address him by name, suggesting brands that he might like to consume right now, presumably based on analysis of his past purchasing behaviour. This level of targeting in social media advertising may not be as effective as social media brands claim to advertisers, but it is accountable in the sense that views, clicks, likes and shares can be counted, and boardrooms around the world like to see calculations of return on investment (ROI) for marketing and advertising. Of course, these numbers do not correspond to sales, market share or revenue, but they are often used as a proxy simply because they can easily be measured. Conventional advertising, in the form of a striking 30 second television spot or stunning print display, with below-the-line support from sales promotion and/or direct mail and outdoor advertising, is not going away any time soon. But the dynamics of making money out of this communication form for brand clients and agencies are changing. Today, real-time TV audiences have dwindled since those viewers who do still watch TV can record, stream and buy on-demand service to watch their favourite shows whenever they like on mobile devices as well as on digital TVs. As a result, big televised events such as the Superbowl or the Oscars offer increasingly rare large-scale, real-time media audiences for advertisers. The attraction of live audiences of many millions is driving sports business, in particular, through bigger and bigger sponsorship and TV viewing rights deals.

As noted above, if ad agencies want to keep their place at the centre of the marketing world, they have to respond to the new reality of the convergent media environment creatively by re-organising, by evolving new skills and techniques, and by developing new ways to get business. For example, according to some visionaries, web blogs have become the most important source for new agency business, as clients and agencies struggle to find time for the traditional pitching process. Blogging has, in fact, become a key marketing strategy and many agencies have embraced this trend on their own websites (Hackley, 2009a). Many others are placing digital communication at the centre of their planning process by hiring digital account planners in response to the demand from internet providers for many forms of creative content. Still others are adapting to the logic of branding and proclaiming their ability to craft brand stories that will resonate with the relevant consumers and can be shared across social media.

Advertising agencies cannot survive without being able to offer creative digital services, but their problem is that clients do not like to pay for digital. They reason that tweets or Facebook pages are free, and even sponsored posts, programmatic advertising and SEO (search engine optimisation) don't cost very much. It isn't easy for advertising agencies (or even for specialist digital agencies) to generate revenue from original digital content. Where digital comes into its own, in the form of branded microsites, games, apps and other branded media content, it can be difficult to offer clients a clear sense of its strategic value. What is more, the 'freemium' business model so prevalent among internet brands means that consumers often resist advertising on free-to-use social media websites (Armstrong et al., 2016). Freemium refers to giving away a basic level of information and service in the hope that this will attract clients willing to pay for a higher level of service. LinkedIn, the professional networking site, is one example of this approach. Many advertising agencies themselves are using a partial freemium model by offering case studies and other information sources free of charge via their website in the hope that clients will be attracted to pay for a deeper engagement with the agency (as do many law firms, accountants and other professional services companies). Social networking sites like Facebook and YouTube have tried to get their user traffic to accept a certain level of click-through, pop-up, auto-play video or banner advertising, and increasingly they are turning to forms of 'native' advertising, that is, sponsored content that is 'native' to the page and looks much like normal, non-sponsored content.[1] The value of digital native advertising is that it is more acceptable to the media consumer because it does not disrupt the experience of viewing entertainment, reading news features, watching videos and so on, and it implicitly has some of the source credibility of editorial.

Many agencies have re-organised their account teams, for example by incorporating digital planners, or in some cases by cutting out a layer of account management. Others have crossed into new areas, for example some direct mail and direct response agencies have expanded their service offer, even producing broadcast advertising. Increasing numbers of media agencies are also trying to move into advertising. As advertising morphs into 'content' they see an opportunity to leverage their specialist expertise in media to encroach on the ad agencies' field of work. Some advertising agencies have developed new revenue streams by re-positioning themselves as ideas companies and developing creative projects as diverse as comics, movies and stage plays. There are ongoing experiments with new agency forms, such as the 'social-media' agency that attempts to handle all the brand communication via the internet.

From the client side, non-traditional styles of advertising are taking a greater share of promotional spend because of the need to engage consumers in ways that offer a more clearly defined ROI than traditional advertising. In particular, clients need their agencies to offer an integrated communications solution that offers value and impact by using different communication channels in a single campaign. For example, this may take the form of a television advertisement supported with dedicated brand microsites containing consumer forums, games, access to company information, and creating presence for the brand in other areas through media coverage, sponsorship, branded apps, direct marketing or sales promotion activities. Within the flux of change in the advertising environment, then, advertising agencies cannot be expected to be the experts in every communication channel but they are in a prime position to generate and to co-ordinate new models of creative and brand communications strategy.

SNAPSHOT 1.2

Social media brands and the dilemma of monetisation

Social media brands wrestle with the problems of generating operating revenue and profit from their audience traffic. Their offer is free to users, so why should users pay? One solution for some platforms has been the concept of freemium, which means giving away free basic content to encourage consumers to pay for enhanced services, and this has become associated with second-generation interactive services. LinkedIn, for example, the professional networking site with almost half a billion members worldwide that was acquired by Microsoft for $25 billion in 2016, utilises the freemium concept to add value to services that can only be acquired by customers paying a premium. Freemium can generate considerable audience reach through **electronic word-of-mouth (EWOM)** very quickly as new users rush to the site. The problem with this is that it can be difficult to add enough value to the basic service to encourage users to pay, if they're content with the basic service. Freemium has the obvious advantage over subscriptions in that it does not inhibit the growth of the platform as new users join. Social networking and video sharing websites, blogs and wikis exemplify web-based business concepts that are enriched by open access and free user participation. In many cases, such sites generate huge user traffic, but many (including, notoriously, Twitter) have struggled to monetise this other than by trying to get users to accept a certain amount of paid-for advertising. Twitter, founded in 2007, gained 7 million users in the USA alone in the first two years, a figure that has grown to around 320 million active users worldwide today (2017). It is a free service that generates relatively small revenues from sponsored tweets yet it was valued at $250,000,000 when it raised money in 2007, and subsequently its market capitalisation was estimated at some $35 billion before collapsing in 2016, to somewhere between $8 and $15 billion.[2] Twitter has struggled to justify its market valuation with appropriate revenues. The difficulty of translating this audience reach into large revenue streams – in other words, the problem of how to monetise audience traffic – is the key problem of internet business models. Nonetheless, having a huge active user count has a value in itself because of the segmented data this can deliver to advertisers. Facebook, with about 2 billion users, leads the way, with platforms such as Instagram (about 400 million), Google + (300 million), Pinterest, LinkedIn and Twitter following. As for traditional mass media brands such as TV shows and newspapers, they have a double problem: firstly, how to shift their resources to the internet site to make up for losses in print sales and reductions in viewing figures, and secondly, how to generate revenue from their web traffic. A small number of media brands, for example the UK newspaper site *MailOnline*, seem to have cracked this particular issue with an astute combination of sensational news coverage and showbusiness gossip that entices more than 60 million unique users per day, making *MailOnline* the world's most popular newspaper website (Hackley, 2013a).

CAN AD AGENCIES SURVIVE IN THE CONVERGENT MEDIA LANDSCAPE?

If advertising agencies are to survive into the next century, they have to engage with new client priorities and broaden their strategic and consulting skills as well as develop creative branded content, including advertising, that can translate across new media channels. Of course, it is easier to say that ad agencies need to acquire expertise in unfamiliar, non-advertising promotional disciplines, than it is for them to do so. They sit alongside other communication disciplines such as PR, sales promotion, digital and direct mail, OOH promotion, branded content and others, many of which still have their own professional routes, qualifications and skills sets. Nonetheless, difficult as it may be, the logic of media convergence dictates that the disciplines of promotional communication will also need to converge. The battle is on as to which form of agency turns out to be the most fluent at developing brand storytelling and other creative craft skills that address clients' needs for integrated campaigns. Promotional communication now often entails transmedia brand storytelling that resonates with consumers and translates across media platforms (Jenkins et al., 2013). For example, whiskey brand Jack Daniel's in its storytelling of American's hillbilly sub-culture romanticises the sub-culture of 'hooch' distilling in a small Tennessee distillery and the ideology of masculinity and anti-industrialism that it supports (see Holt and Cameron, 2010). Coca-Cola's 'Content 2020' initiative demonstrates via YouTube videos how the brand intends to develop storytelling across different forms of content into the next decade. Brand storytelling demands creative craft skills such as scriptwriting, narrative development, characterisation, screenplay development and visualisation that span analogue and digital media.

What will result from the current changes in the advertising environment is anyone's guess, but advertising agencies might well retain their importance, albeit with a very different agency model than is typical today. However, the demise of advertising agencies has been confidently predicted for some 25 years. They're still here. Since they began as brokers of classified advertising space in the early press publications, they have added many new skills and techniques such as copywriting, creative production, business strategy, brand strategy, consumer and market research and media planning. They have been at the centre of the evolution of marketing as a discipline and they remain in a positive position to continue their evolution into the new, convergent, media environment.

WHAT IS ADVERTISING?

This is a question with two possible responses – a short one and a long one. The short one is that advertising is a paid-for promotional message from an identifiable source transmitted via a communication medium. This, at least, is a typical, and typically narrow, definition of advertising that distinguishes it from the other elements of the communication mix. Advertising is conventionally seen as one sub-element of promotion, which is itself one of the four elements of the marketing mix, the others being product, place (distribution) and price. The marketing mix element of 'promotion' embraces any promotional communication, and can include advertising, public relations, personal selling, corporate communications, branded content, direct mail and direct response, point-of-sale (or point-of-purchase) and merchandising, sales promotion, exhibitions, SMS text messaging and other forms of mobile marketing, email advertising, internet banner advertising, all forms of digital execution such as websites, blogs, vlogs and video content, programmatic advertising, social media and more.

There are many forms of advertising execution, and we will explore numerous examples of these in the book. In order to create effective advertising transmitted via print in newspapers or magazines, or on OOH street billboards, on vehicles or on bus shelters, or on any other medium, ad agencies need to deploy a range of medium-specific creative craft skills. TV advertising still presents the highest profile platform for advertisers, with live sports events offering large real-time viewing audiences to advertisers. As seen in the Chapter 6 case study, one of the last major real-time TV advertising opportunities is the American football season finale, the Super Bowl. It has been reported that TV advertisers charged up to $5 million for a 30 second spot to reach the 100,000 audience.[3] Production costs can be even higher, and much thought and planning goes into making a big budget Superbowl TV ad.

Television is by no means the only medium for short advertising films – there is advertising shown in cinemas before the main feature, and, of course, advertising that is produced and aired over the internet and on video sharing websites. Then, there is advertising that integrates intertextually with TV and social media. For example, the Yeo Valley yoghurt brand created a TV ad using a specially created boy band,

'The Churned', who sang an original song in a spot during the UK TV talent show *The X Factor*. The item became a worldwide trending topic on Twitter and a viral hit on YouTube, and the song was an iTune chart hit.[4]

Forms of advertising and promotional communication such as these are very flexible and can be used for many different kinds of creative execution and many different kinds of appeal. This is where the creativity comes in, to make one ad stand out and get viewers' attention by being resonant, whether that is because it reflects an insightful truth for its audience, because it is beautifully made and diverting, or because it is funny, striking or challenging. Some advertising may be designed specifically for direct mail or direct response campaigns, while radio advertising is yet another category that demands complex and medium-specific craft skills in order to effectively reach the desired target audience and convince them to take a second look at the brand.

And that was the short answer. The longer answer will take the rest of this book to explore. There are two reasons why the longer answer is important. One is that, to most people, advertising is a word that covers any kind of promotion whatsoever. To professionals in the field, the various promotional disciplines are important because individuals might spend an entire career in one of them as a professional in, say, PR, direct mail, sales promotion, or indeed, advertising. The professionalisation of marketing and management disciplines developed in the post-war period in response to increasing gross domestic product (GDP) in the West and many, including advertising, developed their own professional trade bodies, training schemes, qualifications and scientific techniques (Davis, 2013). But the professionalisation of disciplines is driven by bureaucratic demands and the politics of organisations – for laypeople, for consumers, all promotion is advertising, of one kind or another (Percy and Elliott, 2009). That in itself isn't a good enough reason to conflate the various disciplines of promotional communication under one heading, but along with the next reason, it may be. As noted above, the media infrastructure for advertising is undergoing profound changes driven by digital communication, and this is changing the very way advertising is conceived. Advertising remains an important discipline, but integration is now the watchword, and major campaigns are now typically expected to embrace a number of different media channels, especially digital channels, with different but thematically connected creative executions. In many cases, large organisations treat the different communication disciplines as separate functions with different departments handling, say, corporate communications, direct marketing, advertising or sales. Yet in the new advertising environment, and from a management point of view, the logic of integration is compelling. Media audiences now access more media platforms than ever before, and in different proportions. Newspapers and television still retain their place in the advertising scene, but they have given up a lot of ground to the internet through social media. In response, brand clients want promotional campaigns to be integrated across media channels and across promotional sub-categories. Given the entrenched professional and organisational separation of the various marketing communication techniques and channels, the ideal of fully integrated marketing communication (IMC) management remains only partially realised. As we write, there is a shake-out going on in the promotional communication industries, which include not only advertising agencies but direct mail, sales promotion, media and branding agencies, and even creative hot shops, film studios and digital agencies. The winners will be the ones that adapt most successfully, and most profitably, to the logic of IMC.

Under the influence of IMC, advertising creative executions are changing and moving towards a broader category of 'content'. The goal is no longer only to create short-term sales but to maintain long-term brand presence and market share. Hence advertising is moving closer to publicity and entertainment as brand owners seek to activate the recognition of consumers across different media platforms in ways that are likeable, challenging and engaging, and that generate social media sharing and brand engagement (Wolf, 2003; Thielman, 2014). Brand owners want to create content that is subtly branded but that will engage consumers, whether that is in the form of a 30 second TV advertisement that is then shared on social media, or a tweet or a viral video, or a piece of branded content on YouTube, or a branded game that can be downloaded as an app on a mobile device … the list is limited only by the digital imagination, and as varied as the technology. In this book, then, the term 'advertising and promotion' is used as an umbrella category for all forms of mediated promotional communication on any media channel or platform.

BLURRING THE DEFINITIONS OF ADVERTISING AND PROMOTION

The ingenuity of advertisers and the flexibility of advertising as a communication form often render attempts to define it in one sentence trite, or tautologous. As noted in Snapshot 1.2, the internet is creating new forms of advertising that don't conform to the old definitions. Advertising often sells something, but often does not, since a great deal of advertising promotes not only branded products and services but political candidates and political parties or ideologies, public services, health and safety issues, charities or other non-profit issues. Advertising is often an impersonal communication, distinguishing it from personal selling, but there are many ads that are eye-to-eye sales pitches delivered by actors or celebrity endorsers in a mediated imitation of a personal sales encounter. Advertising is usually paid-for, appearing in a media space set apart for promotional communication. But, increasingly, as noted above, advertisements may be sponsored on social media platforms or shared because viewers actively search out advertisements they may find entertaining or amusing. In other cases, video sharing is utilised to expand the audience for the ad. For example, UK TV aired a novel ad break in which all the scheduled ads were enacted by Lego characters, as a promotion for a forthcoming *Lego* movie.[5] The ad break was posted on YouTube[6] with a view to sharing for cross-promotion of the ads, the Lego brand and the movie. This is a novel twist on advertising that is extended through social media, but, increasingly, the mass media advertising is being treated as strategically subordinate to non-advertising promotion that is implicit rather than explicit, such as sponsorship, advertainment, advergames, or product placement. Consequently, attempts to define advertising in concrete and exclusive terms are usually more notable for what they leave out than for what they include.

Advertising can sometimes be distinguished by genre elements that set it apart from other forms of mediated communication (Cook, 2001; Leiss et al., 2005; Danesi, 2006). Overheated sales pitches from improbably coiffed spokespersons, deliriously happy housewives singing irritatingly catchy jingles at the kitchen sink, unfeasibly attractive models excited by chocolate confections all spring to mind as advertising clichés. But then again, many advertisements contradict advertising stereotypes. As we have noted above, American advertising guru Bill Bernbach is credited with inventing irony in advertising in DDB's iconic Volkswagen campaign of the 1960s (see Photo 1). And many advertisements now subvert conventional genres and eschew the rhetoric of over-selling in favour of postmodern irony, understatement or narrative designed to create presence and generate word-of-mouth for the brand, as opposed to trying to sell it (Sherry, 1987; Scott, 1990, 1994a, 1994b; O'Donohoe, 1994, 1997; Tanaka, 1994). Some in the industry today feel that Bernbach's 'creative revolution' has faded away along with the *Mad Men* and the swinging sixties depicted in the hit TV series, and has been replaced by sterile business accountability, measurement and **big data** analytics. Others feel that creativity is still around in advertising, but the way it is conceived has to change along with the changes in media infrastructure. Consumers today sometimes like to be passive consumers of entertainment, but often take a much more active part in advertising campaigns, adapting, criticising, re-making, and even contributing to story development when brands crowd-source ideas. User generated content has transformed the notion of how consumers engage with advertising and marketing. The millennial consumer doesn't just sit in the back row of the movies. She and he have ideas of their own and the means to express them. In such a scenario, creativity in advertising has to be seen as something that is no longer a matter of individual creative genius, if it ever was, but as something that is collaborative, dynamic, iterative, and even participative, to suit the era of the participative economy (Jenkins, 2008).

So, a narrow definition of what advertising is can obscure consideration of what advertising does. We might categorise a given piece of communication as an advertisement in terms of its parallels with a vague and fuzzy mental prototype of what an ad should look or sound like, but the norms of advertising media, genres and payment methods are being revised by changes in the industry (see Rosch, 1977, cited in Cook, 2001: 13). Advertising may be a communication that at some level has a promotional motive, but this doesn't prepare us for all the kinds of promotional messages we are likely to encounter. Neither can it prepare us for the subtlety of motive that underlies many hybrid promotional forms, such as a post-match interview with a logo-wearing sporting star, a free download of a trial version of a new computer game, free content from a magazine's website you can download to your mobile phone, or a 'courtesy' phone call from your bank. Each can be regarded as a promotional communication, or by a lay person as, simply, a piece of advertising. Textbook definitions of advertising are being outpaced by innovations in digital communication technology and by hybrid promotional genres. A realistic study of advertising and promotion cannot hope to put all the parts in neatly labelled packages. And that is no bad thing. Advertising takes the enquirer on a journey that is all the more fascinating because it defies boundaries.

STUDYING ADVERTISING – CONSUMER, MANAGERIAL AND SOCIO-CULTURAL PERSPECTIVES

THE CONSUMER PERSPECTIVE

In this book, then, we try to take a 360 degree look at advertising and promotion by taking in three distinct perspectives: these are, the consumer perspective, the managerial perspective and the socio-cultural perspective. Advertising and promotional communication are central to the production of consumer culture (Wernick, 1991; Hirschman and Thompson, 1997; Powell, 2013). It is important for us to educate ourselves about this decidedly contemporary form of communication because of the influence it has on our lives. It is equally important to appreciate that consumers are fully integrated into the consumer culture process. The culture industry revolves around the meaning-making practice of consumers and the most successful brands use their advertising to follow the contours of consumer cultural myth and ideology (Lash and Lury, 2007; Holt and Cameron, 2010). Of course, even though the power of a single advertisement to change individual attitudes or behaviour is frequently exaggerated or misunderstood, advertising is clearly a powerful managerial tool that articulates organisational strategies. Students of business and management, and of other social science disciplines, might profit from learning something of the how and why this tool is deployed, or at least how and why it is justified in brand boardrooms and planning meetings. The managerial perspective is complementary to the consumer and socio-cultural perspectives, since our understanding of advertising is incomplete without an insight into the material conditions from which it emerged (Alvesson, 1998; McFall, 2004; Kelly et al., 2005).

As a consumer, take a moment to think about the advertisements you have seen or heard this week. At whom do you think they were aimed? What, exactly, were they trying to communicate? How did they make you feel? Did you immediately rush to buy the brand? Did you tell your friends about the ad or share it on social media? Which medium conveyed the ads? Did you see them on a passing vehicle, on outdoor poster sites, on the television, hear them on the radio, read them in the press, see them on your Twitter feed or Facebook newsfeed, or on some other website? Did you see other forms of promotion on your clothing, smell them in a promotionally enhanced shopping environment, see them on product packaging, on an air balloon in the sky or on the back of a bus ticket? It is difficult to remember more than a few of all the hundreds of promotions we experience each week, at least if we live in urban areas and have access to televisions, smartphones, tablets and computers. Advertising has become such a feature of daily life that sometimes it seems as if we hardly notice it. Advertising often seems to pervade our cultural landscape and we carry on our lives taking it for granted.

We are struck, then, when particular promotional campaigns become topics of general conversation, whether that conversation is critical or approving of the campaign. For example, Coca-Cola aired a TV ad during Super Bowl 2014[7] in which people of many ethnicities were filmed to a soundtrack of 'America the Beautiful', sung in different languages. The ad caused a storm on social media with many supporters lauding its multicultural theme, but many others claiming that it did not reflect their idea of a predominantly white, English-speaking America. Of course, this storm of controversy was the tip of an iceberg of discord around race, nationality and identity, which has been playing out in American politics, as in politics around the world, and continues to do so. At the time of writing, in mid-2017, Nike announced its first high performance sports hijab, the Nike Pro. The social media comment has included high praise for the product from Muslim sportswomen, and fierce objections from some consumers who claim they'll boycott the brand. From Nike's perspective, the sports hijab is potentially a vast and lucrative market they would be remiss to ignore, and it has apparently made the decision to engage with the cultural tensions around the hijab. Brand advertising, then, is often dismissed as a trivial, mendacious and irritating form of communication, yet there are times when it catches the cultural zeitgeist and articulates issues of social importance, and social tension, in ways that other media simply cannot do. Of course, one can ask how culturally important debates about the Coke ad or Nike's hijab are, since, ultimately, we are talking about fizzy drinks or an item of clothing. Yet, the fact that, through advertising, the business of selling fizzy drinks can become entwined with some of the most pressing social and political issues of our time says something about the cultural force of brands, and of advertising. It is at times like this we realise that advertising occupies a contradictory social space – we take it for granted, and yet it is sometimes a disruptive and incendiary form of cultural communication (Cook, 2001).

Advertising is, of course, so potent precisely because it is taken for granted. There are frequent press features that reflect our puzzled fascination with the latest iconic or controversial ad. The TV show dedicated to the funniest or most outlandish ads has become a mainstay of popular TV programming in many countries. Advertising has become part of mainstream entertainment, while entertainment media make use of advertising styles and techniques, reflecting advertising's dynamic character as a perpetually evolving form of social communication (Leiss et al., 2005). The hard-sell ads remain, but there are also new narrative advertising forms of ever-greater subtlety, variety and penetration. Sometimes, deliberately or through serendipity, these advertisements tap into and articulate acute cultural conflicts and, as Holt (2002) suggests, these can sometimes be understood as conflicts of identity. Brands tap into consumers' senses of cultural identity and it is advertising that often articulates this most powerfully, as Holt and Cameron (2010) demonstrate in many examples, from Marlboro to Harley Davidson. As consumers, we might resist the commercial pressure to express our sense of identity through branding, but it is clear that advertising can excite us with the possibility of new identities (Olsen, 2016).

SNAPSHOT 1.3

Advertising or storytelling?

The genre conventions of what an advertisement should look like are being eroded (Cook, 2001). Above, we mention Coca-Cola's 'Content 2020' initiative,[8] which was intended to express the brand's intended conceptual shift away from traditional advertising towards iterative brand storytelling on multiple platforms. Contemporary advertising often departs from the conventional sales narrative to tell a story that may be only tangentially linked to the brand. For example, UK bank Nationwide created a 2016 TV advertising campaign[9] that consisted of unknown poets reciting poems about their lives to camera in an attempt to generate a sense of authenticity for the brand and move away from advertising clichés. Such campaigns are more accurately described as media content than advertising given that they do not conform to any of the standard genre conventions of an advertisement. They tell a 'story', about the brand by inference, not necessarily in a conventional narrative arc, but in a way that is intended to engage the consumer emotionally.[10] Media content that is entertaining and engaging gets shared and discussed on social media and this gives the brand an increased share of media voice, even if the conversation isn't specifically about the brand itself. The lack of a direct and explicit product pitch lends such content a stronger sense of authenticity than a more conventional advertisement for consumers who are tired of being oversold to by overbearing brands. In another example, in mid-2013 David Beckham starred with digital reproductions of himself in a piece of promotional content for Sky Sports,[11] and he is often seen in imagery displaying brands with no overt promotional pitch. Beckham does dozens of these passive and implicit endorsements, and brands pay him handsomely merely to be seen in his blessed presence (Said, 2013: Hackley and Hackley, 2015). The lack of an overt sales orientation in advertising is designed to build goodwill, presence and authenticity for the brand, and this can translate in the long term to sustained or increased market share.

THE MANAGERIAL PERSPECTIVE

For organisational managers, advertising and promotion are seen as indispensable tools for supporting a wide variety of marketing, corporate and business objectives. There are many professionals on the client side who are deeply sceptical about the claims made for advertising as a business tool, unless they are backed up by statistical evidence of attitude change, recall, or, preferably, sales response. Brand managers are usually under pressure to account for their advertising budgets by linking them to sales or market share in the short to medium term. They often have little use for theories of advertising based on building long-term brand equity. This is understandable, because in the long term, they are in a different job, or out of a job. Many others in the marketing business feel that they have to match competitor adspend for fear of losing market share if they don't. Even though much advertising activity is driven by organisational politics and competitive neurosis, many of the world's major brands would be hard to imagine without advertising, as Holt and Cameron (2010) document (Kover and Goldberg, 1995).

Neither can it be doubted that the commercial fortunes of some brands, and in some cases the size of entire markets, have been transformed through powerful and creatively compelling advertising campaigns. Even though there are many documented advertising success stories, there are persistent questions hanging over advertising's effectiveness and the genuine return it delivers on investment. As a consequence, the advertising budget is often the first to be cut in difficult economic times and mutual insecurity can colour the relationships between clients and advertising agencies. Like a star-crossed relationship, most high volume consumer businesses can't live with advertising, and they can't survive without it.

THE MANAGERIAL USES OF ADVERTISING AND PROMOTION

Industry professionals tend to regard advertising as a necessary marketing tool that often does not deliver. It is a means of persuasively communicating with and to large numbers of customers and potential customers, along with other interested stakeholders. But advertising's ability to persuade people to buy product in the short term is often overstated. Instead, it is often used in much the same way as publicity, to generate and maintain market presence and to reassure consumers, while also reminding shareholders, employees and competitors that the brand remains salient (Ehrenberg et al., 2002).

A strategy of long-term brand building may not always grab the imagination of the brand manager who has weekly sales charts waved in his or her face at the regular board meetings, but soft sell can translate to sales simply by being remembered in the right way by enough consumers. Human beings have a short-term memory capacity of about six or seven items (psychologists call this Miller's magic number seven, after George A. Miller's theory about short-term memory). It used to be axiomatic in advertising practice that consumers would typically make a choice between three alternatives for most purchases, and the internet increased this to five. Most purchases are not researched exhaustively, so we will often choose from the brands we can recall without effort, and which are easy to find. Factor in consumer markets of many millions of people, and it seems self-evident that the most memorably, and the most persistently, advertised brands will take the top few places in the market, provided they are readily available, competitive in quality, and subjectively seen as giving value. Given the possibility that sales dynamics might conform to some degree to this kind of loose model, the aforementioned shift from advertising towards non-advertising branded content is easily explained. We should add that this 'model' of how advertising works is not one of the many that compete for space in the top journals. It is derived from informal conventional wisdom in the advertising industry and, if it has any credence, it has several implications, which we go into in the next chapter. For now, we can simply leave it as given that in spite of the multi-million dollar scientific research projects that have been conducted into how advertising 'works', there might just be a fairly prosaic general explanation for the sustained success of the top brands in each market. Having said that, this is a post-hoc explanation that explains relative market share in mature markets protected by financial barriers to entry better than it explains the success of new market entrants.

It must be acknowledged that the purposes advertising serves may differ somewhat under different economic and cultural conditions. In the USA, for example, TV advertising seems to serve its economic function to communicate offers with typically direct and forthright advertising, much of which is focused on relatively local markets.

The huge size of the country, the competitiveness of its markets compared to smaller countries such as the oligopoly-dominated UK, and the fragmented nature of its media markets frame the style and content of its advertising, Superbowl advertising being the exception (see the Chapter 6 case study). In the UK, on the other hand, TV advertising tends to be less direct and more of a soft sell: it tells branded stories, and that may be because UK consumers are already familiar with many of the offers in our oligopolistic supermarkets, we just need them to be made to seem more interesting so we'll keep buying baked beans. Another difference between the advertising markets in the UK and the USA is that state-controlled, non-commercial media outlets (mainly the BBC) occupy dominant positions in the UK media infrastructure, limiting the capacity for advertising and also perhaps limiting the capacity for consumers to tolerate it. That is not to suggest that there are no offer-based retail advertisements in the UK – there are very many, especially before Christmas (for food) and after (for holidays). We are simply suggesting that advertising, and consumers, are subject to regional variations.

The informal theory of advertising as a matter of getting into the 'evoked set' of six or seven recalled brands implies that the creative content of the ads is not necessarily of critical importance. There will always be examples of ads that capture the public imagination and build brand presence out of all proportion to their budget, and of branded content that achieves millions of social media shares in days, but these are rare. The truth is, much advertising needs only to be good enough in order to maintain market share and brand presence, and it is quite rare for entirely new brands to break into the top few places in established product or service markets because of the financial and technical barriers to entry. While all this is a simplification, it might help explain the popularity of some leading brands of fast food and household detergent whose ubiquitous advertising campaigns are often excoriated for their cliché-ridden narratives and deplorable creative standards, but they are hard to forget and they seem to play a part in the success of the brand.

THE SOCIO-CULTURAL PERSPECTIVE

The managerial perspective in advertising and promotion is not confined to profit making activities. 'Social marketing' is a genre of promotion that addresses issues of social concern, and is typically funded by charities, lobby groups, and government departments (Kotler and Roberto, 1989; Kotler and Zaltman, 1971). Many public services, charities and government departments use advertising campaigns to try to promote their causes or to change behaviour with respect to, for example, alcohol or cigarette consumption, safer driving, sexual practice, domestic violence or social prejudice towards disability or ethnicity. Social marketing, and specifically social advertising, can sometimes shout louder than commercial advertising. In terms of impact, it can do so by shocking audiences into paying attention, at least for the duration of the first ad. Social campaigns are allowed by the regulatory authorities, at least in the UK, to push the boundaries of tasteful depiction further than brand advertising, because of their ostensibly virtuous motives (also see Chapter 9). Ads on UK television depicting car crashes, child abuse and drug taking have been pretty hard-hitting, but their aims of reducing car crash injuries, reducing violent or sexual abuse of children and reducing addiction to illegal drugs are deemed by the UK advertising regulator, the Advertising Standards Authority (ASA), to be worth supporting and therefore they are allowed to be quite shocking. Whether or not shocking social advertisements are actually effective in achieving their aims, or in merely getting PR profile for the cause, is a difficult question to answer.

In some cases, social marketing and advertising have been turned to commercial use, where a brand decides that linking its values with a cause or a particular charity might help its commercial brand **positioning**. For example, Unilever's Dove brand in the UK has created a long running and successful campaign based around the idea that women are misrepresented in cosmetics and personal care products advertising. The Dove 'campaign for real beauty'[12] includes a charitable foundation supporting women's interests and promoted the idea that 'real' women need not try to conform to the idealised stereotypes of typical, photoshopped cosmetics advertising (see Chapter 10 case study).

Questions of what kinds of advertising 'work' and deliver the best value to shareholders, taxpayers and other stakeholders depend for their answer on one's perspective. But no one has a definitive answer. The effectiveness of a campaign invariably depends on many factors, including its objectives, its audience, its budget, its timing and media channel, the quality of the creative execution, and many other environmental factors such as market price and competitive behaviour. In Chapter 2 we will examine some of the many theories of advertising that have been developed to try to find answers to the question of how, and if, advertising 'works'.

ADVERTISING AND TRUTH

Advertising is regarded by many people as a communication form that is inherently deceitful and debased, and occasionally offensive. Yet, considering the tenaciousness with which corporations pursue profits, remarkably few ads tell literal untruths. Of course, some do, but most advertising satisfies typical social conventions, and regulatory requirements, of tact and truthfulness. It must be acknowledged that this may not be setting the bar high enough. What is more, advertising is particularly good at inferring, as opposed to claiming. In other words, what is not said but is hinted at in advertising can be telling. The interaction of consumers with advertising and promotional communication is usually too complex and subtle to be thought of as, simply, a matter of either fact or fiction. If an ad implies that a man's sexual attractiveness and social status will be enhanced by shaving with a Gillette razor or deodorising with Lynx body spray, surely this is merely preposterous rather than untrue? Who would possibly take such an idea seriously? To be sure, consumer perceptions and beliefs about brands are self-sustaining to some degree: we believe what we want to believe, sometimes in the face of contradictory evidence. Do smokers really cough less using low-tar cigarettes? Are we slimmer because we put calorie-free sugar substitute in our coffee? It can hardly be denied that there is an important element of wish fulfilment in what we choose to believe in advertising. The advertisers provide the suggestion, and, as consumers, we complete the gestalt. Gestalt psychology refers to the way people complete the circle of meaning from partial cues or prompts. In other words, our inference goes beyond the evidence. Advertising plays with the grey area of meaning, using implicit connotation and suggestion as well as making explicit claims (Tanaka, 1994; Cook, 2001). The socio-cultural perspective attempts to delve beneath the literal interpretation of advertising messages to access their symbolic codes and generate insight into their cultural meaning (Mick, 1986; Sherry, 1987; Danesi, 1994; McCracken, 2005).

THE SOCIAL POWER OF ADVERTISING

The nice thing about teaching advertising is that it is such an immediate part of daily experience it is relatively easy to get a sense of student engagement with the subject. Few people do not have opinions on advertisements they have seen. This can give the subject of advertising great resonance as a subject of study that is suitable for a wide variety of practical and theoretical treatments. Beyond the classroom, advertising can occasionally have an astonishing power to grasp widespread attention and, in a few celebrated cases, change entire markets. For example, the legendary 'Laundrette' ad that agency Bartle Bogle Hegarty created in the 1982 campaign for Levi's 501 jeans[13] used American provenance to revolutionise the denim jeans market in general and sales of Levi's in particular for the following decade. It has been claimed that the campaign increased sales of denim jeans by some 600%. Other campaigns have become so talked about they have changed language, for example when a campaign for Budweiser beer increased market share for the brand and earned valuable free publicity simply because they added a word ('Whassup')[14] to the vernacular of American English (and even earned a listing in *Longman's Dictionary of Contemporary English*).[15] Advertising has always had the potential to capture the popular imagination in a way that feels a very intimate part of peoples' lives. Social media now leverage this aspect of advertising, the potential to be talked about, adding an air of cultural charisma to advertising as the most enigmatic of creative industries. For example, in 2015 a picture depicting a dress the colour of which was a matter of argument became a popular social media meme. The UK-based charity, the Salvation Army, produced an anti-domestic violence social advertising campaign depicting a bruised and battered woman wearing a similar dress with the strapline, 'Why is it so hard to see black and blue?' The campaign leveraged the popularity of the meme and generated much comment and discussion in the mainstream media. An amusing social media meme and the personal tragedy of domestic violence were linked through advertising in a hugely unlikely but striking juxtaposition, illustrating the extraordinary capacity for advertising to sometimes punch above its weight in cultural significance.

Advertising and promotion, then, constitute a vivid cultural presence in capitalist economies, influencing and inter-penetrating social and cultural values. This is important – too many academic studies conceive of advertising in terms of a narrow cognitive influence on individual consumer decision making, but advertising does not exist in a cultural vacuum. It is ineluctably a form of social communication and the socio-cultural perspective draws on concepts and theories from semiotics, cultural anthropology, literary studies and sociology to try to articulate the various ways in which advertising mobilises, exploits and contributes to cultural meanings (Leiss et al., 2005). Advertising agencies know this, and most duly employ people from many disciplinary backgrounds, including cultural anthropology, ethnography and sociology, alongside history, philosophy, psychology, literature, art, aesthetics and business graduates (Hackley, 2013b).

INTERPRETING ADVERTISING: HUMOUR AND HYPERBOLE

One peculiarity of advertising is that consumers are expected to be able to distinguish between untruth and humorous hyperbole, but the advertisers make every effort to blur this distinction. This is just one reason why this sophisticated communication form is rightfully a part of literary academic study. Advertising performs an essential economic function in capitalist economies. It communicates offers to facilitate consumer choice and market competition and stimulate demand, but for it to perform this function well, it demands a relatively sophisticated level of discernment from consumers who have learned the reading strategies demanded by advertising (for example, see O'Donohoe, 1997). Advertising is rarely a significant part of the school curriculum, yet negotiating a way through the advertising landscape is important to the economic and social competence of citizens. Advertising is often accused of exploiting the vulnerable, the less educated, the very young, the very old and those with access to fewer resources. Advertising professionals are sometimes characterised as unwitting tools of capitalist domination, smoothing the way for global corporations to exploit the world's consumers. What cannot be doubted is that advertising is worth studying, for all these reasons and more, yet the ways in which advertising texts communicate are still relatively poorly understood and under-examined, especially as regards the roles of implicit meanings, such as irony and humorous hyperbole. Who can doubt that this is so at the time of writing when 'fake' news, propaganda and outright untruth dominate discussion of political advertising and promotion. There has never been so much information available to any who can use the search function on a smartphone, yet the confusion is palpable as voters try to negotiate their way through the claim, counterclaim, smear and innuendo that characterise much contemporary political advertising. Advertising has been accused by some of contributing to this confusion by normalising the crass persuasive strategies of brand advertising until voters can no longer relate to reasoned political argument.

To take a lighter example of a campaign that exploits innuendo, a long-running theme used by the male personal care brand Axe, known as Lynx in the UK, implies that men who use Lynx/Axe become instantly irresistible to women (see photo 2). The ads assume that the viewer will understand that it is all just a joke: the plots are clearly intended to be funny. Lynx is pointing at the narrative conventions of male grooming brands and laughing at them with the viewer. But the high production standards of the ads show viewers that, in fact, the marketing campaign is deadly serious. Viewers agree – Lynx is the leading brand in several male grooming product segments. Could it be that knowing the ads are not serious strengthens rather than weakens the message, that using Lynx deodorant might just make the user more sexually alluring to the woman of his dreams? According

PHOTO 2 Lynx/Axe

Image Courtesy of the Advertising Archives

Axe (branded as Lynx in the UK and Ireland, Australia and New Zealand, and China) launched a line extension of their deodorant with a TV campaign called 'Even Angels Will Fall', in 2010. With beautiful videography the films told a fantastical story of angels tempted by the man wearing Axe body spray, evoking the Biblical story of The Fall. Advertising claims that are implied rather than explicitly stated are not usually taken seriously by regulators, especially if they are preposterous. Enough men did seem to take the claims seriously enough to make Axe/Lynx the biggest men's toiletry brand in the world. In 2016 Lynx/Axe updated to a fourth-wave feminist re-brand.

to some theorists it is enough that audiences are aware of the implied message in an ad for the communication to be persuasive – they do not have to believe it. The area of implied meaning in advertising is very difficult for regulators, since this is exactly the area advertising exploits. It is conventional wisdom that 90% of face-to-face communication is dominated by implicit signals, body language, facial expression, tone, gesture and so forth. Why, then, do advertising regulators often focus on the literal message in advertisements, ignoring the other 90%?

The issue highlights the problem advertising regulation has with implicit meaning in advertising. In many cases, especially in areas of public concern such as alcohol advertising, the ASA has made judgements on the implicit meaning that could be read into advertisements, even though the explicit content of the ads did not contravene any of the ASA codes of practice. Researchers have drawn attention to the rhetorical force in advertising of what is implied rather than explicitly stated. Tanaka (1994) argues that 'covert' or implicit communication allows advertisers to make claims that they could not get away with making explicitly. The point here is that implicit communication is not accidental or incidental to advertising but a carefully considered element of advertising creative strategy. As McQuarrie and Phillips (2005) note, some advertising messages that would be illegal if verbalised can, instead, be implied visually. Crucially, researchers say that we do not have to consciously believe implied meanings in ads for them to register with us: we only have to understand what the implied message is in order for it to appear persuasive.

ADVERTISING'S CONTESTED CULTURAL STATUS

Advertising is a topic that often inflames public debate, dissent and disagreement. Advertising is blamed, by some, for many social evils. It is blamed for causing obesity, for causing anorexia, for causing bad manners, reckless driving, excessive drinking – the list is long. Yet, paradoxically, advertising is also widely regarded as trivial. It tends to occupy a lowly status in our cultural hierarchy, beneath popular art, literature, movies, even stand-up comedy performers. Yet its lowly cultural status is belied by our fascination with it. We enjoy TV shows about the funniest ads and we often talk about the latest ads in our daily conversations. Cook (2001) notes this duality about advertising's cultural status. It is regarded as both trivial and powerful, banal and sinister, amusing and degrading. Even though advertising is a familiar form of communication in developed economies, we still struggle to come to terms with its contradictions. In spite of its putative triviality, it is clearly a powerful cultural presence.

Although the level of popular interest in advertising is great, there is little consensus about its role in society. Some argue that it corrupts cultural life with its insistent, hectoring presence cajoling us to buy ever-greater quantities of goods and services. Advertising intrudes into ever more social spaces, both public and private. Many schools, especially in the USA, now accept fees to give exclusive rights to commercial organisations to advertise and sell their goods on campus. Even religious observance is not immune from advertising's influence. Advertising-style slogans in brash colours promoting religious observance can be seen outside many places of worship. Evidently, advertising influences the communication norms of the very culture of which it is part. But while some have a political objection to advertising in all its forms, many people are irritated not by advertising in general but by what they see as its excesses, whether these are to do with its ubiquity or with the offensiveness of particular creative executions. Even acknowledging advertising's unique ideological force in promoting consumerism as a lifestyle, legitimising capitalism and framing everyday experience does not necessarily imply an extreme anti-advertising stance (Williamson, 1978; Marchand, 1985; Elliott and Ritson, 1997; Wharton, 2015). Few can deny that advertising is intrinsic to the creation of wealth through capitalism. Many would argue that it has an equally significant role in the free and untrammelled expression of ideas, a socially progressive exchange of 'ideas for living', to adapt John Stuart Mill's phrase.[16] In the USA, advertising is protected under the first amendment of the constitution as a branch of free speech. Of course, there are also counter-arguments that position advertising at the nexus of a capitalist system of domination that commodifies social relations and stifles human creativity rather than articulating it (Lash and Lury, 2007; Davis, 2013).

Even for many who accept the economic inevitability of advertising, though, its forms and styles provide particular sources of annoyance. 'Pop-up' internet ads, autoplay videos, programmatic algorithms that link ads to our social media browsing, uninvited SMS texts and email 'spam' are a continuing irritation for many internet users. Unwanted junk mail annoys millions of householders daily. Roadside poster sites are sometimes accused of polluting the urban environment or even of distracting drivers and causing road accidents. Even conventional spot advertising is intolerable to many people because of its 'interruptive' nature – it interrupts the flow of the entertainment or news programming we were watching. Consumers go to some lengths to avoid advertising interrupting their enjoyment of media. In addition to intruding on our private time and visual amenity, advertising can be a source of ethical transgression. Organisations are often accused of using advertising unethically for commercial advantage. There is persistent criticism of advertising's effect on children's health and moral development, a topic discussed at greater length in Chapter 9. The rise of 'pester power' as a marketing technique and the distortion of childhood values into those of adults are two of the trends that ad agencies have been accused of initiating, or at least exploiting. All these issues reflect concern with the social responsibility, ethics and regulation of advertising.

The diversity of views advertising attracts reflects its role at the centre of what Wernick (1991) called 'promotional culture' (see also Davis, 2013; Powell, 2013). Within promotional culture, we grow accustomed to spending significant sums of money on items that are not essential for survival. We associate happiness with consumption, indeed, in many ways we define our existence in terms of consumption. As advertising and promotion make continuous consumption of inessential branded items a culturally normalised practice, other competing cultural values that encourage abstention from consumption are relatively reduced in status. Today, at least in advanced economies, over-indulgence is the norm and waste is everywhere, in spite of powerful movements against environmental waste and resistant to the global dominance of consumer culture. Changes in cultural norms and practices of consumption in some countries (such as, in the UK, the relative decline of families eating home-cooked meals together at a set time) to some extent may reflect the influence of promotional culture. Deeply held values and practices are undermined and finally overthrown, partly, though not entirely, under the influence of advertising. Advertising's apparent triviality as a sub-category of popular art should not distract us from its profound cultural influence in framing and changing, as well as reflecting, the way we live.

According to some critics, advertising offers the illusion that one can live 'the good life' by buying material goods (Belk and Pollay, 1985a). Yet advertising is also an easy target to blame for the weaknesses that have characterised humanity since its beginnings. Advertising and promotion are, in the end, necessary to economic growth, wealth creation, and consumer choice. How we manage the advertising that we make and see has deep implications for the wider world in which we live and it is incumbent on consumers, managers, advertising practitioners and policy makers to have a better understanding of the ways in which advertising wields its influence, in order to make informed choices about advertising policy, regulation and practice. Advertising is both a managerial discipline with profound implications for the wider economy and for the general standard of living, and (arguably) one of the most far-reaching cultural forces of our time.

THE ROLE OF ADVERTISING IN BRAND MARKETING

It is important to appreciate advertising's place within an inter-connected tissue of mediated communication. Marketing communications in general, and advertising in particular, are sometimes seen as the major source of competitive advantage in consumer markets (Shimp, 2009). Other elements of the marketing mix occur prior to promotional communication, yet it is the communication that stamps the brand identity on a market. In a world of near-instant communication and rapid technology transfer, it is difficult for brand owners to police their global intellectual copyright. The brand has to stand out as a communication, so that consumers will recognise it and actively seek it out for the symbolic values it represents (Gardner and Levy, 1955). In this way, successful branding creates a quasi-monopoly and a basis for earning what economists call 'supernormal' (i.e. higher) profits. In a sense, it is a mere tautology to draw an equivalence between the most successful brands and their promotion. It makes sense for the most successful mass-market brands to protect their market share by spending more on advertising than rivals can afford. Coca-Cola, for example, seems to owe much of its success to its advertising (Holt and Cameron, 2010). Much of the advertising paid for by major brands is not about persuading individuals to buy, but it is about building a market presence and, in the case of some iconic brands, a cultural presence (Holt, 2004). Many people have never owned a Mercedes, shaved with Gillette, or walked in Jimmy Choos, but many of those people would be able to describe the brand values if asked, and they might buy it if they had the means to do so. All the totality of communication about and around a brand informs the cultural meaning of that brand for both consumers and non-consumers.

Brand management is a painstaking art and attention to detail is often paramount for brand management. Decisions on pricing, design, packaging, distribution outlet and even raw materials are often taken with one eye on the brand's core values and how these might be perceived in the light of media coverage of the brand. As we note, the term media coverage now includes citizen journalism, internet publications, weblogs, video blogging, chatrooms, Facebook pages and scores of other social media forums, as well as copy produced by professional journalists for established print publications, band blogs or other digital publications. It is an overstatement to argue that communication is all there is to brand marketing, but it is a truism that advertising and marketing communications have assumed a key importance in the destiny of brands and their producing organisations (but see Wells, 1975; Schultz et al., 1993).

Advertising alone does not make the brand but the successful consumer brand is, nevertheless, closely identified with its portrayal in advertising and other marketing communications media. The brand 'image' and its symbolism have come to represent dynamic and enduring sources of consumer interest (and company revenue) that brand management are keen to try to shape or control (Levy, 1959; Ogilvy, 1983). Marketing communications do not simply portray brands: they constitute those brands in the sense that the meaning of the brand cannot be properly understood in separation from the consumer perceptions of its brand name, logo, advertising, media editorial, its portrayal in entertainment shows, peer comment on social media and the other communications associated with it. Whether brand A is better designed, more attractive, easier to use, or more useful than brand B is frequently something that cannot be decided finally and objectively. It is usually, to some degree, a matter of opinion. This is where advertising acquires its suggestive power. It occupies a realm in which consumers are actively seeking suggestions to layer consumption with new social significance. Advertisers offer us this symbolic material. As consumers we are not passive dupes being taken in by exaggerated claims, we are complicit in our own exploitation. We get something out of being sold intangible dreams and unrealisable fantasies. We find that life becomes more interesting when our choice of deodorant or sugar substitute becomes a statement of personal identity and lifestyle aspiration. We must do.

FUNCTIONALITY, SYMBOLISM AND THE SOCIAL POWER OF BRANDS

In order to understand the role of advertising in brand marketing it is important to focus not only on the promotional sales message but also on the symbolic meanings incorporated into the brand (Gardner and Levy, 1955; Levy, 1959; Mick and Buhl, 1982; Belk, 1988). Brands have functionality – they do something for consumers, they solve problems. They also have a symbolism that is largely articulated through advertising and promotion. Brands communicate symbolically in the sense that they are signs or combinations of signs (words, music, colours, logos, packaging design, and so on) that convey abstract values and ideas. For consumers, the world of marketing is a kaleidoscope of communication, the component parts of which are impossible to disentangle. When commentators say that marketing, and marketing communications, are inseparable, they are making an important point (Schultz et al., 1993: 46; Leiss et al., 2005; Shimp, 2009: 4). Every aspect of marketing management (price, distribution, product design) can carry powerfully suggestive symbolism. In an important sense, consumers occupy a symbolic economy in which the meaning of symbols is negotiated and traded through a mediated market. Marketing in general can be understood as the management of meaning, and marketing meanings are mobilised primarily through advertising and promotion, in all their forms (McCracken, 1987, 1990).

Anthropologists have long noted the importance of ownership and display of prized items for signifying social identity and status in non-consumer societies. In economically advanced societies, brands take this role as a 'cultural resource' that enables and extends social communication (Holt, 2002: 87; see also Belk, 1988; Elliott and Wattanasuwan, 1998; McCracken, 2005). The influence of brands is such that even resistance to brands has become a defining social position. The 'social power' of brands refers to the meaning that goes beyond functionality and is a symbolic reference point among consumers and non-consumers alike (Feldwick, 2002: 11). This symbolic meaning is powerfully framed by advertising and sustained through other forms of communication such as word-of-mouth, public relations, product and brand placement in entertainment media, sponsorship and package design, and through the brand's presence in social media.

Those marketing professionals more concerned with logistics, supply chain management, order fulfilment, customer service operations, quality management, production engineering and the many other concrete and prosaic activities that bring products and service to the market might not experience marketing in such terms on a daily basis. Brands are material entities and they have functional attributes. But they operate in a consumer plane in which the functional and the symbolic interpenetrate. We might convince ourselves that our purchases are based on a cold-eyed appraisal of a brand's material and functional qualities, but the market dominance of some brands over other, equally functional but less symbolically resonant ones, tells a different story. One marketing legend holds that Pepsi consistently beats Coke in blind taste tests. Whether or not this is true in all cases, it articulates the truism that a brand is far more than a tangible product.

The functionality of a brand, then, refers to what it does: the symbolism of a brand refers to what it means. One is not necessarily implied in the other. Advertising and promotion are central to the creation and maintenance of the wider symbolic meaning of brands. This wider meaning can give brands a cultural presence that goes beyond purchase and ownership. Brands such as Marlboro, Mercedes-Benz, Gucci, Prada and Rolls-Royce have powerful significance for non-consumers as well as for consumers. Branded items are recognised, and they carry a promise of quality and value. But the symbolic meaning the brand may have for friends, acquaintances and strangers cannot be discounted as a factor in its appeal. For example, a simple item of clothing such as a shirt will sell in far greater numbers if it is bedecked with a logo that confers a symbolic meaning on that item. Wearing a branded shirt, as opposed to an unbranded one, can be said to confer a symbolic status on the wearer because of the values of affluence and social privilege and taste the brand represents (Schor, 1998: 47, cited in Szmigin, 2003: 139). As with implied meaning in advertisements, we may be fully aware that this, seen literally, may be a risible or preposterous notion, but that does not necessarily undermine the communicative force of the brand's symbolism. Brands have a cultural resonance that is not limited to their materiality (Schroeder and Salzer-Morling, 2005; Danesi, 2006: Campbell, 2013).

Marketing is replete with symbolism in many forms. Marketing activities of all kinds can be seen to combine signs that resonate with cultural meanings (Williamson, 1978; Umiker-Sebeok, 1987; Barthes, 2000). The futuristic design of a Dyson vacuum cleaner or the clean, aesthetic lines of an iPod have the powerful appeal of implied values that are very important to the consumer. A Rolex watch might be a well-made jewellery item with time-keeping utility but the Rolex brand is best known as an ostentatious symbol of wealth. Rodeo Drive in Beverly Hills, California, Madison Avenue, New York, and Knightsbridge, London, are home to many designer stores because these locations have become culturally identified with prestige retail outlets. The location and architecture of the retail outlet, as well as the price, can often carry a powerful symbolism for the brands.

BRANDS AND INTEGRATED MARKETING COMMUNICATION

Many other aspects of organisational activity not usually categorised as communication can carry particular meanings. Perhaps the most visible aspects of commercial communication for consumers are advertisements placed in **above-the-line** media such as TV, outdoor, the press, cinema or commercial radio. But organisations know that consumers' experience of brands is integrated in a powerful sense: consumers will not normally distinguish between different communication channels when they think of a brand or an organisation. So, organisations need to be conscious of the way that their various communications can be interpreted and of how consistent these interpretations may be with those from other communication sources. This is the logic of the IMC process (Schultz et al., 1993).

For example, as consumers encounter corporate communications through vehicle liveries, letterhead design, corporate advertising, staff uniforms, telephone conversations with organisational staff and press coverage of the organisation's activities, they will assimilate these experiences into their overall understanding of the brand. They will also assimilate news coverage, social media chatter, blog comment, press and PR and any number of other sources into their aggregated idea of a brand. Corporate identity is a distinct field of research and practice but much of its importance lies in the connection consumers make between corporations and their brands in an IMC landscape (Melewar and Wooldridge, 2001). More broadly still, in advanced economies, marketing activity can lie behind a huge majority of the images we see. The ways in which we interpret, understand and use them are central to our experience of marketing and consumption (Schroeder, 2002). In a promotional culture media brands interpenetrate each other and commercial logic permeates media content. It is in this multi-dimensional mediascape that brand managers have to try to maintain some kind of stability of meaning for their brands. Social media have facilitated consumer activism and engagement around brands as never before, and control over the brand image is now a highly nuanced and iterative process. To this end, the integration of different but thematically linked brand communications across a number of media channels is now a default position for most promotional campaigns.

There are yet more subtle dimensions of communication to consider. In the Veblen effect ([1899] 1970), demand for a product reacts inversely with price changes. Price signifies the quality positioning of the brand and this can be an important influence on demand for very expensive, prestige items. Although it is anti-competitive for manufacturers to enforce prices on retailers, nonetheless many brand owners do not like to have their product discounted because of the potential threat to consumers' perceptions of quality. The high price of prestige brands is an essential part of their brand positioning, although, increasingly, even prestige brands are broadening their markets by supplying stock of slightly inferior quality for 'discount' outlets.

The architecture and floor design of retail stores can also carry heavy signification. In the early 1900s US department store retailers were well aware of the power of impressive architecture in creating environments that inspired consumers to consume (Marchand, 1998). The interior design of retail outlets is also a powerful signifier in the marketing process. Retail organisations often commission detailed research into in-store consumer behaviour in order to help the design to cohere with the brand image of the store and to enhance sales per square foot of floorspace. For some fashion retail brands, such as the currently fading clothes brand Abercrombie and Fitch, every detail, from the volume of in-store music (60 decibels) to the look of the 'models' (i.e. retail assistants), is part of the brand symbolism.

As consumers, then, we understand brands holistically by assimilating meanings from many diverse channels of communication. Media editorial, direct mail shots, customer service encounters, television and press advertising and retail store displays, brand logos, social media and website news and opinion, product design and price relative to competition all converge to inform the consumer's understanding of a given brand. Include word-of-mouth and personal experience of brand usage, and it becomes clear that we cannot normally remember which particular communication or experience was significant in forming our enduring impression of a particular brand. Brands subsist symbolically as a nebulous and mutable, yet enduring, memory of many kinds of consumer experience. Brands have a tangible, concrete reality, of course; they are created through human and technological processes, they require resources and they usually (though not always, as in the case of virtual corporations) occupy office or factory space. But, most importantly, a brand also has a secret life, as symbolic abstraction. This abstraction, sometimes called the brand image, in ad man David Ogilvy's (1983) term, acts in concert with its more tangible dimensions to frame and support the overall idea of that brand.

The integrated perspective of this book does not intend to conflate disciplines or media channels that are, rightly, considered by managers to be separate and distinct. Rather, it acknowledges the blurring and convergence of communication media sources in consumers' outlook. It also acknowledges that communications act interdependently: ideas can be reinforced through more than one channel, providing more than one route to consumer activation. The assimilation of brand advertising and marketing into mainstream entertainment media, discussed in detail in Chapter 6, is perhaps the most telling aspect of marketing in the era of media convergence (Hackley, 2003a, 2013a).

CHAPTER SUMMARY

This chapter has discussed some broad themes of the book and outlined some of the major changes taking place in the global advertising environment. These changes are behind a radical shift in advertising management as advertising agencies try to think of process innovations and try to acquire the new skill sets that will keep them at the centre of the brand and marketing communications world amidst stiff competition from other media, branding, content marketing and many other agency specialists who have their eye on the ad agencies' turf. The changes they face focus around the impact of social media, mobile devices and the convergence of media channels via the internet, and the accompanying changes in media consumption patterns. Consumers are drifting away from traditional mass media, and newspapers, magazines, TV and radio channels are all trying to develop new business models based around web presence and digital communication. Advertising isn't going away, but what we understand as advertising is broadening as many hybrid forms of promotional communication emerge on social media. The chapter also discussed general issues of advertising concerning its economic, social and business function. Finally, the chapter looked at the nature of brands and the importance of advertising and promotion in framing brand symbolism. Now the topic has been introduced, Chapter 2 will look at the long history of theorising about advertising.

REVIEW QUESTIONS

1. Make a list of all the forms of advertising and promotion that you have encountered or heard of in the last month. Does the list surprise you? Can you think of any social spaces that have not yet been exploited by advertisers?
2. After reading this chapter, has your view of advertising's social role changed? Make a list of arguments in favour of advertising and contrast it with a list of arguments against advertising. Convene a study group to discuss their implications: can the opposing viewpoints be reconciled?
3. List all the communication sources you can think of that might potentially influence your perception of a brand. Can you think of ways in which your perception of three brands has been so influenced? In your view, which communications channel was most influential in forming your impression of the brand? Why was this?
4. Gather all the promotional material you can for two brands. What meanings do you feel are implied by the imagery, the typography and the other features of these promotions? Could the meanings be interpreted differently by different people?

VIDEO QUESTIONS

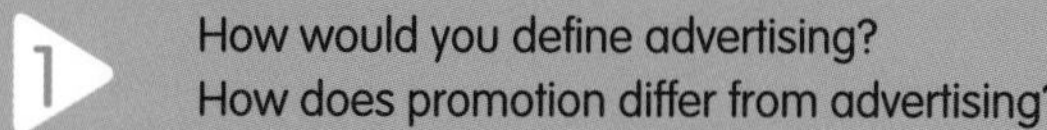

1 How would you define advertising?
How does promotion differ from advertising?

2 What does the new media landscape look like in terms of advertising?
What factors are responsible for the changing media landscape?
How do the advertising agency model and brands respond to these changes?

3 What other techniques and examples can you think of where the line between advertising and prmotion has been blurred?

CASE STUDY

A Rose by Any Other Name – is all video content, advertising?

Video content in general seems to have particular force as an advertising medium on social media. It can be a powerful way for brands to reach new audiences and connect more authentically with existing consumers. A short film that is shared on social media can become a resonant piece of brand publicity that is enjoyed for its own sake, with concomitant benefits accruing to the brand in the form of share of media voice, market presence and brand salience for existing consumers. In late 2016 BMW launched *The Escape*[17] co-starring Dakota Fanning and Clive Owen, as an homage to its industry-changing movie series of some 15 years before, called *The Hire*. *The Escape* is a short but stunning action film, which happens to also star the new BMW 5 Series. In effect, it is a product placement opportunity with full creative control. It was launched without a major publicity drive on the BMW website and YouTube channel, and has accumulated some 6 million views in four months at the time of writing. *The Hire*, directed by Guy Ritchie in 2001, entailed pop star Madonna being driven erratically to a gig by the aforementioned Owen. Made with Hollywood production standards, Hollywood stars and a budget to match, these movies generate a lot of trade press and fan comment, and extend the brand creatively in imaginative ways. BMW, the car manufacturer, is now in effect a sponsor of the movie arts, a major player in action films, and, most importantly, a generous provider of visual entertainment to millions who might never own one of the cars. From a strategic marketing perspective, the exposure in a self-made movie must compare well with, for example, exposure in a Bond movie (in which BMW cars have been historically well represented) but with the added benefit of total creative control.

In 2012, Jaguar got into the movie business to accompany the launch of its new F Type model in 2012. The F Type was Jaguar's first new sports car in 50 years, according to *Advertising Age*. *Desire* starred *Homeland* actor Damian Lewis and the plot revolved around a car chase through a Chilean desert. To top off the tie-ins, Lana Del Ray, no slouch in viral marketing herself, released a new song to go with the movie. Ms Del Ray, or Ms Grant, as she was formerly known, launched her career with a huge YouTube hit. *Desire* airs through video sharing on social media, principally YouTube, and, as with the BMW movies, the plot includes no product promotion at all, other than the presence of the car as the real star.

In an example of video content of a different style, pop star Miley Cyrus created a huge media splash with a clip of a performance at the 2013 VMA awards show that went viral and turned Miley, formerly widely known by the name of her TV character Hannah Montana, into a global star. This kind of content is very much a marketing entity – it was carefully staged and planned, and the clip was soon followed by a record release that rode to number 1 on the publicity wave. The Miley video clip was voted top content of 2013 by the Huffington Post UK and Ogilvy PR.[18]

Video content generates 'earned' media (as opposed to bought advertising spots) through social media shares. This is valuable to brands because it reflects genuine consumer engagement (though not, necessarily, sales). The logic is often that a brand can earn favour with its audiences and cultural 'share of voice' by giving away entertaining stuff for free. At its best, video content evinces all the things great advertising should be about. It's a blank slate, or a blank screen, waiting to activate consumers through great writing, creativity, wit, technical adroitness, visual and musical imagination, and spectacle. The fact that video content is not an advertisement, as such, adds authenticity to its creative appeal. Video content has to be regarded by audiences as credible and resonant, and if it is, then this reflects positively on the brand.

The examples above refer to free-standing narratives that share a style and imagery that resonate with the brand. They might also be regarded as iterations in the brand story in new narrative forms. As such, they could be seen as a reflection of the influence of transmedia storytelling, a narrative technique that has migrated from the movie business into marketing and advertising (Pratten, 2015). Transmedia storytelling normally refers to developments or chapters of one story that are told across different media channels. However, brand stories that are not connected to each other narratively are connected by the brand. Each story is a chapter in the brand story.

Case questions

1. List all the examples of branded video content your group can think of. Which do you feel were commercially more effective? Why?
2. Social media shares have become more than merely an extension of viewing or reader figures for an advertisement, but a proxy for consumer engagement. In what ways do you feel that social media shares of video content might reflect benefits to brands?
3. Bought media space refers to advertising space that has been paid for by the brand. Earned media space refers to social media shares of a piece of promotional content, such as a video clip. Compare and contrast the benefits to advertisers of bought media space and earned media space.
4. Design a concept for a social networking website. How would you make your concept popular, and, if you were successful in building significant traffic, how do you think you could monetise that traffic ('by selling the site to Google' isn't an acceptable answer).

USEFUL JOURNAL ARTICLES

(These Sage articles can be accessed on the companion website.)

Ciochetto, L. (2011) 'Advertising and value formation: the power of multinational companies', *Current Sociology*, 59 (2): 173–85.

Cronin, A.M. (2004) 'Currencies of commercial exchange: advertising agencies and the promotional imperative', *Journal of Consumer Culture*, 4 (November): 339–60.

Hsu, S.Y. and Barker, G.G. (2013) 'Individualism and collectivism in Chinese and American television advertising', *International Communication Gazette*, 75 (8): 695–714.

Kilbourne, W.E. (2004) 'Sustainable communication and the dominant social paradigm: can they be integrated?', *Marketing Theory*, 4 (September): 187–208.

O'Donohoe, S. (2001) 'Living with ambivalence: attitudes to advertising in postmodern times', *Marketing Theory*, 1 (March): 91–108.

Stuhlfaut, M.W. and Davis, C. (2010) 'The teaching of advertising management: essential, elective, or extraneous', *Journalism & Mass Communication Educator*, 65 (3–4): 265–82.

FURTHER READING

Dholakia, N. (2012) 'Being critical in marketing studies: the imperative of macro perspectives', *Journal of Macromarketing*, 32 (2): 220–5.

Hackley, C. (ed.) (2009) *Advertising*. Sage 'Library in Marketing'. London: Sage. 3 volumes: Volume 1: *Advertising Management*; Volume 2: *Advertising Culture*; Volume 3: *Advertising Science*.

Hackley, C. (2013) *Marketing in Context: Setting the Scene*. Basingstoke: Palgrave Macmillan.

Jenkins, H. (2008) *Convergence Culture: Where Old and New Media Collide*. New York: New York University Press.

O'Reilly, D. (2006) 'Commentary: branding ideology', *Marketing Theory*, 6 (2): 263–71.

Powell, H. (ed.) (2013) *Promotional Culture in an Era of Convergence*. Abingdon: Taylor and Francis.

NOTES

1 'Ask the Pro: what is native advertising and is it effective?', www.youtube.com/watch?v=az3vifgUvBQ (accessed 28 March 2017) see also Steve Payne, 'Your simple guide to the native age', 23 February 2015, www.huffingtonpost.co.uk/2013/10/21/guide-to-the-native-age_n_4136861.html (accessed 27 March 2017).

2 Douglas A. McIntyre, 'Twitter market value tops Target and CBS', 31 January 2014, http://247wallst.com/media/2014/01/31/twitter-market-value-tops-target-and-cbs/ (accessed 8 February 2017); Vikram Nagarkar, 'Why Twitter has lost nearly half its market cap since IPO', 3 February 2015, www.thestreet.com/story/13032325/1/why-twitter-has-lost-nearly-half-its-market-cap-since-ipo.html (accessed 29 March 2017).

3 Chris Woodyard, 'Super Bowl ad costs soar — but so does buzz', *USA Today*, 7 February 2016, www.usatoday.com/story/money/2016/02/07/super-bowl-ad-costs-soar----but-so-does-buzz/79903058/ (accessed 10 July 2017).

4 Ian Burrell, 'If you want to watch X Factor ... You'll have to watch The Churned', 10 October 2011, www.independent.co.uk/arts-entertainment/tv/news/if-you-want-to-watch-x-factor-youll-have-to-watch-the-churned-2368637.html (accessed 19 March 2017).

5 Mark Sweeney, 'The Lego Movie rebuilds ITV ad break', 7 February 2014, www.theguardian.com/media/2014/feb/07/lego-movie-itv-ad-break-lenny-henry (accessed 8 February 2017).

6 *The Lego Movie* ad break, www.youtube.com/watch?v=HSbYBzUEQlc (accessed 8 February 2017).

7 Patrick Kevin Day, 'Coca-Cola Super Bowl ad stirs controversy,' 3 February 2014, www.latimes.com/entertainment/tv/showtracker/la-et-st-coca-cola-super-bowl-ad-stirs-controversy-20140203,0,1361331.story#axzz2sbl6JaIo (accessed 6 February 2017).

8 'Coca-Cola Content 2020', www.youtube.com/watch?v=LerdMmWjU_E (accessed 28 March 2017).

9 Tom Connelley, 'Nationwide calls on poets to relay the "Voice the People" in new campaign', 14 September 2016, www.thedrum.com/news/2016/09/14/nationwide-calls-poets-relay-the-voice-the-people-new-campaign (accessed 28 March 2017).

10 www.nationwide.co.uk/voices (accessed 6 July 2017).

11 'Watch new David Beckham ad for H&M as Lisbon is turned into city full of Becks clones', 28 January 2016, www.dailyrecord.co.uk/entertainment/celebrity/watch-new-david-beckham-ad-7262659 (accessed 6 July 2017).

12 About Dove, www.dove.us/social-mission/campaign-for-real-beauty.aspx (accessed 29 March 2017).

13 Levi's 'Laundrette' ad, www.youtube.com/watch?v=wT4DR_ae_4o (accessed 2 February 2017).

14 Budweiser 'Wassup' ad, www.youtube.com/watch?v=UDTZCgsZGeA (accessed 4 February 2014).

15 *Longman Dictionary*, 'wassup', www.ldoceonline.com/dictionary/wassup (accessed 5 February 2014).

16 Mill, John Stuart (1869) *On Liberty*. London: Longman, Roberts & Green; Bartleby.com (1999) www.bartleby.com/130/ (accessed 8 February 2014).

17 BMW Films, *The Escape*, www.youtube.com/watch?v=jzUFCQ-P1Zg (accessed 26 March 2017).

18 'From Miley Cyrus to the Snowden Files – the best content of 2013', 23 January 2014, www.huffingtonpost.co.uk/2013/12/11/best-of-2013_n_4425766.html (accessed 28 March 2017).

ADVERTISING THEORY

CHAPTER OUTLINE

This chapter is concerned mainly with theories that attempt to explain the influence advertising and promotional communication may have over consumers' attitudes and behaviour. The chapter opens with a discussion of the uses of theory. It then outlines three overlapping traditions of advertising theory. These are 1) managerial theories that originated from advertising practice, 2) academic theories from communication and psychology research that were imported into advertising practice, and finally 3) academic theories that have been largely dawn from sociology, literary studies and cultural anthropology to try to explain advertising from a broader perspective. The chapter highlights some of the continuing contradictions raised by advertising theories as they play out both in academic research and professional practice.

KEY CHAPTER CONTENT

Why theorise advertising and promotion?

Practice-based advertising theory

Cognitive information processing theory in advertising

Socio-cultural theory in advertising

Levels of explanation in advertising theory – cognitive, social and cultural

Want a primer? Go to https://study.sagepub.com/hackley4e and watch...

Campaign Principles **to learn**
How the different advertising theories impact on the message and form of delivery

The New Frontier of Digital **to learn**
About the impact on advertising of the death of the USP

Foods and Brands that Matter **to learn**
How relevant the AIDA model is to the media landscape today

Implicit Advertising **to learn**
What polysemy is, how it looks in advertising and explore your own examples of this and intertextuality

... to tackle the video questions at the end of the chapter.

WHY THEORISE ADVERTISING AND PROMOTION?

Marketing textbooks are replete with theories, but practitioners seldom find them useful when describing their work (Ardley, 2008; Ardley and Quinn, 2014). Advertising is no different – practitioners typically articulate and construct their experience of their work in their own words without recourse to theoretical ideas (Hackley, 2000; Svensson, 2007). However, this does not mean that theory is unimportant in practical settings, and nor does it mean that it serves no purpose. Far from it. There are two reasons why theory is important in organisations. The first is that we cannot do without it. We need theories as rules of thumb to frame policies and actions. We might not be very good at articulating them, but marketing policy can often be said to be based on implicit theory (Hackley, 1999a). Advertising can be understood as a field of applied human science, since it involves implicit predictions about the ways in which humans will react in their behaviour to external stimuli (that is, to advertising and promotional communication). Even if actions are not based explicitly on theoretical assumptions, it does not mean they are not there (Kover, 1995; Hackley, 2003b). For example, a director of creativity (DOC) might say that they 'like' a particular scene in a proposed ad – but what they are really saying is that they think the target consumers will like it. But how does the DOC know the consumers will like it? Presumably, the DOC is making a prediction based on his or her accumulated experience and professional judgement, and that is enough for most practitioners (and, to be fair, all they usually have time for). But if the practitioner was an academic, they might have the time to think about the implicit assumptions they are making about the target audience and its reaction to the communication, and to apply some research studies to try to gain some more explicit and evidence-based understanding of the mechanisms involved. Of course, there is a great deal of research that goes on in advertising for this very purpose, when time and budgets permit (as we discuss at greater length in Chapter 10).

The second reason why theory is important, linked to the first, is that theory is a source of power. Management and marketing in general are largely constructed through words, with help from numbers, in reports, presentations, charts, meetings, arguments, negotiations, strategy documents and so on (Brown, 2005). Actions and strategies have to be argued for, applied, explained, tested and justified. The winner of the argument gets to have their ideas put into action. Whoever can control which theory is deemed credible in an organisation, and which theory is deemed suspect, can influence decisions on policy. This is the case in advertising agencies no less than in any other type of organisation, whether a social services unit, manufacturing plant, a psychological therapy agency, a political party, a school, or a university (Cook and Kover, 1998). Theory is used to justify certain courses of action over alternatives – theory acts as a discursive resource to be drawn upon to win arguments (Burr, 1995; Berger and Luckman, 1966; Billig, 1996). There may not always be a very accurate match between the theoretical justification and what is actually done in certain organisations, but that doesn't necessarily matter – theory is political. Once the argument is won, it's all over. Of course, in engineering, physics and chemistry it is pretty important for the theory to match up with what is done in its name, otherwise bridges will fall down, satellite rockets will malfunction and drugs won't do as doctors wish. In issues of strategy and policy, though, it is a different matter. For example, prevailing theories of education become more or less highly regarded over time but, regardless, schools still function, and pupils still graduate. Similarly, theories of domestic or international political policy, of psychological therapy, even of economic policy management are in constant competition as some are discredited and others become popular for a time. Yet, politicians still make policies, therapeutic psychologists still practise, and economists still earn a lot of money. The kinds of theories such professionals use may be very different. A politician might be wedded to free trade and market liberalism, or alternatively to socialist policy and collectivism, and these theories would be used to justify their policy prescriptions. A psychologist might prefer person-centred therapy or perhaps Cognitive Behavioural Therapy, and an economist might be a Monetarist or a Keynesian. The theories people espouse don't necessarily reflect their day-to-day behaviour, because everyday decision making tends to be pragmatic and easily changed. The point is, if professionals espoused no theories at all, they probably wouldn't win many arguments.

This isn't a whimsical point. Marketing in general can be seen as a rhetorical enterprise in which those with the most powerful arguments, and the most persuasive ways of expressing them, win the day (Tonks, 2002; Miles, 2013, 2014, 2015; Nilsson, 2015). Advertising is a field particularly engaged with theory and theories are often used as resources through which interested individuals and organisations stake claims and negotiate a sense of professional identity (Case, 1999; Hackley, 2003c). Which theory gains currency at a particular time wins resources and taps into revenue streams for consulting, training, book sales and more. For the fortunate individuals espousing the right theory at the right time, promotion might be won.

Take, for example, **neuromarketing** (Lee et al., 2012). This has become very popular among global brand conglomerates, many of whom have bought **magnetic resonance imaging** (MRI) scanners and hired teams of neuroscientists to operate them. Neuroimaging can help management make policy decisions by, for example, comparing the central nervous system response of a consumer to alternative advertising images to see which image excites the most positive neurobiological reaction. The idea is that our consumption decisions are motivated to some degree by unconscious, physiological and neurological responses to marketing initiatives such as advertisements, packaging, taste, or product design. Brain scans can tell the neuroscientist whether the response is greater between alternative stimuli. Some might argue that as human beings we are capable of overriding our neurological impulses with emotion and reasoning, and if this is the case, then some of the great expense and time taken to develop neuromarketing might not be fruitful. Again, it doesn't necessarily matter. The science is generating investment and jobs, and it can be used to justify policy decisions in organisations, even if some astute senior managers might sometimes use the science to justify their hunch.

So, theory is important, even for managers who claim that they have no interest in it. Economist John Maynard Keynes made this point when he suggested that politicians are usually more influenced by economic theorists than they realise. Marketing and advertising professionals, too, often fail to recognise the historical antecedents of their contemporary professional practices, or, technology notwithstanding, there is little that is really new in marketing (Bartels, 1988; Brown, 1995; Jones and Tadajewski, 2015; Tadajewski and Jones, 2016). For practical people, the term 'in theory' is often used in a pejorative sense to refer to ideas that are seen as irrelevant, impractical or obscure. But theory can be viewed as a form of everyday understanding that allows us a sense of control over our world and, sometimes, helps us to predict outcomes based on previous experience, or evidence-based assumptions. Rudimentary theories allow us to understand our world in ways that are not possible if we are solely concerned with concrete experience.

THEORIES, MODELS AND RULES-OF-THUMB

The terms theory and model are misused a lot in marketing studies, and we will not try to put that right here. What a theory is and which theory is better has been debated intensively and continues to be so both in academia and in practice (see, for a small example of discussions, Anderson, 1983; Arndt, 1985; Belk, 1986; Bartels, 1988; Hunt, 1991, 1992; Wilkie and Moore, 2003; Brown, 1996, 1997; Brownlie et al., 1999; Baker, 2000; Arnould and Thompson, 2005; Tadajewski and Saren, 2008). In advertising, and marketing more generally, there are ideas that are regarded as basic theories but which would not stand up as social science theories because they are based on experience rather than evidence. Theories such as AIDA (Attention–Interest–Desire–Action, see below) in advertising, or, in marketing, the marketing concept, the product life cycle, portfolio analysis and so on act as rules of thumb or practical heuristics (Hackley, 2009a). More formal social scientific theories, such as theories of attention, perception or behavioural intention are sometimes used as a basis for research in advertising (Ajzen, 2002).

There is no shortage of disagreement about theory in marketing and advertising. In advertising practice, for example, there can be enormous tension between quantitative research findings, which often guide clients' decisions, and the more qualitative forms of understanding, which often guide the work of creatives and planners (as we discuss in Chapters 4, 5 and 10). For our present purposes, we will treat theories, or models, as devices that, on the face of it, enable some degree of informal explanation and prediction. We all live by implicit theories: knowing that rain gets you wet therefore you should put on a coat before you leave the house may strike you as obvious, but it involves an abstraction from particular experiences of getting wet and it informs our behaviour. It may not be as complex as a theory of relativity but it is the kind of theorising that most of us are familiar with. Practical theory guides behaviour and action in the workplace even though it may be implicit rather than explicit. Noted advertising man turned academic Arthur Kover (1995) studied the implicit theories of communication used by creative professionals in New York advertising agencies. They each had their own implicit theory of communication and this guided their problem solving strategies in addressing creative briefs. In another study account team professionals in London agencies worked to differing implicit models of the consumer (Hackley, 2003b). These models implied quite different ways of understanding, and therefore of communicating with, consumers.

Theorising informally allows us to use our imagination to move from the concrete to the abstract and to attempt to generalise from the particular. We can compare and combine ideas and speculate on new ways of understanding the world. Our understanding of any social phenomenon requires some theoretical dimension in order to raise it beyond the trivial. For example, one can say without fear of contradiction that books are made up of printed words, but to compare different books and to offer views on their qualities one has to invoke informal theories of literary criticism on matters of, say, prose style ('this book is well written'), theories of narrative ('the plot was exciting') or theories of dramatic characterisation ('the characters were not believable'). We have an opinion of what constitutes good writing or effective characterisation even though we may not be at all familiar with the intellectual traditions of literary criticism. Theory does not necessarily have to be complex, and neither does it have to be divorced from everyday understanding.

Advertising is perhaps the management sub-discipline that has made most use of academic theory in its practices (Cornellisen and Lock, 2002). Advertising lends itself to theoretical treatments as applied psychology (Strong, 1929; Dichter, 1949; Packard, 1957; Heath, 2012; Hackley, 2013b), or cultural anthropology (Sherry, 1987), semiotics (Mick, 1986; Umiker-Sebeok, 1987), visual aesthetics (Scott, 1994b; Schroeder, 2002), literature (Stern, 1993b) or, indeed, as a number of other disciplines. As we shall see in this chapter, academic theory in advertising has drawn on the disciplines of cognitive and social psychology, sociology, anthropology, cybernetics, mathematics, communication science and literary theory, to name just a few. In this book, then, theory is not considered as a byword for obscurity, irrelevance or unnecessary abstraction. At a rudimentary but decidedly non-trivial level it simply allows us to articulate the world in ways that go beyond the unimportant or the obvious. In more complex analyses, theory allows us to achieve a more nuanced understanding of how different phenomena are connected.

DIFFERENT STAKEHOLDERS IN ADVERTISING THEORY

As we note above, theory is political in the sense that, in organisations, knowledge is power. But, knowledge is invariably contested, therefore, it is truer to say that what counts as knowledge is power. Clients would like proof that their investment in advertising gives them a good return, and they are not always convinced when advertising agencies claim to have proof (Ewing and Jones, 1990). Ad agency account planners would like theories that give them strategic insights into consumers' deep motivations, passions, fears and fantasies (Holbrook and Hirschman, 1982; Hackley, 2003b; Feldwick, 2007; Griffiths and Follows, 2016). Agency creatives would like theories that show why their idea should get made – they feel that their experience, intuition and talent are more effective than any theory (Hackley, 2000; Gilmore et al., 2011). Yet, creatives have theories too, even if they don't acknowledge them as such (Kover, 1995, 1996; Hackley and Kover, 2007). Regulators, consumer groups and policy makers would like theories that help them to understand the effect advertising has on socially problematic phenomena such as drinking alcohol or eating healthily (Hackley et al., 2015). There is no shortage of theoretical perspectives that some would tout as the solution to all these questions.

Unfortunately for all these stakeholders, advertising remains an enigma in spite of its 100-year history of practice, thought, theory and research. As consumers, we often disagree with our friends about what advertising means, what it does, or how it does it. From the practitioner side, too, there are stark disagreements about how, and indeed if, advertising 'works' (see Vakratsas and Ambler, 1999; Heath and Feldwick, 2008; Hackley, 2010); in what ways it influences consumers (or doesn't) (Ehrenberg et al., 2002); what role creativity plays in effective advertising (Smith and Yang, 2004), how advertising planning should be crafted for best effect (Rossiter et al., 1991), and on which advertising agency philosophy is most effective (West, 1993). The best that advertising agencies can do is to write up case studies of their campaigns to show how their clients' objectives were achieved through the agency's work, although even though many case studies are highly detailed they usually amount to circumstantial evidence rather than scientific proof. Spending money on advertising and promotion remains, to some extent, a leap of faith for clients, even in the era of programmatic advertising and big data.

The advertising industry has enjoyed global growth and influence on a huge scale in spite of uncertainty about its theoretical foundations. It is unrealistic to seek a general theory of advertising, given the complexity of this communication form. Advertising is many things and it 'works' in many ways (Feldwick, 2015). Advertising has to serve many stakeholders, including main board executives, shareholders, advertising agencies, consumers, regulators, governments and citizens. It is applied in many different situations. As a communication form it is complex, since it can combine music, visual imagery and written or spoken words in a huge variety of narrative forms and on a wide range of media channels (Umiker-Sebeok, 1987; Scott, 1990, 1994b; Schroeder, 2002). Even tiny elements of an advertisement, such as the choice of font, the colour of a background, or the intonation with which an actor recites a script, could potentially influence the interpretation of that communication. Advertising speaks to a huge variety of different demographic, ethnic, national, socio-economic and sub-cultural groups. Theories serve different vested interests, depending on what they want to say about advertising – that it sells product, that it doesn't, that it operates on consumers in unethical ways, that it doesn't, that it causes social ills, or that it doesn't, and so on. Theory is essential to understanding, but it is equally essential that we understand the limitations of theory.

Agencies are always looking for a competitive edge and theory often lends itself to claims that one agency can deliver better value for the client's advertising budget. Cornelissen and Lock (2002) have argued that theoretical developments in advertising do influence practice, not always by changing it but by supplying new conceptual vocabularies to articulate practice. For their part, agencies are quick to latch on to the latest buzzy concept, whether that is account planning, semiotics, **psychographics**, programmatic advertising, influencer marketing, buzz, viral, context marketing or another, to help convince clients that they, unlike other agencies, have the inside track on how advertising works (Danesi, 1994; Sawchuck, 1995; Hackley, 2003f, 2003g; Danesi, 2006).

PHOTO 3 Strand Cigarettes

Image Courtesy of the Advertising Archives

The 1959 TV, cinema and print campaign for Strand Cigarettes, called You're Never Alone With a Strand, was an astonishing success in every respect but one. People didn't buy the cigarettes. The background instrumental to the TV ad, The Lonely Man Theme, became a UK chart hit and the actor in the ads, Terence Brook, became a star. The creative execution might have been evocative and slick but it lacked a coherent strategy. The TV ad showed a man lighting up alone at night on London Bridge. But people want brands that make help them attract friends and admirers. The campaign became a notorious failure and the brand was subsequently withdrawn.

SNAPSHOT 2.1

How do advertisements convey meaning?

For McCracken (2005), marketing is the art of managing meaning. Ask any three people what they think about a particular promotional communication, and you may well get three different interpretations. This presents both a problem and an opportunity for advertisers. The problem arises if they want to be certain that everyone in their target audience will take exactly the same meaning from a given advertisement. This is very difficult to do without reducing an advertisement to a very unappealing instruction. For example, the words 'Buy Shoes from Smith's Shoe Shop' on an otherwise blank poster are probably quite difficult to interpret in any way other than as an exhortation to buy the shoes provided by Smith's, but they are hardly striking or persuasive. On the other hand, in a more creative communication consisting of, say, a picture and some metaphorical language, there is likely to be scope for **polysemy**, that is, a range of different possible interpretations (Bengsston, 2002; Puntoni et al., 2010; Scott, 2012). Advertisers can play with polysemy to get their audience to engage in the game of interpretation, but it is important that the team working on the ad thoroughly understand their target consumers and pay great attention to detail, or it can all go wrong.

One historical example of an advertisement that was interpreted in an unexpected way concerned a UK campaign for Strand Cigarettes, in 1960 (see Photo 3). The ads featured an actor alone on London Bridge at night, mock heroically lighting up a Strand cigarette to the accompanying strapline, 'You're never alone with a Strand'.[1] The ad was hugely popular but the sales were weak because consumers felt that the brand was targeted at lonely people. Today, there are many creative executions that generate complaints and are rapidly withdrawn, in spite of the layers of quality control that apply before major brands allow their ads to be launched. For example, in early 2017, Airbnb withdrew and apologised about a series of OOH ads in San Francisco, USA, that struck the wrong tone in suggesting that the accommodation agency should not be charged hotel taxes. In another example, during the TV coverage of the 2015 American Superbowl, insurance company Nationwide aired a poignant ad about a boy who drowned in the bath to highlight the dangers to children of preventable accidents. The brand, no doubt, wanted to strike a tone of sober authenticity amidst the Superbowl party atmosphere, but viewers felt that the ad was morbid and exploitative and the company's Chief Marketing Officer (CMO) soon left his job. Machines are little better at managing the meaning of ads – there are countless examples of algorithm-driven programmatic ads on social media that juxtapose a hugely unsuitable or insensitive ad next to a piece of news content and lend a whole new, unintended, meaning to the brand. In spite of the science that often goes into the creative development and targeting of advertisements, advertisers still cannot easily manage the meaning of advertising.

DOES ADVERTISING COMMUNICATION HAVE TO BE EXPLICIT?

The importance of the implicit in communication may seem self-evident, given the widely acknowledged role of the implicit in human face-to-face communication, yet the concept that has dominated research in advertising has been the idea of a clear, explicit, verbalised and unproblematic 'message' (Heath and Feldwick, 2008). Of what this message is comprised, though, is hard to say. As noted in the previous chapter, advertising can be seen as a form of 'social communication' that operates on many dimensions (Leiss et al., 2005). As a complex communication form, advertising can be understood not only in terms of an engineering model of 'information' transmission, but also in terms of a vehicle of meaning that is interpreted in symbolic ways by different audiences (Lasswell, 1948; McCracken, 1987; Sherry, 1987; Ritson and Elliott, 1999).

One problem facing advertising theorists has been finding a popular and accessible way to theorise both its explicit and implicit elements. Human face-to-face communication has been shown to be about the gestures, vocal tone, emotional timbre, poise and gravitas, facial expression and social context, as well as about the verbal content. Words are important; they are the infrastructure around which persuasive arguments are built. But what listeners take from such communication is not determined solely by the words, by any means. Advertising theory, both practitioner and academic, has tended to privilege the verbalised or printed linguistic elements of promotional 'messages', the explicit communication, and underplay the elements of communication that are implicit, or those to which conscious attention is not paid (Heath and Feldwick, 2008).

One reason for this is the powerful influence of the personal selling–advertising analogy propagated by early theorists like Kennedy (1924). Advertising is still often conceived as a quasi-verbal message that is processed consciously by individual receivers who make conscious and rational evaluations to compare consumption choices. Another reason is that acknowledging the implicit elements of advertising and promotion opens up controversial issues of 'subliminal' or hidden influence. Much advertising theory has been conceived with one eye on the latent public unease articulated by Vance Packard's (1957) idea of advertisers as 'hidden persuaders' engaged in sinister and underhand manipulation (Hackley, 2007). Packard highlighted the use of depth psychology by advertising agencies to reveal the deep and unconscious motivations of consumers (including, to Packard's alarm, children) in order to exploit them. Packard was able to articulate a deep suspicion of the manipulative and underhand techniques of persuasion used by marketers. A focus on the rational, the conscious and the verbal, deflects the charge of manipulation quite neatly, but at the considerable price of grossly over-simplifying the subject matter. Hence, there is a political reason why, in the marketing of marketing theory, some pretty weak ones, like AIDA, have been highly popular in organisations for almost 100 years. Such theories of advertising focus on the consumer's rational and evaluative behaviour and ignore the more difficult-to-conceptualise margins of advertising communication, the implicit meaning, the irrational and emotional appeals, the dark arts of persuasion, and hence they serve a sociological purpose of legitimising advertising.

So, having outlined some of the problems and possibilities of advertising theory, Chapter 2 will now begin to explore the topic in terms of three traditions of theory: practitioner theory, information processing theory and socio-cultural theory (Hackley, 2010).

PRACTICE-BASED ADVERTISING THEORY

'REASON WHY' AND 'USP' ADVERTISING

The surprising thing about advertising theory is that, in spite of the huge volume of academic and practitioner research, significant elements of it have changed little in a century. Early advertising theory was based on direct experience, though informed by psychological studies. It was focused mainly on improving practice. John E. Kennedy (1924) is credited with one of the earliest attempts when he wrote that advertising was 'salesmanship in print'. Kennedy was at the Lord and Thomas agency, later to become the biggest agency of its era in the world. This was where American advertising pioneer Albert D. Lasker started the first school of advertising copywriting, applying Kennedy's principles. The idea that a direct analogy could be drawn between face-to-face selling and advertising on a medium (that is, on a technological means of communication) appeared self-evident to advertisers of the time.

Kennedy subsequently developed the 'reason why' approach to copywriting, a technique that led to Rosser Reeves's idea of the unique selling proposition (USP) some decades later (Fox, 1984; McDonald and Scott, 2007). The USP is the single thing that gives the consumer a reason to buy. Advertising agencies today often refer to the 'proposition', by which they mean the premise of an advertisement, the single idea that they want consumers to get from the ad. The 'proposition' is still the key concept in the creative advertising development process today (Heath and Feldwick, 2008). Of course, reason to buy and propositions are both features of basic personal sales techniques. The sales person is taught that prospects (consumers) who have expressed some interest in a purchase are simply looking for a reason not to buy, and it is the salesperson's job to give them a reason to buy and answer all their objections to purchase. The aim is to give the consumer a reason not to feel negative about their purchase decision. Advertising devised on this model makes a clear claim about the brand, perhaps that it is the most powerful cleaner, the best value, the most aesthetically appealing in its market. Testing such ads entails surveys that ask consumers post-exposure to rate their attitudes to the brand.

CREATIVITY AND PRACTITIONER THEORIES OF ADVERTISING

Other well-known developments in practitioner theory for advertising include Bill Bernbach's emphasis on creativity, David Ogilvy's 'brand personality' and Leo Burnett's use of dramatic realism, using images of housewives at the kitchen sink, but looking impossibly glamorous, in advertising that reached out to consumers' daily experience. Creativity in advertising is a contentious topic (and we discuss it at greater length in Chapters 4 and 5), since there is little agreement on what it is or on whether it is useful. For some hard-headed practitioners, the idea of creativity smacks of the kind of self-indulgence that can lead agencies to try to make advertising that forgets about the client and instead make advertising that is 'arty' for its own sake. For others, creativity is the fundamental contribution advertising agencies make to business: they are, after all, ideas factories, and creativity is the stuff they sell, however it may be conceived. For still others, creativity is a component of the best advertising that must be used judiciously alongside more pragmatic considerations. After all, countless ads today turn out to have been copied from internet videos, or they use the latest photographic or animation technique for visual effect – advertising certainly need not always be creative in the sense of being original. On the other hand, for many creative professionals in advertising, the purpose of advertising is the same as the purpose of art – to activate the audience, to inspire them and make them think (Hackley and Kover, 2007; McLeod et al., 2009). Creativity is then about advertising agencies acting as cultural curators (or cultural intermediaries; Cronin, 2004) in selecting imagery, text and music in a combination that will tap into the cultural consciousness of the target group to engage and activate, and motivate, them. If the resulting communication is not really very creative in itself that is not the point – advertising, after all, is not art, supposedly. Advertising's purpose is not to draw attention to itself for its own sake but to draw the right kind of attention to its sponsor, the brand.

One commonplace distinction that is often used with regard to advertising is between 'hard' and 'soft' sell. Sometimes, compelling creativity is thought to establish and build the brand equity, anthropomorphising the brand in value terms that stimulate responses of affection, and perhaps loyalty, from consumers. The other side, the 'hard sell' theories, follow the tradition of Kennedy and Reeves, and the equally noted Claude Hopkins, and are not associated with stunning creativity. They tend to be direct sales appeals that rely more on rational persuasion than creative activation, in keeping with their objective of generating a spike in sales in the short term (McDonald and Scott, 2007).

COGNITIVE INFORMATION PROCESSING THEORY IN ADVERTISING

Other practitioners in advertising soon began to burnish their informal theories with academic work. Of these, Edward Strong (1929) and Harry D. Kitson (1921) can probably claim the longest legacy. Strong's book *The Psychology of Selling and Advertising* and Kitson's (1921) *The Mind of the Buyer* melded psychological principles to the evolving work in theories of personal selling. Their work was influential and added some scientific starch to a rudimentary theory of persuasive communication known as AIDA, which is still repeated in almost every textbook on advertising and marketing, including this one. The AIDA model for personal selling, adapted to advertising, remains by far the most influential theory in the field. AIDA is often cited alongside the 'transmission' model of mass communication from mathematical communication science, also known as **linear information processing** theory. Both are described below.

Another important academic influence on advertising theory that is worth mentioning here came from one of the originators of behavioural psychology, John B. Watson. Watson (1924) was a psychology professor who left academia and applied his theories of learning and reinforcement to a successful career in advertising with J. Walter Thompson and later the William Esty agency. Watson's ideas may have fallen out of vogue long ago, but of all the advertising theorists, he is possibly the most well known and his approach can be seen today in some learning systems.

THE SHANNON–WEAVER COMMUNICATION MODEL

'Information processing' is a term that sums up a vast tradition of advertising theory. It encompasses not only a theory of communication but an implied theory of human cognition. The information processing model was originally devised to model the mathematical efficiency of technical communication channels (Shannon, 1948; Weaver and Shannon, 1963) but was applied to mass communication (Lazarsfeld, 1941; Lasswell, 1948; Schramm, 1948; Katz and Lazarsfeld, 1955). Applied to human communication, the theory assumes that humans 'process' data in much the same way as computers or other machines. It is also called the 'transmission' model since data are transmitted to the receiver. It is linear, in the sense that it can be modelled as if there is a straight line from sender to receiver and back.

There are many variations on the model but its basic components remain the same in most applications. There is a sender, or a 'source', and a receiver. The message is encoded into a form that allows transmission, and then is sent via a medium or channel of communication to be decoded by the receiver. There is a feedback loop in the model, so that it can be determined whether or not the message was efficiently delivered. If the message was encoded accurately, and transmitted via the correct medium, the only reason for miscommunication would be 'noise', which refers to anything that interferes with the transmission or decoding/encoding process.

Whether or not the classic information processing model (Figure 2.1) is appropriate for human communication is a highly contested matter. Nevertheless, in most marketing textbooks and those of many other disciplines including communication studies, it is reproduced faithfully and presented as if none of its key elements nor its founding metaphor is in any way problematic.

It is easy to see how the analogy between machine communication and human communication could be applied to a simple model of advertising. An advertisement can be conceived as a message, especially if one refers to the ideas of Kennedy and Hopkins. The message has to be encoded by the sender (the advertising agency creative team) into a form that will be decoded successfully by the receiver, who is of course the consumer. Encoding will put the message into a form in which communication is possible on the available media channels. In Kennedy's day, this would consist of print advertising. With the development of broadcast media it would be possible to include sound and, later, moving pictures. The challenge for the advertising creative is that they want the receiver to decode the same message that the advertisers encoded into the communication in order to retrieve the meaning intended.

The surrounding environment may have 'noise' of various forms that distracts from the message. Noise can be construed metaphorically as anything that might disrupt the communication by, say, distracting the attention of the receiver, or confusing their decoding process. In an aural communication it may be literal noise that disrupts the communicative process. With visual communications such as roadside advertising poster sites, noise may be all the activities of an urban road that might distract a person's attention from the poster, such as pedestrians, cars, shops, stray

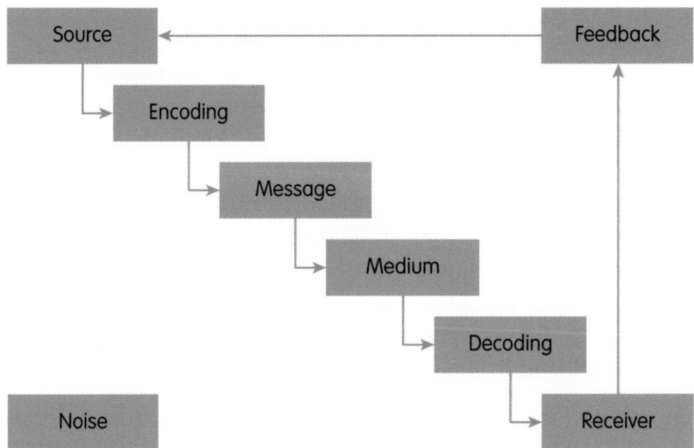

FIGURE 2.1 The classic transmission model of communication

dogs, or anything else. This simple conceptualisation of advertising communication has many descriptive uses. It has been a mainstay of marketing communications and advertising texts because of its economy and descriptive scope. It can be applied to almost any communications scenario and will have a degree of superficial applicability. The idea of the advertising 'message' still drives much thinking in advertising, and as a practical construct the linear information processing model has proved useful. But as a theoretical explanation for what is happening in advertising communication it has serious limitations.

THE AIDA (ATTENTION–INTEREST–DESIRE–ACTION) MODEL

A theoretical model is no more than a textual representation that captures by analogy some, but by no means all, of the features of the phenomenon it purports to represent. In other words, models as theoretical representations have weaknesses. Before discussing these in more detail, though, we will revisit the AIDA model of persuasive advertising communication. This maps easily onto the classic information processing model of communication because of its linearity and its cognitive focus, and it has generated a host of variations that fall under the category **hierarchy-of-effects theories** in advertising (Barry and Howard, 1990). AIDA, which, as noted above, was designed as a theory of personal selling before it was co-opted to model mediated selling through advertising, is based on a simple set of sequences that are supposed to take the consumer from a state of indifference to one of commitment, when they buy the product or service that is being advertised. Firstly, the advertiser must get the consumer's attention. An indifferent consumer will not become a customer. Following that, the ad has to generate the consumer's interest. The next stage in the persuasive process is to elicit desire for the product or service being sold. Finally, the consumer is moved to take action, by buying the item (see Figure 2.2).

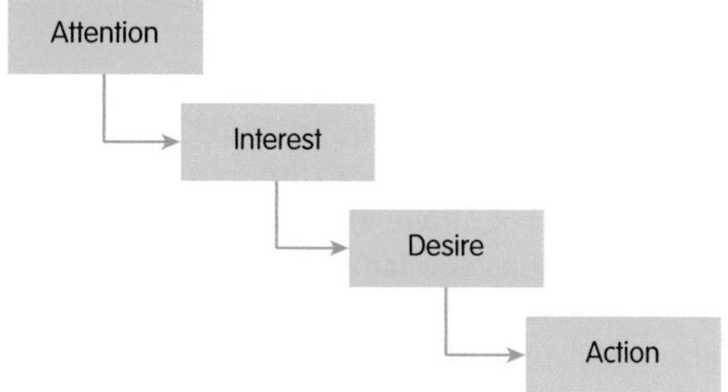

FIGURE 2.2 The Attention–Interest–Desire–Action (AIDA) model of persuasive advertising communication

The AIDA model assumes that consumers are essentially indifferent to the offer and need to have their attention grabbed. After that, they (and we) have to be pushed along a continuum of persuasion until we buy the product. When the AIDA model is conceived in terms of mass communication to thousands or millions of potential consumers through advertising, this process can be seen in terms of a gradual and incremental effect. As consumers we have many communications competing for our attention. If an advertiser wants to sell us a new product or service, then on this model they first have to get our attention. This could take many attempts – we might view an advertisement many times before we find ourselves sufficiently interested to pay explicit attention to it. Once we have done that it may take many more exposures, or even many more campaigns, to elicit our interest, evoke our desire for the brand, and finally to provoke us into actually acting on the message by purchasing the advertised brand.

HIERARCHY-OF-EFFECTS

The logic of AIDA, extended from a face-to-face sales conversation to a mass mediated advertising market, takes the human consumer as an entity that is resistant to persuasion but susceptible to a successive accretion of persuasive inputs. In other words, we are gradually persuaded to accept the sales message as our resistance is undermined by the accumulation of messages. The 'hierarchy-of-effects' theory represents 'compounding probabilities', as each step in the process is a necessary condition for the subsequent step (Percy et al., 2001). The hierarchy-of-effects tradition has spawned many theories that are designed to improve the efficiency and effectiveness of campaign planning (Barry and Howard, 1990; see also Lavidge and Steiner, 1961; Vaughn, 1986; Rossiter et al., 1991). Most importantly, they all conceive of advertising persuasion as a rational and self-conscious process through which an individual consumer can eventually be persuaded to buy by the force of the message. The assumption is that any advertisement can be reduced analytically to the notion of the univocal 'message'. There is no scope in AIDA or information processing theories for implicit communication or contested interpretations of advertising.

COGNITION, AFFECT AND CONATION MODELS

Some variations on advertising theory have incorporated emotion, humour or other intangible elements into an over-arching information processing scheme. One well-known generic model incorporated emotionality into purchase decisions by using a three-stage conceptualisation: cognitive, affective and conative, known colloquially as 'think–feel–do' (for discussions see Lutz, 1977; Bagozzi et al., 1979; Barnard and Ehrenberg, 1997). The cognitive element persuades the consumer on a rational level by including facts about the product or service qualities. The affective dimension gets the consumer to respond emotionally to the appeal, by, say, including images of attractive, happy families or by making the consumer laugh, and therefore encouraging affection towards the brand. Finally, conation refers to the behaviour elicited by the advertisements, for example by including a direct response coupon or telephone number for the customer to call.

Many automobile advertisements seem to conform to the cognitive (thinking), affective (feeling) and conative (doing) model when they picture a beautiful car to strike at the prospect's sense of aesthetics and aspiration, slot in an attractive driver or happy family to promote projective identification and elicit desire, underpin the picture with detailed information about petrol consumption and speed, and finally add a direct response mechanism for the consumer to send off for a brochure or apply for a test drive.

The think–feel–do scheme tells us why many ads combine rational with emotional appeals. It cannot tell us which of those appeals will prove more powerful or what the right balance of rational–emotional appeal should be to create a successful advertisement. In other words, like many theories and models in marketing it may have some explanatory value, but no predictive or normative value. It cannot tell which ads will be successful and which will not, and it cannot tell us how to construct a successful ad. Consumers do not conform to convenient textbook models. Some drivers buy a car for its colour, some for its speed, some for its practicality. Many are influenced by the brand image, and many drivers buy the same brand of car repeatedly even though there are many others from which to choose that perform equally well. More and more car ads like to play with the 'emotional realm', examples include Honda's 'Choir', Skoda and VW ads.[2] Clearly, there is no formula that fits every model or every buyer (Percy and Elliott, 2009).

ADVANTAGES OF INFORMATION PROCESSING THEORY

The information processing model and its associated theories of persuasion, notably AIDA and the other hierarchy-of-effects family of theories, have some advantages. One is that they allow the complexity of advertising communication to be reduced to a simplified and easily recollected model that appears to fit any communication scenario. The shared assumptions of AIDA and the transmission mode of communication mean that any construct of cognitive psychology can be the subject of research into 'intermediate' advertising effects. For example, attention is a sub-field of psychological research and theory with relevance for this model. So are the psychological research fields of memory, attitude, emotion and behaviour. Research into intermediate advertising effects focuses on the elements that appear to be sequentially necessary in order for persuasion to take place. For example, it is assumed that if consumers like an advertisement because of its humour they are more likely to respond emotionally to the brand, and therefore more likely to change their attitude from negative or indifferent to positive. The assumption is that purchase is then more likely to result. Many studies are conducted on consumer memory to try to understand which advertising formats prompt the best recall scores, on the assumption that remembering an ad is a stage in the process leading to purchase.

CRITICISMS OF INFORMATION PROCESSING THEORY

The use of information processing models of communication in advertising, and related linear theories of persuasive communication such as AIDA, has been criticised on many grounds (see Stern, 1993a, for an overview, and also Buttle, 1994; Heath and Feldwick, 2008; Hackley, 2010). They are based on assumptions that are not always clearly understood because of the extent to which they have become regarded as the key theories of advertising by default and their origins forgotten.

For example, do these theories correspond in any meaningful sense with the way human communication actually happens? Do we process information serially or one piece at a time, and consciously, so that we are fully aware of each piece of communication we encounter? Advanced research in artificial intelligence (AI) has modelled serial as opposed to linear information processing: computers can process input data through more than one channel at a time. Intuitively, we know that paying attention to more than one sensory input at a time is difficult for a human, but it is certainly possible. It is easy to argue that most advertising is screened out at the attention stage. But is it really? Do advertisements occupy some part of our peripheral vision and hearing, even if we are paying more explicit attention to something else? Or, rather, might advertisements deliberately attempt to seduce our unconscious mind and by-pass our conscious reasoning altogether, as Robert Heath (2012) suggests?

ADVERTISING AND THE SOCIAL CONTEXT

AIDA and the hierarchy-of-effects models of advertising persuasion tend to focus on a single advertisement seen by an individual consumer, which is not surprising given that they were developed from a model of face-to-face sales communication and later adapted to mass advertising communication. Some authors have pointed out that advertising is seldom viewed by an individual in an experimental viewing booth. More typically, advertisements are seen in social contexts, in the company of other communications and, often, in the company of other people. What is more, they are often the subject of social interaction. Indeed, long before social media sharing became so important for advertising, it was acknowledged that one of the key elements of success for an ad is to get it talked about (Dichter, 1949, 1966). Consequently, some researchers have argued that advertising is better understood as a social, rather than a cognitive phenomenon. Theories that posit one sender and one receiver of an advertising message, then, lack naturalistic validity in the sense that they do not necessarily reflect the way that consumers consume advertising.

Another much-criticised aspect of the linear information processing approach to theorising advertising is its assumption that advertising communication occurs mainly in one direction towards a passive consumer who will be acquiescent towards an unambiguous message if they process it correctly. In Chapter 1 we discuss the role of consumers in the participative economy and the extent to which social media are accelerating the reversal of production into consumption and vice versa (Toffler, 1980). Put simply, we can say that it has always been simplistic to model consumers as if they read advertising messages passively and hegemonically – human beings, after all, are interpreting creatures. The empty vessel theory of education (pupils are empty vessels that simply need to be filled up with facts) was discredited long ago, yet the AIDA model remains popular in marketing communications texts even though it is also a version of the empty vessel theory. Not only do consumers interpret, re-interpret, resist and question advertising, they also fire back now that social media have given us the means to do so.

This leads to another criticism, which is that AIDA and other cognitive theories assume that the message and the meaning of the advertisement are synonymous. In other words, there is no theoretical scope for different consumers to interpret the ad in unexpected ways. Advertising is a text to be read, and AIDA allows no ambiguity, not scope for interpretation – there is, simply, the message, and either the receiver encodes it correctly, or incorrectly. As we see from many examples throughout the book, the message in a communication is rarely stable or unambiguous.

Finally, there is a key assumption in AIDA that the object of any advertisement is, always, a sale. As we have noted, sales, at least in the short or medium term, may not always be the best measure of a campaign's success. Advertising cannot sell – it is a mediated communication. It cannot answer your objections to purchase as a personal salesperson can. We can ignore it, when it is far more difficult to ignore a good salesperson. An advertising campaign might assist in creating a sense of brand positioning, or in informing consumers of new offers, or in attaching abstract values to brands that might chime with the sense of identity of particular consumer segments. These are intermediate states to sales – a sale is not a direct result of most ads but a by-product.

'STRONG' AND 'WEAK' THEORIES OF ADVERTISING EFFECT

Before discussing socio-cultural theories, there is another informal theory of advertising that is relevant here, and which we touched upon briefly above. The distinction between advertising and promotion that is designed to sell product, and advertising that is designed to build brand presence, has been expressed in terms of 'strong' and 'weak' theories (Jones, 1990). A popular analogy we have already noted expresses the same idea in terms of 'hard sell' and 'soft sell'. Theories of advertising that assume its main purpose is to persuade a potential customer (a 'prospect' in sales jargon) to buy, are called strong theories. AIDA falls into this category, since it is premised on the assumption that an advertisement is designed to persuade the viewer to change their behaviour and buy the product. Theories that take a less sales oriented view and allow that advertising may have a similar effect to publicity as a long-term builder of brand presence and brand positioning, are called weak theories.

Strong theories are more compelling to many clients of advertising agencies who really want to see the sales graph spike upwards within a few days of the campaign launch. The problem is that a direct causal relationship between an advertisement and a sale cannot be proven beyond doubt, however persuasive the circumstantial evidence, because sales can be affected by other variables such as trends, fashions, weather events, seasonal sales, or changes in disposable income. To add to the difficulties for strong theories, even if there is a sales increase as a result of the campaign, the time lag between advertising exposure and sale is impossible to predict.

ADVERTISING AS PUBLICITY

As we have noted, many contemporary ads eschew the strong sales pitch format in favour of a less direct narrative that is designed to build long-term brand equity, and to remind or to reassure existing customers. Ehrenberg et al. (2002) have suggested that advertising seldom actually persuades a non-buyer to buy in the short term, but more typically acts like publicity to reassure existing buyers that the brand remains relevant and current. Many car brand ads for, say, BMW or Mercedes-Benz, evince general brand values as well as promoting particular models because consumers may only buy that car brand once or twice in a lifetime, if at all. They need to be consistently reminded of the brand's relevance and values for the time when they might be in a position to buy. For example, Mercedes's innovative Twitter campaign YOUDRIVE, first launched during *The X Factor* TV show in 2012, gave viewers a chance to engage interactively in a driving game.[3] The *X Factor* audience might not be the primary market for Mercedes sales, and there was no sales pitch as such, the campaign was just a fun way for a wider audience to engage with the brand. Sponsorship in general acts in this way, to publicise a brand in particular contexts that the brand managers feel will meet with favour from the target audience. Benetton's hugely controversial advertising in the 1980s and 1990s was not sales oriented and contained no product information, yet it generated a huge amount of publicity and, consequently, sales. As we note in Chapter 1, if a brand is top of mind for large numbers of people, that usually translates into sales. It may not be always true that all publicity is good publicity, but P.T. Barnum certainly knew the value of it (Brown and Hackley, 2012). Publicity has a value for brands, and it doesn't necessarily need a sales pitch in order to result in a sale.

A great deal of theory in advertising has been devoted to understanding persuasion (O'Shaughnessy and O'Shaughnessy, 2004). But there is a question of what persuasion in advertising entails. Does it entail directly changing someone's attitude or behaviour through the force of reasoning? Or does it mean presenting brands in a generally persuasive light by inferring that they enhance personal lifestyle and act as symbolic resources for the production of social identity (Elliott and Wattanasuwan,

1998)? Weak theories of advertising assume that the advertising cause and the sales effect are linked, but over a much longer time period and through different mechanisms to strong theories. An important function of branding is that it is a badge of reassurance for the consumer (Feldwick, 2002). Consumers are often insecure about making difficult purchase decisions. None of us wants to get our purchase home to find that it is defective in any way or that our peers regard it with disdain. Brand names offer reassurance for the consumer that the purchase we have made is safe in the sense that the brand is credible and the quality good. Brand advertising, then, supports this sense of reassurance by reminding consumers that the brand is current, relevant and successful.

SNAPSHOT 2.2

'Weak' advertising appeals

John Philip Jones's (1990) research paper that conceived of 'strong' vs 'weak' advertising appeals roughly maps onto the popular distinction between, respectively, 'hard sell' and 'soft sell'. Hard sell is perhaps best understood as a direct and forceful appeal to purchase. Examples might be ads that focus on price, quality or superior value over competitors. Weak advertising appeals, on the other hand, would cover a wide variety of ads that tell brand stories rather than trying to persuade the consumer to buy the product or service by reason, argument and evidence. One of the most popular ads in the UK in the last 20 years was a 2007 Cadbury's ad (by agency Fallon, London) featuring a man in a gorilla suit playing the drums.[4] The ad went worldwide and formed part of an integrated campaign with print, TV and social media. There was subtle branding on the ad but no sales appeal or product features. It was all for fun. It was reported that the Cadbury's brand image was enhanced and market share increased. It is probably fair to say that the most popular ads do tend to be fun and likeable, in other words they appeal to emotion, rather than conforming to a sales pitch narrative. They might also meet with strong resistance from clients because they don't work well in pre-tests – the Cadbury's Gorilla almost didn't get made.[5] Cadbury followed up 'Gorilla' with several more 'feel-good' ads, including their hugely successful 2009 film 'Eyebrows', the 'Not-so-secret secret' and their Crispello ad, 'A lovely little naughtiness', in 2013.[6]

SOCIO-CULTURAL THEORY IN ADVERTISING

AIDA and other hierarchy-of-effects theories remain influential in advertising, but advertising agencies also make considerable use of socio-cultural theory in their practice. Many agencies employ account planners with backgrounds in cultural anthropology, sociology, literature, psychology or ethnography. Academic studies of advertising often have different aims from professional practice, but there are many to be found in all these disciplines (e.g. Sherry, 1987; Scott, 1990;

Mick and Buhl, 1992; Stern, 1993b; Scott, 1994a; Schroeder, 2002; Cronin, 2008; for an overview, Hackley, 2009c).

For example, the implied passivity of the consumer as a receiver of a one-way advertising message has been a criticism of the information processing models. This assumption is left unstated in 'transmission models' of mass communication but nevertheless implies that audiences 'receive' information, much as a computer receives data. In contrast, drawing on literary criticism, advertisements can be understood as texts, like other reading matter, to be read, with the same elements of judgement and interpretation. Academic studies applying reader–response theory to advertising suggest that audiences actively interpret, critique and/or resist advertising messages. Consumers are by no means passive receivers of advertising (e.g. O'Donohoe, 1994; Scott, 1994a). This, of course, is truer than ever in the age of social media.

Critiques of the passive consumer assumption have engaged with the transmission model of communication. For example, Stern (1993a) undertook a thorough critique of static transmission models of communication in advertising, arguing that the model over-simplifies the communication process. Other work that has indirectly opposed the idea of a passive consumer posits the consumer as an active reader of text, as noted earlier, or an interpreter of signs (Mick, 1986; Scott, 1994b). Researchers working from the standpoint of linguistics have pointed out that what is implicit in communication is often more persuasive than what is explicit. When this principle is applied to advertising communication, the limitations of a focus on explicit messages become all too apparent. For example, Tanaka (1994) analysed advertisements in detail to illustrate the rhetorical force of implied connotation and denotation in advertising.

ECONOMIC RATIONALITY AND EMOTION IN BUYING BEHAVIOUR

A further criticism of linear models of advertising persuasion is that they overplay the role of economic rationality in the consumption of advertising and ignore the role of emotion. Subsequent models have incorporated stronger elements of consumer emotionality not as a mediating influence but as a guiding motive in the buying process, reflecting the often irrational and quirky motivations behind consumer behaviour (Holbrook and Hirschman, 1982; Holbrook and O'Shaughnessy, 1984; Elliott, 1998; Dermody, 1999). Many of us go shopping when we feel down. Buying things can be therapeutic. Rationality plays little part in addictive or mood shopping, or in compulsive or impulsive consumer behaviour like excessive drinking (Hackley et al., 2012).

Our rationality as consumers can also be challenged by unconscious contextual effects (Hackley, 2013a). We can be swayed in our interpretation of communications through the other communications that are juxtaposed with an advertisement. The medium influences the way that the message is interpreted and understood (McLuhan, 1964; Cook, 2001). Our perceptions can be framed by the wider context, and the ways we 'read' marketing signs can be influenced by environmental cues. Advertisements are interpreted in the light of the context in which they are viewed, including the medium, the media vehicle, the other ads wrapped around the ad in the slot, the programming and so on. Advertising acquires meaning not only by its content but also its context.

Cook (2001) suggested that the contexts of advertising include the following:

- the physical material or medium that carries the text (such as the cathode ray tube, newsprint or radio waves)
- the music and pictures that may accompany the text
- the gestures, facial expressions and typography that constitute the 'paralanguage' of the text (in the UK, TV ads for Nescafé Gold Blend instant coffee featured romantically linked characters who created a sexually charged atmosphere, while interacting in settings that suggested affluence and social poise)
- the location of the text in time and space, on an outdoor poster site, in a magazine or during a commercial TV break
- the other texts that connect to that text such as the other ads in the same magazine or the other brands appearing or mentioned in a TV show
- the connections with other social **discourses** implied in the ads (for example, **intertextuality**)
- the participants, that is, the intended audience, the apparent originator or sender of the ad and their respective assumptions, intentions and communicative idiom (ads sometimes have a particular 'voice' designed to confer authority, such as when ads for children's toys feature adults speaking the voice-over in the tone and patois of children).

Clearly, this list of the contexts of advertising implies that research studies which analyse the recall and attitude of an individual consumer to a single promotion by exposing that consumer to the ad in a viewing booth risk ignoring some of the most powerful influences on how ads are interpreted and understood. The contextual influence on advertising interpretation can have serious implications for advertising regulation.

SNAPSHOT 2.3

Emotion and advertising

Advertising theory has been focused mainly on consumer reasoning and decision making, and this seems odd when one considers that marketing began as a discipline that dissented from the economist's fixation with consumer rationality. Some thinkers felt that microeconomics lacked the conceptual penetration to assist in clearing markets because consumers were far less rational and more variable in their wants and needs than the economist's notion of utility allowed. Hence, marketing was born as a university discipline at the turn of the twentieth century (Hackley, 2009a). And yet, marketing itself, along with advertising, seems to have largely forgotten the founding principle of the discipline, since so much research and thinking assumes that consumers buy with conscious reason, rather than with unconscious emotion (Elliott, 1998). In the 1980s there was a movement in consumer research that revived the sense of consumption as something motivated not solely by cold reason but by a need for feelings, fantasies and fun (Holbrook and Hirschman, 1982; Holbrook and O'Shaughnessy, 1984; Elliott, 1997). The advertising world has, from time-to-time, also remembered the importance of emotion in consumption. A 2013 article in *The Economist* magazine[7] credited Nobel prize-winning psychologist Daniel Kahneman with turning advertisers on to the notion that emotion could be more important than reason for consumers. Or, to be more accurate, some advertisers have picked up on Kahneman's ideas to justify what many in advertising knew already. Kahneman posits that human brains operate in two systems: system 1 is an intuitive and emotional system, while system 2 is rational. According to his (very simplified) theory, our behaviour is governed by system 1 to a far greater extent than system 2. This might explain why many of the most popular advertisements are just feel-good pieces with no rational product appeal, and also why so much market research that asks consumers to explain their thoughts and feelings around a particular brand or advertisements turns out to be wrong.

MEANINGS AND MESSAGES IN ADVERTISEMENTS

Information processing models tend to focus on the communication of a message, while socio-cultural theories of advertising communication focus on meanings rather than messages. The difference is important, since the idea of a message emphasises the power of the sender to control the way that a communication is received, while the idea of meaning in communication emphasises the power of the receiver. In literary theory, this difference is sometimes referred to in terms of hegemonic readings, that are intended to be accepted unconditionally, and negotiated or resisted readings, in which the reader/consumer might re-interpret or dissent from the message as it is intended. The concept of a message is often used broadly to refer to the content of an ad, that is, to the creative execution, but in advertising theory it is often used more narrowly to refer to a communication in terms of a single, unequivocal and uncontested meaning. In other words, in AIDA and similar linear schemes of advertising communication, meaning and message are assumed to be identical. Alternative theories of communication challenge this notion.

A similar distinction can be made between advertising as meaning, and advertising as information (McCracken, 1987). An advertising 'message' would typically be conceived as some information that is intended to constitute a persuasive argument that will appeal to the rational (Kahneman's system 2 – see Snapshot 2.3) part of a consumer's brain. If, on the other hand, an advertisement is conceived as a vehicle for meaning, this indicates a broader but deeper conceptualisation that taps into the consumer's need for meaning within a cultural system.

POLYSEMY IN ADVERTISING

Advertisements carry meanings that may be interpreted differently in different situations, or by different consumers. The capacity for a communication to have more than one possible interpretation is called polysemy. The meaning of some ads is indeterminate: none of the meanings in a given ad is necessarily prior to, or stronger than, the others. There is an interpretive space through which consumers can engage creatively with the ad. This gives advertising a particular power. It is us, the audience for advertising, who impose particular meanings on a given ad, helped, of course, by the cues placed in the ad by the creative people. This freedom to interpret advertising and to use it creatively in our own lives gives advertising communication a dynamic and iterative character that is particularly suitable for social media engagement. If people enjoy an ad they might want to discuss its possible meanings through social media and video sharing. All this engagement benefits the brand.

Advertising agencies, far from being limited by the complexity of advertising meaning, exploit the ambiguity of advertising to create an intimate and personal engagement with consumers (Pateman, 1983, in Forceville, 1996). In other words, polysemic advertising can be a deliberate strategy rather than a failure of communication. Ads can be artfully designed so that the curiosity of a designated target group of consumers is excited. Ads that are deliberately obscure can seem inaccessible to older consumers and, by implication, aimed at younger consumers. Ambiguity of meaning in ads can be used as a deliberate strategy to engage a target group by allowing them to feel part of an in-group who 'get' the ad. In addition, carefully coded ads can create a sense of conspiracy by communicating in a way that excludes non-targeted groups. As we note throughout the book, there is a shift in advertising towards polysemic content that does not hammer out a sales message, which people would find uninteresting, but instead seeks to engage by being entertaining, intriguing or simply fun. The more an ad is discussed and shared on social media, the wider the audience it reaches.

SNAPSHOT 2.4

Open versus closed advertising texts

As we have noted, advertisements can be understood in literary terms as texts that have to be read. We look at an ad and try to read and interpret it just as we would a poem, a novel, a comic strip, an art object, a movie or a piece of graffiti on a wall. Some ads attempt to create a hegemonic reading by hammering home a clear message that the advertiser hopes will be interpreted in the same way by all readers/consumers who encounter it. Other ads are less determinate, like a piece of art they actively solicit the reader's involvement in interpreting the meaning of the ad. This can be termed as closed versus open advertising texts (Yannopoulou and Elliott, 2007). Open advertising texts have more than one possible interpretation – they are polysemic (Scott, 2012). The ways in which open advertising texts might be interpreted need not be entirely arbitrary. The creative team can encode certain cues within the ad to appeal to a particular sub-cultural group or consumer community. For example, there is a long tradition of polysemic ads for the clothing fashion line Diesel (photo 25) that are open to many possible interpretations, but are also targeted at a young, style-conscious in-group. Many of its ads, including the 'Be Stupid' campaign, have won industry creative awards.[8] Guinness is another brand famous for the open text character of much of its advertising over many years[9] (see Photo 4). Guinness ads have been designed to inspire with visual spectacle and heart-warming stories of human creativity and achievement. They focused on creating pieces of entertaining content long before the term 'content' came into fashion in marketing and advertising.

PHOTO 4 Guinness

Image Courtesy of the Advertising Archives

Guinness has a peerless reputation in creative, brand-building advertising. This waterfall image was part of their Bring It To Life campaign. Many Guinness ads are polysemic in the sense that they carry no explicit message but are open to alternative interpretations. This print ad also intertextually references the TV ads in the campaign. Guinness ads tend to carry no sales message and no product information, yet they have succeeded over many years in turning a local Irish beer with an acquired taste into a global brand.

COVERT AND OSTENSIVE COMMUNICATION

The examples of polysemic and open text advertising we have noted above make their point by using implicit as well as explicit communication. The presence of both explicit and implicit elements in advertising communication has complicated the task of theorising advertising. Forceville (1996: 105) refers to a distinction made by Tanaka (1994: 41) between 'ostensive' and 'covert' communication in advertising. This distinction allows us to theorise what is implied in ads, as opposed to what is clearly and unambiguously claimed. The ostensive communicator makes the intention of the communication clear. The covert communicator does not. Many ads combine both ostensive (or explicit) and covert (or implicit) elements.

As we have noted, it is the capacity of advertising to deploy implicit communication that gives it its cultural force as a system of communication. This important dimension is neglected by linear theories of advertising communication and persuasion. The implicit dimension creates a problem for advertising regulators. Advertisements under industry regulation are strictly constrained from making claims that are untrue or preposterous. They get around this inconvenience by implying covertly those claims that could be seen as ridiculous or would open them up to criticism if they were made explicitly. The Lynx/Axe campaigns mentioned in Chapter 1 make absurd claims about how men's sexual attractiveness is increased by using the product, but this is implied in the narrative of the advertising, not stated explicitly as a feature of the product. In this particular case what is implied is clearly intended as a joke, although, as Tanaka (1994) notes, even if a claim made about a brand is absurd, the fact that it is understood makes it persuasive on some level.

Advertising cannot compel us to believe particular claims or to accept that certain values are embodied in a given brand. Rather, advertising suggests, implies and hints. It places images and words in a suggestive juxtaposition to imply that consuming a given brand will symbolically confer certain qualities and values. If you use a Gillette razor you are enjoying 'The Best a Man Can Get' (at least, according to the ads), and you might even acquire some of the characteristics and lifestyle of the actor in the ads. Driving a prestigious motorcar brand such as a Toyota Avensis will (we are invited to infer from the TV ads) confer a symbolic social status on us that reflects our success and desire. The ads don't actually say these things: they merely imply them, hoping that viewers will read the desired implication.

Ads frequently imply that consumers will be more sexually attractive, more powerful, more happy, or will appear more materially successful if they consume a given brand. Where branded products are juxtaposed with images of attractive, happy and successful people, the link between the two is implied but not stated. Most importantly, knowing that these suggestions are absurd does not necessarily undermine their force. Watch brand Omega, for example, is well known for pairing the brand with celebrities such as Nicole Kidman and Bond stars Pierce Brosnan and Daniel Craig in movie product placement and advertising, and it sponsors major events, such as the London 2012 Olympic Games. Omega also deploys feel-good advertising with aesthetically beautiful images in its advertising.[10]

PHOTO 5 Omega Watches

Image Courtesy of the Advertising Archives

Wrist watches feature prominently in Ian Fleming's James Bond novels. Bond wore Rolex watches in the movies until 1995. This print ad intertextually evokes the movie as actor Daniel Craig strikes a classic Bond pose. In Craig's 2006 debut as Bond in Casino Royale he made a scripted reference to the Omega watch he was wearing. This clunky brand reference was derided by film buffs. Undeterred, the producers piled more and more product placement deals into the movie franchise. Craig's fourth appearance as Bond in the 2015 release Spectre was alongside an estimated 17 featured brands, including Heineken, Bollinger and Sony.

VISUAL METAPHOR IN ADVERTISING

Covert meaning is often conveyed in advertising though pictorial, auditory or linguistic metaphor. If a branded bottle of alcoholic drink is pictured juxtaposed with scenes of fit, young, affluent people, then the metaphoric link is clear. For example, alcohol brand Martini used to be advertised in the UK as a drink enjoyed by swimsuited young men and women diving from a yacht moored at a tropical island. The juxtaposition of a branded alcohol drink with apparent wealth, attractiveness and physical fitness is exactly the opposite of what one might reasonably expect, since alcohol drinking is quite likely to make exponents fat and unfit, and may also make them poor if they drink enough. The **covert communication** in this campaign was preposterous but nevertheless clear. The Martini brand was used as a metaphor for sexual attractiveness and the good life. It matters little that the drink may often be consumed in social contexts that are, on the face of it, as far from the good life as one might wish to be. One can see the same implied suggestions in countless ads for alcohol, cigarettes and cosmetics.

Consumption is, significantly, not only a verbal phenomenon but a visual one. Images can communicate with great economy and force, and advertising is pre-eminently a visual phenomenon. Yet the particular qualities of visual communication have been very much under-theorised in the field. One notable exception comes in the work of Jonathan Schroeder (2002), who draws on art history and aesthetics to help us understand the complex ways in which advertising communicates visually. Schroeder (2002) argues that we do not only consume the branded products and services that are advertised, we also 'consume' the visual images of advertising and promotion.

For example, many perfume ads in lifestyle and fashion magazines make no direct reference to the odour; instead, they juxtapose sensuous images with an enigmatic strapline or slogan that evinces some abstract notion of the brand. The visual organisation of image and copy is carefully designed to rhetorically support the implicit claims made about the brand. A UK press ad for an Estée Lauder perfume portrayed a woman with flowing hair against images of waves, scattered flowers and sunlight with the copy, 'Introducing the new fantasy in fragrance' and the brand 'beyond paradise' with the explanation that it offers 'an intoxication of the senses'. The ad had visual impact: it made a striking image when placed in a double-page section immediately inside the magazine cover. By its size and page location the ad was rhetorically declaring that its subject matter was important, more important, perhaps, than the magazine's editorial. The woman's face engages the reader eye to eye with a questioning and provocative expression that seems to be asking, 'Dare you join me in paradise?' The face rhetorically supports the idea that this brand transports the ordinary woman from the everyday to a different world in which she can be free to be any self she chooses. The French brand name draws on the cultural idiom of style and sophistication to imply that the perfume has those qualities and so, by association, will the reader who buys the brand. Of course, consumers will decide if they like the odour, but the odour is designed to be pleasant. Once again, the powerfully suggestive aspect of this ad is not only in its message but also in its creativity. The ad is rhetorically organised to support certain implied meanings.

The visual rhetoric of ads is not, then, confined to the copy. An ad is an argument, a persuasive communication. Every part of it must support the main argument, must be persuasively suggestive. A press ad for Retinol Actif Pur face cream used a clever visual metaphor to support a claim that the cream reduced facial wrinkles. The ad featured two juxtaposed images of a beautiful (Caucasian) woman. She was wearing what seemed to be a white robe, folded over one shoulder like a Roman toga. In the background was a pure blue sky and a suggestion of white pillars, of the kind found in a Greek temple. One picture was cracked, like the surface of an old oil painting. The other was smooth. The metaphoric reference was clear: the cracks suggested wrinkles, but in an elegant way that was complimentary, not demeaning, to age. Old paintings are things of classical beauty, but the paint does tend to crack with age. The ad was designed to draw the eye across aesthetically appealing images while giving the reader heavy hints about the classic beauty they might aspire to if they were to consume the brand.

ADVERTISING AND THE CULTURAL CONTEXT

Advertising is not merely a force acting upon us from some other place. It is part of our cultural scene – we draw on our cultural knowledge to interpret and understand, to 'read', advertising, just as advertisers draw on the very same cultural milieu to find ways to articulate brand stories visually and verbally. Research studies have drawn attention to the ways in which advertising occupies the same cultural space as consumers. In other words, advertising does not simply do things to consumers – consumers also do things with advertising. This insight was perhaps a more novel one 20 years ago when most advertising theory within academic marketing took a linear communication approach. Today, in the context of social media, the active involvement of consumers in adapting, re-making, discussing, re-interpreting and satirising advertising seems impossible to ignore.

Theorists such as Stephanie O'Donohoe (1994) and Grant McCracken (1986), and before them Ernest Dichter (1966), point out that advertising is ineluctably a cultural as well as a cognitive communication phenomenon. We consume and discuss advertising in a social and cultural context, not in an individually isolated experimental viewing booth. Ritson and Elliott (1999) showed how important advertising can be in the everyday conversation of adolescents. By expressing preferences and finding certain ads funny or enjoyable the researchers found that the adolescents were also expressing their sense of social identity and group membership.

Advertising's meaning, then, draws on the cultural environment within which it is framed. A key concept in understanding this aspect of advertising as social communication is intertextuality (also discussed in the Chapter 2 case study below). Intertextuality refers to the ways in which one text refers to other texts (e.g. O'Donohoe, 1997). Intertextuality might be invoked when, say, an ad uses a style of cinematography more commonly used in news or documentary filming, or when an ad includes a visual or verbal reference to a TV show, a movie, or a topical event. When celebrities are used in ads it can be seen in terms of an intertextual reference to the celebrity's persona outside of advertising, as, say, when a former sporting star is used as a spokesperson for a brand. Intertextuality can also be invoked as a discourse, that is, a particular way of talking about or representing things, say, where an ad takes on the stereotypical sales conversation style of a company representative talking direct to camera, or an authoritative grey-haired man in a white lab coat invoking the representational style of science to make claims about the scientific properties of a product. Intertextuality is far from an arcane literary concept but a typical way that advertisements communicate with their target audiences.[11] Most importantly, though, consumers must have the relevant cultural knowledge to decode the intertextual references in advertisements – they must know about the movie, the topical event, the actor to which the ad refers in order to *get* the ad. By the same token, advertising agencies must understand the cultural reference points of their target consumers in order to design creative executions that are loaded with relevant cultural cues.

Our understanding of ads then, and the brands they promote, is formed in the light of the social contexts within which such communications subsist. This inherently social aspect of human understanding reflects a broader concern with the socially constructed character of social reality and of individual psychology (Berger and Luckman, 1966; for introductions see Burr, 1995; Nightingale and Cromby, 1999). In important respects we maintain that brands and their advertising cannot be properly understood simply as self-sustaining entities. They must also be understood as entities that exist in the realm of social interaction, sustained through the way they are talked about and used. In other words, brands can be seen as social constructions. A great deal of marketing activity can be seen to have a socially constructed character in the sense that it has an existence that is sustained in the social world beyond the tangible realities of product features, packaging and price (Hirschman, 1986). A brand's meaning as portrayed or implied in advertising subsists in the social space between the organisation, the advertising and its **interpretive communities** of consumers. In the convergent media era, this truism plays out in very tangible ways and consumers actively participate in the negotiation and renegotiation of brand meanings.

SNAPSHOT 2.5

Advertising context and regulation

A good illustration of the importance of the context of advertising for the meaning we construe from it can be found in a UK campaign for a perfume brand. A magazine ad for Yves St Laurent's Opium perfume featuring model Sophie Dahl, apparently naked, elicited little comment. Such ads are common in lifestyle and fashion magazines. When the print ad was blown up into a poster and featured on roadside billboards it elicited such a large number of complaints that even though the campaign was launched in 2000, in 2012 it still ranked in the top ten ads most complained about to the UK Advertising Standards Authority (ASA).[12] The magazine ad was, presumably, seen as sensuous and witty in the context of many such ads for perfume in fashion and lifestyle magazines. The same ad on posters was widely considered to be obscene. The complaints to the ASA were predominantly from young women, exactly the readers of the magazines in which the press ad had featured. The meanings we impute to ads are, it seems, highly influenced by the interpretive context in which the ad is placed.

ADVERTISING AND SEMIOTICS

Semiotics deserves a brief mention because of its considerable influence in studies of advertising (Mick, 1986; Mick and Buhl, 1992). Semiotics is the study of signs and their meaning. American influence (particularly that of Charles Sanders Peirce) has broadened the field from the study of linguistic signs, also called semiology, to include the study of any signs whatsoever (Peirce, 1958; de Saussure, 1974; introductions in Danesi, 1994; Hackley, 1999b). Advertising and marketing have attracted much attention from semioticians (Williamson, 1978; Barthes, 2000). Ads are seen as 'strings of signs' in the service of the brand (Umiker-Sebeok, 1987). Such signs (copy, typeface, soundtrack, positioning, image, colour, objects) rhetorically support the sub-textual or covert meanings that are central to the persuasive force of advertising. The meaning of a given sign depends on the context, the receiver and the communication codes that form the cultural expectations of the sender and receiver.

The sales message, if one can be discerned among the cacophony of signification in many ads, is only one part of the complex process of communication that is going on when a consumer engages with an ad and attempts to interpret its meaning. For example, another way of analysing polysemic ads is to look at the signification properties of each part of the ad. These will include the copy and the other visual elements: colours, print quality, actors, props in the scene, the clothes, the juxtaposition of images, the intertextual references, and so on. Semiotics seeks to recover the communicative codes through which we receive messages from word, visual, auditory or other signs.

Marketing as a whole is a rich source of symbolism that reaches into the most intimate areas of our lives to transform the meaning of everyday signs (Sawchuck, 1995). The acts of shaving, washing and even personal cleanliness are superimposed with marketed values. Advertising lies at the fulcrum of marketing's semiotic mechanism, symbolically articulating the brand values contrived by the strategists. We will return to some of these concepts as the book progresses through its account of the advertising and promotion field.

LEVELS OF EXPLANATION IN ADVERTISING THEORY: COGNITIVE, SOCIAL AND CULTURAL

In the book we hint at the vast range of theory in advertising. To conclude Chapter 2 it is worth briefly discussing the role and purpose of theory in the context of social science, given that scholarship and research in advertising are concerned both with managerial issues and matters of social policy. The difficulty of this is that theory and research in management and business are derivative. Management and business do not have their own theories and methods but borrow them from social science. This creates problems of ecological validity. To express this with an example, why should a theory of emotion developed in general psychology be appropriate for advertising? All too often, social scientific theories are bolted onto advertising contexts without any adaptation.

The marketing field in general has a tendency to use theories without reference to their original context. It has adapted, and often caricatured, theoretical and conceptual developments in many other social disciplines, such as economics, psychology and sociology (O'Shaughnessy, 1997; Foxall, 2000; Hackley, 2003c, 2009a; Gronhaug and Kleppe, 2010). Theoretical work in advertising has, as we have seen, similarly adapted work from other fields. Much advertising research draws on assumptions from mass communications research, which had, in turn, borrowed ideas such as linearity and the concept of the internal mental state from early research in AI and computing.

Much research into advertising has drawn on the arts and humanities, for example, literary theory (Scott, 1994a, 1994b), feminism (Stern, 1993b), anthropology (Sherry, 1987), ethnography (Ritson and Elliott, 1999), applied linguistics (Cook, 2001), critical theory (Elliott and Ritson, 1997), and so on. All this diversity begs the question of whether one can fairly evaluate a social theory without also understanding the assumptions about the audience for the research and the rightful aims of that research. To try to accommodate something of the diversity of theory in advertising in a way that reconciles the different kinds, it will be useful to draw on the notion of 'levels of explanation' in social research, which has been used in social psychology education to integrate differing kinds of theory (Stevens, 1996).

THE COGNITIVE LEVEL OF EXPLANATION

Advertising works at a cognitive level in that it influences the individual cognitive functions of perception, memory and attitude. Theories that focus on the cognitive levels of explanation also emphasise rational, conscious consumer thinking. The scope of explanation in such theories extends to the internal mental state of the individual and the assumed connection between those internal states and observed (consumer) behaviour. **Copy-testing**, experimental research designs and attitude research attempt to isolate the internal mental states which act as causal variables that motivate consumers to act on the advertising they see. This level of explanation offers succinct and measurable results, but its weakness is that it risks distorting the way consumers engage with and understand advertising to fit a set of convenient research methods.

Much cognitive research into advertising has taken the individual consumer as the unit of analysis (Holbrook, 1995: 93, citing McCracken, 1987: 123; Ritson and Elliott, 1999: 261; Hackley, 2002: 214). Unlike computers, humans depend heavily on social interaction for meaning. People born blind who have sight restored in middle age have to learn to perceive structures and images from a jumble of visual sensory data. In other words, they have to learn how to see. People who are raised in social isolation cannot naturally learn speech and people who live in a culture without mediated communication cannot 'read' advertising. The way that we understand advertising is deeply informed by the cultural understanding we can only acquire in social interaction. The experimental research paradigm that attempts to isolate individual physiological or attitudinal responses to advertising cannot easily capture this dimension.

THE SOCIAL LEVEL OF EXPLANATION

The social level of explanation offers an account of advertising that accommodates its social character. Advertising is not encountered in a social vacuum but in a given social context, and it occupies a place in public discourse. How we think about advertising is strongly influenced by what we hear others say about it. How many times has someone asked you if you have seen this or that ad? As ads become part of social discourse they assume the characteristics of social constructions, in the sense that Berger and Luckman (1966) described. Research and theory that focus on internal mental states (such as memory or attitude) fail to grasp the essentially malleable nature of these states. One's attitude towards an ad is not arrived at in isolation but is constructed in a social context. Social constructionism disputes the validity of the internal mental state as a construct and suggests that such states subsist in social discourse (see also Burr, 1995; Hackley, 2000). In practical terms, this implies that it is not sufficient to measure memory or attitude in experimental laboratories; rather, advertising research needs to look at consumer thinking and behaviour in its normal social context, in interaction.

It is hugely significant that advertising agency professionals understand this intuitively. But politically, many agencies still struggle to justify this form of understanding to clients and account managers who are concerned with measuring consumer attitudes to advertising. This fundamental difference of mentality is a central issue in advertising and promotional management, but many existing research approaches perpetuate the differences instead of providing possibilities for reconciliation (Hackley, 2003d).

THE CULTURAL LEVEL OF EXPLANATION

We have seen that advertising can be regarded as a form of cultural text. It takes the symbolic meanings and practices of non-consumer culture and recreates them in juxtaposition with marketed brands to suggest contrived brand values and to portray a brand personality. For advertising to be construed in this way there needs to be a symbolic aspect to the way consumers engage with advertising. We must understand advertising in terms that transfer symbolic meanings from our broader cultural experience to advertised brands (Belk, 1988; Mick and Buhl, 1992). This level of analysis broadens a socially constructed notion of advertising to accommodate the wider cultural influences that are the preconditions for local social discourse.

At this level of analysis power is an inevitable part of the picture. Brand marketing corporations have the economic and political power to impose contrived meanings upon cultural practices. Brand advertising, cleverly designed and expensively produced and exposed, can work to normalise particular social practices (such as cigarette smoking, alcohol drinking for females, fast food consumption for children) and invest these practices with symbolic values such as personal independence, power and coolness. In this way advertising can be seen to operate as an ideology or, indeed, as the 'super-ideology' of our time (Eagleton, 1991; Elliott and Ritson, 1997).

A detailed exposition of advertising as ideology lies beyond the scope of this book. It is worth pointing out, though, that an intellectually viable appraisal of how advertising works is incomplete without an understanding of advertising's ideological power to render consumption practices normal and everyday in an infinite variety of appealing portrayals, to invest these practices with rich cultural significance and to place the interests of brand marketing organisations at the forefront of social life. If marketing as a whole can be seen as a vast semiotic vehicle constituting experiences and identities, then advertising is its engine, providing a continuous stream of new images, ideas and portrayals of consumption in juxtaposition with marketed brands (Williamson, 1978; Wernick, 1991; Elliott, 1997; Elliot and Ritson, 1997; Brownlie et al., 1999; Klein, 2000; Lash and Lury, 2007).

CHAPTER SUMMARY

This chapter has discussed the importance of theory in advertising and outlined three overlapping but contrasting traditions: the practitioner tradition, the information processing tradition, and the socio-cultural tradition (Hackley, 2010). It reviewed practice-based advertising theory, some of which is still well known in the advertising world, such as the idea of the USP. The chapter then discussed linear information processing theories of persuasive communication and the hierarchy-of-effects theories that they underpin, most notably AIDA. Finally, it reviewed a number of concepts from what it broadly labels as socio-cultural theory. The key distinction in the chapter reflects a contentious and long-running debate in marketing studies as a whole. Can marketing best be conceived as art, or as science? (See Brown, 1996 and 2001, for an overview.) There is a parallel debate in advertising, although the two perspectives achieve a tense but largely productive co-existence in most advertising agencies. This topic is explored again in Chapter 10 on research in advertising. For the present purpose, Chapter 2 has attempted to present an outline of some of the complex though highly influential issues in theorising advertising. These issues have very practical implications for advertising and promotional strategy, and are therefore central to the book.

REVIEW QUESTIONS

1 Choose three print advertisements and three TV ads. For each, construct descriptions that distinguish the covert from the ostensive meanings in the ad. Compare your interpretations with those of colleagues: do they differ?

2 What is meant by polysemy? What is its importance in advertising? Collect several magazines: can you find ads that appear to be polysemic?

3 Choose one print ad and form a group with three collaborators. Try to pick out all the individual signs that might carry meaning in the ad. These might include the copy (the words, the position of the copy in the visual and the typeface or font that is used), the models, the props in the set, the background, the relation of objects and bodies to each other, the gestures, the quality of paper and use of colour and the other brands advertised in the magazine. What is the meaning of each in its context?

4 What is a message? To what extent is meaning carried unequivocally within an advertisement? Compare three ads to discuss this.

5 Choose three ads. Try to discern the message and conceptualise the ad in terms of the stages of AIDA. How effective is your conceptualisation in explaining how the ad might 'work'?

VIDEO QUESTIONS

How do the different advertsing theories impact on the message and the form of delivery?

Do you agree that we are facing the death of the USP? If so, how would this impact on adversting?

How relevant is the AIDA model to the media landscape today?

What is polysemy? How does it look in advertising? Can you think of other examples? What is intertextuality in advertising? Can you think of other examples?

CASE STUDY

Polysemy and intertextuality in advertising

Do advertisements carry meanings that can then be injected, as it were, into the consumer, via the hypodermic of a media channel? Or are attempts to eliminate ambiguity in communication (reflected in linear information processing theories and AIDA) based on a fundamental misunderstanding of the nature of media, as Marshall McLuhan (1964) argued? Socio-cultural theories in advertising have adapted some concepts from literary criticism to illuminate some of the ways in which advertising can generate meaning in interaction with readers in a given cultural context. In this case we look at two – intertextuality and polysemy. What these concepts enable us to do is to talk about the ways that advertisements sometimes use ambiguity as a strategic tool. The cognitive paradigm of advertising theory cannot do this because it acknowledges no role for ambiguity in advertising.

Advertising, like all communication, can only become meaningful by virtue of the context in which it is transmitted and received. It is essentially a 'parasitic' communication form in the sense that it draws from, and refers to, styles, genres and discourses of textual and visual representation that are not exclusive to advertising but subsist in other cultural areas (Cook, 2001). The idea of intertextuality originated with Julia Kristeva and the French poststructuralists in discussions of literature but has been adapted to advertising by many academic researchers (e.g. O'Donohoe, 1997; Feng and Wignell, 2011; Torres, 2015; Al-Siyami, 2016). The literary concept of intertextuality refers to the idea that no text is entirely original or autonomous but consists of references, conscious or not, to other cultural texts. Just as in speech a phoneme generates meaning only in the context of other phonemes, a text is said to generate meaning in the context of, and in relation to, other texts. For example, a TV advertisement might be accompanied by a song that was a hit in the 1960s, or by some news footage of iconic events, such as the Beatles at Shea Stadium, or President J.F. Kennedy's assassination. Such intertextual references, whether auditory, visual or verbal, would be designed to make the target audience turn its head to watch or to listen – especially if the target audience happens to be baby boomers who recall these events, images or songs. Intertextual references do not have to be to events beyond advertising – in contemporary media, they may be references to other media texts. For example, a 2016 UK TV campaign for a price comparison website had furry meerkat characters acting out the hit movie *Frozen*,[13] while an earlier example from Cadbury's played on the TV series *Dallas*.[14] Intertextual references can act as an implicit targeting device by using references that are within the cultural understanding of one group, but not another (O'Donohoe, 1997). Intertextuality can also be used to communicate implicitly what cannot be stated explicitly. For example, cigarette brand Silk Cut famously deployed the technique when the UK government applied tighter regulations on cigarette advertising in the 1970s. The posters consisted merely of a sheet of silk with a cut in it – but the targeted audience knew exactly what was being advertised. The fact that the audience has to do a little work to retrieve the meaning from an enigmatic image made it all the more engaging.

Polysemy overlaps conceptually with intertextuality and many advertisements display elements of both. Polysemy refers to the capacity for a communication to have two or more possible interpretations (see Snapshot 2.1). The use of intentional ambiguity or 'purposeful polysemy' in advertising is common not only in the fashion and fragrance sectors but also in many others (Puntoni et al., 2010). The intention is to draw the viewer into the game of interpretation and thus increase their engagement, perhaps to the extent of prompting them to discuss it with friends. The generation of all advertising meaning is dependent on shared cultural reference points between the makers of the ad and the audience. Polysemy plays with the shared cultural knowledge, nudging the viewer into the pleasurable sense of recognition as they 'get' the reference, and the intended meaning of the ad. The Diesel clothing brand has made much use of purposeful polysemy in many campaigns with intriguingly absurd visual and textual juxtapositions that defy explanation, but implicate the brand in a sophisticated but whimsical game. As Cook (2001) suggests, perhaps one of the most important roles served by advertising is to fuel a need for play, and much advertising certainly tries to do that.

Case questions

1. Choose any three print or broadcast advertisements. Can you identify the intertextual elements in each? What does this tell you about the intended target market segment?
2. What kinds of cultural knowledge do you feel are required in order to identify the intertextual elements in your chosen advertisements?
3. Is one implication of intertextuality that advertising cannot be interpreted in the same way by people from different cultures? If this is so, how can you explain, for example, the global success of the Diesel brand, which often uses the same campaign globally without adaptation?
4. Choose three ads that seem to combine intertextuality and polysemy and interpret their meaning. What might be the benefits to the brand of this strategic ambiguity (Puntoni et al., 2010)?

PHOTO 6 Silk Cut Cigarettes

Image Courtesy of the Advertising Archives

In advertising, as with other forms of rhetoric, what is not said is sometimes more powerful than what is said. This ad for Silk Cut cigarettes featured in outdoor billboards, magazines and newspapers. The tobacco industry had responded cleverly to the ban on TV advertising for cigarettes by becoming more creative with their print and outdoor campaigns. In this example the well-known Silk Cut brand is evoked simply with an image, one of a series that used intertextuality and polysemy to engage consumers in a sophisticated game of visual interpretation. This visual metaphor became iconic in UK advertising.

USEFUL JOURNAL ARTICLES

(These Sage articles can be accessed on the companion website.)

Campelo, A., Aitken, R. and Gnoth, J. (2011) 'Visual rhetoric and ethics in marketing of destinations', *Journal of Travel Research*, 50 (1): 3–14 (first published 19 March 2010).

Cova, B., Maclaran, P. and Bradshaw, A. (2013) 'Rethinking consumer culture theory from the postmodern to the communist horizon', *Marketing Theory*, 13 (2): 213–25.

Miles, C. (2007) 'A cybernetic communication model for advertising', *Marketing Theory*, 7: 307–34.

Nan, X. and Faber, R.J. (2004) 'Advertising theory: reconceptualizing the building blocks', *Marketing Theory*, 4 (June): 7–30.

Phillips, B.J. and McQuarrie, E.F. (2004) 'Beyond visual metaphor: a new typology of visual rhetoric in advertising', *Marketing Theory*, 4 (June): 113–36.

Schwarzkopf, S. (2011) 'The political theology of consumer sovereignty: towards an ontology of consumer society', *Theory, Culture & Society*, 28 (3): 106–29.

FURTHER READING

Arnould, E. and Thompson, C. (2005) 'Consumer culture theory (CCT): twenty years of research', *Journal of Consumer Research*, 31: 868–82.

Danesi, M. (2006) *Brands*. London and New York: Routledge.

Hackley, C. (2003) *Doing Research Projects in Marketing, Management and Consumer Research*. London: Routledge.

Hackley, C. (2010) 'Theorizing advertising: managerial, scientific and cultural approaches', in P. MacLaran, M. Saren, B. Stern and M. Tadajewski (eds), *The Sage Handbook of Marketing Theory*. London: Sage, pp. 89–107.

Holt, D. (2004) *How Brands Become Icons: The Principles of Cultural Branding*. Boston, MA: Business School Press.

NOTES

1 '1959 Strand Cigarettes – Lonely Man', www.youtube.com/watch?v=WjBHUQEiTPw (accessed 18 March 2017).

2 Examples of emotional car ads are: Honda's 'Choir', see www.youtube.com/watch?v=gjyWP2LfbyQ; Skoda Fabia's 'Cake – Full of Lovely Stuff', see www.youtube.com/watch?v=k_uyUAR8nZE; Volkswagen's 'Stay in Safe Hands', see www.youtube.com/watch?v=vGPrfVeA0G0 (accessed 26 June 2017).

3 Mercedes-Benz ad, www.youtube.com/watch?v=VXO_WKe54jY&list=PLv2mhXe6zUJuEuoh0T8Le5j8eOes_NwxD (accessed 19 March 2017).

4 Cadbury's 'Gorilla' ad, http://vimeo.com/73564800 (accessed 11 February 2017).

5 Jo Caird, '"I was basically told: you are never showing this" – how we made Cadbury's Gorilla ad', *The Guardian*, 7 January 2016, www.theguardian.com/media-network/2016/jan/07/how-we-made-cadburys-gorilla-ad (accessed 29 March 2017).

6 'Cadbury's Dairy Milk: The Not-So-Secret Secret', see www.youtube.com/watch?v=aAymavc19Zs (accessed 29 March 2017).

7 'Nothing more than feelings', *The Economist*, 7 December, 2013, www.economist.com/news/business/21591165-admen-have-made-marketing-guru-daniel-kahneman-prizewinning-psychologist-nothing-more (accessed (11 February 2017).

8 'Diesel: Be Stupid Advertising Campaign', www.creativeadawards.com/diesel-be-stupid-advertising-campaign/ (accessed 11 February 2017).

9 Guinness: Advertising, www.guinness.com/en-gb/advertising/ (accessed 29 March 2017).

10 'Omega Co-Axial Chronometer', www.youtube.com/watch?v=ctj-RDbTBMU (accessed 18 March 2017).

11 Some visual examples of intertextuality in advertising: www.bing.com/images/search?q=intertextuality+in+advertising&qpvt=intertextuality+in+advertising&qpvt=intertextuality+in+advertising&qpvt=intertextuality+in+advertising&FORM=IGRE (accessed 29 March 2017).

12 Bibby Sowray, 'YSL Opium advert is eighth most complained about', 30 May 2012, http://fashion.telegraph.co.uk/news-features/TMG9299894/YSL-Opium-advert-is-eighth-most-complained-about.html (accessed 29 March 2017).

13 'Oleg's Magical Dream', www.youtube.com/watch?v=rmxvmS0gpx4 (accessed 6 July 2017).

14 Cadbury's Fingers ad, www.youtube.com/watch?v=J2quHgLgepQ (accessed 11 February 2017).

BRANDS AND PROMOTIONAL COMMUNICATION

CHAPTER OUTLINE

The brand is the central concept of consumer marketing, and integration of promotional campaigns across different media channels, both on and offline, is the key theme of contemporary advertising in the convergence era. This chapter explores the notion of the brand in relation to the promotional communication upon which many brands depend for their continuing salience. The chapter focuses on the management task of conceiving, planning and communicating brands, it touches on the theme of integrated marketing communication and explores distinctions between marketing strategy and advertising strategy in a broad examination of the ways in which advertising and promotional communication can support brand marketing objectives.

KEY CHAPTER CONTENT

- Branding basics – origins and conceptualisation
- What advertising and promotional communication can do for brands
- The strategic brand management process and communication planning
- IMC planning
- Limitations to IMC

Want a primer? Go to **https://study.sagepub.com/hackley4e** and watch...

Strategic Branding **to learn**
How you define brands, their impact and importance, the reasons brands are created and the advantages of having a strong brand

Brands as Broadcasters **to learn**
How the relationship between brands and advertising has changed

Strategic Brand Management **to learn**
The elements and factors that go into the strategic brand management process

... to tackle the video questions at the end of the chapter.

BRANDING BASICS: ORIGINS AND CONCEPTUALISATION

In Chapter 3 we turn from the complexities of theorising advertising and promotion campaigns to the underlying purpose of most campaigns – the promotion of a brand. We note that the idea of a brand has become extended from a product, to services, to non-profit, entertainment, government, health and almost anything else. In Chapter 2, we noted a number of theoretical perspectives on advertising that illustrated how difficult it is to impose meaning on an individual consumer through an advertisement. Part of the enigma of the advertising business is that we may not fully understand how it works, but it does, nevertheless, seem to do so and there are many striking examples. Indeed, it is hardly possible to conceive of the world's most prominent brands without advertising. In this chapter we focus on the management task of conceiving, planning and communicating brands. Firstly, it is important to reflect a little on the central concept of integrated advertising and promotion – the brand.

Brands and branding, like most areas of marketing, are not short of definitions, few of which are helpful in capturing the nebulous entity they seek to describe. The American Marketing Association (AMA) offers numerous definitions in its website dictionary resource, including this one: A brand is a name, term, sign, design, symbol or any other feature that identifies one seller's good or service as distinct from those of other sellers. As Keller (2012) points out, this definition ignores something that marketing practitioners regard as very important – a brand is nothing until it is recognised as such by a meaningful number of consumers. In other words, a brand is more than the name or symbol, but is a reputation, a set of recognised values, a presence in the marketplace, what Keller calls the industry's concept of a brand with a capital B. The capital B is often generated through advertising and promotional communication, but service, quality and reliability are also indispensable in generating WOM endorsements that build reputation. De Chernatony et al. (2010) also emphasise the augmented aspect of the essential brand as something that adds customer value to the name, symbols and basic functionality. Lury (2011: 137) cites Wang (2008) suggesting that a product is made in a factory, but a brand is bought by a consumer. The perception of the brand is what appears to be the key notion here – it matters little if Daz soap powder really does 'wash whiter', as the strapline insisted – what matters is that the consumer remembers the strapline and, by association, the brand name.

Rosenbaum-Elliott et al. (2015) draw attention to the brand as a sign that is rich in potential signification, alluding to the semiotics of signs and symbolism (Umiker-Sebeok, 1987; Danesi, 2006). It is implied in the work of management theorists such as Keller that brand management can, in principle, design the desired signification into the brand and impose it on the perceptions of consumers. Advertising is a rich vehicle for signification in juxtaposition with brands and the suggestive power of brand communication invests products with the potential to act as resources for identity projects (Belk, 1988; Goldman and Papson, 1994). But, as we saw in Chapter 2, the fact that communication may be crafted by the brand owner does not necessarily mean that the meaning of the brand can be injected unproblematically into the mentality of the consumer. Brands are considered to be co-creations of organisations and consumer culture (Zwick et al., 2008). This possibility poses a

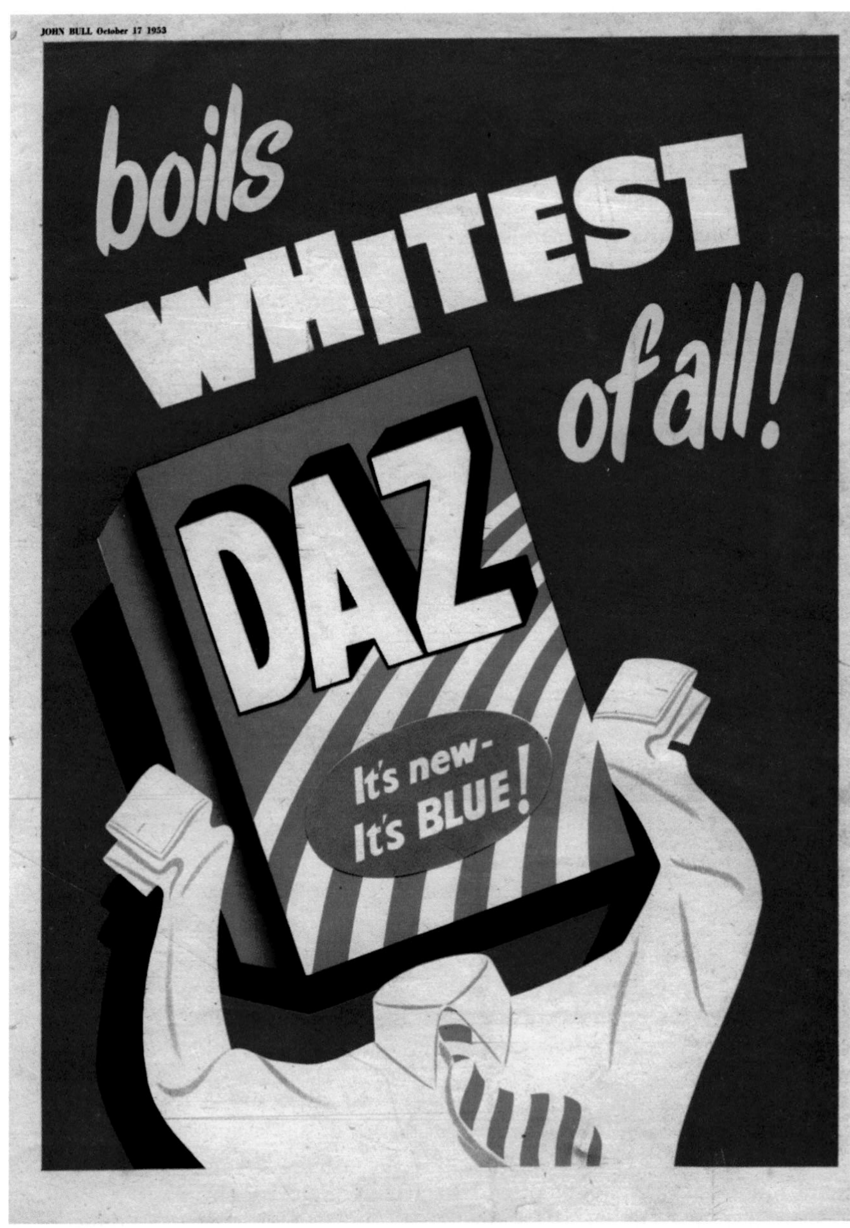

PHOTO 7 Daz Soap

Image Courtesy of the Advertising Archives

This 1950s magazine ad for Daz detergent played on the USP (unique selling proposition) formula in a simple but economical creative execution. It told readers that Daz washes clothes whiter than any other detergent (a claim which, in the best advertising tradition, was impossible either to prove or to refute). It used a bright cartoon image that anthropomorphised the grateful shirt to give energy and appeal to the message. The commodity is named, and brought to life with an anthropomorphic image and a slogan that make it irresistibly memorable, whatever its qualities.

problem for the hypodermic model of brand management. Holt (2004) goes further in proposing that brands are constituted by the stories that are circulated about them. These stories emanate from companies, from culture, from intermediaries such as trade press and salespeople, and from consumers. Holt notes that the idea of brands as psychological phenomena based on perceptions is a popular one, but he suggests that, 'what makes a brand powerful is the collective nature of these perceptions; the stories have become conventional and so are continually reinforced because they are treated as truths in everyday interactions' (Holt, 2004: 3). The notion of brand storytelling has become a prominent theme in marketing practice, especially in the world of branded content, and it plays neatly into the related ideas of brands as cultural constructions that can be sustained through iterations of their stories. Or, as Feldwick (2015) suggests, the brand is a circus, and the task of brand management is to keep the audience in their seats. What better way to do this than to articulate compelling stories around the brand. For Holt brand stories can be culturally encoded through OOH promotion, advertising, store design, brand names, design, and many other consumer touch points.

Branding as a metaphor originates from the physical process of burning identification marks into livestock, but the modern understanding of branding has a shorter history. In 1867 Harvey Proctor re-named his white soap Ivory Soap in one of the earliest examples of branding as we understand it today. Proctor's imagery of the distinctive branded packaging, and the slogan that went with the posters ('99 and 44/100 % pure') was soon recognised as a powerful aid to recalling and recognising the brand (Danesi, 2006). It was quickly learned that named products outsold generic products. Others soon followed with some, like Parker Pens, converting their trademark into a brand name. Among the first named brands in the UK grocery market at the turn of the twentieth century were Hovis, Bovril, Cadbury, Fry and Kellogg. Brand names were soon extended from groceries to technical products such as Singer sewing machines and Raleigh bicycles, and by around the 1920s brands had become the focus of advertising. Branding, evidently, is central to the emergence of consumer culture as brands can be conceived in different ways. For example, Holt and Cameron (2010) argue that brands are essentially ideological entities that draw on cultural myths to resolve identity dilemmas. They are ideological in the sense that they entail a number of beliefs and values that do not necessarily have a material basis. For example, Holt and Cameron cite Marlboro as an example of a brand that was rather unremarkable as a women's cigarette, but was transformed through advertising in a symbol that drew on myths of American masculinity. As American men felt that their power in society was waning, the cigarette brand symbolically restored it. Rosenbaum-Elliott et al. (2015), in contrast, emphasise the extent to which brands can be understood as psychological perceptions that are overlaid with emotional and symbolic elements. Keller (2012) goes further to argue that these perceptions can be imposed on consumers through managerial action because, he suggests, branding is a science of management control.

While conceptualisations of the brand differ, it can hardly be denied that what constitutes a brand has changed radically. The early branded grocery and machine products were manufactured innovations that had a material basis – sewing machines sewed clothes, soap cleansed, bicycles moved people from A to B. Later on, branding moved into more abstract entities such as services (Vargo and Lusch, 2004) and experiences (Gilmore and Pine, 2011), particularly, experiences of entertainment (Wolf, 2003; Lehu, 2007; Sayre, 2007). Today, the notion of the brand has been altered along with the economics of branding. Iconic social network Facebook has about 2 billion active users, yet it produces no media content of its own. The world's biggest taxi firm, Uber, is based on an owner-driver business model and therefore owns few cars of its own, other than the driverless ones it is reported to be trialling at the time of writing, in March 2017. Alibaba, the world's biggest retailer, owns no stock. Twitter is credited with fomenting revolutions, fuelling regime changes and driving political populism, yet it remains a resolutely loss-making business enterprise. The internet has changed business models and, with them, the very nature of branding.

Traditionally, the brand can be described as a badge of origin, a promise of performance, a reassurance of quality, and a transformation of experience (Feldwick, 2002: 4–9; de Chernatony et al., 2010). Brands trigger recognition which, if accompanied by a sense of reassurance about the value the brand brings to a consumption practice, enables consumers to avoid a lengthy and time-consuming search every time we wish to buy something. This recognition can be loaded with cultural values that ostensibly differentiate the brand from alternatives and make it more meaningful to particular consumer groups. What is more, brands transform experience through these cultural values. Drinking a Coke, for example, is far more culturally loaded than merely slaking thirst, since the brand evokes echoes of many advertising campaigns promoting it in juxtaposition with its American provenance and a sense of friendship, joy and togetherness. Similarly, drinking a coffee with Coffemate, washing one's hair with L'Oréal, driving a BMW or drinking PG Tips tea all transform the prosaic acts themselves by layering them with second order meanings (Schroeder and Salzer-Morling, 2005; Danesi, 2006). Advertising and promotion are key to these meanings.

Brand strategy is often conceived in terms of what Holt and Cameron (2010) call a 'mind share' model, the psychological model we touch upon above. Attributing this type of approach to authors such as Aaker (e.g. 1995, 2004), the brand is said to have a personality (an idea originally attributed to advertising man David Ogilvy, 1983), which is created by the brand management and then communicated to the target market through advertising and promotion. The brand personality (sometimes referred to as its identity in similar models) should have values and attributes that distinguish it from alternatives in the market, and therefore it should occupy a distinctive place in the consumer's mind (hence, 'mindshare'). The brand is essentially seen as a psychological construct. All the aspects of the brand that might impact on its identity or personality are referred to as brand equity, and the management task is said to be to manipulate these elements in order to maintain the brand's distinctive positioning in the consumer's mind. As Keller has suggested, there is no universally agreed definition of brand equity, but it has become a much-used if nebulous term. Rosenbaum-Elliott et al. (2015) state that brand equity has been described variously as 'the value of the brand to the customer', 'the additional cash flow achieved by

PHOTO 8 Marlboro Man

Image Courtesy of the Advertising Archives

The Tattooed Marlboro Man in this 1955 print ad was a predecessor of the iconic cowboy Marlboro Man. Marlboro was regarded as a woman's cigarette when manufacturers Phillip Morris hired Chicago agency Leo Burnett to reposition the brand to men. They tried images of cattle ranchers, sailors and working men such as Mr Hand Tattoo above before settling on the cowboy. The Marlboro Man tapped into a powerful myth of American masculinity. The campaign is a fine example of how advertising, as a cultural intermediary, is capable of taking symbols and ideologies from consumer culture and combining them in new and novel ways.

associating a brand with the underlying product or service', 'the value that resides in a brand name, trade mark or product', 'the beliefs consumers associate with the brand', and 'the net value of the brand image', among other definitions (2015: 89–90). The risk of the notion of brand equity is that it reifies the brand into a fixed entity that must be preserved, and this can lead to a loss of market salience for the brand.

Holt and Cameron critique this approach for being too one-sided. They suggest that brands are cultural constructions that subsist not in individual psychology but in wider culture. Holt suggests that marketers and brand managers often think of brands as 'psychological phenomena which stem from the perceptions of individual consumers. But what makes a brand powerful is the collective nature of these perceptions; the stories have become conventional and so are continually reinforced because they are treated as truths in everyday interactions' (Holt, 2004: 3). Hence, in order to succeed, brands must tap into cultural currents and mobilise identity myths. Crucially, the implication is that brands cannot simply inject a desired brand identity or personality into the consumers' mind as if advertising and promotion were some kind of hypodermic. Instead, they must earn a deep anthropologically inspired understanding of what the brand means to the target consumers (McCracken, 1990; 2005).

On this reasoning, the brand is not a fixed entity created by brand management and inserted into the consumer's psychology but a cultural construction that subsists in the social spaces between people (Rosenbaum-Elliott et al., 2015). There is a concrete materiality in what the brand represents, whether that is the tangible elements of a service or a physical product, but the symbolic extension of the brand is a fluid entity. Brands tap into identity myths and, sometimes, mobilise a sense of shared experience among otherwise divergent members of brand communities (Belk, 1988; Muñiz and O'Guinn, 2001; Holt, 2002, 2004; Brodie et al., 2013). Brands are able to do this because their communicative meaning is not confined to their material functionality but extends to the meaning they are able to symbolise (Gardner and Levy, 1955). So, for example, the Marlboro Man became one of the most iconic symbols in American consumer culture through the advertising in which he symbolised a myth of American masculinity. The cigarettes, which were previously known as a women's brand, became a powerful symbol of this masculinity myth by association.

Brands are valuable (see Snapshot 3.1) because consumers seek them out, recognise them and buy them instead of alternatives. In effect, a successful brand acts as a quasi monopoly, because a proportion of consumers will seek out a particular brand, while ignoring the claims of other brands. As a result, brands allow companies to charge higher prices and make higher profits. They also enable the same companies to sell longer production runs and therefore produce at lower marginal costs. In competitive markets, this can mean lower consumer prices. Branding, marketing and advertising are not necessarily costs borne by the consumer. They can underpin economies of scale by improving productive efficiency. Put simply, brands earn greater revenue by doing one of three things: getting existing customers to pay more, getting them to buy more often, or getting more people to buy (Sharp, 2010). Brand management is about more than advertising and promotion, but the communication elements of brand strategy can be central to achieving any of these aims.

SNAPSHOT 3.1

The world's top brands by global revenue

Brand consultant Interbrand compiles a list of the top global brands each year by value.[1] In 2016 they placed Apple and Google at number 1 and number 2, with values of $178,000 million and $133,000 million respectively. The rest of the top ten were Coca-Cola, Microsoft, Toyota, IBM, Samsung, Amazon, Mercedes Benz and GE. Amazon and Facebook (at number 15) were the fastest growing brands in the top 50 by value. *Forbes*[2] magazine produces its own list with a different methodology, and also puts Apple at number 1, with Microsoft at number 2. Few would claim that advertising and promotion alone built these companies. Clearly, there have been important and essential elements of technical innovation, ownership of intellectual property and historical accident – Western brands seem to have an advantage because of its economic dominance. Most of the world's top brands are less than 50 years old but brands can be highly enduring over time. Nestlé's KitKat has been the market leading countline in the UK for over 50 years, while many European luxury brands have histories in excess of 100 years (Lu, 2008). Sharp (2010) has suggested that brand loyalty is less important in building and maintaining market share than often supposed. Instead, he argues that occasional, and fickle, purchasers are key to market share, provided the brand can attract enough of them. One implication of this is that target marketing might be over-rated, since the large periphery of consumers who shift from one brand to another are more important to the overall value of the brand than the hard core repeat customers. The revenues of the top global brand exceed the GNPs of some entire countries. For example, Apple's global revenue exceeds $200 billion. The stakes are high and advertising and promotional communication can make the difference.

Brands communicate values, attitudes, identity positioning and discernment, and hence they constitute a shared symbolic cultural vocabulary. We would get little out of owning and displaying brands as symbolic objects if we did not know that others also speak the same vocabulary. Advertising and promotion are key parts of this cultural vocabulary. For example, in Spotify's 2016 campaign, the company took social media comments that consumers had left and incorporated them into their advertising, thus leveraging (reflecting and also amplifying) the social media conversation that was already taking place. This reflects a growing awareness among brands that consumers are deeply invested in the brand and their stories can usefully be incorporated into the brand stories via social media (Gensler et al., 2013).

The notion of brand personality reflects the attempt to generate a sense of affinity between consumers and brands by anthropomorphising the brand, giving it human characteristics (a 'personality') in order to stimulate affective and emotional responses from consumers towards the brand. Many brands are anthropomorphised through fictional characters while others use celebrity spokespeople to give the brand a human face (Brown and Ponsonby-McCabe, 2013; Hackley and Hackley, 2015). The goal overall is to make it easier for a consumer to respond affectively to the brand as if it were human, by liking, not liking, being loyal to, being fond of or even loving, the brand. Some brand consultants even speak of a brand having a 'soul', but this is really further entrenching the idea of the brand personality in a silo. The notion that a brand has some essential soul or essence that can potentially be revealed, or perhaps just intuitively understood, is very misleading. The brand does not exist at all on a brand-planning document – it exists only in the social spaces occupied by consumers and as such there is no 'soul' or 'essence'. The brand is a relation and its cultural meaning will shift along with the cultural worlds of its consumers.

In keeping with the importance of brand anthropomorphism, social media and convergence mean that brands can respond in a dialogue with consumers in order to reinforce the sense of an interactive, two-way communication between consumer and brand (Ashley and Tuten, 2015; Armstrong et al., 2016). Some brand communication, such as advertising and promotion aired on bought media spots, can be controlled from one side, even if the ways it might be interpreted by consumers cannot necessarily be controlled. Other elements of brand communication, such as social media sentiment and press coverage, are, in principle, beyond the control of brand management. Brands have to react and respond to social media and other communications that emanate from the consumer side. Brands have to ride cultural currents and respond creatively to shifts in the popular sentiment or to topical events, in order to try to maintain their cultural resonance and remain relevant to their target audiences. The key issue for brand management is for managers and their advertising agencies to continuously work to understand the cultural milieu of their consumers so that their brand communications are cast in the same cultural idiom used by their consumers, so that they can make a connection with their consumers' cultural experience.

For some, advertising that encourages us to think that our choice of detergent is important to our sense of social status, our identity, even our happiness, is ridiculous. It may be absurd, but through advertising, brands acquire this strange power to transform an everyday activity into something more meaningful that connects it to the wider symbolic world, at least if we suspend our scepticism for a little while. The brands themselves are often competing with similar commodities for our attention and our repeat purchases, and they will try to be as alluring as possible to us in order to be able to compete with their market rivals. Advertising and promotion are central to the realisation of the cultural resonance and market potential of brands. In a fundamental sense, communication doesn't simply pass on messages about the brand – it constitutes the brand.

SNAPSHOT 3.2

IMC and B2B: Slideshare and B2B content

Integrated marketing communications remains discussed in academic texts but it has long been regarded as a default position in the marketing industries. In order to achieve the necessary audience reach and salience brands have to be prepared to use multiple channels, and somehow they have to co-ordinate their channel communications, creatively and strategically. This is not confined to consumer marketing. As Dr Owen Matson of Texas company MarketScale has pointed out, social media for business-to-business (B2B) has moved beyond LinkedIn and Slideshare is one of the means through which B2B brands are sharing content. Matson (2017) points out that Slideshare is one of the top 120 websites in the world with some 60 million unique visitors per month. Slideshare is free to use, including its data analytic tools, and it has video functionality, which means better SEO. Video is key to content and the astonishing potential reach of video sharing (as we saw in Chapter 1 with the multiple million audience reach of some YouTube influencers) can be added to Slideshare presentations to enhance engagement. B2B content is a different genre to consumer-based content, but nonetheless it too is transformed in the convergence era. Some strategic skills, though, remain as old as advertising itself. The most resonant creative ideas are founded on genuinely penetrating consumer and market insight.

WHAT ADVERTISING AND PROMOTIONAL COMMUNICATION CAN DO FOR BRANDS

Advertising's role in marketing is often under-emphasised. It is easy to see why. Advertising and promotion are, too often, the very last things marketing or brand managers think about, after product development, market testing, business analysis, production planning, material sourcing, distribution and so on. Yet it is a mistake to assume that the sequence of managerial activities involved in bringing a market offering to the consuming public reflects their relative importance. Advertising and other forms of marketing communication are not in themselves sufficient for successful consumer brand marketing, but in most cases they are necessary to the success of the venture. From a managerial perspective, advertising and promotion are the final step in bringing an offering to market. From a consumer perspective, advertising is often the only visible aspect of the marketing chain, and, via social media, it is often seamlessly linked to purchase and delivery. Of course, few consumers will concede that we are susceptible to the suggestions of advertising. We prefer to think of ourselves as heroically resisting the manipulative intent of brand marketing. To be sure, consumers are not dupes and we engage critically with the marketing we encounter. The issue is that the key decisions have already been made when we engage with marketing. Financial and other barriers to market entry meant that our choices are framed by our consumer cultural environment (Hackley, 2013a). Advertising is often our point of entry into the long chain of brand marketing planning and co-ordination, and it is inherently a narrow one. We are presented with limited sets of choices and our wellbeing is framed in terms of consumption. The advertising helps to establish a set of assumptions that the consumer will bring to all other aspects of their engagement with a given brand.

Advertising and promotion are not only produced for the benefit of consumers and, concomitantly, shareholders. They are also important for the confidence and morale of other parties who have a stake in the a brand, such as sales staff and other employees, intermediaries, suppliers, regulators, business and consumer journalists, and investors. Advertising provides tangible evidence of the financial credibility and competitive presence of an organisation. Corporate communication is a distinct discipline in itself. But in a broader sense every ad is a reflection on the corporation that sponsored it because of the cumulative influence on its commercial credibility. Tangible benefits from this credibility might include longer supplier credit periods, greater influence over suppliers' prices, better employee retention and more effective recruitment, and greater confidence among stock market players.

Advertising's corporate influence can spread far beyond the brand. As a device of marketing strategy, advertising and promotion can also be both subtle and precise. The UK Institute for Practitioners in Advertising (IPA)[3] claims that among other business aims, advertising can:

- defend brands against own-label growth
- effect change internally as well as externally to the company
- increase the efficiency of recruitment
- transform entire businesses by generating new markets for a brand
- revitalise a declining brand
- reinvigorate a market
- stop line extensions cannibalising existing sales
- change behaviour
- influence share price
- make other communications more cost-effective
- generate rapid sales increases
- increase growth of a mature brand in a declining market
- address crises in public relations.

With creative ingenuity and careful targeting, advertising can support many kinds of marketing objective. It must be remembered that advertising itself is communication: ads cannot sell anything as such, because they cannot answer 'objections' to purchase as a personal salesperson can although advertising on social media certainly has interactive properties that traditional mass media advertising before social media did not (Gensler et al., 2013; Armstrong et al., 2016). What they can do is place particular ideas in the public realm to publicise offers in juxtaposition with a brand name, values and images. Advertising can support marketing strategies such as positioning and repositioning, market **segmentation**, launch and relaunch, raising brand **awareness** or rebranding, and fulfilling corporate communication objectives.

NON-COMMERCIAL BRANDING

Consumer marketing is by no means alone in using integrated marketing communication planning. For example, while political parties have long deployed techniques from marketing, including market research, advertising, targeting, branding and PR (O'Shaughnessy, 2001; Peng and Hackley, 2007; Ormrod et al., 2013) in recent years social media marketing has now become central to political marketing (Cogburn and Espinoza-Vasquez, 2011; Towner and Dulio, 2012). Many other organisations have adopted marketing and advertising for ostensibly socially beneficial outcomes such as, for example, health departments of governments who deploy advertising and other marketing tools to try to encourage healthier alcohol consumption practices (Kotler and Roberto, 1989; Hackley et al., 2015).

The uses of political advertising and marketing in the UK date from the late 1970s. Initially, there was some resistance to it. For example, the UK Labour Party and the trade unions were historically unsympathetic to advertising because they associated it with a sell-out to capitalism. As a result, such organisations were unable to promote themselves effectively. A change of viewpoint eventually emerged, significantly because of the involvement of the DDB London chairman at the time, Chris Powell (Peng and Hackley, 2009). This change of view about using advertising to promote left-wing politics and issues coincided with the political revival of the Labour Party. One poster campaign called 'Labour Isn't Working' produced by Saatchi & Saatchi for the UK Conservative Party for the 1979 general election has been described as the most successful political advertisement of all time,[4] since it was credited with winning the election for the Conservatives.

Non-profit advertising including charities, public sector, health services and public safety and information campaigns have collectively become a significant sector of the advertising business. For a time, under the Labour government of 1997–2010, the government through its Central Office of Information was the largest single spender on advertising in the UK, out-spending even the largest consumer goods conglomerates. The use of advertising in public service campaigns, though, can be seen as problematic, and it is questionable how effective it is in public health issues such as alcohol consumption (Szmigin et al., 2011). Campaigns in these areas are subject to similar planning processes as commercial advertising and promotion. The differences lie in the fact that each sector serves different stakeholders and, therefore, has different objectives to fulfil and different expectations to meet.

ADVERTISING AND SEGMENTATION

Marketing management texts have popularised the term 'segmentation' to refer to the need for categories of consumer to be broken down for easy identification, surveillance (through consumer research) and targeting (Kotler and Keller, 2015). Consumers are often complicit in this categorisation, since we eagerly seek out ads and images that we feel cohere with our sense of social identity and resonate with our individual aspirations and fantasies (Holbrook and Hirschman, 1982; Belk, 1988; Elliott and Wattanasuwan, 1998). Most importantly, this entails creating a sense of otherness towards categories of consumer that are not us. In a given TV or poster ad, the casting, the set, the scene props and the dialogue are all powerful signifiers of the kind of human that is supposed to favour a given brand. Through advertising and promotional communication we are offered resources from which to produce a sense of identity through consumption (or through resisting consumption) (O'Donohoe, 1994, 1997; Ritson and Elliott, 1999). This sense of identity through consumption is liminal in the sense that it can give us a sense of social and personal change, even if the change is symbolic and illusory (Olsen, 2016).

It is a cliché in advertising that half the budget is wasted, but no one knows which half. The value of segmentation to organisations is that it is designed to improve marketing ROI by reducing the amount of the marketing budget that is misdirected at undesired consumer groups. Clearly there is a potential drawback to targeting a given segment. If the target group is wrongly identified then there is a risk that the entire marketing budget might be misdirected, instead of only half of it. What is more, many brands have a cultural resonance that leverages their presence among many people who do not and will never buy the brand, such as car brands Mercedes, BMW and Jaguar (see Chapter 1 case study). As we have seen, brand planners might see sales increases as a long-term consequence of a strongly sustained brand personality. An over-emphasis on targeting might neglect to project the brand personality to non-consumers. This could be an important omission given that the brand personality depends as much on the perceptions of non-consumers as of consumers.

ADVERTISING, BRANDS AND DIFFERENTIAL ADVANTAGE

Competitive brand management demands differentiation, however that is achieved. The emphasis might be placed on managing brand 'equity' through a carefully constructed brand 'architecture', or it could be placed on a 'mindspace' positioning designed to create a sense of differential in the consumers' perceptions (Keller, 2012; Rosenbaum-Elliott et al., 2015). Or, indeed, it might entail both. Arguably, the decisive source of differential advantage for brands in competitive markets is often communication. This is not to suggest that product and service design, innovation, quality, access to distribution channels, merchandising, service, and so on cannot each be decisive in particular cases. However, these can potentially be matched by competitors given the relative ease of international technology transfer, deregulated markets, rising affluence across developing markets, international trade in raw materials, the ease of information access via the internet, the popularity of international payment systems, global distribution and the difficulty of enforcing intellectual copyright. Not only this, but even brands with an apparent advantage in technology, design or cost are not necessarily perceived as being of a better quality or value than competitors. Furthermore, in developed economies consumer markets are increasingly sensitive to the actual or perceived links between public events, personalities and news stories, and brands. This makes the brand vulnerable to unexpected changes in public taste. In short, it can be argued that communication is the single most important element in the creation of sustainable competitive advantage (Schultz et al., 1993, 1996; Shimp, 2009).

It is important to note that most consumers will gain their knowledge of most brands through communication, and probably from advertising and promotion in some form, since most consumers do not buy most brands. To put it another way, markets for even popular brands consist of relatively small proportions of populations. For example, car maker BMW sold about 150,000 new cars in the UK each year between 2014 and 2017. The population of the UK is about 65 million, roughly 52 million of whom are of driving age. Therefore, most UK drivers do not own a BMW. They are likely to be quite familiar with the brand because of its long history and prominence in the worlds of motor racing, rallying and Hollywood movies, not to mention the branded content movies discussed in Chapter 1. Many citizens are likely to be able to recognise a BMW in the street. Nonetheless, the great majority of people in the UK do not own one and may never have ridden in one. The task of BMW marketing and communication, then, is not to make potential owners aware of the brand, nor to make claims about the performance of the car or the quality of the service. Major global car brands tend to be very competitive on quality, reliability and service, and earning a clear sense of differentiation on those bases is difficult. Rather, the task is to communicate a sense of the distinctiveness of the brand in creatively compelling ways so that next time a driver is considering replacing their car, they might consider test driving a BMW.

Consider the oft-repeated taste tests that place Pepsi ahead of Coca-Cola, yet Coca-Cola consistently outperforms Pepsi in market share (Yglesias, 2013). Leaving aside the fallibility of consumer research, advertising communication is an essential component of brand marketing. A brand lives on through consumer perceptions that are formed in engagement with advertising communication. The distinctive positioning, segmentation and targeting that is so difficult to achieve and sustain through other means can be achieved symbolically through advertising and promotional communication. The point that communication is integral to how consumers understand and engage with marketed brands does not necessarily imply that a brand is all about superficial 'puffery' and short-term publicity. 'Puffery' is the name given to advertising copy that is so clearly hyperbolic that no reasonable person would take it literally. It is also sometimes used as a derogatory term for advertising in general. Most advertising conveys something about a brand's values and characteristics, but this is not all there is to brand marketing. Brand managers will normally argue that communications are like the tip of an iceberg, just visible above the waterline with a far more substantial structure, unseen, beneath. This invisible structure includes production, staffing, training, operations, logistics, supply and material sourcing, and all the other activities without which a branded product or service could not reach a marketplace. The communications dimension, the tip of the iceberg, is all that the general public can see and that is why it is so important.

Most brands have a concrete existence as businesses with plant, machinery and personnel, but they also have another existence as an idea in the collective public mind. Some brands, such as Virgin,[5] exist primarily as an abstract entity covering many diverse businesses (an airline, a cable TV and phone supplier, music production company, tourism and space travel operator and many more). In some cases, such as Virgin, corporate brands act as a family branding system, even if there may be no connection between those different businesses, other than the corporate branding. In other cases, such as Unilever or P&G, the corporate branding may often be invisible and individual product market offers are branded as distinct entities.

Brand advertising and communication, then, should not be thought of as a trivial or superficial activity in a marketing context. It is central to success in consumer, and increasingly industrial, B2B and services marketing. For consumers the brand image or personality, the values and associations linked with the brand, the way the brand is talked about by friends and acquaintances, the way the brand is represented in press editorial and TV coverage, and the memory of personal experience of consuming the brand, are all aspects of a holistic engagement with this entity, the brand. A consumer brand is a fine exemplar of the notion of social construction since a brand is more than the sum of its parts, it is the ways in which it is understood, perceived and talked about (Berger and Luckman, 1966). What is more, the perceptions of the brand become reality in the world of mediated communication, just as, in Berger and Luckman's (1966) example, a book can assume a separate but parallel existence through the way it is perceived and talked about. Influencing the way this abstraction is thought and spoken of is clearly a task in which communication is a primary tool.

SNAPSHOT 3.3

Brand positioning and integrated communication

Positioning refers broadly to the values and associations, both tangible and intangible, that are linked with a given brand in relation to its competition (Kotler and Keller, 2015). Positioning can be described with concrete qualities of the brand, price differentials, service enhancements, but consumer perceptions of these elements are what matter. Hence, positioning is often described as a psychological notion that differentiates the brand from its rivals in the perception of consumers. Positioning can be conceived graphically, as a positioning 'map' in which competitors are mapped according to two dimensions, say, price and quality. Positioning can also be conceived linguistically in terms of metaphors that connect the brand to its values and associations (De Chernatony et al., 2010). Brand marketing organisations take great care to articulate the positioning of brands so that the necessary values and associations can be reproduced through all levels of communications and marketing. Some, such as Unilever, who market some 1,000 brands globally, undertake detailed analysis of some of their brands to delineate its 'essence'. The components of this essence include: an analysis of the competitive environment; the target consumers; the key insight that makes the brand distinctive; the consumer benefits (tangible or intangible) conferred by the brand; the values and personality of the brand; the way the brand supports those values and why consumers should believe them; the features that differentiate the brand from its competitors; and the single concept that sums up the brand 'essence'. Unilever would need to draw out these issues for brands such as Colman's mustard, Pot Noodle snack food, Birds Eye processed foods, Surf detergent, Domestos bleach and numerous others. Each would differ depending on the brand positioning and the competitive conditions in each particular market. All major brand organisations use brand planning conceptual frameworks to emphasise the distinctive characteristics of each brand they market, and to enable them to maintain the same brand values and positioning through all their integrated communications.

BRAND POSITIONING

'Positioning' (see Snapshot 3.3) normally refers to the abstract psychological attributes and associations that a brand may evoke for consumers. It is inherently a relational concept since the positioning is relative to other brands in that marketspace. Positioning can also refer to more tangible characteristics of a brand that ostensibly differentiate it from others, such as the logo, packaging colour, frequency of and reason for use, and any other characteristic. Positioning is linked to the benefit, tangible or intangible, the manufacturer wishes to associate with consumption of the brand. For example, the chocolate countline KitKat has been positioned for many years through its advertising as a reward for hard work, epitomised in the famous strapline, 'Have a break – have a KitKat'. In contrast, rival countline brands such as Bounty bars or Cadbury's Flake are positioned as sensuous indulgences, not rewards for hard work but rewards for just being you. The differentiation is echoed in all advertising and brand communication since it is this differentiation that is essential to maintaining the brand's market share.

Positioning can also refer to the usage occasions appropriate for a brand. For example, advertising can be used to signal to consumers that a brand can be used in an alternative way or by different people in relation to the previous norm. The chocolate snack Mars Bar was advertised for many years with the strapline, 'A Mars a Day Helps You Work, Rest and Play'. This reflected the brand's positioning as a tasty snack that gave one energy to cope with a busy life. Like many chocolate snack ads it was presented as a solitary pleasure rather than a social one. A later advertising campaign showed a group of happy-go-lucky young people pushing a broken-down car to a garage, cheerfully chomping on Mars Bars, thus repositioning the brand's somewhat dated image for a younger and more socially oriented consumer. Mars Bar consumption was now positioned as a social event and re-positioned to a younger audience. The breakfast cereal Kellogg's Cornflakes was the subject of an ad campaign that showed people enjoying cornflakes in non-breakfast scenarios. A couple enjoyed a romantic late-night bowl of cornflakes, and another consumer used the brand as a TV dinner. The aim was to increase sales to existing consumers by showing that you can eat cornflakes at any time. The brand was thus re-positioned as an anytime snack as well as a breakfast cereal.

THE STRATEGIC BRAND MANAGEMENT PROCESS AND COMMUNICATION PLANNING

For Keller (2012: 58), the strategic brand management process entails four main stages:

1. Identifying and developing brand plans.
2. Designing and implementing brand marketing programmes.
3. Measuring and interpreting brand performance.
4. Growing and sustaining brand equity.

Step one might entail, for example, developing a positioning based on a perceived gap in the market. Once this positioning is established and delineated, it must be clearly signified to consumers. The core brand associations are designed and the points of brand competitive differential established. Keller (2012) infers that these elements can be designed and imposed top-down on consumers by organisational management, while Holt and Cameron (2010) suggest that the process is rather different and entails identifying cultural disruptions that brands can exploit. Step 2 entails designing creative marketing programmes (especially advertising and promotion) that will articulate the desired values and positioning to the target audience. Step 3 is the business process of evaluating and auditing brand performance, while Step 4 distils the key points of brand differentiation in order to extend them across the other offers of the organisation in a co-ordinated way. Keller (2012) refers to this broadly as designing the brand architecture for long-term management of brand equity.

It is in this process that major confusion can occur between brand management and communication agencies, because the brand management objectives and goals need to be translated coherently into communication objectives and goals. There can be confusion between brand clients and advertising agencies about what, exactly, can be achieved through advertising communication. There is certainly some overlap between marketing and communication, but they are not the same. For example, a marketing plan might set an objective of achieving a 3% increase in market share over two months. A communication cannot deliver market share, because it is a communication. What it can do is to support the marketing objective by, for example, motivating consumers by giving them a reason to buy the desired brand instead of its rivals. This distinction may be nuanced but it is important. Exactly how a communication might motivate consumers would depend on the consumer target group characteristics, the product or service market in which the brand is operating, the distribution channels, the current competitive conditions, and so on. The relation between a marketing objective and a marketing communication objective is important and closely linked, but it can be subtle.

As an example, in one long-running campaign for car manufacturer Volkswagen, a London agency, then known as DDB Needham, devised a campaign based on the creative idea that Volkswagen cars were not as expensive as people thought. The **qualitative research** revealed that consumers perceived VW as high quality, and high price. In fact, the prices of the models were competitive with rivals in each car class. The marketing objectives were to increase market share by 3% in each class (family saloon, small car and executive saloon) across Europe, and to refresh the brand. The communication objective was to persuade consumers that they could have VW reliability and prestige without having to pay a high price. The **advertising strategy** had to put across the idea that VWs were not as expensive as people thought. The agency found amusing and low-key creative executions that informed consumers that, in fact, VWs were indeed less expensive than they thought. One ad showed an audience at a tennis match, losing focus on the ball when they see a VW poster. Another showed workmen wrapping up a lamp-post with a rubber cover because a distracting VW billboard has been placed by it, just as a man is about to walk into the lamp-post because he's looking at the billboard.[6] The market share increase was indeed achieved and the campaign ran for many years, winning many industry awards for creativity and for effectiveness. In this case, the marketing objectives, the communication objective and the advertising strategy were not exactly the same but they were mutually supportive. Naturally, the objectives would not have been achieved if the other elements of the marketing mix, the product (including service and after-sales, warranties, reliability, image and performance) and the distribution through the service centres, had not been up to scratch.

There is a great deal of scope for confusion and misunderstanding between the marketing plan and the marketing communication plan. This is one reason why the client–agency relationship is such a fraught advertising area. The problems can be managed if there is frequent dialogue and a mutual appreciation of the differences between marketing and communication. One of the key elements of integration in marketing communication is to ensure that all communications portray consistent and coherent brand values through all media and across all product ranges. So it is essential that the marketing planning and the communications planning do not conflict. For example, if an advertising campaign builds a high level of awareness and anticipation for a new brand launch in the chewing gum market, all that effort and those resources will be wasted if the chewing gum has not made it into the stores by the time the campaign is launched, as happened in one instance. As another example, if the brand is positioned at the low cost, low quality end of the market, it would not be useful for the advertising to imply that the quality is excellent.

STRATEGIC AND TACTICAL PLANNING

It is useful to note a semantic distinction that can be important in brand planning. This is the distinction between strategic and tactical planning. Broadly, strategy refers to longer-term objectives that demand significant resources, while tactics refer to shorter medium-term objectives demanding fewer resources. However, the distinction between strategy and tactics is not always so clear-cut. Promotion is one quarter of the marketing mix, along with physical distribution, price and product, but it can command extensive resources and can also be the most important element of competitive success in some circumstances. Management is, after all, as much art as science and the use of terms is far from precise or universally agreed (Brown, 1996, 1997). In the VW example above, the use of advertising clearly had a strategic implication since it represented a major and long-term investment (the campaign helped achieve strategic corporate goals in European market share). The distinction between strategy and tactics is typically based on timescale and importance to the overall profitability of the organisation. It is a mistake to assume, as some marketing texts do, that all promotional effort is merely tactical just because it is promotion (Holt and Cameron, 2010). Advertising and promotional campaigns have, in many cases, attracted substantial resources and achieved strategic objectives for brands and for whole companies.

For example, a marketing strategy might be to achieve market leadership by being the most innovative and high-quality supplier, and the promotional communications would have to find a way of supporting that. A marketing tactic might be to spoil a rival's promotional campaign by having a short-term, 10% price discount offer.

Again, the communications would have to support the price-based promotion. In many organisations, the ideal plan would have strategic aims and objectives operating at the level of the corporation, with operational plans designed for each individual product market. The various levels of business and marketing objective would, ideally, dovetail into each other. So, for example, if the corporation was dealing in motor cars and positioned itself as the innovator in the market, then the various car brands it sold in each motor car segment (family saloon, small car, utility sports vehicle, etc.) would have different plans tailored to their particular target market and competitive conditions, though all would need to have a degree of fit with the overall corporate strategy. Honda and electronics giant Sony have become known for expensive, entertaining and high profile advertising campaigns that focus on the corporate brand values of quality and innovation, while they also have individual campaigns for particular models. The corporate level of communication sets the tone for the product–brand level of communication in advertising.

IMC PLANNING

The phrase **integrated marketing communications** or IMC reflects managerial interest in co-ordinating different media channels to optimise the effectiveness of brand marketing communications programmes (Schultz et al., 1993, 1996). If brand communications reflect coherent values, themes and imagery that have a connecting thread through differing media channels, then the hope is that these might act in a mutually reinforcing way. Not only that, but using different media channels in a co-ordinated campaign might also reach much larger potential audiences. A third perceived advantage is control. The portrayal of the brand has become the dominant issue in marketing communication, and IMC holds out the hope that brand representatives might be able to control the way the brand is portrayed from the centre of communication strategy, instead of having to cede some of that control to different media specialists. In practice, IMC is far from realised for reasons that we will discuss below, but it remains a useful descriptive tool for marketing education.

As we have noted, brand clients typically want to see the brand values communicated across several platforms simultaneously in **through-the-line** or ‘integrated’ campaigns (although these terms are frankly becoming redundant as integration becomes the default approach in the digital era). Above-the-line (ATL) media are mass media: TV, radio, press, etc. Below-the-line (BTL) refers to media that did not attract commission payments from media owners, such as sales promotions, logo-bedecked balloons, pens, direct mail, OOH, etc. Through-the-line (TTL) campaigns use both, in an integrated way. Interest in IMC has developed partly because of the view (noted above) that marketing communication offers the ‘only sustainable competitive advantage of marketing organizations’ (Schultz et al., 1993: 47). IMC places the brand at the centre of strategy, rather than on the periphery as an afterthought. Once, advertising and promotional communication was conceived on a linear model as an effort to create one-way communication that would influence the attitudes and behaviour of target audiences (Shimp, 2009). In the convergent media environment, in contrast, brands are considered in relational terms as nodes of interaction between brand owners, consumers and other stakeholders. IMC represents the attempt to co-ordinate brand stories and content through all media channels, especially social media.

There have been pressures in the industry pushing ad agencies towards integration. Advertising agencies consider traditional advertising to be their core activity, but the larger, full-service agencies are increasingly finding that clients expect them to offer expertise across the marketing communication disciplines. Consumers, moreover, do not generally make a strong distinction between the differing media that carry advertising. As Percy et al. point out, 'people generally look at all marketing communications as "advertising"' (2001: v). The rise of brand marketing makes the advertising medium secondary to the brand personality (to use ad man David Ogilvy's expression), an entity that can be expressed through many differing forms of creative execution and communicated through different media. Integrated advertising campaigns utilise the qualities of different media in a communications effort designed to maintain consistent brand values regardless of whatever communication source the consumer encounters.

The blurring of the lines between marketing communications disciplines is part of a radical change in the media infrastructure coming from developments in electronic communications technology and the rise of global business. Global brands now cross borders and resonate with the consumers in many countries. Mass media, above-the-line advertising is often regarded as the strategic element of marketing communications, the one communication technique that can transform the fortunes of corporations, create brands and change entire markets. Although there are still good reasons for holding this view, there is also a strong case for managers to consider advertising from a strategic, integrated and media-neutral perspective, which acknowledges that the rationale for brand communications drives the pragmatic development of integrated creative executions and media strategies. On this logic, mass media advertising is not necessarily the centrepiece of every campaign.

The idea of integrated marketing communications, then, reflects the need to take a global view of the brand and to ensure that brand communications across all media are consistent in terms of the brand image, values and personality, and that the media channels used are complementary with regard to segmentation, positioning and targeting. IMC has become more popular because of various factors, notably the **fragmentation of media audiences** and changes in the media consumption patterns of these audiences in the light of an explosion of new media channels and vehicles. Concomitantly, IMC reflects a shift in power from manufacturers to consumers, a shift from mass to niche media channels and vehicles, the emphasis on data-driven marketing and the move to 24/7 consumption.

Integration of media implies the use of online and offline media channels. Offline media channels could include the traditional 'old media' of television, print (newspapers, magazines), radio, cinema advertising and also outdoor advertising, direct marketing, public relations, personal selling and sales promotion. Online channels could include dedicated websites, optimisation of search engine results, email, banner and click-through advertising, podcasts, blogs and other web-based exposure.

SNAPSHOT 3.4

Advertising creativity and the dramatic portrayal of consumption

A major challenge for IMC is to devise a creative approach, the creative execution, that will translate across different media channels. Many creative approaches are channel-specific in the sense that they will work best on a particular medium. For example, one of the major creative movements in advertising since the 1960s has been dramatic realism (Marchand, 1985). Ad agencies use imagery and metaphors from classical art and literature to create aesthetically inspiring dramatic portrayals of the product along with 'an account of … the social benefit that the consumer could be expected to derive' (Leiss et al., 1997: 79). Demonstrating the social benefit is most effective if the consumer can be portrayed in their everyday circumstances, but with the heightened dramatic effect contributed by portrayal in a medium with high production values such as a glossy magazine or TV ad. This takes consumers' daily activities and portrays them in an altogether more dramatically interesting light. For example, an everyday situation such as dirt on clothes might be portrayed as a problem that the model housewife solves with the help of a branded detergent. The picture accompanying the advertising text would be carefully drawn as graphic art, perhaps with an attractive model in a striking pose, in juxtaposition with the brand logo and packaging. Dramatic realism helps the consumer identify with the creative themes in the ad. Advertising agencies recognised consumers' needs for aesthetic stimulation and symbolic self-expression and bridged the gap between manufacturers and creative artists. In this way the design of American advertising and the products themselves were improved (Leiss et al., 1997: 81). Consumers were treated to advertising that was aesthetically attractive and a product that could express something about consumer personality and social identity. Mass media were especially suited to this kind of execution, so part of the challenge for IMC has been to adapt the creative logic of mass media advertising into new media channels.

TWO DIMENSIONS OF INTEGRATION FOR BRAND COMMUNICATION: THEMES AND CHANNELS

It is important to understand the rationale behind integration of marketing communications. One key issue has been noted above: that is, the primacy of the brand as the concept that drives marketing activity. All marketing activity is designed to support, enhance and reflect the brand as a symbol of certain values and characteristics that differentiate it in the market. Consumers seek out brands, we recognise them and we pay more for the reassurance that quality brands offer. The brand may comprise many tangible things, and consumer preferences may be developed through the direct experience of buying it. But there is also a powerful element of communication involved since brand image is built up not only through direct personal experience of the brand's utility but also through less tangible attitudes and perceptions, which are influenced by the communication we read, hear, see and express about the brand.

The management effort to ensure a co-ordinated and coherent approach to integrated brand planning rests on two overlapping and connected dimensions: (1) brand themes, and (2) media channels.

The first dimension, the themes, concerns the need to manage the distinctive brand values and personality as they are expressed through all communication, from corporate to product–market communication. This focuses on the visible elements of the brand, including its colours, logo, typeface, and other aspects of the visual representation. So there should be particular themes that reflect and portray the brand positioning, which can run through all marketing communication for a given brand and ensure that the brand is recognised and its positioning is distinctive. This is no easy task when campaigns may have many parts, perhaps designed by different sub-contracted agency specialists. Nevertheless, it is the key task of brand planning to ensure that the brand retains its integrity whatever the medium or creative execution may be. The second dimension concerns channel integration. We live in a world of integrated and interlocking media. If we have a favourite TV show we don't just watch the show. We can read weblogs posted by fans or critics, we can go to the show website for stories about the characters and the actors or to buy merchandise. We can even download episodes via the internet, to listen to by podcast or on a mobile device. We can buy magazines that carry articles for fans of the show, follow the show's Twitter feed and like its Facebook page. And so it goes, a given brand, whether it be a car, a watch, or a clothing range of a movie or syndicated TV show, can be exposed on many different media channels. It is therefore incumbent on the brand management to utilise these different media channels in promotion of the brand, and to try to manage the brand image through these channels.

THE INTEGRATED MARKETING COMMUNICATIONS PLAN

There is no definitive formula for planning or implementing IMC. The precise composition of an IMC plan will differ according to the particular market and communication context, and according to the custom and practice of particular organisations. A plan is not a prescription nor is it a checklist. It is a guide for action. Typically, an IMC plan would have the following general elements. There are many possible variations on the IMC plan (see, for example, this useful example of one from Coca-Cola):[7]

- executive summary
- brand research and competition analysis
- target audience
- communication objectives
- advertising strategy
- creative approach and creative brief
- media plan
- action plan and tactics
- budget estimates
- effectiveness evaluation.

Brand research and competition analysis

It is rare for brands to require a radical re-positioning that distances the brand from its earlier manifestations. In most cases, the brand needs some continuity from one campaign to the next to reflect the coherence and stability of the brand personality. This is why it is so important for the agency to research the brand and the client organisation in order to try to fully understand its history and values (Holt and Cameron, 2010). This includes looking at previous promotional campaigns. In addition, it is important to thoroughly understand the competitive context in which the brand is operating. Brand values and personalities must be understood in the context of alternatives – the reason for the brand is to differentiate the offer from competitors, so it must be understood in relation to competitors. This differentiation expresses the brand's positioning, and it reflects the attitudes and values that consumers project onto the brand. So for integration in brand communication to be achievable, it is a prerequisite that the advertising agency has a deep understanding of the brand.

In many cases, the agency will take two or three weeks over this research and analysis stage. The account team will rely mainly on secondary sources but they may also make use of primary sources in the form of **focus groups** with consumers and in-depth discussions with the client staff. After all, if a client thinks its brand values are different from those the consumers thinks it has then there is a fundamental communication problem to address. Advertising agency staff are fond of relating stories about clients who didn't understand their own brand. It is easy to understand that internal organisational values and politics might make it difficult to face reality if, for example, consumer perception of a brand personality has been distorted through negative media coverage. Sometimes a dispassionate agency view can highlight incoherence between the brand values as envisaged by the client and those as perceived by the consumer. Whether the client can accept such advice is another matter. Either way, the first element in the process of creating an integrated marketing communications campaign is for the agency to gain a thorough and insightful understanding of the brand, its history and values, and its competitive context.

Target audience

Advertising agencies need to know to whom the client wants them to speak. This refers to the tasks of segmentation and targeting. But knowing who the target audience is, is not enough. A conscientious agency will also want to understand the lifestyle preferences, consumption habits, media consumption patterns, values, attitudes, drives, aspirations, income, priorities and influential **peer groups** of its target segment. Qualitative research in the form of discussion or focus groups, or surveys, can be of assistance in this stage of the process. Secondary data sources detailing demographic and other information important to segmentation and targeting can also be invaluable. If the mentality, lifestyle, demographic characteristics and buying preferences of the target group are understood, then this can form the basis for a creative execution that speaks to its members in a way they will recognise. Defining the target audience is a difficult task with major implications. Once the audience is defined, this will drive the media plan and advertising schedule. It will also heavily influence the advertising strategy and creative execution. Get it wrong, and all the effort is wasted. If the defined audience is too narrow then opportunities for consumer engagement will be lost and the campaign will not yield the desired return on investment. If the target group definition is too wide, then impact may be lost or the campaign might be scheduled on a medium that the real targets don't use.

Communication objectives

Building on the above information and insights, the account team will be ready to formulate communication objectives. These will guide the overall approach and should dovetail into the client's marketing plan objectives. Communication objectives are key because they will form the bridge between the marketing plan and the integrated marketing communications campaign. They will clarify how communication can support the marketing objectives. Life in brand marketing and advertising agencies consists of a lot of meetings at which every step in the planning process is debated and discussed. Each element of the IMC plan will be interrogated for coherence and viability. The elements of the brand personality and its 'essence' are so difficult to pin down that this kind of process is necessary in order to keep attention focused on the key brand values and personality and to ensure that they are superimposed throughout all communication channels and mix elements. Communication objectives might, for example, be to engage the interest of the target audience and inform them about the kinds of problem-solving challenges entailed in active army service. Whatever the objectives are, they should be something that can be achieved through communication and which supports the marketing objectives.

Advertising strategy

Advertising has to have a purpose in order to succeed. If no one knows what they want to achieve by a campaign, then success is not possible because there will be no yardstick by which to measure it. The advertising strategy is important because it guides the creative team and encourages them to produce creative work that can motivate the desired consumers in a way that supports the overall communication objectives. To be effective, the advertising strategy should be expressed in simple terms without jargon, so that creatives (who have no patience with marketing jargon) can understand it (Hackley, 2000; Percy and Elliott, 2009).

The advertising strategy should explain what the ad is to do. For example, should it motivate an immediate response? Does the client want people who engage with the ad to contact the company? Or is the aim to encourage an emotional response from the viewer in the interests of building long-term brand equity? Is it to persuade the consumer to trial the product, as the Korean Dunkin' Donuts campaign did in the Chapter 3 case study below, or to convince consumers that the brand is better value/cooler/higher quality than competitors? Is the strategy to change consumer attitudes or buying habits? The advertising strategy will inform the creative brief, which is the document the creative team has to work from. It is therefore essential that the advertising strategy, the reason for advertising, is clear, coherent and consistent with the overall brand personality and communication objectives.

Creative approach and creative brief

We discuss this element of the advertising development process in greater detail in Chapters 5 and 6. For the present, it is important to introduce the process in order to set the broader context for the brand communication strategy. Once the marketing and communication objectives have been decided and the advertising strategy devised, arguably the most important part of the whole process is undertaken – this is the creative approach (also called the creative execution). The creative approach can undo all the careful planning and waste the budget, or it can leverage the brand and generate the benefits of positive publicity far in excess of expectations. A campaign that is talked about and shared on social media will receive unsolicited attention that spreads the brand values and reinforces the brand presence. A creative execution that is ignored because it's regarded as boring might lack impact and resonance for the target group. On the other hand, with some campaigns and some brands it is more important to portray the brand values in a clear and coherent way than it is to be creatively striking. As with all other elements of the IMC plan, the precise marketing and communication objectives in the context of the brand's values, positioning and competitive position, inform the creative approach.

The creative approach is decided with reference to the creative brief. The creative brief is an important document that is discussed in detail in Chapter 5. It is the guide from which the creative team will work and it represents an agreement between the agency and the client regarding what the advertising should achieve. The brief disciplines the creative work to ensure that the creativity is not over-indulged simply because it looks great or because it's so funny. The aim of advertising is not to win awards for creatives or to gratify their creative urges but to generate business for clients. The creative brief is the document that represents the client and agency interest in the campaign. It is the creative expression of the communication strategy.

The creative team must express the brand values and the advertising strategy in a way that attracts the right kind of attention from the target group. The creative approach also needs to consider practical issues such as the budget, length or size of ad, medium or channel. Most importantly, it needs to be focused according to the particular type(s) of person to whom the advertisement must speak. Creatives tend to claim that if they know their audience, whatever kind of person that is, they can produce a piece of work which motivates that audience. So the brief has to be based on careful research and clear commercial reasoning.

Media plan

In any advertising campaign there are important decisions to take regarding media, and many issues to consider. Most media buying agencies are now independent of advertising agencies, but media should have been kept in mind from the beginning of the IMC process because media and creative execution are interdependent. How can the target group be reached most efficiently and with the greatest impact? Do media choices have to accommodate a direct response element? Does the budget allow for broadcast media, or does it confine the campaign to local print media?

The media plan (discussed more extensively in Chapter 6) is an important document that directs the campaign to the right target audience with the maximum impact and reach, at the lowest possible cost per thousand consumers reached. Some campaigns burst onto the scene saturating all media channels for a week, and then disappear. Others are planned to drip the communication into consumers' consciousness in short exposures at longer intervals over a protracted period of time. Still others are focused on seasonal demand issues, such as where chocolate manufacturers spend a large proportion of their advertising budget in the UK over the Christmas period because of the high concentration of chocolate sales at that time. The media schedule depends not only on the budget but also on the brand, the market, the target audience or segment, and the campaign objectives.

Budget and effectiveness

In reality, in many cases, the budget has been set by the client before the first stage in the IMC planning process has begun. Where the agency does have scope for action is in accounting for the success, or the failure, of the campaign. Any campaign can be assessed against the objectives set for it, though doing so is not always a simple task. Calculating ROI is a difficult but important task in marketing and advertising since it reflects the effectiveness of different kinds of marketing intervention and the implications go straight to the bottom line of profitability. The ROI is also important in deciding in the future what budget to allocate to particular forms of advertising.

As noted above, well-planned campaigns have clear and achievable objectives precisely so that their achievement (or lack of it) can be judged. For example, if the communication objective of a campaign were to change attitudes towards eating a brand of breakfast cereal so that consumers would start to eat it in the evening as a snack, it would be relatively easy to conduct a street survey asking respondents when they ate this brand of breakfast cereal before and after the campaign. Before and after surveys of attitudes or behaviours are common methods of measuring campaign effectiveness. Another common approach is to use internal company records to look at sales patterns or new customer enquiries that might be linked in principle to advertising exposures. Many measures of effectiveness rely on long-term data regarding market share or sales volume, so the true effect of an advertising campaign can often not be fairly judged until many months after the campaign.

SNAPSHOT 3.5

Tracking the effectiveness of BT's 'It's Good to Talk' campaign

An example of effective campaign tracking involves the use of a statistical technique called multivariate analysis to try to establish a strong correlation between a campaign and a change in customer behaviour. A famous UK campaign (called 'It's Good to Talk') conducted for British Telecom (BT) attempted to change the telephone usage habits of domestic British customers. The advertising agency's consumer research had established that the average length of British domestic telephone conversations was significantly shorter than those in other countries such as the USA, Italy and Germany. It seemed that there was a British mentality that saw talking on the telephone as a cost that should be minimised. In fact the cost was and is small as a proportion of household income. In many other countries (such as Germany, Italy and the USA) domestic telephone users seemed to regard telephone conversation as a necessary expense and spoke for far longer on average on each call. This consumer research insight formed the basis for the campaign. A series of TV ads dramatically portrayed the typically succinct British phone user as someone lacking in empathy and warmth. The message was that it was kinder to talk at greater length, especially when talking to loved ones. The ads also suggested that telephone communication could strengthen bonds of family and friendship if people used it generously. It was claimed that the campaign resulted in a major social change: domestic telephone usage habits in the UK were substantially altered. A near 60% increase in call revenues to BT was claimed. The agency used multivariate analysis to correlate the electronic data on telephone conversation length with the exposure of the TV ads.

LIMITATIONS TO IMC

IMC has made a big splash in academic journals but its resonance for practitioners is variable (Eagle et al., 2007). The idea that all brand communication can emerge from a single strategic platform remains powerful for the potential benefits to ROI and the advantage of centralised control over the brand image. On the one hand, practitioners tend to agree that integration is a given in contemporary advertising planning. The use of new media is essential if clients are to fully leverage the promotional budget. On the other hand, many professionals dispute whether it is possible or desirable to formalise IMC. This intersects debates within strategy and marketing on the virtues and practical difficulties of planning per se. In many cases, business plans are created through an internal process that focuses minds and helps to disburse resources, but often departs to some extent from what actually takes place. Plans tend to rest on assumptions, the full implications of which only become apparent when the action is under way. This is not to argue that planning is irrelevant in business and administration, it is merely to point out that while planning is a necessary and fundamental part of managerial processes it does have its limitations.

With regard to IMC, many industry professionals ask whether it can ever be more than partially achievable. Media integration is something that depends very much on the circumstances of the brief, on the creativity and lateral thinking of the teams involved, and on the objectives for the campaign. How can there be general theories or principles of IMC if each brief is so very different? What is more, from a practical perspective, should there be an assumption that IMC is a necessary virtue for any campaign?

It is by no means clear that integration will benefit every brief. Some 20 years after IMC became a popular **buzz word** in marketing, some leading ad agencies still handle a large proportion of business in which they are asked to produce an advertising campaign without any digital component. It is a standard part of advertising planning that there is an evaluation of media channels in terms of segmentation and targeting, audience reach, resonance and cost per thousand target consumers. In this regard, some practitioners argue that IMC is nothing new. The media channels have changed and the media vehicles have multiplied, but advertising has always been subject to such changes and has adapted accordingly. It has always been conventional wisdom in advertising that media channels are used selectively: why use every channel just because they are there?

One reason might be that media consumption patterns have changed in such a way that reaching a target consumer through all possible channels is now feasible, where it wasn't before. But even this is dubious. The ideal of controlling the message through every medium through which the target audience might access brand communication is all very well in principle, but there are many barriers. Firstly, absolute control of brand communication is not possible – there will always be leakage between media, say through media editorial coverage. User-generated content such as blogs and wikis, twittering, and so forth, occupies much internet space and neither this, nor everyday news stories connecting with the brand, can be controlled. They can be reacted to and incorporated into communication plans, but this is a reactive process largely charged to the media relations function.

Furthermore, absolute control over brand communications on every medium may not even be desirable, even if it were possible. Brands are products of culture. They result from the interactions of consumers in the social context in which they are seen and used. They are not entirely the creation of the brand owner. Many brands, indeed, are building user-generated content into their strategies through social media consumer engagement initiatives. For example, in 2011 Coca-Cola posted a video demonstrating their content marketing strategy through 2020 on YouTube, and a central part of this is to engage consumers in brand storytelling and to incorporate consumer ideas into future strategies.[8] Arguably, this is less about a top-down, one-way model of brand communication control and more about a collaborative style of opening up the brand to consumer engagement, which, in turn, feeds back into brand and communications planning.

Where there is less argument is around the need for advertising and promotional planning to integrate creative themes across different media platforms. This is dictated by the logic of branding – a brand must represent distinctive values and these are linked with certain conventions of visual and auditory representation. Put more simply, a brand ought to be distinguished by the same colour scheme or signature tune whatever the medium, so that consumers recognise it as that brand. But many professionals regard this as a given, a default position, and no more than professional commonsense, rather than a theoretical or formal planning principle. IMC is undoubtedly an area that professionals in communication cannot ignore. It is perhaps not surprising that academic and scholarly research focuses around trying to gather general principles or theories, while professionals are focused more pragmatically on client briefs that can be utterly different from day to day.

Naturally, if academics can generate a theory of IMC that helps practitioners get more out of their clients' budgets then there would be less scepticism and much applause from the industry. But like so much research and theory in business and management, the ambition of IMC scholarship and research isn't yet realised in terms of its relevance and effectiveness for practice. Nonetheless, several factors will ensure that IMC as an idea continues to receive attention from all sides. One factor concerns the possibilities for greater efficiency and accountability opened up by digital advertising media applications and the increasing advertising potential of mobile. While this area may not be accessible to a general theory, it is certainly one in which practitioners will be open to any useful general insights or principles. In particular, the economic recession and the consequent squeeze on promotional budgets will mean that greater attention will be paid to **cost-per-thousand** (CPT) and return on investment criteria. These returns can be measured most effectively through new media.

Another important factor driving integration of campaign planning concerns the fragmentation of media audiences and changes in media consumption patterns, which mean that advertising and promotional planners often have to deploy integrated campaigns simply in order to reach sufficient numbers of their desired market segment. Finally, the increased attention being paid to consumer engagement with brand communications also pushes planners towards new media that facilitate such engagement in cost-efficient and user-appealing ways.

CHAPTER SUMMARY

This chapter has introduced the integrated marketing communication process. It discussed the central role of the brand in this process, and explained the distinctions between marketing objectives, communication objectives and advertising strategy. It also discussed distinctions between marketing strategy and tactics, and noted that advertising and promotion can be strategic as well as tactical. The two main dimensions of integration were explained, these being integration of brand theme across channels, and integration of media channels in advertising campaigns. The chapter then listed the basic stages in a typical IMC plan. Each stage in the plan has been outlined in Chapter 3 while many of them are developed in greater detail in other parts of the book. Finally, limitations and caveats around the somewhat fashionable notion of IMC were discussed. Chapter 4 will move on to discuss the internal processes and roles of advertising agencies engaged in this process.

REVIEW QUESTIONS

1 Collect ten video, radio or print advertisements and divide them between two groups. Each group should try to ascertain what each of their ads was intended to accomplish. In other words, what was the planning rationale behind the ads? Then the two

groups should swap ads and perform the same exercise on the other group of ads. The two groups combined should discuss their respective analysis of each ad and decide which analysis seems the most likely to be accurate. The intention behind the ads should be considered in the light of such issues as: (a) the likely target audience for the brand; (b) other possible stakeholders; (c) the apparent brand positioning indicated by the ad's creative approach; (d) the choice of medium; and (e) other marketing issues concerning this brand.

2 List as many examples as you can of marketing objectives that might be supported with advertising and promotion. Be prepared to justify your choice with examples or reasoning.

3 Is the role of communication in marketing primarily tactical or strategic? Give reasons for your answer.

4 Develop a scenario in which your group has been asked to outline creative ideas for the launch of a new brand of chocolate confection called 'Slick'. Focus on the segmentation, targeting (especially media) and positioning issues.

VIDEO QUESTIONS

How would you define brand?
What is the impact and importance of brand?
What are the reasons that brands are created? What are the advantages of having a strong brand?

How has the relationship between advertisng and brands changed?

What elements and factors go into the strategic brand management process?

CASE STUDY

Channel integration in action

Integrated campaigns that operate across media platforms still need to satisfy the basic rules of successful creative advertising. That is, they need a creative execution that resonates with the target audience. One questionable example was the launch campaign for the eleventh generation Toyota Corolla, the biggest selling car brand in the world. It was launched in 2014 with an integrated marketing communication campaign called 'Elevate' from Saatchi & Saatchi Los Angeles, targeted at the 'Millennial generation, while still appealing to Baby Boomers', according to the press release.[9] The key broadcast ad was a 60 second spot called 'Style Never Goes Out of Style', shown on TV and in cinemas.

PHOTO 9 Snickers

Image Courtesy of the Advertising Archives

This TV ad for Snickers (formerly known as Marathon) chocolate and nut snack used actresses Joan Collins and Stephanie Beacham in a 2012 comedy sketch as part of the You're Not You When You're Hungry campaign. The campaign, targeted mainly at men, used laddish humour to bring wit and camaraderie to the brand. Humour is a reliable advertising appeal, but clients are sometimes suspicious that creatives are making funny ads to feature in TV shows and to be shared on social media, rather than to sell the brand. Of course, ads can be funny and effective if the strategy is clearly conceived.

The ad placed the Corolla at the hub of pop culture since its launch in 1968. The print campaign showed crowds of people cheering the car, while content clips of battling DJs and a hip-hop music producer were shown on digital. LED highlighted OOH signs and billboards in major US cities had a built-in chip that enabled consumers to go on a virtual test drive via their smartphone. An advergame mobile app added to the excitement, while 6 second Vine videos and 15 second Instagram videos showed dance styles including the signature 'Elevated' dance from the broadcast commercial. The agency hoped that viewers would share content via the hashtag CorollaStyle.[10] Experiential and activation included events and games at cinema showings of the ad, and opportunities for test drives. Some industry bloggers[11] were unconvinced about the youth-oriented street style of the campaign. The Toyota Corolla was known, said the bloggers, as a reliable, trustworthy workhorse of a car – not a cool style leader. In contrast, the Nike 'Find Your Greatness' campaign was hailed as a strong creative idea grounded in a powerful consumer insight,[12] as was the Snickers 'You're Not Quite You When You're Hungry' campaign and another campaign for Foster's lager that played on laddish humour. In each case, the writer claimed that the foundation was a great idea based on a consumer insight.

A campaign that was less creative but highly effective for Dunkin' Donuts in South Korea took the activation element one step further with 'flavor radio'. Every time the brand's jingle was played on the radio in public buses in Seoul, a flavoursome artificial coffee smell was released in the bus. Sure enough, Dunkin' Donuts stores near bus stops grew sales by 16% while the chain as a whole saw a 29% sales increase, according to the Huffington Post.[13] Koreans are coffee aficionados and coffee shops abound in Seoul. The brand was associated more with donuts than with coffee, so there was plenty of competition. The campaign began with radio ads that told commuters about Dunkin' Donuts stores that were near bus stops. The commuters then heard the ads while travelling on the bus, and smelt the coffee aroma. On alighting the bus, they found the bus stops peppered with outdoor ads pointing to the nearest store. The seamless alignment of integration with activation led a proportion of the estimated 350,000 consumers who were exposed to the campaign on a short journey from exposure to the radio ads, all the way to the store via their daily commute.

With thanks to Dr Henri A. Weijo of Bentley University, for additional material.

Case questions

1. In a small group, design an IMC campaign for a new brand of car. The name, brand positioning and target market are your choice. Try to integrate as many media channels as possible, and unite them with a key idea. What are the key problems that emerged in this task?
2. Does IMC re-write the rules of marketing, or merely offer increased opportunities for good marketing practice to reap rewards?
3. Does IMC change the game of advertising and promotional communication, or does the tension between creativity and effectiveness still remain just as it does for mass media advertising?
4. List all the circumstances you can think of in which an IMC campaign would not be appropriate for a brand. Give reasons to justify your list.

USEFUL JOURNAL ARTICLES

(These Sage articles can be accessed on the companion website.)

Haytko, D.L. (2004) 'Firm-to-firm and interpersonal relationships: perspectives from advertising agency account managers', *Journal of the Academy of Marketing Science*, 32: 312–28.

Kaptan, Y. (2013) '"We just know!": Tacit knowledge and knowledge production in the Turkish advertising industry', *Journal of Consumer Culture*, 13 (3): 264–82.

O'Boyle, N. (2012) 'Managing indeterminacy: culture, Irishness and the advertising industry', *Cultural Sociology*, 6 (3): 351–66 (first published December 14, 2011).

Rossiter, J.R. (2012) 'Advertising management principles are derived mostly from logic and very little from empirical generalizations', *Marketing Theory*, 12 (2): 103–1.

Spotts, H.E., Lambert, D.R. and Joyce, M.L. (1998) 'Marketing dèjá vu: the discovery of integrated marketing communications', *Journal of Marketing Education*, 20: 210–18.

FURTHER READING

Belch, G. and Belch, M. (2011) *Advertising and Promotion: An Integrated Marketing Communications Perspective*. New York: McGraw-Hill.

Hackley, C. and Hackley née Tiwsakul, R.A. (2013) 'From integration to convergence – the management of marketing communications', in H. Powell (ed.), *Promotional Culture in an Era of Convergence*. Abingdon: Taylor and Francis, pp. 70–87.

Holt, D. (2004) *How Brands Become Icons: The Principles of Cultural Branding*. Boston, MA: Harvard Business School Press.

Percy, L. and Elliott, R. (2009) *Strategic Advertising Management*, 3rd edn. Oxford: Oxford University Press.

Schultz, D. (2003) *IMC – The Next Generation*. New York: McGraw-Hill.

Schultz, D. and Kitchen, P. (1997) 'Integrated marketing communications in US advertising agencies: an exploratory study', *Journal of Advertising Research*, September/October: 7–18.

NOTES

1. 'Best Global Brands 2016 Rankings,' http://interbrand.com/best-brands/best-global-brands/2016/ranking/ (accessed 24 March 2017).
2. 'The World's Most Valuable Brands', www.forbes.com/powerful-brands/list/ (accessed 24 March 2017).
3. www.ipa.co.uk/ (accessed 13 February 2017).
4. 'The poster that won the election', 8 September 2002, http://backspace.com/notes/2002/09/the-poster-that-won-the-election.php (accessed 13 February 2017).
5. www.virgin.com/ (accessed 13 February 2017).
6. 'VW "lamp post" by BMP', 1 July 1998, www.campaignlive.co.uk/thework/920833/ (accessed 12 February 2017).

7 'IMC of Coca-Cola', 24 October 2013, www.slideshare.net/OnkarDhongade/imc-of-coca-cola (accessed 28 March 2017).

8 'Coca-Cola Content 2020', www.youtube.com/watch?v=LerdMmWjU_E (accessed 13 February 2017).

9 'Integrated marketing campaign elevates 2014 Toyota Corolla to new heights', 5 September 2013, www.prnewswire.com/news-releases/integrated-marketing-campaign-elevates-2014-toyota-corolla-to-new-heights-222503921.html (accessed 13 February 2017).

10 Lauren Johnson, 'Toyota accelerates Corolla campaign with multiple mobile engagements', www.mobilemarketer.com/cms/news/strategy/16115.html (accessed 13 February 2014).

11 Jonathan Salem Baskin, 'Toyota's ad demonstrates how not to sell cars', 18 September 2013, http://adage.com/article/cmo-strategy/toyota-s-ad-2014-corolla-shows-sell-cars/244201/ (accessed 13 February 2017).

12 'Nike launches "Find Your Greatness" campaign', 25 July 2012, http://news.nike.com/news/nike-launches-find-your-greatness-campaign-celebrating-inspiration-for-the-everyday-athlete (accessed 23 March 2017).

13 'Dunkin' Donuts flavor radio: chain releases coffee scent when ads play in South Korea', 31 July 2012, www.huffingtonpost.com/2012/07/31/dunkin-donuts-flavor-radio_n_1724869.html (accessed 21 March 2017).

4 THE CREATIVE AGENCY MODEL

CHAPTER OUTLINE

As Chapter 1 explained, the agency model for advertising is under threat in the convergence era. This book takes the position that the craft skills of creative advertising development that have been honed in advertising agencies continue to be relevant. The fact that non-advertising agencies are moving into advertising highlights the need for wider understanding of these craft skills as they try to bring their core skills to the advertising party, whether their core skills are brand consultancy, direct response, media strategy or other specialisms. Therefore, this chapter offers a largely descriptive introduction to the key roles and processes of ad agency work, before focusing more closely on the creative advertising development process in Chapter 5.

KEY CHAPTER CONTENT

Advertising agencies as cultural intermediaries

The advertising agency in evolution

Advertising agencies and the pitch process

Account team roles and responsibilities

Want a primer? Go to https://study.sagepub.com/hackley4e and watch...

Neil Quick – Analyzing Data **to learn**
About the challenges facing the advertising agency

Brands as Broadcasters **to learn**
How these challenges force the agency to evolve

Andrew Peake – Advertising and Brand Transformation **to learn**
How challenges are creating opportunities in advertising agencies

Advertising Design and Neil Quick – Analyzing Data **to learn**
How the two agencies are similar, how they differ and how typical they are

... to tackle the video questions at the end of the chapter.

ADVERTISING AGENCIES AS CULTURAL INTERMEDIARIES

Ad agencies are deeply interested in everyday consumer culture, and cultural theorists have been very interested in ad agencies, although there have been surprisingly few studies of the social dynamics of advertising development that explore the experiences of the people who create advertising (exceptions include Blake et al., 1996; Fowles, 1996; Alvesson, 1998; Hackley, 2000; deWaal Malefyt and Moeran, 2003; Nixon, 2003; Cronin, 2004, Kelly et al., 2005; Leiss et al., 2005; McCracken, 2005; Deuze, 2007; Svensson, 2007; Cronin, 2008; Gilmore et al., 2011). Operating at the interface of culture and commerce, advertising agencies can be seen to have a powerful ideological role in promoting consumption as a lifestyle and in framing and normalising all kinds of behaviours (Williamson, 1978). This is not to suggest that we are helpless against the power of advertising – far from it. Indeed, the very fact that advertising sometimes seems to have such power is a tribute to the cleverness of advertising professionals in creating so many iconic campaigns.

In this chapter we offer a largely descriptive introduction to the key agency roles and processes of advertising and promotional communication. The account draws on 20 years of research to try to distil the major feature that agencies commonly share. On the face of it, this seems a pretty straightforward task. However, once one grasps the odd state of the cultural intermediary, the straightforward task becomes layered with rather deeper implications. Anyone can think of a cultural reference or two. But how does one encode them into a persuasive communication that has very specific strategic objectives? To some extent, this is where the mystique of advertising reveals itself. For all the textbooks and industry analyses, models and prescriptions, the power of advertising remains something of an enigma. By appreciating a little of the role of the cultural intermediary, we can at least earn some insight into the complexity of the superficially straightforward process of creating advertising that stirs emotional and behavioural responses in consumers.

One of the major planks of the traditional agency model has been that the agency acts as intermediary between the brand and its consumers, filtering and controlling the communications. Clearly, under convergence the advertising agency's role as intermediary between brand marketing organisations and consumers is being undermined by the immediacy and ubiquity of social media. There is a risk that social media and programmatic advertising, search engine optimisation and other algorithm-driven approaches shift the focus to clicks and likes with the core skills of advertising becoming forgotten. This is why we focus in this book on those very core skills. The advertising agency's role as cultural intermediary is under threat because the technology exists to allow anyone to produce content that looks pretty cool. The algorithms can place this content in social media contexts (i.e. individual newsfeeds and timelines) that superficially appear to be relevant. This can lead to the conclusion that anyone can produce good content. This has been called the democratisation of creativity in advertising (Oetting, 2015). It cannot be forgotten that the brand's relationship with the consumer is now direct – the brand cannot exist at arm's length and must engage fully in a social media conversation with consumers or risk being seen as aloof and out of touch. However, the efficacy of programmatic advertising is unproven – after all, we avoid these annoying interventions into our social media experience by skipping past them. Carefully crafted creativity is more important than ever because without it the huge volume of ads we encounter will disappear into an amorphous mass of annoying media froth. This is the real challenge for the challenges to the agency model – how to generate strategically astute content.

Leaving aside for the moment the many acute problems of targeting social media advertising, the advertising agencies have a job to do to retain their role as cultural intermediaries for advertising in an era when everyone has the technology to produce content (Gensler et al., 2013; Ashley and Tuten, 2015). The immediacy of consumer access to brands via social media erodes the time agencies need to plan and design their strategy. As a result, brands often need to work with a variety of agencies or bring their advertising operations in-house in order to achieve the agility they need to respond in real time to market shifts and consumer sentiment. What is more, advertising agencies can no longer focus purely on advertising and communication and neglect the other aspects of the client's business. The business focus must be central to agency concerns otherwise the client will simply feel that the agency is not fully engaging with their needs. In a sense, this takes advertising agencies full circle, as they need to once again become strategic partners to clients, as they were in the halcyon days of the dominant full service agency back in the 1960s. The way they do this has changed though and they must be able to bring their core skills to a multi-media world. This means taking 'media neutral' planning to the next level – agencies have to be honest with clients in order to deliver the 360 degree solutions clients demand.

Advertising agencies have to give clients full attention and top quality service, yet they also have to pitch competitively for ever greater amounts of business to make up the falls in revenue per account. This is another major challenge to advertising agencies' business model. They need personnel to commit to clients, but winning new business is also a major challenge that demands hours of agency time. In addition, agencies need to think about the pool of talent from which they recruit – agency work is gruelling at the best of times, but advertising continues to attract talented and committed individuals because of the job satisfaction entailed in creating good work and the material rewards of doing so successfully. Agencies have a major task in preserving these elements of the job in order to continue to recruit the talent upon which the industry depends. Advertising as an industry has always faced challenges in maintaining and expanding the diversity of its recruitment. It has to meet this challenge head-on in order to broaden the skill set it owns and to employ staff who more closely reflect the markets and consumer audiences with which agencies need to engage.

Regardless of the changes in the media environment, advertising and promotion, broadly conceived, remain the primary means by which brands acquire their cultural resonance. The mechanisms through which they do this tend to be largely ignored in marketing texts and courses. To be sure, a great deal of advertising seems to lack much depth or complexity, especially when it is driven by artificial intelligence – what is there to analyse in a 10 second video ad inserted in a timeline making a price appeal for a local car retailer, or a print ad declaring that the kumquats from one supermarket chain are always fresh and juicy? But, as we have noted, there are deeper aspects to advertising. For one thing, the aspects of communication we take most for granted are often the most enigmatic, once we start to notice them. In particular, what is not expressly stated but implied in ads can often be the most powerful (Tanaka, 1994). For another, it seems clear that a lot of advertising is not merely a cheaply made and simply conceived sales pitch, but is thoroughly planned and conceived at an abstract level to subtly perpetuate brand values and associations. Advertising agencies are regarded as key institutions in twentieth-century capitalism, and they along with other agency specialists have collectively been and continue to be a major influence on contemporary consumer culture. As we have seen, most global brands cannot be conceived without the advertising that is central to their success. Not only what they do but also how they do it are important topics in marketing and advertising.

Advertising agencies have been described as 'cultural intermediaries' in the sense that they seem to take elements of culture such as art, language, music, fashion and popular trends, and then use them in juxtaposition with brands to make up new forms of communication aimed at a selected audience (e.g. Cronin, 2004). Culture in this sense is meant broadly to mean not only high art, classical music and serious literature, though these are very much part of the advertisers' vocabulary, but also aspects of everyday culture such as current affairs and media news stories, popular fashions, fads and trends, and anything else that might feature in the habitus of the consumer. Advertisements take culture and reflect it back at itself, marketising the most mundane of daily routines by adding symbolic value (Davis, 2013). At least, that is one way of conceiving of the role of advertising.

Advertising is often the target of criticism because of its putative influence over behaviour and cultural values. But on the other hand, advertising uses culture as its material – it takes what is already out there and combines it with images of consumption. So the question of whether advertising causes certain things or merely reflects them becomes a circular one because of its role as cultural intermediary, mediating between brands and taking language, behaviour, values and trends from everyday culture and transforming them into messages of consumption. Advertising may sometimes magnify or even distort social practices, behaviour and values that are already out there, but whether it deserves the bad press it sometimes gets is open to argument.

SNAPSHOT 4.1

Advertising agencies transforming for the digital era

Many advertising agencies[1] have had to learn to produce content in multiple platforms and media channels in addition to their traditional mass media advertising channels, and their websites now reflect this change. WCRS of London positions itself as a creative agency producing work that will engage people whether through advertisements, apps, digital games, or programming. Red Bee, a former entertainment marketing content producer that has turned into a multi-purpose content producer, describes itself as a 'content and design agency born in entertainment'. It sees its creative leverage coming from its background in entertainment, because it believes that 'brands that entertain have a competitive edge'. Red Bee operates in the areas of content and integrated advertising campaigns, design and brand strategy. Ogilvy London describes itself as an 'agency community' which 'make brands matter'. Ogilvy's background in advertising is well known after its eponymous founder, and its PR operation is fully integrated into the London advertising agency. The agency website lists no less than 29 marketing disciplines offered to clients, including but not limited to, advertising, activation, behaviour change, branding and design, content and production, data and digital marketing, integrated management consulting, promotional marketing (which you might think covers all the above), research and insight, retail and social, and **UX**, which means user experience design. Irish International simply states on its website that it comprises 96 people using their imaginations to help brands grow. Like many other contemporary agencies, it wants to emphasise to clients that it has moved on from the position that it deals in communication and the marketing is the client's responsibility. Rather, contemporary agencies take responsibility for the role communication can play in supporting and delivering marketing objectives. From this small selection of advertising agency websites, it seems clear that leading agencies are taking the changing landscape for advertising very seriously indeed by attempting to reinvent the concept of full service for the digital era.

ADVERTISING LANGUAGE, DISCOURSE AND CONSUMPTION PRACTICES

However advertising and promotion are conceived, they remain textual forms of communication. There is a need for communication to be encoded into language, and digital does not change that fundamental. Part of the fascination of advertising and promotion for practitioners is that it entails solving problems of communication when the main basis of communication, language, is continually adapting to express new kinds of experience and to accommodate new influences. The English language is especially popular in advertising the world over, probably because of its flexibility and global familiarity as the language of business. Of course, advertising's use of imagery and music makes it a richer device of communication than language alone. Indeed, as we have noted, part of advertising's uniqueness as a discourse form derives from its capacity to combine language with music, pictures and substance or medium (Cook, 2001). But language itself carries meaning within its context: there is a medium of transmission (written or aural) and meanings are nuanced through the combination of language with tone, gesture and other aspects of context. Advertising and promotion offer forms of communication that not only set language in any social context with which we are familiar, but also invent new contexts through novel combinations of imagery, words and music. The possibilities for novelty in advertising communication seem limitless.

PHOTO 10 Gillette

Image Courtesy of the Advertising Archives

Advertisements can offer insights into cultural history. Many print ads of the 1950s and 60s can appear to the modern reader to be loaded with incongruous cultural values, especially regarding gender and relationships. This 1958 poster by British designer Tom Eckersley was similar to many in that it showed a woman fawning over a man, in this case, because he had a smooth face. Later Gillette campaigns were a little (but not a lot) more subtle with the 'The Best A Man Can Get' campaigns. These ads included cars, jet planes, fast cars, and even children, as accessories to the successful man, as well as women.

Advertising can be seen as a form of discourse since it is an identifiable form of communication that can be described. As a discourse, advertising is defined by its conventional narrative forms, but these do evolve and adapt to new media. As we have noted, advertising and communication agencies produce cultural texts that portray consumption by drawing on social practices and symbols extant in the wider, non-consumption culture. For example, at the most simple level, a promotion that pictures people riding on a public bus cannot communicate anything unless viewers of the ad are familiar with the cultural practice of riding on a public bus. Riding on a bus is not merely an act: it is a cultural consumption practice because it is subject to agreed rules that are seldom stated. There are conventional ways of paying one's fare and of interacting (or not) with the driver, ways of taking one's seat (or not taking one and standing up), ways of disembarking at the correct stop, even ways of speaking to fellow passengers or to the driver. If one tries to take a bus ride in a strange country with an unfamiliar language the importance of these conventions becomes all too apparent and one can look, and feel, socially inept because one does not know them. As Goffman (1959, 1979) has underlined, there is a quality of performance to social interaction of which we tend not to be consciously aware, except when we are in a situation where we do not know the social conventions. It is part of advertisers' job to act as informal applied sociologists to reveal and understand these social conventions, in order to communicate with consumers using a cultural idiom that consumers will recognise and respond to.

THE ROLE OF CULTURAL KNOWLEDGE IN INTERPRETING ADVERTISING

Advertisements, then, presuppose the consumer's cultural knowledge of local social practices so it is essential for the creators of advertising to share or understand the social milieu of the consumers so that the ads they create will be invested with social significance for the viewer (Iser, 1978; Bakhtin, 1989; Thompson et al., 1994; Brown et al., 1999; Hackley, 2002, citing Scott, 1994a and 1994b). In portraying everyday activities in rather dramatically enhanced and sometimes glamorised ways, advertising and promotion reveal us to ourselves. The ordinary things we do are portrayed in film and photography, video and other forms of hybrid media content, from taking a shower to buying a coffee. No doubt advertising's use of high-quality cinematography and print techniques and elaborate sets, together with its prominence in the contemporary consumer experience, make our everyday activities portrayed in this way seem dramatically compelling and loaded with significance. Taking a shave with a Gillette wet razor, for example, is portrayed in some of the brand's advertising as a symbolic statement of social status and material aspiration, and a gender performance that confers a powerful (symbolic) sexual attraction on the (male) shaver. Advertising, regardless of medium or platform, adds symbolic value to brands by layering consumption practices with cultural meaning.

Underlying all advertising communication is the implicit message that it is consumption, and not merely its portrayal in advertising, that can make our experience of life ostensibly more fulfilling. For this communication to work there has to be a shared cultural vocabulary between the makers and consumers of advertising. Advertising and promotional agencies operate at this cultural interface, continually reprocessing cultural meanings to create this communication between brand marketing organisations and consumers. Advertising is, of course, a formidable commercial tool as well as a form of popular communication art. Mass advertising can be a powerful marketing blunderbuss, browbeating consumers into compliance by conditioning through repetition. As we saw in Chapter 3, it also has the flexibility to support many kinds of marketing and business objectives with tailored specificity. It can reflect and magnify social changes and is an important cultural influence. The ways in which advertising and promotion are produced and consumed are constantly changing, reflecting rapid and far-reaching innovations in technology, media and the organisation of agencies. A useful account of advertising practice, then, must be able to accommodate some of this complexity.

SNAPSHOT 4.2

Los Angeles – creative 'content epicentre'?

Los Angeles is well known the world over as the location of Hollywood and the globally recognised American movie industry. Since Horkheimer and Adorno (1944) located their Frankfurt School of critical theorists in LA to write *Dialectic of Enlightenment*, it has been regarded as the key centre of the global creative and cultural industries, continually reinventing itself to remain relevant in the face of rapid developments in the technologies of digital communication and concomitant changes in the working practices of the cultural industries (Lash and Lury, 2007). It is a key centre for advertising in the largest single advertising market in the world, and in the convergence era, the two aspects for which LA is most recognised, entertainment and advertising, are merging, as the skills demanded by each also converge. For some, Los Angeles is the 'creative capital' of the world,[2] although there are other cities that would also stake a claim. LA has the advantage of having been a centre for the global cultural industries for many years, and it has attracted key actors and agencies to build a stock of organisational expertise. There is a revolving door for movie-makers, actors, musicians and writers between advertising and the movie and music worlds. Once, these different worlds were separated by a perception that advertising was low culture, and movie making was art. Not anymore. They have morphed into a seamless source of cultural production that produces content that is entertaining, promotional and profoundly intertextual. Advertising agencies' role is changing accordingly, and leading practitioners assert that this role is becoming broader as agencies have to move away from being 'media fillers' and towards becoming content creators[3] for brands from a multi-disciplinary and multi-media perspective. This does not mean that the traditional agency roles and working practices are redundant, but it does mean that they have to evolve in the convergence era.

THE ADVERTISING AGENCY IN EVOLUTION

This chapter, then, will use the traditional, **full-service agency** as its point of departure for describing the craft skills and working processes of the advertising and promotion business.

However, as we have noted, there are many threats to the traditional agency model. Clients are demanding **integrated solutions** and advertising agencies are coming under increased competition from other specialists such as brand, strategy and communication consultants, media agencies and direct mail and direct marketing agencies. The environment for advertising is changing and the ways in which advertising is commissioned, created and consumed are also changing as agencies morph into all-purpose media content creators (see Snapshot 4.1 above).

The portrayal of advertising executives in popular culture has contributed to the enigmatic and slightly sinister image of the advertising profession (see Packard, 1957; also Deuze, 2007; Hackley, 2007; Hackley and Kover, 2007). From *Mr Blandings Builds His Dream House* to *How to Get Ahead in Advertising* and, of course, *Mad Men*, advertising in movies and TV shows is the domain of the mendacious, avaricious, driven, superficial, brilliant, and often alcoholic, maverick. In reality, there is less alcohol and less money, but probably just as much angst. It is perhaps fair to say that advertising does not enjoy the same kind of professional prestige as, say, medicine or architecture, or perhaps even politics. Yet there is also a certain glamour attached to working in advertising and promotion, even though the heyday of the *Mad Men*[4] of Madison Avenue is long gone. Competition for graduate trainee or creative positions in agencies remains intense because careers in the area are so prized.

Advertising people are sometimes caricatured in popular entertainment because it is difficult to categorise and its professional activities are not widely understood. It occupies an industrial sector of its own; it is a service but it is also more than that, it is almost, but not quite, a branch of entertainment. It is a business, but then again, not exactly like other businesses. It is part of the creative industries, but quite unlike a theatre company or publishing house. The task of managing the different skills, sensibilities and temperaments that have to work together to produce good advertising has always been somewhat fraught, and it isn't getting any easier.

The integration of marketing communications has been a recurring theme for consultants and academics for some two and a half decades (Schultz et al., 1993). The industry of advertising and promotion has been slow to move on from its traditional demarcations, but, as we have seen, many are beginning to try to evolve in response to the demands and priorities of the convergence era. As well as advertising agencies and their traditional emphasis on above-the-line mass media, there are, still, smaller agencies that specialise in below-the-line sales promotions, word-of-mouth and **viral marketing** communications, direct and database marketing, and also public relations, consumer and market research, industrial or business-to-business advertising, new product development, sponsorship, merchandising, strategic brand planning (including those dedicated solely to new brand names), corporate communications and internal marketing, internet-based promotion and interactive communications, media buying and strategy, and so on. These narrow specialists are finding it difficult to maintain their positioning without a loyal roster of clients, and many are finding that they must either absorb broader skills and move into new areas (such as direct response agencies moving into advertising) or be absorbed into larger agency groups.

The full-service advertising agency is transforming to reinvent what full-service actually means. Their primary expertise may lie in advertising, but their strategic perspective covers, in principle, any communications discipline, and they may buy in specialist talent in other marketing communications areas for help in executing an integrated, through-the-line campaign. Agencies are developing a more laterally integrated way of thinking about client problems. Many have acquired in-house expertise in other disciplines such as direct marketing, digital and PR, and they incorporate these into their offer alongside their core advertising expertise.

EARLY ADVERTISING AGENCY PRACTICE

The activities of advertising agencies can be better understood in the context of their historical evolution. Advertising agencies emerged as space-brokers, simply buying advertising space in the press on behalf of clients (McDonald and Scott, 2007). Gradually, they extended their activities to provide more services to clients and to add value to their business. So they provided artists to draw up the ads for clients as an improvement on text alone. They acquired expertise in typography and print technology, graphic art and photography. With the development of broadcast media, some agencies developed expertise in media planning, scriptwriting and radio production and, later, film production. Many agencies found that because of their location they attracted certain types of business such as retail advertising in the local press or sales promotion. In these cases, many regional agencies developed as specialists in particular categories of work, serving mainly local clients.

Advertising is a fast-moving field but few of its techniques are entirely new. Examples of advertising have been noted since the origin of writing itself. In fact, writing may have developed to facilitate marketing (Brown and Jensen-Schau, 2008). Classified advertising has existed since the advent of print technology and newspapers. It is a common mistake to suppose that, because early advertising was limited to the printed word, it was merely informative rather than persuasive. Detailed research has shown that this is not the case (McFall, 2004; Harbor, 2007). It is another mistake to suppose that techniques such as product placement and branding are modern inventions. For example, British pottery entrepreneurs were keen to get their pottery dinner sets into royal portraits in the Victorian era, and they made use of techniques of segmentation and targeting (Quickenden and Kover, 2007). In another example, a British entrepreneur of the 1800s, Thomas Holloway, pioneered the use of advertising and branding to sell his patented medical remedies. Holloway was said to have employed outdoor posters as far away as China to advertise his health tonics. Holloway was ahead of his time in other promotional techniques too. He managed to get references to his brands inserted into the script of some of the popular plays of the time. He is even said to have asked Charles Dickens to insert a reference to a Holloway brand into his classic novel *Dombey and Son*. Dickens declined. Holloway made a fortune and used it in philanthropic activities. Among them was the building he financed that is now a college of the University of London, called Royal Holloway.

ADVERTISING AGENCIES AS STRATEGIC MARKETING EXPERTS

The scope of activities ad agencies became involved with, and the expertise their staff developed in a variety of disciplines and markets, gave them yet another dimension. Their skills in artwork and typesetting became useful to media owners since they were able to produce advertisements of a quality that visually enhanced the publication. In addition to the skills of art, design and copywriting, agencies developed expertise in strategy and brand planning. Advertising agencies had to understand consumers in varied markets, and they also had to understand the businesses of their many clients. On top of that, they grew to understand media markets. They understood marketing in a way that was free of the practical constraints that limited the thinking of manufacturing organisations. They had a special understanding of the powerful role communication could play in exciting the interest of consumers, and they knew which kind of consumer read which publication. They had, therefore, a special vantage-point from which to offer strategic advice to clients on general business strategy, product development, brand planning and brand communication, possible new markets to enter, market segmentation issues and so on.

So, advertising agencies began to offer strategic advice to their clients as well as simply designing and placing advertisements. By so doing they were able to add value to their offer. The insights acquired in advertising are valued – many advertising agency account planners and strategists move 'client side' in their career to manage the brand planning process from inside the client organisation. It should be noted, though, that advertising agencies are not regarded as strategic partners by all clients in all regions of the world. Many clients, especially bigger ones, prefer to treat ad agencies as service providers who are required to deliver creative ideas, not consulting advice or research.

ADVERTISING AGENCIES AND MEDIA

The media strategy and planning tasks are discussed in greater depth in Chapter 6. Here we need to note a few initial points. Contemporary advertising agencies supply strategic communication ideas and, increasingly, production skills. They also normally possess media expertise and have a voice in deciding how ads will be targeted at selected consumers through particular media channels. Some ad agencies will handle media buying for a client, but media planning is increasingly handled at arm's length from the ad agency by specialist media agencies. Media buying originally formed part of full-service ad agencies' remit but many media departments were eventually sold off to become free-standing specialist businesses divorced from creative services.

In many countries, media buying services are provided by a limited number of companies because of lateral mergers and high concentration in the media industry. It can be convenient for media owners to sell advertising space to a small number of buyers rather than to thousands of individual clients. However, lateral mergers between communications groups mean that advertisers can be faced with monopoly suppliers in particular media and this places them in a poor bargaining position. For example, in the UK, licences to provide regional television or radio services are sold on a strictly limited basis so that local advertisers often have only one company to buy from. This, advertisers argue, maintains an artificially high cost for certain kinds of advertising medium.

Some media agencies, not content with being the back-room players in the advertising world, are broadening their remit under convergence and adding creative services, to encroach on ad agencies' business. Like advertising agencies, media agencies boast a wide range of expertise, for example, in consumer research, strategic analysis and brand planning. Convergence demands an understanding of different media channels and media agencies are, of course, well placed to exploit their deep knowledge of consumers and media. The advertising agencies are not usually overjoyed to find that they are pitching against a media agency for advertising business.

THE LEADING AGENCY BRANDS

Given the scope, public profile and economic importance of what advertising agencies do, it is perhaps paradoxical that the names of most agencies are virtually unknown to those outside marketing or communications fields. Ad agencies do not generally advertise themselves. A few of the world's top agency brands[5] do have a high profile presence in corporate life (see Table 4.1) but most are not nearly as well known among the general public as their client brands. This is partly because client organisations prefer the consuming public to be unaware of the talented intermediaries producing the creative executions that add lustre to the brand. It would be a little like the backing singers getting as much publicity as the star. Agencies have had to learn to be discreet about their abilities: successful advertising must always be about the client, not about the agency. Agency success lies in bringing success to clients. Another reason for their shadowy character in commercial life is that they operate in what is essentially a business-to-business environment where much work is gained through word-of-mouth, relationships and reputation among a small community.

Dentsu dominates Japanese advertising but is placed at number 6 in the global consolidated agency networks of 2015, behind Y&R, DDB, MCCann Erickson, BBDO and Ogilvy (in Adbrands[6]) (see Table 4.1). Y&R includes digital and direct marketing agency Wunderman and is a subsidiary of WPP. McCann Erickson was one of the first advertising agencies to move into other marketing communication disciplines and today includes customer relationship management (CRM), PR, sales promotion and branding businesses, and many more. DDB was founded by the legendary ad man Bill Bernbach and is a subsidiary of media conglomerate Omnicom, while Ogilvy & Mather was also founded by an advertising icon, David Ogilvy. BBDO generates more revenue than any other agency in the world's biggest advertising market, the USA, and since 2005 the BBDO agency network has won more creative awards than any other. It includes the top UK agency AMV BBDO.

TYPES OF ADVERTISING AGENCY

Worldwide agency networks, such as BBDO, McCann Erickson, Leo Burnett or Saatchi & Saatchi, often have local offices in many different countries. One dynamic behind the evolution of the international agency networks was the need for global conglomerates

TABLE 4.1 Top agency networks by estimated worldwide revenues, 2015

1	Young and Rubicam (Y&R)
2	DDB
3	McCann Worldgroup
4	BBDO
5	Ogilvy
6	Dentsu
7	TBWA
8	Publicis
9	Havas Worldwide
10	FCB
11	JWT
12	Leo Burnett

Source: www.adbrands.net/top_advertising_agencies_index.htm (accessed 27 February 2017)

to manage campaigns in many different countries for each of their individual brands, hence the development of multinational agency networks. In many cases, they have acquired other agency businesses offering specialisms in other promotional disciplines. A second category of agency consists of smaller networks, usually based on distinctive strengths in creative work. These might have just a few offices worldwide. Examples include Bartle Bogle Hegarty, Wieden & Kennedy and M&C Saatchi. The third category is the most typical; these are individual agencies that might be owned by a larger group but operate independently. Some are large and offer a full agency service, while others are more specialist **creative boutiques** with distinctive creative skills, often in a particular medium such as digital or television.

The global communication holding groups generate very big business. For example, the London-based WPP advertising and marketing group posted billings of $55 billion and revenues of $14.4 billion in 2016.[7] Holding groups such as these own many individual agency brands, reflecting the increased industry concentration through mergers and acquisitions. WPP owns such agency networks as Ogilvy & Mather Worldwide, JWT, Y&R and Grey. Omnicom owns BBDO, DDB and TBWA. Some agencies build reputations for creativity, usually based on the creative awards they win[8] (see Table 4.2).

The one commodity advertising agencies feel that they own, above all other marketing and media disciplines, is creativity. Ad agencies are nothing if not their ideas, and their creative craft is what sets them apart. Even though they operate in a somewhat closed culture, agencies do have some interest in self-promotion. If they can enhance their reputation in the industry they are more likely to be invited to pitch for new business. To this end, some agencies try to build a reputation in the communication and marketing industry by entering case histories of their work to try to win

TABLE 4.2 World's top ten agency networks (2012) by creative awards (points)

1	BBDO (including Proximity) 3,349
2	Ogilvy (including OgilvyOne, Ogilvy Action) 2,837
3	Leo Burnett 2,104
4	DDB (including Rapp) 1,868
5	Y&R (including Wunderman) 1,762
6	TBWA (including Tequila) 1,055
7	JWT 8858
8	Saatchi & Saatchi 707
9	Publicis 688
10	Euro (including Havas) 670

Source: www.adweek.com/news/advertising-branding/bbdo-again-tops-big-won-awards-tally-146645 (accessed 15 February 2017)

Note: The 2012 rankings are based on 4,459 campaigns or pieces of creative work that won awards at 39 shows around the world.

industry awards (and publishing them in bound volumes), publicising their history and their successes in coffee table books and producing copies of their ads. Many agencies adopt particular creative techniques or advertising development styles and promote their expertise to differentiate their brand to clients. Frequent social events for awards, campaign launches, annual reviews and so on are an essential part of the networking that is integral to the industry. Advertising is a small community and awards shows and other events create a sense of specialness and exclusivity that is important to the industry in order to offset the lack of wider recognition for advertising expertise and accomplishment. This tendency for advertising professionals to award each other prizes seems important, sociologically, to the industry and it also reflects a self-referential insularity. It is especially important for the creatives. Creatives want their ads to win creative awards, sometimes, it is rumoured, even more than they want their ads to sell product. Creative awards burnish not only creatives' reputations but that of their agency, and are highly prized.

SNAPSHOT 4.3

Advertising careers

The influence of convergence can be seen on the recruitment pages of some leading advertising agency groups. Ogilvy UK,[9] for example, offers careers in advertising and digital, relationship marketing, business-to-business marketing, direct marketing, public relations, retail, experiential and sales promotion, internal communications and social media, media planning and buying, branding, design and production services. Agency groups have evolved through successive mergers bringing formerly outsourced services in-house, and some even bring them under the same roof, and in some cases into the same room. For example, Kaper,[10] an integrated digital and PR agency, has experts in digital, social media, creative and research working together in its enormous London office. Agencies want to solve communications problems with creative thinking so their people need a diverse set of skills and knowledge. As a consequence there isn't a definitive background for an ideal advertising person, they have a wide range of educational backgrounds – a degree is usually essential, but it doesn't necessarily matter in what specialist subject. The key requirements are to be passionate about advertising and have great analytical, communication and interpersonal skills.

ADVERTISING AGENCIES AND THE PITCH PROCESS

Advertising and promotion agencies are slightly mysterious places. They have great (and often under-recognised) importance in capitalist economies. They produce work that is often striking and resonant, and they attract some of the brightest and best-educated people to work in them. Yet, explaining exactly how this work results from the hive of activity that is an advertising agency is not an easy task. The advertising world remains an enigmatic one in spite of its importance to the economy.

Marketing and advertising textbooks and research are remarkably vague about exactly how advertising is created, and even committed and highly skilled advertising professionals themselves are not quite sure how precisely to explain their work. Like much human organisation, the fact that it turns out to be productive can be hard to explain given the messiness, the conflict and the confusion surrounding it. This is more true of advertising than most fields, given the collision of creativity and business that has to be reconciled for advertising to be produced. The enigmatic character of ad agencies means that a descriptive account of roles and working procedures may appear glib. A list of the components of a TV set in no way serves as an account of what it produces. Nevertheless, this chapter outlines these roles and processes while acknowledging that there is much flexibility and indeterminacy in the processes. What is more, as we assert many times in this book, the business of advertising and promotion is in a flux as media convergence throws all the old certainties into question and agencies are experimenting with new forms of organisation and process management in response. Advertising is a creative industry. The superficially chaotic character of agency life may be seen as a reflection of the high intellects and professionalism of advertising folk. Some clients take a different view and regard communications agencies as poorly managed, un-businesslike places that need close direction and cannot be trusted to be prudent with clients' money.

The account that follows is organised broadly around the sequence of activities that agencies must undertake in the course of acquiring and executing client business. The first step, therefore, will be to look at the nature of the agency as a business brand and how this might influence its 'pitches' for business.

Advertising is a very substantial business that punches well above its weight in terms of its contribution to the economy in relation to the size of the sector by number of employees. The American Association of Advertising Agencies (AAAA)[11] put global adspend in 2016 at some $550 billion.[12] This amounts to a great deal of employment and wealth generation. If all forms of marketing communication and media agency are included, the estimated number of advertising and promotional agencies is around some 100,000 and more in the USA alone. The UK has perhaps some 700 advertising agencies, but the figure is difficult to establish because so many different kinds of agency are now coming into the advertising scene, as disciplines formerly regarded as non-advertising promotion such as direct mail, sponsorship, PR and mobile are subsumed into an integrated advertising and promotion industry. UK advertising spend, the amount spent on advertising by clients, is estimated at around £20 billion for 2017, driven mainly by large increases in adspend on TV and internet.[13]

The traditional way for ad agencies to get business has been to 'pitch' for new accounts. One of the UK trade associations for advertising, the IPA, has listed the elements of the pitch process, adapted in Table 4.3.

Table 4.3 illustrates how time-consuming and labour-intensive the pitch process can be for both client and agency. The ten stages listed could develop into many more with iterative meetings possible from each stage. Three months would be a typical timescale for this process, but it could be longer. The eleventh stage is the decision. The client will have to arrange further meetings to inform the agencies of their decision. In this discussion we will focus mainly on the actual pitch conducted on pitch day. The stages of the process include 'chemistry' meetings, at which the client and the agencies will meet to decide if they can establish the chemistry or rapport for a good working relationship, and 'tissue' meetings, which are for establishing whether

TABLE 4.3 An outline of the pitch process

1	Client brief
2	Identification of potential agencies
3	Gathering credentials
4	Shortlisting agencies
5	Chemistry meetings
6	Pitch briefing sessions
7	Tissue sessions
8	Negotiations
9	Pitch day
10	Field testing
11	Decision and meetings

Source: www.thegoodpitch.com (accessed 27 March 2017)

or not the agency's thinking to date coheres with the client's vision for the campaign. The client will brief the agencies on the pitch nearer the pitch day, and, once the agencies have pitched their ideas, the client will take some time to field test those ideas in order to decide which are best.

The process of pitching may be preceded by an invited credentials presentation in which selected agencies will try to persuade the client that they are a credible and professional organisation. Track records of successful accounts are important here, as are the reputations of the star personnel. If the agency is already a leading brand then so much the better. The client no doubt has an advertising department and public relations office of its own and needs to be reassured that the agency can add specialist expertise that it cannot provide for itself.

For establishing credentials, agencies have begun to add more and more content to their websites and often contribute to industry blogs. The agency website is a shop window and blogs can also be important in generating comment and presence in the industry. Such presence might lead to an invitation to pitch for business. The client issues a client brief to the agencies it deems worthy to pitch for the business. The client brief contains the background information the client feels is essential to the task, such as the brand name and the category of the product, the company, the desired market and segmentation strategy, the price, the distribution channel and, most importantly, the budget. The selected agencies take the brief, decide how they might solve the client's problem and present their ideas.

SNAPSHOT 4.4

The client brief

The client brief is an important document that sets out what the client wants the agency to do. A written brief facilitates communication and helps each party understand the requirements of the other. The UK Advertising Association suggests that a client brief should include: situation analysis (expressed as 'Where are we now?'); objectives ('Where do we want to be?'); and marketing and communications strategy ('How do we get there?'). Other essential topics include consumer segmentation and targeting ('Who do we need to talk to?'); effectiveness measurement ('How will we know when we've arrived?') and practical issues. The entire project should be managed with clear lines of communication and individual accountability, and not left as an informal, ad hoc or implicit arrangement. Following these principles reduces the risk that the client–agency relationship may become unsatisfactory or unsuccessful.

The pitch itself is a piece of theatre. As with all presentations, it should be well prepared, convincing, succinct and it should have impact. The ad agency team must come through it appearing to have a deep grasp of the client and their needs, and the level of competence to execute the tasks with creative flair, within budget and on time. Pitching for business is an everyday activity for most advertising agencies.

The impact of the presentation is everything; appearances are important and presentational poise and social skills are to the fore. The agency will be judged partly on the creative flair of its ideas, as well as on the strategic planning and professionalism of the pitch. It is the responsibility of account managers and account planners to make sure their pitch presentation is highly professional so that the creative work and strategic thinking are seen in the best light by the client. From the 1960s on, it became common for the creatives to be excluded from the pitch, and from all direct contact with the client, but this convention is increasingly dispensed with today. Creatives are expected to be professional in their dealing with clients, and clients want to have close relationships with the people who will actually be creating the campaign.

If the client does not like the work, the account person who presented it may be accused by creative staff of not trying hard enough or of failing to do justice to the quality of the work. In some cases agencies may toil for two or three weeks on a pitch only to see the business given to another agency. Even worse, it is not unknown for ideas to be stolen, and used without attributing their source. The agency may charge the client for the work they put into the pitch but ultimately will do this work in hope of winning the business rather than with any realistic expectation of a profit from the pitch itself. Exceptionally, an agency might refuse to divulge creative ideas in a pitch, on the grounds that these could be stolen, and in any case, it is a little premature for an agency to pitch creative ideas based only on a client brief. Agency BBH are known for taking this stance. They feel that their reputation should be enough to show the client that they will come up with striking and commercially resonant creative ideas, if they are given the business.

The key elements of the pitch can often be the intangible ones. It is especially important for the client to feel confidence in the agency personnel, and if the agency team can strike a rapport (the aforementioned 'chemistry') with the client team, it can be a basis for trust. The best advertising tends to result from the best client–agency relationships. The agency account team and the client team will have to spend a lot of time together in meetings, so the relationship side of things is very important. The chemistry meeting is an opportunity for each team to appraise each other.

Effective pitches must give the client a strong sense that their wishes and priorities are being listened to with close attention.[14] The agency team has to get and keep the client team's attention instantly, so presentation skills are at a premium. This does not necessarily mean a flamboyant visual show with super-dooper PowerPoint slides. It can come down to the personal styles of the presenters. They have to have confidence in order to make the client team feel confident in them, without appearing to be over-confident. They also have to sing from the same hymn sheet. If agency staff talk across each other or appear not to understand or agree with each other's positions, it can look very bad to the client.

The outcome of the pitch might occasionally be that a new or a small agency gets the business rather than the huge multinational agency group. The nature of the brief will influence the kind of agency that is chosen. Some clients want a full strategic communications service, in which case a larger full-service agency is more likely to be chosen. Other clients may be more interested in getting help with specific activities such as creative, production or media strategy and so may choose a smaller agency. A client who, for example, wishes to advertise a brand launch across international boundaries may have more confidence in an agency group that is already operating internationally. The rise of the big communication conglomerates has been driven by the need for major multinationals to manage campaigns in scores of different countries.

THE CLIENT–AGENCY RELATIONSHIP

Advertising agency professional bodies emphasise the importance of the client–agency relationship. Industry professionals argue that the most effective work results from strong relationships and clear lines of communication between the client and the agency (see, e.g., West and Paliwoda, 1996). Continuity in these relationships gives each the time to understand the other and the business. Agencies claim that a foundation of success is longevity and mutual trust in client relationships, and would prefer reliable clients and repeat business to 'promiscuous' clients. Agencies post news of their campaigns on their websites to publicise their success with prominent clients and to encourage new ones.

The client is effectively the invisible member of the account team. The client's wishes and aims are represented in the client brief. As we noted in Chapter 3, communication and marketing are different things, and client briefs can often require a lot of work by the agency because the client may not have a very clear rationale for communication. This can be a cause of tension in the relationship. It is up to the agencies to research the client brief in order to understand fully the nature of the client's business, markets and brands. Client briefs can come couched in marketing jargon that communication professionals find obscure and misleading. Marketing directors tend to compartmentalise marketing management functions. This leads to elements like pricing strategy, product design, distribution and promotion being considered separately without reference to each other. But advertising professionals have the benefit of a more dispassionate perspective on the marketing process and they recognise that the elements of marketing management and strategy are interdependent. Brand name, price, product design, packaging and distribution outlet all have relevance for the brand communications. Advertising that is able to portray a coherent brand strategy that makes sense to the right consumers has a far greater chance of success than advertising that is trying to use creativity to make up for an ill-conceived marketing strategy. If the account manager (known as the 'voice of the client' in the agency) can act as a consulting partner to a client and gain in-depth knowledge of the marketing function, this will help the agency devise a coherent and successful campaign.

It is axiomatic that agencies traditionally regarded mass media advertising as the answer to every marketing problem. If a client is dismayed at falling sales and allocates a large advertising budget to address the problem, the agency should really concede that advertising may not be the answer to the client's problem – it may be that, say, poor customer service, flawed distribution or poor product design are the cause of the client's problems. Account managers understandably feel under pressure not to turn business away but if a campaign cannot succeed because it addresses the wrong problem then it is wise to advise the client rather than risk the ignominy of a failed campaign. But clients have to be handled sensitively. Some will not accept that they have misunderstood the nature of their own business and will not be protected from their folly. Agencies today are expected to be 'media neutral' in their approach to clients' communication strategies. In other words, they are expected to find and solve the right problem regardless of what the solution might be. Since advertising moved away from the commission system of payment and began to incorporate more elements of non-advertising expertise in their agency groups, media neutrality has become more achievable, and less costly, for them.

The decision to allocate an advertising budget and appoint an agency is a highly political one for client organisations. Client relations are always a sensitive area for agencies and demand astute management skills from account managers. The senior board-level account director will be responsible, along with other agency heads, for deciding whether to accept a client brief. There may be reasons for declining it at the client brief stage, if, for example, the agency's research reveals that communication is not the client's problem. More plausibly, the agency will need to decide if a new client will fit with existing clients. Agencies need to try to ensure that they are not open to conflicts of interest when, say, representing two clients who compete in the same market. Agencies will also have to decide if a client's business fits with their agency brand for ethical reasons. If the pitch goes well, then the agency will be awarded the client's advertising business, called 'the account'.

ACCOUNT TEAM ROLES AND RESPONSIBILITIES

Work in advertising, media and marketing services agencies is normally organised through account teams. These are the vortex of the advertising development process. The account team roles reflect different yet often overlapping areas of responsibility. The major account team roles are those of account management (also called client services), account planning, analysis and strategy, and creative. In addition, there are ancillary roles. These include media planning and buying, discussed in more detail in Chapter 6. Another essential ancillary role is **traffic controller**, now more commonly called production or project management. Their responsibility is to allocate work, monitor progress and ensure that tasks are co-ordinated to deadline. The traffic controller also ensures that there is a paper trail showing the continuous progress of all the component parts of development. If, for example, the production of a TV ad requires a script to be finished, artwork to be completed and a research brief to be fulfilled before the production company can be given the go-ahead, it will be the traffic controller's job to monitor progress and chase up the staff responsible in order to meet deadlines.

Other staff may be engaged in creative production in artwork, digital, print or TV/ video production. They are required because creative teams are there for the ideas and creative logic they can supply; they do not necessarily have production skills. Staff with expertise in graphic art and computer-aided art production, animation and animatronics, website or mobile app design and other production activities can be very useful for agencies to have in-house because they can make the creative ideas happen.

THE ACCOUNT MANAGER

If an agency is appointed by a client then the account manager (sometimes called the 'account executive' or 'account director', or simply 'account man' regardless of gender) will be the client's first point of contact in the agency. The account manager is essentially the business manager for the accounts held by that account team. Reporting to the client services director, he or she is responsible for liaison between the client and the other account team members to ensure that the campaign is planned, developed and produced on time, on brief and on budget. The account manager is often regarded as the business person or, less respectfully, as 'the suit' (Hackley, 2000, 2003f). He or she has to manage the various personalities and tasks to ensure that the work generates revenue for the agency. Consequently, he or she requires skills in relationship management, project management, planning and co-ordination. Account managers will normally have a good working knowledge of the whole advertising development process. The account manager is normally closer to the client than any other person in the agency. In most agencies he or she will have primary responsibility for client liaison and may speak to the client daily.

In some agencies it is common for the account person to be the only contact point between agency and client. The account manager is consequently regarded as the voice of the client in the agency since he or she acquires a strong sense of what the client wants and will accept. This can present conflicts of interest when the creative staff want the account manager to argue strongly in favour of a creative execution that the client may not want to accept. Account managers will sometimes admit that there are occasions when they do not fight as strongly for their creatives' idea as they might, simply because they know that it is not what the client wants. The specific tasks account managers undertake during the creative development of advertising vary from agency to agency, and from account to account. In many cases they will take the lead in interpreting the initial client brief and developing and presenting the pitch for business. Once the account is won they will convene the various planning and progress meetings to discuss and agree strategy. Either alone or with the account planner they will discuss, research and write the creative brief. In many agencies account managers, rather than account planners, commission consumer and advertising research and interpret the findings at various points in the creative advertising development process. The account manager ultimately holds the responsibility of ensuring that an account is, firstly, won and then retained for as long as possible. Along with the account planner (see below), the account manager will often have responsibility for measuring the effectiveness of the campaign against the objectives that were set for it.

SNAPSHOT 4.5

Implicit theory in advertising account teams

Advertising is a practical business, but as noted in Chapter 2, theory has a role, even if its role is often implicit. Kover (1995) found that creative staff hold differing implicit theories of communication while Hackley (2003d) found that account team members work to differing implicit models of the consumer. Agency working practices entail lengthy meetings and considerable communication. These two research studies illustrated how difficult it can be for agencies to articulate all the implicit assumptions that guide professional communications practice. The three main account team roles of account management, creative and planning often approach marketing communications problems from intellectually incompatible perspectives. While this is a strength of the team approach it is also a source of conflict because the differing perspectives are not well understood.

ACCOUNT PLANNING

Traditionally, advertising and promotional agencies have been organised hierarchically, with the account manager leading the account team. Research was once conducted behind the scenes by a specialist researcher who serviced the account manager. Strategy and planning were conceived mainly by the account manager. However, some advertising professionals saw this as a problem since research insights were not necessarily integrated into the creative advertising development process, and the account manager was not necessarily the best person to commission and analyse research. A new discipline called account planning was invented. This discipline, in principle, gave the account planner equal status with the account manager.

The account planning role was initiated in the 1960s in London at JWT (by Stephen King) and at BMP, now DDB London (by Stanley Pollitt), and adapted in the USA by New York agency Chiat Day (Steel, 1998; Pickton and Crosier, 2003; Feldwick, 2007; Griffiths and Follows, 2016). The name 'account planning', a misnomer really, was conceived at a JWT awayday and stuck. The account planner was charged with generating consumer insights through research and with ensuring that these insights were integrated into every stage of the creative advertising development process (discussed in Chapter 5). The account planner, therefore, had to be the intellectual in the agency, the 'boffin' (Hackley, 2000) who was at ease with all types of social research, and who was able to articulate these techniques and their findings with clarity. Good account planners often have a wide range of analytical, linguistic and advocacy skills that enable them to articulate the strategic thinking for brands that contributes to the longer-term management and development of the brand vision.

The role was conceived also as a buffer between creative and account management, resolving or deflecting tension and aiding creativity. It would therefore be a politically important role because it would moderate the tension between creative and account management by offering an authoritative voice based on evidence-driven research (Feldwick, 2007). Originally conceived as the 'voice of the consumer' within the agency, the account planner's role has broadened with the rise of brand marketing (Pollitt, 1979). He or she is now often seen as the brand custodian charged with ensuring that the brand's core values and personality are maintained through all associated marketing communications. The planning discipline has also broadened across new areas such as digital and direct marketing, media, and communications and PR. Planners have always had to be robust though, in making their case, and that hasn't changed, since not all agencies fully support the concept of the planner. Some agencies are almost evangelical about the account planning ethos and the benefits it brings to the agency. Others in the industry are sceptical about the claims made for account planning and ask whether it really constitutes a distinct discipline, or just, as cynics say, a great way to get new business. These agencies use job titles of 'strategist' or 'analyst' instead of account planner. The account planners have a professional body, the Account Planning Group (APG),[15] which tries to address confusion about the discipline by offering training courses, case studies and awards.

DIFFICULTIES OF THE ACCOUNT PLANNING ROLE

There have been three persistent problems facing the account planning discipline, which proves unfortunate when, in the words of one account planner, they see their own role as 'helping creatives and making the work better'. One problem is the hostility of many creative staff towards research (Hackley and Kover, 2007). When the researcher was a lowly backroom person, there was less threat, but when research is a responsibility of the account planner, it has management status. The account planner is a soft target for the angst of creative staff who feel that judging their work against research findings misses the point of what makes advertising appeal to consumers (Kover, 1996).

Secondly, not only do account planners find themselves at odds with creative staff, they may also be at odds with account managers who feel that their status is undermined. Account planners do many of the tasks that were formerly the sole responsibility of the account manager, such as deciding what research to conduct, liaising with the client and writing the creative brief. In agencies implementing the account planning philosophy there often results a three-way power struggle as creatives and account management, comfortable in their mutual contempt, find common ground in their hatred of account planners.

As if these problems were not enough, thirdly, account planners have a credibility problem in the industry as a whole. Just as those agencies that espouse the account planning ethos are convinced of its positive value, those that are not, argue their point of view with vigour. Account planners can be vulnerable to the charge that they cannot easily answer the question of what craft skills they bring to the advertising development process. Many are expert researchers with substantial educational attainments. Others are not, but have found their way into the post through a facility with words and ideas, and a sense of curiosity about people. While creative staff have creative skills, and account management have business skills, account planners are sometimes unfairly seen to have no particular skills that justify their status and power on account teams. Because of these difficulties, account planners require skills of tact and sensitivity in order simply to do their job. As researchers, they require sensitivity to consumers' attitudes, predispositions and preferences, and an ability to work these out from carefully gathered qualitative and quantitative research data.

DIGITAL PLANNERS

Some agencies (see the Chapter 4 case study below) have introduced a new role, digital planner, as part of their effort to instil digital thinking into account team practice. The digital planner has two main roles. One is to understand digital platforms and contribute ideas to the integration effort right from the client brief, rather than as a service function. This means that the implications for digital can be understood immediately any creative idea is put forward, instead of weeks later. Their second role is to educate internal and external colleagues (especially clients) about what is or is not possible on digital.

The truth is, digital platforms are changing so quickly that digital specialists' technical expertise has a time limit. Even they can get left behind, but they have the advantage that they can still baffle colleagues with their technical knowledge. Their status as planner also means that the technical details need not be important, if they understand the broad principles and can apply those to strategic thinking. Some industry bloggers have even suggested that account planning could become redundant in an age of social media, unless the discipline is informed by an understanding of digital and social media.[16] The digital planner, then, apart from just being a fancy new frill for some agencies to boast about, might even move into the centre ground of account planning.

CREATIVE TEAMS

The advertising creative person is a topic of myth and legend. In the *Mad Men* era of the 1960s, creative individuals could emerge, win big reputations and become feted like rock stars, and paid like them too. These individuals could be childish, temperamental, self-indulgent, capricious, frequently late or absent, and it would all be tolerated as long as they kept coming up with ideas the client loved. No longer. Today, creative professionals in advertising have to be team players, they have to be well organised, and in many agencies they even have to attend business meetings. They are, though, no less important to the agency.

Advertising agencies produce and sell ideas. The quality of their creative output is the benchmark of their standing as an agency. The creative team is responsible for this output, and in many agencies the creative work is organised into teams of two people. There may be one creative person who specialises in words (copywriting, scriptwriting, music jingles) and another who deals in images, and undertakes, for example, visualisations of story boards for TV ads, press ad layouts, poster design, typography and so on. Sometimes, these roles are referred to respectively as 'art director' and 'copywriter'. In US agencies it has been traditional for the term 'copywriter' to be used to refer to the originator of any creative input, the assumption being that a copywriter without visualisation (that is, drawing) skills would simply instruct a designer or production artist to put his or her ideas into visual form. Quite often, the two members in a creative team have interchangeable skills. In some cases, creatives prefer to work alone (McLeod et al., 2009). The creative professionals (the 'creatives') typically swim to a different current than other employees. They draw their cultural influences from art, aesthetics and popular culture. Their business is to know what movies people are watching, what cars they're driving, what they're talking about, thinking about and wearing. As a generalisation, though, it is becoming more widely recognised that advertising is a collaborative process, and creatives are part of a team all of whom have to have a strong sense of the cultural zeitgeist.

SNAPSHOT 4.6

Creative stars and agency culture

Creative professionals in advertising need to have a big ego. It is a career that demands considerable personal drive and confidence. However, where a creative becomes so successful that he or she (most commonly it is a he, although the agency world is slowly becoming more diverse in its employment practice and more female creative stars are becoming established) comes to dominate the agency with their personality, it can destabilise the working process and undermine the objective-driven creative advertising development process. Creatives live and die by peer recognition, marked by the awards they win, but clients are more interested in their marketing objectives than in creative awards (Hackley and Kover, 2007). In some creative-dominated agencies, clients' briefs may go straight to the creative star without any initial planning or research taking place. This can be fruitful when the creative person's intuition about the market and its consumers results in an effective creative execution. However, it is a high-risk approach since there is no clearly researched basis for creative work and no carefully thought through strategy. In such a situation, clear criteria for assessing campaign effectiveness might also be disregarded, to the potential detriment of the clients' interests. The creative brief and the layers of account management and planning that buffer the creative from the client are intended to militate the risks of wayward creativity.

LIFE AS AN AGENCY CREATIVE

Becoming a creative is very difficult indeed. Young creatives often study specialised courses then work as interns for little or no pay just to gain the experience they need. There are more talented and passionate creatives than there are jobs, unfortunately. In many agencies, creative teams operate at arm's length from account management. They often occupy their own sub-cultural space in the agency (Hackley, 2000; Gilmore et al., 2011). Creative staff often feel disempowered by the advertising development process since the worth of their ideas is judged by other, non-creative people (Kover and Goldberg, 1995). However, creatives who win awards for their work can quickly acquire a star reputation that brings them (and their agency) considerable prestige. In some cases, star creatives can come to dominate an agency.

Creative staff might not be brought into the process until the initial market and consumer research and strategic planning have taken place. They are then presented with a brief and asked to offer creative executions that satisfy the requirements of the brief. This brief is an important document that should inspire creative staff and excite them about the creative possibilities for an account, while also providing them with parameters to work within, which are derived from the research and strategic thinking that have gone into developing the strategy for advertising. This should ensure that the creative execution will support the desired marketing objectives of the client (Kelly et al., 2005). When creative work has been approved internally by the agency team (usually by the internal director of creativity) it is presented to the client by the account manager. If the client likes it and agrees that it fulfils the criteria set out in the brief, then the work will be produced and offered for public consumption.

Creative staff enjoy a privileged existence within agencies. They must have the discipline to produce ideas to a deadline, starting with a blank piece of paper. While younger creative staff are often very good on ideas, the task of the creative professional requires both experience and resilience, the former of which is necessary in order to know what will work as an execution in different media. Creative work requires strong craft skills aligned to a knowledge of different media and their properties, along with an intuitive sense of the excitement that consumption generates. Creative staff have to be resilient because, in the words of one experienced creative interviewed by the author, 'of every ten ideas, only one will get made'. Creative staff must accept that the great majority of the ideas they come up with will be rejected as unsuitable for a huge variety of reasons. The creative brief in particular is supposed to discipline the creative work so that it serves the clients' marketing objectives rather than the fetid imagination of the award-hungry creative. In most cases, clients would wish advertising to be based on a more transparent footing, with a business-like approach to planning and accountability.

CHAPTER SUMMARY

This chapter opened by detailing some of the major threats to the advertising agency model in the era of convergence. It maintained that the craft skills of the creative advertising development process remain relevant regardless of the medium of execution, and subsequently outlined the account team system and the pitch process. It explored the role of agencies as cultural intermediaries, operating in the interface between culture and commerce. The chapter also touched on the current state of the industry with its many kinds of agency and layered agency networks. The following chapter will develop more detail on the creative advertising development process, planning and strategy.

REVIEW QUESTIONS

1. List the main functional roles in a typical full-service advertising agency. How does each of these roles contribute to the creation of an advertising campaign?
2. Form account team groups, one person each taking the role of creative, account manager and account planner. Draft an outline communications plan for the launch of a new brand of long-grain rice. Then each account team should compose a pitch for the business based on their initial ideas. The pitches should cover the likely target market, the major marketing issues, the possible media plan and creative ideas.
3. List, explain and discuss some of the major problems of management and control in advertising agencies. How have agencies tried to resolve these problems?
4. Research five major advertising agency websites. To what extent, and how, does each bring out the theme of integration?

VIDEO QUESTIONS

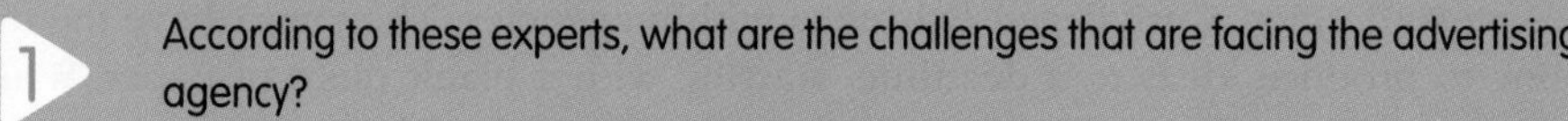

1 According to these experts, what are the challenges that are facing the advertising agency?

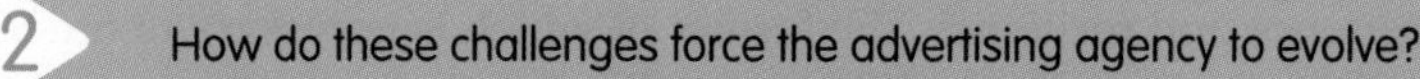

2 How do these challenges force the advertising agency to evolve?

3 How are these challenges creating opporiturnities in advertsing agencies?

4 How are these two agencies similar? How do they differ from one another? How typical do you think these agenices are?

CASE STUDY

Ad agencies: evolution or revolution?

As we noted in Snapshot 4.1 above, it is apparent from their websites that even agencies with a long and distinguished tradition in advertising recognise the need to change what they offer to clients and how they operate. Ad agencies now use sub-contracting, lateral integration and recruitment of new staff/internal re-organisation of work units to broaden their offer to clients across genres, media and disciplines. Some commentators accuse ad agencies of drifting along making cosmetic changes but really offering the same services that they always did. A very few recent case studies exist that delineate the culture and climate of the truly multi-media content agency, such as Grainge and Thompson (2015) who discuss the movement of an entertainment-branding and video-focused production agency into the wider world of advertising and marketing. For agencies that are historically grounded in the full service ad agency model, the question is whether evolution is going to be good enough?

Leo Burnett is one of the world's most famous advertising agencies, with multiple creative awards since its beginnings in Chicago in 1935. Today it is a worldwide agency group with offices in 102 countries and offers clients numerous services including brand consultancy, content, design, experiential, direct, sponsorship and B2B.[17] One of the authors [C.H.] was kindly invited to spend a week in Leo Burnett London talking to account team people in late 2011.[18] Even then, the agency incorporated several disciplines as separate but connected businesses, under the same roof. In addition to Leo Burnett London, a full-service advertising agency with extensive creative production facilities in-house, these included social media specialist Holler[19] and ARC, a brand activation and retail specialist that appears from its website to be a separate business now.[20] The agency created one of the most talked about campaigns of 2016, the Like A Girl campaign (see Photo 11), which was designed to empower young girls and reinforced the agency's claim that it tries to create a cultural impact.

In 2011 Leo Burnett London had introduced an innovation into their account team role. The role of digital planner was incorporated into the heart of account teams. This was unusual at the time and represented one element of the industry's attempts to deal with media integration by placing it at the heart of their thinking. The digital planner had a difficult task. Not only were they expected to keep up with the rapid developments in digital media production, but they also had the responsibility of explaining the implications of these developments to colleagues and also to clients. The presence of the digital planner in the team from the initial client brief meant that every idea mooted in strategy meetings could be looked at from a digital perspective. This is important because activation and engagement are now seen as inherent elements of advertising strategy, and digital media are central to the way this works. For example, a broadcast ad might be shared on social media and added to with iterative storylines on video clips. These might include something, say an app or a game, that drives interested consumers to the brand website, where they might also find opportunities to engage further by signing up to updates or trials. Digital media demand different creative craft skills from other media, so digital specialists are needed to tell other account team colleagues what creative execution will or won't work on digital, and how or why.

The agency places a high priority on creativity, but there seems to be an understanding that creativity must have a context. In a convergent media environment, creativity is collaborative, and, as the agency claims, 'a good idea can come from anywhere', which means that it is not only the creatives who can be creative. This attitude could be intimidating to some creatives, who need the credit for creative work because that is all that is in their portfolio. The creatives at Leo Burnett enjoyed working on some of the world's biggest accounts and seemed to be entirely comfortable with the collaborative nature of the work. In other agencies there are many stories of account planners and account managers who came up with the key creative idea in a meeting, but the credit was given to the creatives. These stories usually come from account planners and managers, who claim to be content with their role as creative 'midwives' (Hackley, 2000, 2003g).

C.H. has not been back to Leo's since they were kind enough to let him explore their working culture in 2011. What seems apparent from the agency's website is that the agency offer has been transformed, along with the offer of most major ad agencies. It is not known how the role of the digital planner evolved – at a guess, it may be that every account planner (and perhaps every creative) now needs to be literate in digital executions. It remains an open question as to whether adding roles and skills to the account team will be enough in the long run to maintain the ad agency's edge, or if entirely new organisational structures are emerging.

PHOTO 11 Always

Image Courtesy of the Advertising Archives

This 2016 ad was part of a high impact #LikeAGirl campaign for P&Gs tampon and feminine hygiene brand Always. Leo Burnett Canada developed the key idea based on research that showed girls experience a reduction in confidence at puberty. The expression 'like a girl' is often derogatory when used by boys, and the agency realised that it could be used ironically to speak to the empowerment and confidence of girls and women. A YouTube movie launched the campaign and generated some 85 million views from more than 150 countries. The campaign developed many more virals, ads and social media memes, and received creative awards whilst increasing the brand's equity.

Case questions

1. If 'a good idea can come from anywhere', is creativity in advertising now dead?
2. How might it help an account team to have a digital specialist in every meeting? Could there be downsides to this extension of the account team?
3. A lot of people would like to work in advertising, but few get the chance. What kinds of skills and qualities do you feel are needed?
4. Every ad agency now claims to be (a) creative and (b) integrated. How have things moved on since the interviews upon which this case is based?

USEFUL JOURNAL ARTICLES

(These Sage articles can be accessed on the companion website.)

Alvesson, M. (1998) 'Gender relations and identity at work: a case study of masculinities and femininities in an advertising agency', *Human Relations*, 51: 969–1005.

Gotsi, M., Andriopoulos, C., Lewis M.W. and Ingram, A.E. (2010) 'Managing creatives: paradoxical approaches to identity regulation', *Human Relations*, 63 (6): 781–805.

McLeod, C., O'Donohoe S. and Townley, B. (2009) 'The elephant in the room? Class and creative careers in British advertising agencies', *Human Relations*, 62 (7): 1011–39.

Moeran, B. (2009) 'The organization of creativity in Japanese advertising production', *Human Relations*, 62 (7): 963–85.

Sinclair, J. (2009) 'The advertising industry in Latin America: a comparative study', *International Communication Gazette*, 71 (8): 713–33.

Svensson, P. (2007) 'Producing marketing: towards a social-phenomenology of marketing work', *Marketing Theory*, 7 (3): 271–90.

FURTHER READING

Ardley, B.C. and Quinn, L. (2014) 'Practitioner accounts and knowledge production: an analysis of three marketing discourses', *Marketing Theory*, 14 (1): 97–118 (first published November 20, 2013).

Deuze, M. (2007) *Media Work*. Cambridge: Polity Press.

Hackley, C. and Kover, A. (2007) 'The trouble with creatives: negotiating creative identity in advertising agencies', *International Journal of Advertising*, 26 (1): 63–78.

Hackley, C. and Tiwsakul, R.A. (2011) 'Advertising management and professional identity in the digital age', in Mark Deuze (ed.), *Managing Media Work*. London: Sage, pp. 209–16.

Jones, J.P. (1999) *The Advertising Business.* Thousand Oaks, CA: Sage.

Packard, V. (1957) *The Hidden Persuaders.* New York: McKay.

Pollitt, S. (1979) 'How I started account planning in agencies', *Campaign*, 20 April: 29–30.

Steel, J. (1998) *Truth, Lies and Advertising: The Art of Account Planning.* New York: John Wiley & Sons.

NOTES

1 www.wcrs.com/, www.redbeecreative.com/what-we-do, https://ogilvy.co.uk/ www.irishinternational.com/ (all accessed 27 March 2017),

2 Jennifer Rooney, 'Mad Men of LA: here's what's different about the social advertising world', *Forbes*, 14 August 2014, www.forbes.com/sites/jenniferrooney/2013/08/14/mad-men-of-la-heres-whats-different-about-the-socal-advertising-world/ (accessed 15 February 2017).

3 Ibid.

4 *Mad Men*, www.imdb.com/title/tt0804503/ (accessed 15 February 2017).

5 Worldwide advertisers/agencies, www.adbrands.net/top_advertising_agencies_index.htm (accessed 15 February 2017).

6 www.adbrands.net/ (accessed 27 March 2017).

7 'WPP at a glance', www.wpp.com/WPP/About/WPPAtAGlance/ (accessed 27 March 2017).

8 Noreen O'Leary, 'BBDO again tops 'Big Won' awards tally', 18 January 2013, www.adweek.com/news/advertising-branding/bbdo-again-tops-big-won-awards-tally-146645 (accessed 15 February 2017).

9 https://ogilvy.co.uk/ (accessed 15 February 2017).

10 www.kaper.uk.com/our-work/ (accessed 15 February 2017).

11 www.aaaa.org/Pages/default.aspx (accessed 16 February 2017).

12 'Carat Ad Spend Report: September 2016', www.aaaa.org/carat-ad-spend-report-september-2016/ (accessed 29 March 2017).

13 'The Advertising Association/WARCExpenditure Report', http://expenditurereport.warc.com/ (accessed 27 March 017).

14 Chris Smith, 'Four tips for pitching a new client', 5 April 2013, www.theguardian.com/media-network/2013/apr/05/four-tips-pitching-client-advertising (accessed 16 February 2017).

15 www.apg.org.uk/?page_id=269 (accessed 17 March 2017).

16 Paul Feldwick, 'Account planning: back to the future?', www.marketingsociety.com/the-library/account-planning-back-future#JrWfax02HhytvQ1i.97 (accessed 29 March 2017).

17 www.leoburnett.co.uk/ (accessed 27 March 2017).

18 For this kind invitation I thank Ayesha Datoo, my former student at Royal Holloway University of London, who was at the time an account handler at Leo's. At the time of writing (February 2017) Ayesha is Global Business Director at Grey, London. I'm also grateful to everyone at Leo's who very kindly took the time to talk into my digital recorder.

19 http://holler.co.uk/ (accessed 27 March 2017).

20 www.arcww.co.uk/ (accessed 27 March 2017).

STRATEGY AND CREATIVITY

CHAPTER OUTLINE

Chapter 4 introduced the key roles and activities in advertising agencies, and Chapter 5 goes into the creative advertising development process in greater detail, drawing on 20 years of research in many different agencies to try to distil the common elements. The chapter begins by outlining the steps in the process. It then moves on to strategy development for advertising and integrated marketing communication before addressing the creative process. Finally, issues of evaluation will be touched upon before being dealt with in greater detail in Chapter 10.

KEY CHAPTER CONTENT

The creative advertising development process

Developing communication and advertising strategy

Strategy and IMC planning

Creative development

Campaign evaluation

Want a primer? Go to https://study.sagepub.com/hackley4e and watch...

***Advertising* to learn**
How the creative process at Mr President matches and differs from the basic stages in the creative development process

***Neil Quick – Analyzing Data, Gwyn March – Advertising, Fran Cassidy – Content in Advertising* and *Andrew Peake – Advertising and Brand Transformation* to learn**
How these different experts recommend evalutaing campaigns, what the different possible measures of success identified are, how they each define effectiveness and how the evaluation processes differ

... to tackle the video questions at the end of the chapter.

THE CREATIVE ADVERTISING DEVELOPMENT PROCESS

In this book we take a neutral position on creativity in advertising. Creativity occurs where someone has to decide on what an ad is going to look/sound and/or feel like (or, indeed, what it is going to smell like, as we saw in the Chapter 3 case study on channel integration). Unless they decide to simply plagiarise another ad in all its detail, then what they are doing is making a creative decision. There are persistent debates about the role and purpose of creativity in advertising that we need not dwell on here. It seems merely intuitive that ads that are clever will be more likely to interest consumers, and one can say that a clever ad is a creative one. Some ads are, of course, pieces of popular art, but many are not. Much advertising today is driven by artificial intelligence and hence has no creative element to its targeting, although someone at some point had a creative input into what the ad was going to look like. Hence, we use the term creative advertising development because arguments over whether, why or how advertising is creative seem redundant. It is creative because ideas are encoded and communicated to a brief that starts with a blank piece of paper, and there is no machine or formula than can do this. So, in this chapter we draw on 20 years of research with advertising professionals in many countries to try to distil the process of how ads are developed into its main component elements.

We acknowledge that, in today's advertising environment, this process rests on several preconditions that may not always pertain to the contemporary advertising scene. For example, there is a need for time, personnel and hours (or weeks) of preparatory work to research the client brief and devise the strategy. These may all be luxuries that the small agency or the time pressed client cannot afford. Nonetheless, what we describe here is a tried and tested approach to devising successful advertising and promotion. If clients want great results, they would be well advised to invest in this process or at least in elements of it.

The creative advertising development process, then, in any major agency entails a set of broadly defined tasks that are listed in Table 5.1. Each could be sub-divided into smaller tasks, but for the present we will focus on the broad commonalities of the process. There is, firstly, strategy development. Once the agency has won the work and allocated it to a team, the team must come up with a great campaign. The place to begin is the first step in the planning process. They will need to analyse the client brief carefully and do any additional research or information gathering that may be necessary to have a full understanding of all the issues at stake. The agency team must understand the brand, its history, its markets, its competitors and its consumers: they must understand the client, and most important of all, they must understand the problem or problems the client wishes to solve with communication.

Once the strategy is devised, informed by the careful analysis, the team will be clear about the precise purpose the campaign must accomplish. The strategy will be distilled into one or more objectives. The task of making sure that the team's thinking feeds into the client's marketing strategy is not complete at this stage – that is an ongoing task, normally the responsibility of the account planner. The planner must ensure at every stage of the creative advertising development process that the client's needs,

TABLE 5.1 Basic stages in the creative advertising development process

1	Developing the advertising strategy
2	Developing the media strategy
3	Developing the creative ideas
4	Pre-testing creative executions
5	Creative production
6	Campaign execution
7	Campaign evaluation

crystallised in the communication strategy, remain at the centre of the campaign. At this stage, media strategy is a consideration, but for the purposes of exposition this is dealt with in greater detail in Chapter 6. The issue for many agencies is that media buying will be outsourced to a specialist media agency who will have their own thoughts on media strategy. There can be conflict here. In many cases, media strategy and planning are considered in as much detail early in the process as is necessary for the purpose of developing communication strategy and advertising strategy. This becomes more complex, of course, in integrated campaigns, as discussed below.

The account planner and account manager will then write the creative brief. This document is a key part of the process since it sets out in writing what the campaign must achieve, to whom it must speak, and any other necessary inclusions. The client and agency directors of creativity and client services must all sign off on the creative brief, so it is a very important document for all concerned. It provides a record of what exactly was agreed should the creative development stray from the brief, or should the client later get cold feet about the strategy.

The creative team will take the creative brief and try to develop some good ideas. This is where the magic is supposed to happen. Some more issues around creativity in advertising are discussed later in this chapter. The advertising strategy has to be expressed in a way that reflects all the considerations of the creative brief, including target audience, brand positioning and any mandatory inclusions. The creative team might have scope to do something expansive in a big television commercial (TVC) if the budget allows, but more typically, there will be clear guidelines as to the medium and budget to work to. Within all these constraints, the creatives have to produce good ideas to a (very) short deadline. Advertising creativity, then, may be like artistic creativity in many ways, but it is constrained by many practical and commercial considerations. Hence, advertising creativity demands craft skills and experience.

Draft creative executions will be tested as they develop, until there are ideas that all agree can be moved into pre-production, mocked up and pre-tested in 'link' tests or in another form of consumer 'copy' testing. If the ideas pass those tests, then the ads will go into final production, media planning and buying, before being pre-tested once more before launch. Once the media plan is decided in detail and the campaign is launched, there will be continuous monitoring to evaluate effectiveness against the objectives listed in the strategy. The evaluation of the success or otherwise of the campaign against the objectives that were set for it should then feed back into the strategy development process for monitoring and/or reappraisal.

The creative advertising development process differs in detail in each advertising agency. While these differences are important, it is also true that every agency around the world does broadly similar things in broadly similar ways (Hackley and Tiwsakul, 2008). The differences in management processes between agencies are normally marked by differences of emphasis and tone rather than by more fundamental issues. Ad agencies generate ideas to help clients achieve their objectives through communication. To put this in a long-winded way, ad agencies analyse clients' brands and assess their marketing and communication activities, and then they devise creative communication strategies that aim to help clients achieve their marketing objectives. These strategies might focus on broadcast or print advertising, but, depending on the client, the brief and the agency, could include any element of the communication mix, including, for example, activation or sales promotion, engagement or social media, mobile, public relations or native advertising. Where agencies differ is in their history, their personnel, the emphasis of their process management, and on the particular mix of skills they can access. What follows is a necessarily general but representative outline of the major elements of the process of developing an advertisement.

SNAPSHOT 5.1

When creative strategy goes wrong

Thompson and Coskuner-Balli (2007) describe processes of 'corporate co-optation' whereby brands try to tap into ideological movements in order to galvanise consumer support. Many brands have attempted to do this through their advertising, with varying degrees of lasting success (Holt and Cameron, 2010). For example, in 1971 Coca-Cola used mass media advertising to position the brand as a salve for the world's disharmony, with a famous ad entitled 'I'd Like to Teach the World to Sing'. In April 2017, Pepsi launched an ad called 'Jump In' that portrayed a street protest in which the tension between the protesters and the police is broken when model Kendall Jenner hands a can of Pepsi to a police officer. The ad, produced by Pepsi's in-house content division Creators League Studio, was greeted with a storm of derision on social media. Much anger was directed at the way the ad seemed to trivialise political conflict.[1] Pepsi was trying to tap into a contemporary cultural climate of conflict, over policing, race, inequality and politics, to position Pepsi as a symbol of youth and hope through reconciliation and understanding. But this ad clearly struck the wrong tone. Some critics felt that casting Kendall Jenner was the key mistake – others that the supporting cast lacked ethnic diversity, while still others thought the timing was wrong, as there were raw emotions about current political conflicts around the world. Recent protest scenes were vividly recalled from just a few months before the ad aired, including one that went viral of protester Leshia Evans facing down a group of riot police in a Black Lives Matter protest in Indiana. The ad was seen as exploitative and inauthentic. Pepsi's share price was hit and the company was forced to issue an apology and quickly withdraw the ad. On big budget campaigns for global brands there are detailed checks and balances through which creative development is tested, yet in spite of these something went badly wrong in the execution. The advertising strategy was to position Pepsi as a symbol of those moments in life when we lose our inhibitions to 'jump in' and create an emotional connection[2] that generates a message of unity and reconciliation. There was nothing necessarily wrong with that, but the creative strategy that encodes the advertising strategy was, as it turned out, badly misjudged in the febrile climate of conflict and anger. Perhaps the creative strategy might have succeeded had the ad been cast and filmed with an edgier and more authentic feel of street protest – unfortunately it looked like what it was, a group of well-paid models having fun in the sunshine acting out a fake street protest.

DEVELOPING A COMMUNICATION AND ADVERTISING STRATEGY

To have a strategy means to have a purpose. It has become conventional in management and business studies to use war analogies for business policy; hence, the talk is of strategy rather than purpose. Strategy is distinguished from tactics by its timescale and resources – a tactical plan would normally be shorter term and demand fewer resources than a strategic plan. A strategic plan would often have major implications for the long term, and demand major resources. An IMC plan might be strategic or tactical, or it might include elements of each.

Essentially, a strategic plan asks, and answers, three questions:

1 Where are we now?

2 Where do we want to be?

3 How do we get there?

For an advertising campaign, the starting point could be an analysis of the brand, the market, the client's marketing plan, the client's objectives and the consumer behaviours and lifestyles. This (sometimes cast as a SWOT analysis for internal Strengths and Weaknesses, external Opportunities and Threats) gives the team a background of good information to contextualise the subsequent discussions. The client will have some idea of where they want to be, cast in terms of marketing objectives (say, a 3% increase in market share within three years) and the client and agency will have to resolve the marketing objectives into communication objectives. These will then be expressed as a communication strategy, sometimes refined into an advertising strategy (discussed below).

The strategy might be expressed as a goal or objective, as in this example from a marketing website:[3] 'Convince marketing communication managers that *AdCracker* CD will help them create more effective advertising, faster, and that now is the best time to buy'. There might be subsidiary objectives, as in this example: 'Achieve 50% brand recognition with target audience as defined by the ability to (A) recognise our logo, (B) describe at least one of our products, (C) associate equivalent products when prompted for brand characteristics; achieve a 2% response rate and sales of $500 per 10 direct mail packages within 30 days; achieve a lifetime value of $1500 on each customer within five years'. These objectives are very specific – unusually so. Nonetheless, the more specific strategic objectives are, the more effectively they can be measured. In this example, the campaign is a sales oriented one – in many brand positioning or corporate campaigns it would be very difficult to pin down strategic objectives realistically to such a level of specificity.

The next part of the process is about answering the question 'how do we get there?' This is where the creativity comes in – the creative team have to devise a way of conceiving and communicating the required message that resonates with the target consumers and motivates them to engage with, and respond to, the campaign. Before looking into this process in greater detail, some details of day-to-day agency life need to be noted first. Specifically, just how does strategy get made? The answer, is through meetings. This is a far from trivial point. It is easy to forget that advertising emerges through language and material objects (briefs, research reports, etc.) in human interaction (Moeran, 1996; Alvesson, 1998; Kelly et al., 2005; Svensson, 2007). The ways that particular ideas evolve and emerge can assume a dynamic all of their own once human interaction and organisational politics take effect. The values of an advertising agency can often be implicit and these implicit norms and values can be a guiding rationale for the development of advertising that is as important as the explicit, concrete materials of market analysis reports, consumer discussion group videos, theatre tests and so on (Hackley, 2000).

MEETINGS, MEETINGS, MEETINGS ...

In most ad agencies, campaign planning is conducted through lengthy meetings. From the initial meetings (sometimes called 'plans board' meetings) through to strategy development meetings, views will be heard from all major parties, including the client, creative and board-level account management. These meetings are at the heart of advertising development; promotional campaigns evolve through a process of debate and argument. Although creative work can sometimes be the inspiration of one individual, in an important sense, creative development is a joint effort because of the way ideas develop and reach a certain point through intense discussion. What this means for employees is that ad agencies value people who are socially poised, emotionally intelligent, articulate and also tough – there is a Darwinian attitude to ideas, and egos need to be self-controlled.

This discussion, which sometimes can seem endless, is given direction by the use of documents. In all agencies there are written documents that perform several functions.

They provide a template for practice and thereby act as a tool of management control. Life in agencies is chaotic enough; without pro forma documents, the chaos would be total. Documents provide a paper trail of accountability and a basis for contractual agreement. Client and agency have a permanent record of what, exactly, was agreed. Documents also act as stimulus tools for directing thinking along predetermined lines. They are handrails for advertising development.

An important semantic note is that ad agencies use the terms analyst, strategist and planner to label the people responsible for developing strategy. The role of planner (as described in Chapter 4) is devoted not only to commissioning and analysing research, but also to integrating the findings into strategy development and, ultimately, writing the creative brief. In some agencies, there is a separation of analysis and planning, while in others the analysis is arm's length from the development of the creative brief. For our purposes, we will not distinguish here between planning and strategy – the former is conceived as a broad term referring to the efforts that go into developing the latter. This is slightly different from the use of the terms in media, where media strategy is logically prior to, and conceptually superordinate to, media planning, which is more of an operational function.

THE COMMUNICATION STRATEGY

There has to be a clear marketing rationale, a purpose, for advertising and communication. Many commentators recommend beginning the process with a SWOT analysis, analysing the internal strengths and weaknesses and external opportunities and threats to the brand. However, other process models simply list 'research' at this stage, since the process model is less important than the outcome, which should be that the agency understands the client brand, its history, its markets and its consumers thoroughly. In many cases, this stage can take two to three weeks as the agency team tries to really get under the skin of the brand, the client, the market and the precise problem or issue the client wants to address. The team will use secondary research, drawing on existing sources such as market reports and published consumer research data, and sometimes they will also engage in some primary data generation through small-scale consumer group discussions, just to gain additional insights into the consumer attitudes and behaviours around the brand. The important thing is that the strategy discussions are informed by an astute and comprehensive collective understanding of all the relevant issues.

In many agencies, there is a hierarchy – the communication strategy is conceived as a more abstract and generalised concept into which the advertising strategy will feed. The communication should be expressed in terms 'your mum would understand', as one planner expressed it (Hackley, 2000). A communication objective might be, say, to re-position the brand to a new market segment, while the advertising strategy might be to persuade this new segment to change their consuming behaviour. However, the distinction between the communication objective and the advertising strategy may be merely semantic in some cases – the two clearly overlap. The main case for having both is that a communication objective actively links the purpose of the advertising to the client's marketing strategy in a more general way. Fundamentally, an advertising strategy (as part of the communication strategy) disciplines the account team to think of an advertisement not just in terms of their own personal response to it but also in terms of the behavioural or attitudinal outcomes that it is designed to achieve. Advertising has to do something for the client's brand. The strategy expresses just what it is that advertising and promotion should do for the brand in order to support the client's marketing objectives.

The communication strategy must include an objective, or objectives. The objective will enable the success or failure of the campaign to be evaluated. The objective will be accompanied by a guiding idea, a sense of who the target audience will be, and a budget.[4] It should also include ideas on media. In the integrated marketing communications environment, it is incumbent on agencies to have an idea of which media they plan to use, and why, right from the beginning of the process. The notion of communication strategy has been used by many advertising agencies, but not by all. It is becoming more important in the convergence era, as agencies strive for media neutrality and seek to devise communication solutions of which advertising may be a part, but in concert with other media[5] in IMC or 'through-the-line' campaigns.

THE ADVERTISING STRATEGY

The strategy document, as with all the other documents in the advertising development process, normally poses a series of questions that the account team members, assisted by other interested parties such as the client, are required to address. These usually include:

- What does the client expect the campaign to achieve? (For example, an increased market share, raised brand profile, changed brand identity.)
- To whom is the advertisement to speak? That is, who is the desired target audience? (For example, motorcar drivers between 25 and 69 years of age using ACORN or other segmentation systems.)
- What is the key consumer or market insight that gives consumers a reason to believe the claim made in the advertisement? (For example, that the brand advertised is more reliable/inexpensive/exciting than rival brands.)
- What is the desired reaction the campaign must produce in consumers? (For example, in terms of beliefs, memory, attitudes to the brand and purchase behaviour.)

The advertising strategy is seldom expressed in marketing jargon. Agencies usually insist on jargon-free, simple and even monosyllabic expressions for strategy. The rationale for the advertising must be clearly expressed, agreed by all relevant parties, commercially coherent and easily communicable to everyone involved. As communication professionals, advertising people strive for clarity and simplicity in their own internal communications. This clarity does not preclude a certain flakiness: phrases such as 'inject a dose of adrenalin into the brand' or make the brand 'compulsory equipment' are not uncommon. These were, in fact, phrases used in the advertising strategy for one of the most successful campaigns of all, for

Levi's 501 jeans. The value of such phrasing is that it resonates with advertising people who feel that they know just what is meant.

The strategy for advertising will be the measure of the campaign's success or failure. The advertising strategy will form the basis for the creative brief. We should note that just as there may be some overlap between the communication objectives and the advertising strategy, there may also be overlap in the issues noted in the advertising strategy and in the creative brief. This reflects the interdependence of the steps in the creative advertising development process.

MEDIA STRATEGY AND PLANNING

Media strategy and planning are normally finalised later in the process but it is important that they are considered as factors influencing creativity, especially where campaigns will be integrated across media channels. Creative ideas for advertising creative executions do not happen in a vacuum – as we saw in Chapter 2, the context is important in framing the interpretation of communication. Media issues have moved to the foreground in advertising development with integration and the interactive possibilities of digital media. An additional issue is that media strategy and buying have been pushed out of the agency to media independents (as discussed in Chapter 6). However, broad-brush media and strategy and planning issues can certainly be engaged with by the account team at this stage, taking into consideration the budget, timescale, target group, and advertising and communication strategy and objectives. Creatives will certainly need to know which media channels they have to work within and what kind of media strategy in terms of targeting, timescale and frequency of exposures will be sought.

Some media strategies require very long-term planning – for example, a US company aiming to place a major TVC in a slot during the Super Bowl will need at least a year's lead-time for planning, buying and creative production. A campaign based on radio ads, on the other hand, could be planned, designed, created and launched within a month, while some social media campaigns based on reactions to topical events (sometimes called 'newsjacking') have been launched in real time within hours, such as the tweet that made Oreo the most talked about brand after the 2013 American Super Bowl (described in Hackley, 2013a).

SNAPSHOT 5.2

Creativity and earned media

Earned media resulting from social shares, likes and comments is often associated with programmatic and SEO techniques that require little creativity. The truth is, though, that algorithms can put content on the viewer's social media screen, but they can't make that content engaging or even relevant. The most shared content is the most engaging and relevant, and brands that want to drive engagement need to create content that people will enjoy and relate to. That means making creative content, but the kinds of creativity needed, and how creative content is created, are changing. One brand that has been pretty successful with its content across social media is Oreo. Oreo's 'Blackout Tweet' at the 2013 Superbowl (also see Chapter 6) achieved a claimed 525 million earned media impressions.[6] The tweet, a joke about the stadium power outage that interrupted the play, was created and launched within a few minutes of the lights going out in the Mercedes-Benz Superdome in Louisiana, USA. Subsequently, the brand engaged in other social media initiatives, including one in which the creative content came from the fans. They were asked to submit ideas based on their favourite parts of the Oreo cookie, and the brand received some 46,000 submissions via Instagram within just three days. In addition to earned media, brands can make use of owned media, that is, their own YouTube channel, or social media pages. Oreo now has more than 2 million followers on Instagram – that means they have an instant outlet for creative content that, if it is fun and engaging, will quickly achieve a level of coverage at virtually no cost that would cost millions of dollars to buy on traditional mass media.

CREATIVE DEVELOPMENT

The next step is the development of creative ideas, in order to develop the 'creative execution', what the ad will look/sound like. Once these have been established (discussed in detail below), the creative executions will be pre-tested. That is, they will be subject to audience research to try to predict how they will be received when the campaign is launched. Advertising pre-testing (often called copy-testing) is an area fraught with difficulty. It plays on the insecurities of all concerned. The creatives are insecure about their ideas being blocked on flimsy evidence; the client is insecure because it's their money and they want all the assurance they can find that the campaign is going to be received in the way that they want; account management are insecure because they want the client to feel happy about the campaign, but they also want to back the judgement of their planning and creative team. Copy-testing can be a crude method and many creatives 'hate' it because they feel that it is just a reason not to have their idea made. Copy-testing will be discussed in greater detail in Chapter 10.

STRATEGY AND IMC PLANNING

Communications strategy and advertising strategy are part of the traditional creative advertising development process. They take on a somewhat more nuanced character when applied in an IMC context. The need to have a strategy that defines the purpose of the communication is not less important in IMC, but perhaps greater. The difference is that the strategy must have the flexibility to be applied through different media channels. Maintaining a strategy coherently in a print campaign with four different creative executions is difficult enough. Maintaining the same strategy through multiple media channels is clearly a more complex task, and the difference is not just quantitative. Consumers consume different media channels in different ways and the strategy has to take this difference into account.

IMC, as previously noted, integrates at the levels of both media and creativity. The integration of media implies a carefully timed and co-ordinated media plan that reinforces the brand values through different channels and hence not only triggers greater recognition among the target audience but also extends the audience reach of the campaign. The second level of integration, creativity, is at a more abstract level as the creative themes are iterated through different media in ways that do not, necessarily, simply repeat the same things, but trigger recognition in more subtle ways, perhaps by developing storylines that continue from one medium to another, or more commonly by adapting creative motifs by utilising the qualities and constraints of each medium. For example, a print execution, a TVC and a mobile app would obviously require rather different creative executions. The ways in which the executions are thematically linked would reflect the strategy.

HORIZONTAL, VERTICAL, INTERNAL, EXTERNAL AND DATA INTEGRATION

There are also other ways to consider levels of integration. These are called horizontal, vertical, internal, external and data integration. Horizontal integration refers to the ways in which different business elements communicate values to consumers and stakeholders. So, for example, the retail outlet, the product design and the corporate livery are all important aspects of the brand, but they would need to be integrated cross-functionally for complete co-ordination to be achieved. Vertical integration refers to the need for communication strategy to be integrated from the brand and product/market level to the business unit and corporate levels. Internal integration refers to the internal marketing communications function and the distribution of the same themes and values to employees for communication to stakeholders. External integration is the level discussed most extensively in this book, and concerns the integration by medium and theme of all the advertising and promotional communications that end users and other stakeholders see. Finally, data integration requires a marketing information system through which data can be shared between functions. This is especially relevant for social media communication strategy and planning, given the importance of data analytics in social media.

STRATEGIC BENEFITS OF E-MARKETING AS PART OF IMC

The benefits of integrating different media in campaign planning are tangible. For example, research by the Internet Advertising Bureau has suggested that when an above-the-line media plan was supplemented by online advertising to 10–15% of budget, the overall campaign benefits (however measured) would show increases of 20–30% (Sharma et al., 2008: xiii). This tendency for integration to leverage disproportionately large benefits has been seen in all media mixes. But what particular qualities do e-marketing approaches bring to IMC campaigns? Firstly, it makes sense to examine what is included in the e-marketing category. E-marketing refers broadly to any marketing through electronic media, especially digital media such

TABLE 5.2 Examples of e-marketing techniques

Viral marketing by email or video	Affiliate marketing
Interactive billboards	Social networking and buzz marketing
SMS text messaging	Search engine marketing
Microsites and sales promotions	Interactive product placement
Podcasting	Online personal selling
Advergaming	Use of online consumer communities
Branded e-content	Online advertising, banner, pop-up, embedded video
Brand blogs	Search engine optimisation (SEO)
Online direct marketing	Social media marketing

as the internet, mobile devices and digital television. Table 5.2 gives some examples of e-marketing techniques. This is the fastest developing area of advertising and promotion since new technology and new applications are emerging very rapidly. The internet, in particular, is the fastest growing advertising medium in terms of reach and share of promotional spend. What is most intriguing about the field, from an advertising point of view, is the rate of convergence between electronic media. Mobile devices combining television and internet will become more and more common, with much improved accessibility and quality in the future. Integration is moving on from being a source of strategic advantage in advertising, to being a default aspect of promotional planning.

The meaning of e-marketing is extending all the time. Another old term, viral marketing, has also broadened its meaning beyond email to video, since video sharing websites have become such popular vehicles for viral advertisements. SMS text messaging can make use of location technology to target mobile device carriers when they are in a specific place, such as a particular shopping area. **Affiliate marketing** refers to co-operative ventures that enable sites to market each other's products or provide direct click-through access to related, affiliated brands. Search engine marketing is the practice of making sure that a particular brand features at the top of category searches by paying search engines and ensuring that search terms are connected with the brand. With online personal selling, a pop-up window connects consumers browsing a site with a live sales person. This can also be done via text, so that the audience communicate with the salesperson (or customer service assistant) via a dialogue box. Online advertising includes banner, classified and click-through ads, while many brands will make use of microsites with brand information, offers and opportunities for consumer engagement such as games, competitions, offers and feedback opportunities.

Advergaming refers to three forms of promotion. One is where a game is placed on a company website for the amusement of consumers, and to encourage them to the site.

The second is where a bespoke branded game is created specifically for promotional purposes. For example, companies in both the USA and the UK have created online games to increase recruitment to the armed forces by allowing gamers to utilise the kind of skill and to experience (vicariously) the kind of task they would meet with as a recruit. Thirdly, brands buy presence in existing games, sometimes called virtual product placement or in-game advertising. This is a major category of product placement since many games demand realistic urban scenarios, and players want to see actual brands represented in street advertising hoardings and pitch-side banners at sports stadia.

Another method of e-marketing as part of IMC is interactive product placement, which makes use of a technology enabling viewers watching TV or video online (especially on mobile devices[7]) to click on items in the scene to find out how to buy them. This technology is often deployed on pop videos because they are usually viewed on platforms with cursors that can be run over the desired item. When technological convergence arrives and TV is commonly viewed on screens that also access the internet, interactive product placement could even challenge traditional TV advertising. Search engine optimisation refers to the ways in which places can be bought for certain words or brand names on internet search engines so that they come up on the first page of general searches.

In many cases, techniques such as these emerge from more creative ways of understanding how consumers interact with electronic technology. In others, the techniques are technology-driven. For example, computer games have now evolved beyond hand-held devices so that gestures, speech and body movement can involve gamers in a scenario in which they interact with characters. This virtual world clearly has immense possibilities for deepening consumer engagement in promotional communication. On one level we can simply walk through shopping centres and choose products, or we can become characters in the scenarios depicted on screen. So, for example, you could enter a shopping world and have salespeople talk to you directly, answering queries you have put to them. Or, you could have three-dimensional games designed around a brand.

These are but a few examples in a crowded and rapidly developing area. Part of their appeal is novelty – they are new, and that has an intrinsic appeal, especially to people intrigued by new technology. There are also significant commercial advantages to be gained from using e-marketing communication. For example:

- *Cost*: an e-marketing campaign can be created at relatively little expense when compared to above-the-line media campaigns.
- *Reach*: e-marketing communications can reach huge volumes of potential consumers globally.
- *Accountability*: there is considerable scope for measuring results from direct response mechanisms in e-marketing.
- *Conversion*: e-marketing enables customers to make instant purchases, enabling a rate of converting browsers into customers.

- *Engagement through interactivity*: e-marketing makes it possible to engage consumers in dialogue or interaction, for example where brand-based websites offer games, blogs, offers, news and competitions.
- *Segmentation and database management*: it is possible to link the customer database with the company website and achieve personalised, targeted offers based on tracking pervious purchases and inquiries.
- *Relationship management*: since people are accessing the internet via increasingly mobile means it is possible to target and interact with individuals in ways that are tailored to their personal lifestyle.
- *24/7 service*: there is no limit on the opening hours of a website.
- *Creative scope*: e-marketing offers a creative palate for advertisers almost without limit. Different media can be combined and enhanced through display and visual technology, generating powerful possibilities for engaging consumers.

It has always been slightly problematic to separate marketing activities and processes from marketing communication. Some commentators maintain that the two are indistinguishable – marketing *is* communication (Schultz et al., 1993). After all, what is a market but a forum for communication? For example, the brand positioning, the satisfaction of consumer needs, and indeed the purchase, are all predicated on communication, in some sense. E-marketing technology has made the indivisibility of marketing communication all the more evident since it has collapsed sourcing and logistics, order fulfilment and customer service, and promotion, into one entity. The website connects the customer directly with stock control. Of course, behind the scenes there may be many links in the chain. Delivery, for example, is often outsourced to another company, while there may be many stock suppliers, and multimedia advertising and promotion programmes. But the website offers a seamless integration of all these elements from the customer perspective. Not only that, but company websites can generate additional revenue streams taking advantage of the browsing traffic through affiliate marketing programmes or the trade in customer databases for market segmentation and customer profiling.

IMC PLANNING ISSUES WITH E-INTEGRATION

Developing an e-marketing plan entails much the same sequence of steps as for a conventional advertising or marketing communication plan. Firstly, there is a need to devise the strategy, then define the desired or potential target audience. If there are several potential audiences then they should be ranked in order of importance so that media mix decisions can be made on clear commercial considerations. Objective setting is also important. The objectives can be much the same as for any other kind of advertising, such as increasing the market share of an existing brand, positioning or repositioning, brand launch, change attitudes, reach a new market, building sales through the internet, and so on. Once objectives are established, the optimum e-marketing mix has to be decided upon. There are numerous techniques from which to choose, depending on the precise objectives, and target groups. Budget setting might be the next stage, given that the objectives and e-marketing mix ought to give an idea about the potential rate of return. In many cases, this doesn't happen and the budget is simply a default figure, what is left after essential costs. But this is a short-sighted way of operating since marketing budgets are an investment that will provide a rate of return. True, in marketing the rate of return (often called ROI or return on investment) is notoriously difficult to calculate with precision. But of all marketing media, e-marketing offers the most powerful potential for measuring ROI because of its integration with database management and order fulfilment. The next step in the planning process concerns action, especially tactics. What has to be done to make this plan work? Finally, constant attention to the measurement of results can make it possible to adapt, increase or redirect resources to a particular area where necessary.

BENEFITS OF AND BARRIERS TO IMC

In practice, as noted in Chapter 3, the differing disciplinary traditions and practices of the various communications disciplines make true integration very difficult for organisations to achieve. It is often more feasible to create a degree of commonality that links the various channels with consistent themes and values while allowing for variation within the overall theme. In other words, organisations achieve limited yet significant control over the way that their brand is portrayed across communication channels by establishing common creative themes, such as logos, scripts, colour schemes or musical links.

The implementation of IMC, then, is limited by, as noted, the different cultures, value systems and craft skills of the different communications disciplines. These can act as 'functional silos' that present barriers to the internal integration of management that IMC demands. In addition to the problems of organisational and disciplinary politics, implementation of IMC is limited by the fact it is a difficult task of management co-ordination. Many organisations may lack the necessary personnel and skills.

The benefits of IMC overall are considered to include enhancing a competitive advantage over those brands that do not take an integrated approach by presenting a clear and coherent brand positioning, by reaching a wider audience, by leveraging social media more effectively, by reinforcing the recognition and increasing the chances of acceptance of the message, and by saving money through efficiencies.

CREATIVE DEVELOPMENT

The importance of creativity to successful advertising is asserted many times throughout this book. Advertising agencies are ideas factories, they are hubs for cultural production. However, there is a debate within the industry that places creativity and effectiveness in opposition. For some practitioners, this is hard to understand. Surely, they think, advertising that is not creative will not stand out, will not generate interest, and will not inspire consumers to consume anything. Others, though, see creativity as a code word for advertising that ignores the client's marketing objective and, instead, seeks to make something beautiful for its own sake. Many professionals simply deny the validity of the creativity versus effectiveness dichotomy, because they know it is meaningless. Advertising has to be creative to be good.

There's little point in equating creativity with great art – advertising is a creative craft skill. The potential for creativity to be indulged for its own sake, though, worries clients, even though some research studies have shown how important creativity in advertising is to marketing performance.[8] Clients' idea of what creativity means, though, is likely to be quite different from what ad agency professionals mean by it. Even the most down-to-earth of clients would admit that good advertising needs good ideas. Furthermore, they would admit that it needs good ideas that will work well in specific media, and that these ideas have to inspire and motivate the target consumers. And that is advertising creativity, hence there is no contradiction. Where there may be less agreement is how the creativity can be produced, what constitutes creative output, and even who should make it (see Snapshot 5.2). Experienced advertising and content creatives can indeed come up with ten great ideas before lunch if they have to. But, the demands of IMC and integration today mean that ideas have to go through a lengthy process of iteration as the team discusses how well they fit with the strategy and how well they work within each media channel. All this makes advertising creativity a lengthy and difficult process, that some clients are reluctant to pay for. They don't necessarily see why it should take so long, but they do nevertheless want great advertising.

ADVERTISING APPEALS

Defining an advertising appeal in terms of one characteristic can seem reductionist, a bit like saying that Shakespeare's play *The Tempest* works through a shock appeal,

TABLE 5.3 Examples of advertising creative appeals

Social-emotional appeals	Personal-emotional appeals	Rational appeals
Social status	Fear	Product knowledge
Peer esteem	Security/safety	Detail and factual comparison
Respect/'face'	Humour	Proprietary information
Embarrassment	Happiness	
Belonging	Self-actualisation	
Acceptance	Joy	
Family values	Nostalgia	
Scarcity	Pity	
	Ambition	
	Sex/sensuous pleasure	
	Music/tag lines	
	Celebrity endorsement	

or that the classic Orson Welles movie *Citizen Kane* was a soap opera. As we saw in Chapter 2, advertising communication can be conceived as a text that has some complexity, including implicit and explicit aspects. The 'appeal' may not be reducible to one dimension. Nor is it meant to be – the creative execution is far more than the basic appeal. Nonetheless, the appeal is a common way of conceiving the basic approach advertising creative executions take to attract the attention of target consumers and to motivate them behaviourally or emotionally. As an analogy, one might think of a pitch for a Hollywood movie screenplay, where the author (or author's agent) has to explain the concept to the producer in one, short sentence. It may be a romcom, an action adventure, a period drama. Similarly, an advertisement might play on a rational appeal, an emotional appeal, humour, shock, fear, guilt, sex ... and so on. Advertisements are not high concept – they are ads, and hence the particular appeal taken can be an important part of the creative development that feeds into the strategy. Table 5.3 gives examples of advertising creative appeals.

EMOTIONAL APPEALS

As discussed in Chapter 2, there is an argument that consumption is predominantly emotionally driven, and therefore that most successful marketing and advertising interventions operate on that level. Emotionality can form the basis for an advertising appeal; there may even be a rational component in the ad as well. Emotional appeals are sometimes broken down into two categories: personal and social. Personal emotional appeals might be based on, for example, safety or security and fear, love, humour and happiness, joy, nostalgia, sorrow or pity, pride and self-actualisation, ambition or sensuous pleasure. Social emotional appeals, on the other hand, might be based around social status and peer recognition, respect, embarrassment, rejection or belonging, social approval and acceptance.

Fear appeals are often used for selling home security systems, roadside car rescue subscriptions and insurance. The fear is that a terrible fate might befall the viewer if they do not buy the product. We all like to have 'peace of mind', and consequently many of us are over-insured, because we are sold on the idea that we can buy insurance to prevent nasty things happening, like burglaries or car breakdowns. Fear appeals are also used in the cosmetics industry to play on our personal insecurities about our looks or our body image. Fear appeals are typically personal but can also be social – for example, some deodorant or bad breath products play on the fear that others may think less of us because we might smell bad. Fear and emotional appeals are linked in direct-to-consumer (DTC) drug ads on American TV, in which a sick person is shown enjoying playing with their grandchildren because their life has been extended by a particular branded drug. Fear appeals can become shock appeals if they hit hard enough. Shock is considered to be more effective in getting attention than in generating sales, and it tends to be used more in charities advertising and marketing than in consumer brand marketing.

Humour appeals are very popular as a way to engage consumers' attention and to help us to like the brand. Many of us resent boring advertisements and after we've seen one we just want that 30 seconds of our life back. A humour appeal can help us to forgive the TV station for inflicting that interruption to our entertainment on us. For some clients, humour can seem a creative risk if the ad is so funny it overpowers the reason for consumers to buy the brand. Humour in advertising should not, therefore, be used for its own sake, but should be used when it links in with the advertising strategy.

It is well known that sex sells, and sex appeal has been used in many different ways to sell everything from cars to perfume, from clothes to ice cream, and from soft furnishings to confectionery. Everyone notices a pretty girl, and the less she's wearing, the more she's noticed. As with the humour appeal, this approach to advertising can be risky because the brand is forgotten, or possibly because sexuality and nudity in advertising may be off-putting or offensive to some consumers. For advertisers, it sometimes pays to offend some consumers with sexuality, because it generates controversy and media discussion as people lodge complaints about the ad. Fashion brands like CK and FCUK, and perfume brands like Yves St Laurent Opium and Marc Jacobs, have all made good strategic use of offending some people with their advertising. Sexuality in advertising is subject to very different regulations in different parts of the world, so it is a consideration in international campaigns.

There have been some reactions to the ways in which sexuality is portrayed that had implications for brands. For example, Unilever's Dove brand in the UK created a market-leading positioning by mobilising consumer resentment towards conventional cosmetics advertising with its heavily Photoshopped, size zero models. Dove has been positioned towards 'real' women, reflecting the reaction of some groups against the standards of female beauty and sex appeal set by the fashion and cosmetics industries (see the Chapter 10 case study).

An advertising appeal can also be based on music, in the sense that a very catchy tag-line or melody associated with the branding can be powerful as an aid to recall. In the USA, for example, TV advertising is generally known for its creativity, but there is great pressure for it to be effective. One TV ad for insurance has used a simple but very popular sung tagline 'Like a good neighbour, *State Farm* is there'.[9] Scarcity appeals are a timeless marketing technique, as when Amazon declares under a book 'only two left!' Other common scarcity appeals can be tied to sales promotional tools such as limited time to purchase or limited time money-off offers to motivate the consumer to take immediate action.

SNAPSHOT 5.3

Who owns creative strategy?

In the era of convergence, media integration is a default position for advertising and promotion. This means that creative strategy is no longer just a great idea 'with legs' as it was in the *Mad Men* era of the 1960s. Today, creativity has to be a series of great ideas that can be linked intertextually across media platforms. This means that in one sense nothing has changed in advertising – there still has to be a great idea that can execute an astute and carefully conceived strategy. This is why books like this remain relevant to practice – the core skills of advertising and promotion remain central to brand communication strategies. What has changed immeasurably is the complexity of executing creative strategy across media channels and platforms that are engaged with very differently by consumers and which demand very different craft skills from creatives. Creativity must therefore be collaborative as never before, and this can be seen in many agency websites that promote their cross-media, cross-disciplinary expertise. The creative stars of advertising today can no longer be maverick individuals who are treated like rock stars (Hackley and Kover, 2007). Instead, they have to be seasoned creative culture professionals who are used to working deeply with teams across the marketing communications disciplines to iterate ideas for cross-channel campaigns. This change is also reflected in the senior role of the executive creative director. Where once the occupant of this role would be a single curator (and gatekeeper) for agency creativity, now in some agencies the role is split into teams to reflect the need to manage creativity across multiple platforms.[10]

Celebrity endorsement qualifies as a form of appeal since it is so common, and the precise nature of the appeal is seldom interrogated. Having a celebrity in an ad serves a targeting purpose, since the celebrity's fan base is likely to notice the ad. It also guarantees a degree of social media buzz, since celebrities' every activity is often reported and commented upon in fan forums, including their sponsorship activities. There is often an assumption that fans will be interested in following the celebrity's espoused preferences and will, therefore, buy the product. There have been theories mooted arguing that there must be coherence between the values of the brand and those associated with the celebrity's public persona, their celebrity brand (called the match-up hypothesis). However, celebrity association is increasingly used to create new markets for brands because of their crossover appeal – David Beckham, for instance, enables brands to access new markets and cross international boundaries because of the international span of his fan base, regardless of whether he is promoting underpants, sports shoes, or prestige watches (See Photo 12). As an appeal, using a celebrity can be creatively lazy, and carries the risk of alienating potential consumers who are not fans.

The emphasis of an ad might be on rational appeals for complex and/or high-involvement products and service, for example, financial services products or business-to-business services. A **high involvement** product or service is one that the consumer takes some time and trouble over deciding to buy, as in a house, a car, a medical insurance plan or a pension scheme. Typically, rational appeals in advertising are combined with emotional elements.

If the type of appeal forms part of the strategy it will be incorporated into the creative brief and the creative team will need to find a way to express it through a telling creative execution.

THE CREATIVE BRIEF

One of the key tasks of the account planner and account management is to write the creative brief. As noted earlier, creatives stereotypically don't like briefs, and some claim to throw them all in the office bin. More realistically, experienced creatives rely on the brief to make their work better by giving it the essential context without which it would be meaningless. It is, of course, important that the brief is written well and factually correct. The brief must inspire creatives: a brief that makes the job seem tedious, routine and functional is unlikely to inspire great advertising. For example, traditionally, creatives 'hate' prices briefs; a brief with the strategy focused on the brand's price advantage is often seen as un-creative. In one case, though – a 1990s campaign for Volkswagen cars – the team found a way to make the prices brief seem interesting. Volkswagen has a long and much-lauded tradition of highly creative advertising since Bill Bernbach and DDB[11] started the creative revolution in advertising with their iconic VW campaigns.[12] The agency (BMP DDB London) wanted their creatives to do something creative with a strategy that required consumers to believe that VWs were less expensive than they thought they were. Qualitative research had suggested that consumers mistakenly thought VWs were more expensive than other cars in their class. The campaign addressed this in fun ways that won many awards for effectiveness and creativity over the following decade, with ads like 'Tennis', 'Guard' and 'Lamppost'.[13]

Each agency has its own pro forma documents for strategy and creative briefs. Of these, the creative brief is very important because it is agreed between the client's representative (often the marketing or advertising director) and the agency account management and planning team. Once it is agreed and signed by client and agency, it is given to the creative team as the basis for the creative execution. It must be clear, carefully thought through and motivating. Each agency has slightly different conventions for the brief, though the aims are similar. Like strategy documents, the creative brief poses questions that the account team are required to answer. In many agencies, the account planner will research and write the creative brief in consultation with the client and account management.

The creative brief would normally begin with some background, a short paragraph stating the scenario to be addressed – brand, market positioning, the context for advertising – such as in this example from a model creative brief[14] from website AdCracker: 'This is a test campaign to a selection of Citibank customers. We want them to try Citibank's new "CitiClick" which is available as a mobile app for all operating platforms, from iPhone to Android. This smart app makes online purchases easier and more secure – and we've got a $1 pizza offer to get them started.' This passage is simple, clear and direct, and sets the context for the brief. The subsequent questions in the typical creative brief would be something like those in Table 5.4.

PHOTO 12 David Beckham and Armani

Image Courtesy of the Advertising Archives

David Beckham's fame as a footballer went global (see page 229) when he started modelling. Beckham has had commercial endorsement contracts with Adidas, Breitling, Armani (above), Samsung, Diet Coke and many more. His recognisability is such that brands that hook up with him can get exposed to new market segments, simply because his huge global fanbase follows everything he does. Beckham's earnings are said to have increased since he quit football and focused full time on being a celebrity.

TABLE 5.4 Questions in the creative brief

1	Why advertise?
2	Who is the audience?
3	What must this communication do?
4	What must the advertising say?
5	Why must the audience believe it?
6	What else will help creative development?
7	What is the tone of the advertising to be?
8	What practical considerations are there (e.g. schedule, mandatory inclusions)?

Question number 1 in the creative brief, 'Why advertise?', invites the account planner and account manager to express the rationale for advertising, drawing on the strategy document. Without a clear reason for advertising, there is little chance of a successful campaign. There must be an opportunity for communication to accomplish an outcome that will support and enhance the brand's marketing strategy. In the Citibank example, they state that the reason for advertising is that 'We want people to download the free app and use it within 10 days to buy the special offer, a $1 family size pizza from Papa John's'. This is a clear statement of intent and it gives the creative team a strong steer as to exactly what the ad is required to do.

Question number 2 asks for the target audience to be carefully defined. In the Citibank example, the response is: 'This campaign will be aimed exclusively at existing Citibank customers in three test markets: Sacramento, Houston and Washington, DC. The primary target will be segments of our customer database: male and female, 20–35 years old, with at least one Citibank credit card. The target will be approximately 70% married, with combined household incomes of $85,000 on average. The audience is comfortable with new technology, and quick to test new smartphone apps that save their time. They make multiple purchases monthly'. In this example, the target audience is conveniently bracketed and not difficult to define. It is an affluent target audience with a household income almost double the US median. In more abstract brand campaigns this can be a much more nuanced task, but equally crucial to the success of the brief. The creative team needs to have a very clear idea of the kind of people they need to speak to.

Question number 3, 'What must this communication do?', asks what the outcome of the advertising should be for the consumer. This is often couched in terms of consumer attitudinal or behavioural change. It must be a very simple and clear statement of what the ad must achieve. It is slightly different from question number 1 because it focuses on the outcome (for example, to make people feel more positive about the brand) as opposed to the reason for advertising (for example, sales are suffering because people feel less positive about this brand than they did five years ago). In the AdCracker Citibank example, the response to this question is: 'Citibank will simplify and speed up all of your online purchases, while providing increased security'. From the point of view of the creative team, the outcome might be prosaic and straightforward, but that doesn't mean they should be prosaic and straightforward about getting consumers to make that conclusion. In our list, this question is subdivided into two: question number 4 refers to the bottom-line message of the ad that the client wishes the consumer to get from exposure to the ad. This is sometimes called the 'proposition' or the 'take-out' (for example, this brand is the leader in its class). In the Citibank example, the answer could be something like: 'Citibank value my custom and want to make life easier for me with this app'.

Advertising makes many claims, and can support many different kinds of marketing objective (as we saw in Chapter 3). Good advertising gives consumers a reason to believe the claims. Question number 5 asks the account team to provide evidence to support the claim, a reason to believe. The reason can be emotional or rational, or both. For example, many motorcar ads try to reassure the consumer that the brand is mechanically reliable and technologically advanced. In the case of German car brands, this is not too difficult because in many countries German engineering and technology have an excellent reputation. This attitude can be symbolised economically in TV or print ads, with visual images of working engine parts or a cutaway image of an engine interior. The consumer, primed with cultural knowledge about the quality of German motor engineering, understands the inference implicitly. In our example, the response is given that the consumer should believe the ad because 'it's free, from Citibank, your trusted partner – it's backed with 100% fraud protection guarantee – it has earned rave reviews from real users (with quotes supplied in the ad) – and it is easy to access in seconds via the customer's online account'. The ad, then, has to offer some reason why consumers should believe the claims, and in this example, they have several pieces of evidence.

Questions number 6, 'What else will help creative development', and number 7, 'What is the tone of the advertising to be?', broadly refer to the way that brand values are reflected in the creative and production values of the ad. In the Citibank example, there is an 'insight' that claims: 'People don't like to put their credit card details and shipping details in over and over again when making online purchases. But they also don't like feeling their credit card information is vulnerable to theft. This app is the solution'. This claim might draw on some research carried out in the planning stage. It does, though, contain a hostage to fortune. The software development had better be right, because if the app did prove vulnerable to fraud, the campaign would be completely undermined. Not all creative briefs include a note about the 'tone' of the ad. In some, for example the iconic 1980s 'Laundrette' ad for Levi's 501 mentioned earlier, the response to this question was 'Heroic, but period'. Tone can refer to stylistic aspects of advertising production, including the set, music and narrative, and cinematography. The tone of the ad carries implied values for the brand.

Finally, in terms of practical considerations (question number 8), there is often a schedule detailing deadlines for initial creative sketches, the creative review meeting and more advanced production of creative ideas, e.g. with colour and/or sound, for internal and then external (to the client) creative and media presentations, and finally deadlines for finished art work and creative production. There may also be mandatory inclusions that the creatives must take on board. For example, for many years, it was mandatory that BMW ads featured no human beings; the focus was to be on the engineering and the aesthetics of the car. The Levi's 501 ad mentioned above had a requirement that there be no words but lots of close-ups of the rivets on the jeans. The ad was to be shown in many countries, so language had to be absent. Some ads have contact telephone numbers as mandatory inclusions, website addresses, particular straplines and so on.

THE CREATIVE EXECUTION

As we have seen in Snapshots 5.2 and 5.3, the creative execution refers to the particular way the creative team address the creative brief, considering all the required elements of strategy, target audience, tone, required content and media. The creative execution, in a nutshell, is how the creatives make a great ad out of a particular kind of appeal. The execution must embody and achieve the advertising strategy. The scope of advertising creativity is greater than ever before because of IMC. The creative execution might come in the form of a script for a radio or TVC, a screenplay for a piece of branded video content, a striking piece of photography for a print ad, a piece of animation, a memorable jingle, strapline, slogan or logo, a design for an interactive billboard, a cheap retail flyer, an expensively produced cinema ad; it could be a comedy script, a piece of emotionally tense drama, a one-line gag that captures the public imagination and puts the brand in everyone's consciousness, a blog piece or a piece of native advertising journalism, or any number of other kinds of creative execution. Importantly, the ways in which a creative execution activates the audience can be in the incidental detail or in the tone, such as the quality of acting, the casting or the feel of the film (see Snapshot 5.1), the font that is used in print, or the production standards. Attention to detail is essential.

There is no single best way of producing creative work, every creative has his or her own particular style of working and every team has a different dynamic. Typically, in a traditional ad agency the two-person creative team would firstly generate a list of ideas, usually expressed in sketches, roughs, hand-written notes. They would then develop these by interrogating them against the creative brief. They would narrow the ideas down to a smaller number and discuss the implications of each, how they would work on different media, the costs, the time they would take to produce. Subsequent meetings to discuss outline creative executions would involve more members of the account team, and perhaps the director of creativity (DOC) and/or director of planning (DOP). There would be a further stage of development in which ideas would be developed in a more advanced way, making use of production artists to visualise the ideas more completely. There might be a need for research to test the ideas on a panel of consumers, before making decisions on which ideas to present to the client. If the client likes none of the ideas presented to them, the creatives will go back to work. If the client gives final approval on an idea, then it will go into full production.

PHOTO 13 BMW

Image Courtesy of the Advertising Archives

This print ad adapts the idiomatic English acronym I.O.U. (as in I owe you (e.g. money)) to imply that the car is a reward that the successful person owes him or herself. BMW has a tradition of advertising that features no human beings, but they abandoned that principle in a famed series of short viral action movies first launched in 2001 (see Chapter 1 Case Study) that racked up more than 100 million global views in the first two years. In 2016 they released another, called The Escape (http://bmwfilms.com/) starring Clive Owen and Dakota Fanning. The Escape is lauded as a great movie in its own right as well as a huge marketing success for brand BMW.

THE ENIGMA OF CREATIVITY

How creatives create is one of the abiding mysteries of advertising. As Gilmore et al. (2009) showed in her research with creatives, they tend to be passionate about their work and they see it as something that is important. They are not salespeople, analysts or account managers since they see the problem from a different place, drawing on their own value judgements that are informed by their love of popular art, comic books, graphic design, literature and everyday consumer culture. The fact that they come to communication problems from a space that is not solely sales-driven is what gives them their creativity, but some clients find it unsettling to think that their bottom line is in the hands of a comic book enthusiast or aspiring novelist. The account management and account planning functions are both, essentially, organisational devices to manage (and to discipline) creativity. The tension between the two cultures of art and commerce (to adapt C.P. Snow's famous axiom[15]) lies at the heart of the fascination of advertising, giving rise both to its conflicts and also to its occasionally astonishing outcomes. Advertising is a creative business, with the emphasis on the business (Hackley, 2000). In the UK the IPA has tried to address some clients' misunderstandings around creativity by commissioning a major case study programme of research that shows how creativity and advertising effectiveness can be shown to be linked.[16]

It seems self-evident to laypeople that creativity is what makes advertising good, but many clients still view creativity in particular, and advertising in general, with suspicion. The creative execution fills the space between analysis and outcome. Some commentators argue that Bill Bernbach's famous use of self-deprecation in his early VW ads was not creativity but brilliant strategy. However, as we have seen in the examples above, the two are not so easily separated, hence the term 'creative strategy'. In the case of Bernbach's iconic VW campaigns (see photo 1), there may have been an astute strategy, but it was expressed by a brilliant and, at the time, daring, creative execution that ran against the grain of conventional advertising wisdom at the time. Unfortunately for advertising professionals, there are a lot of marketing consultants and managers who couldn't recognise creativity if it fell on their head, and others who are determined to misunderstand the nature of advertising communication by reducing it to a data input model that is based on information rather than inspiration.

Depending on the media mix employed, the creative team will have, in principle, a multiplicity of ways in which to encode the message, especially in IMC campaigns. In practice, of course, a great deal of advertising is not very creative. For ancient Greek philosopher Aristotle, all art is mimesis, by which he possibly meant that no intellectual output is entirely independent of other outputs with which it is intertextually connected. Advertising is a cultural industry that makes use of symbols and practices that exist in wider culture, so it is not only inevitable but entirely necessary that some ads borrow visual and linguistic idioms from other sources. Of course, it is also possible to view some advertising practice in a dim light since many ads are not really very creative and make use of tired clichés, worn-out stereotypes and outright plagiarism. Not a few award-winning advertising and promotional campaigns began life as a YouTube clip uploaded by an amateur, or at least they look as if they did. Then again, a great deal of advertising is not very good, and as in most fields, true creative excellence is rare to find and difficult to achieve. This does not mean that the worst examples of plagiarism in advertising represent good practice, they really don't.

Creativity can run in cycles, with particular narrative forms or production techniques coming into vogue for a while before being replaced by another. Some creative teams make a career out of one type of creative execution, such as animation or celebrity endorsement. Some creatives exploit their friendship with a celebrity to get some input. Some ads, though, do stand out, and some agencies, and some creative professionals, consistently make ads that stand out from the rest by distinguishing the brand in ways that appear fresh and different, even if they may not be entirely original. The thing that makes these ads stand out is called creativity, for want of a better word. There is art and craft in starting with a blank piece of paper and generating ideas, words or that might be engaging, inspiring and perhaps amusing to a given audience, but which also knit with the advertising strategy and resonate with the target audience. Whether the ad made is another great Guinness ad, a Nike epic, or a corny but catchy execution for a local car dealer, there can be an integrity to advertising work that is best expressed as creativity.

Advertising creatives have to survive in an exceptionally highly pressured professional environment. They bring varied temperaments, backgrounds, motivations and working methods to their tasks, but most are genuinely passionate about wanting to make great work. It would be hard for them to survive in the business if they were not. Just what, though, should be judged as great work is a point of endless debate. Budweiser's legendary 'Whassup' campaign[17] won many awards and was lauded as a hugely notable campaign, but was it great creativity? Great art it certainly was not, but someone had the idea that the idiomatic expression being used by many young American men at that time could be used to link the beer brand with its target audience, and that took a kind of thinking that might be termed creative in the sense that it entailed a conceptual leap from one domain to another (Hackley and Kitchen, 1997).

There are many definitions and theories of creativity but one fact emerged strongly from the psychology research in human expertise. This is, that creativity has a context. Ad agencies sometimes set creativity exercises for graduates competing for their graduate trainee posts like 'how many uses can you think of for a brick?' or 'think of an advertisement for lard'. 'Diagonal thinking',[18] lateral thinking or creative problem solving exercises are all very well but without a context for creativity, a creative output is unlikely to resonate with relevant groups. One of the truisms about creativity is that it is a social accomplishment: it is nothing unless it is recognised as such by others. It takes experience, craft skills and a social presence in a particular milieu, in other words, a network, to have creative output recognised, in any field. This is why creatives in advertising value industry awards from their peers so much. It is also why creativity in advertising must be understood in the wider context of the role and organisation of the whole industry (Pratt, 2006).

The best advertising creatives tend not to complain about having to work to a brief – they realise the creative brief is there to make their work better, and if their work lacks any connection to the strategy, they are unlikely to win awards. There are always exceptions, examples of advertising creativity that breaks the rules and still works. These, though, are rare, and usually result from a bond of trust between client and agency (or more specifically, between ad agency account team and client brand team). In such cases, the brief can be deliberately broad, leaving the creatives scope to do something that might be seen as risky. When this works well, the results can be highly satisfactory for all parties involved. Such situations of trust are becoming more and more difficult to find though, as commercial pressures swarm into every area of the marketing communication business and measurable ROI becomes clients' abiding priority.

CAMPAIGN EVALUATION

Once ads have been produced and the campaign has been launched in selected media, it is important for the campaign's effectiveness to be ascertained. This task is a perennial problem in the advertising industry because of the difficulty of conclusively linking the advertising cause with the purchase effect (Cook and Kover, 1998). It is important, though, because clients want agencies to be accountable for the success or failure of a campaign. Clients need to know their ROI on advertising and media spend, and they need criteria to judge agency performance. For their part, agencies need to know what works and what doesn't, and they need to have feedback on their performance in order to monitor and improve their working methods, and to improve their credibility with clients. Winning creative awards is important, but if the agency is not winning effectiveness awards as well then potential clients will draw their own conclusions. In this section, campaign evaluation will be outlined in brief, and the research methods used in the process will be discussed in greater detail in Chapter 10. Some methods of campaign evaluation are summarised in Table 5.5.

Clients need to be reassured that campaigns are effective in meeting their objectives if they are to continue to pay for advertising and promotional campaigns. As noted throughout this book, even though TV advertising is holding up pretty well, in general, client adspend is shifting away from advertising and towards digital because of the perception that digital gives a better ROI. Digital media can be subject to complex and precise analytics so that a value can be placed on every unit of adspend, and that is very attractive to brand clients in comparison to the leap of faith they have to take with mass media advertising. However, there is a little less to digital ROI than meets the eye. Digital and social media advertising can generate impressive statistics on audience views, reach and engagement, but the central problem remains – these stats cannot easily be linked to sales in a causal relationship. Not only that, but there is sharp practice in the generation of social media metrics. For example, some social media platforms count a 'view' as an instance where a piece of content is in the newsfeed of a target as they scroll by. This is not a 'view' in any meaningful sense. What is more, the role of 'bots' in social media is often downplayed. Media metrics such as shares, likes and Twitter followers can be artificially inflated by non-human elements. The truth in advertising, as ever, can be hard to find.

Moving back to non-digital metrics, ad agencies and professional bodies have done a lot of work in developing evidence bases for advertising effectiveness, but the conventional wisdom is still that a large proportion of advertising spend is unproductive.

TABLE 5.5 Methods of campaign evaluation

Methods of campaign evaluation
Pre- and post-launch street surveys for brand recall/prompted recall
Social media data analytics for brand engagement (e.g. clicks, page views)
Sales data/enquiries/conversion rate analysis
Media content analysis
Mid-campaign audience/reader surveys
Surveys of intermediate attitudes, e.g. intention to purchase, brand preference
Calculation of advertising ROI by ratio of revenue to advertising and media costs
Market share analysis
Focus groups
Case studies

Evaluation of advertising is, nonetheless, an essential component of the process. Evaluation techniques can only be as successful, though, as the strategy allows. If a campaign had a poorly conceived strategy, leading to confused or vague objectives, there is no method that could ascertain its effectiveness. Adding to the complexity, campaign evaluation is always contingent on market conditions as well as on campaign objectives. For example, if sales fall after a campaign, the client will not be happy, but it would be important for the agency to consider seasonal or competitive factors before declaring the campaign a failure. If every supplier's sales fell during the same time period, but the agency's client's sales fell less, then the campaign could be regarded as a qualified success in bolstering sales and increasing market share in a falling market.

Many agencies try to reduce the risk of failure and quantify the risk by carrying out extensive pre-launch testing. When a creative execution has been signed off by the client, it is often subject to one final phase of pre-launch testing before the campaign launch. This is often called 'copy-testing' and is sometimes done through 'link' tests, computerised platforms that allow panels of consumers to access ads remotely and offer assessments on them through an online questionnaire. If the results of the link test are satisfactory to the client, the campaign will be launched and evaluation will continue throughout the campaign via, for example, recall tests, prompted recall tests and street surveys.

One UK campaign was commissioned by a health charity to get more people to go to their doctor to be tested for diabetes. A survey established that most people didn't know the typical symptoms of diabetes. The poster campaign was launched in the London Underground, and a subsequent survey established that the percentage of people who recognised the symptoms of diabetes had risen significantly. In that example, the objectives of the campaign were clear and easily measured in the medium term. Many ads with a simple appeal can be evaluated in this way, either through street surveys or by email or internet surveys, although without face-to-face questioning it is more difficult to ascertain the respondent's credibility. Ads with a clear sales objective can, of course, be evaluated by looking at sales figures at the time of the campaign, but there is often a difficulty of a time lag both in the available figures, and in the sales effect.

Many campaigns are evaluated through intermediate effects, effects short of sales, such as measures of brand recall, of ad recall, measures of attitude to the brand, and measures of 'purchase intention', in which people are asked if they plan to buy the brand in the future. 'Self-reports', as these forms of research are called, can be very imprecise, but they form part of the battery of evidence that ad agencies compile to evaluate the success or otherwise of their campaigns.

CHAPTER SUMMARY

This chapter has reviewed strategy and creativity in advertising. The chapter outlined the entire creative advertising development process before discussing the development of communication strategy and advertising strategy, and then discussed implications of IMC. It then focused on the creative brief and the development of the creative execution. Chapter 6 will discuss the rapidly evolving media environment for advertising, and the implications of convergence for media planning and strategy.

REVIEW QUESTIONS

1 What is the difference between the creative execution and the advertising appeal, and how are they reconciled in the creative brief?
2 Is there a tension between creativity and effectiveness in advertising? How might this be resolved?
3 Devise an advertising strategy for a new-to-market brand of high fashion wear targeted at women aged 18–25 and branded 'Ms Dynamic'.
4 Describe the creative advertising development process and explain the key issues and difficulties at each stage in the process.
5 Why is strategy important for advertising campaigns?

VIDEO QUESTIONS

How does the creative process at Mr President match and differ from the basic stages in the creative development process?

Compare how these different experts recommend evalutaing campaigns.
What are the different possible measures of success identified?
How do they each define effectiveness?
How do the evaluation processes differ?

CASE STUDY

Influencer marketing on video sharing websites

Influencer marketing is celebrity endorsement enhanced for digital media and it is becoming a major part of the promotional mix for global brands. Social media adspend is heading towards the $35 billion mark globally[19] and appears to be in a relentless upward trend. Social media, including video sharing websites, are now exceeding traditional mass media not only in targeting precision and accountability, but also in simple audience reach, and traditional media are being pushed to the margins by the power of digital.[20] TV remains important for advertisers but video sharing websites can now generate audience reach that makes TV look decidedly lame as an advertising medium. Some YouTube channel entrepreneurs boast greater numbers of viewers than national TV broadcasters could ever dream of, in the multiple millions. Advertisers pay handsomely to be associated with these 'influencers'. For example, one blogger, PewDiePie, has been reported to have some 15 billion views and 54 million subscribers to his mix of chat, video games and pranks at the time of writing, in mid-2017[21] (by www.vidstatsx.com). PewDiePie recently lost lucrative deals because of some of his video content, but he remains the biggest YouTube star in the world.[22] Zoella, Ksi, Joe Sugg, Tanya Burr and Alfie Deyes are among the top British YouTube stars who, in addition to their millions of channel subscribers, extend their celebrity across other platforms such as Instagram and Twitter. Celebrities from other domains, especially music, see a YouTube channel as a natural extension of their audience reach. Katie Perry, Justin Bieber, One Direction, Eminem, Taylor Swift all have subscriber figures that guarantee hefty advertising revenue, as do the more general sports, news and entertainment channels. Terrestrial TV cannot approach such figures and advertisers know it. Video channel influencers make money not only by having advertising wrapped around their videos, but also by featuring brands within their broadcasts, either through declared sponsorship and product placement deals, or through undeclared ones. The term influencer, though, can be misleading. It is not necessarily influence that is being bought, but the celebrity's audience reach. Celebrities in general are able to open up new market segments for brands through their fanbase, even though many fans know that their brand endorsements are deeply insincere (Hackley and Hackley, 2015). Some deals with YouTubers breach advertising regulations by not declaring that plugs (brand mentions, appearances in videos) are paid for by the sponsor, but policing such a huge field is a major headache for regulators (Hackley, 2014). At the time of writing (March 2017) some major advertisers are boycotting Google because of the lack of precision in wrap-around video advertising algorithms. Some advertising is ending up in channels extolling extremist terrorism, making serious revenues for the terrorists.[23]

Video channel influencers are challenging the hegemony of television not only because of their vast audience reach and relatively low cost for advertisers, but also because of their perceived authenticity. Their subscribers see their content as personally relevant and authentic, so they are excellent vehicles for advertisers to precisely target particular lifestyle and demographic groups across national boundaries.

The viral possibilities of these sites mean that uploads which people like can spread to millions and even billions of viewers in a short time. For advertisers, media exposure that is 'earned' from shares is a whole lot cheaper than 'bought' media advertising spots. It is also hugely valued because earned media reflects the engagement of the viewer – people share content to their network of social media contacts because they found it particularly resonant for some reason. This is a measure of the involvement of the viewer, and it gets around the problem that many viewers of conventional spot advertising on TV do not find it relevant or interesting and may not even pay any attention to it, but they still appear in the viewing figures on the bill the channel sends to the brand. The difficulty, of course, with video advertising content is that there is no formula for producing engaging content, but that is why so many brands leave it to the influencers, who know what their audience wants. Video influencers are the new celebrities who operate under the radar for many older consumers, yet their power and reach mean that advertisers cannot ignore them.

Case questions

1 How might media planners conceptualise the audience reach of social video sites? Is it possible to break down the target segments by demographic or region, or is it just all about the numbers?

2 Many advertisers are sensitive about the media context in which they are viewed. Does the rise in popularity of programmatic advertising on social media mean that advertisers no longer worry about being juxtaposed to imagery and ideas that might offend their consumers?

3 Does social media advertising change the way creativity should be conceived in advertising?

4 Are video channel influencers changing the way the role of celebrity in marketing and advertising should be understood?

USEFUL JOURNAL ARTICLES

(These Sage articles can be accessed on the companion website.)

Cronin, A.M. (2004) 'Currencies of commercial exchange: advertising agencies and the promotional imperative', *Journal of Consumer Culture*, 4 (3): 339–60.

Loda, M.D., Norman, W. and Backman, K.F. (2007) 'Advertising and publicity: suggested new applications for tourism marketers', *Journal of Travel Research*, 45 (3): 259–65.

Serazio, M. and Szarek, W. (2012) 'The art of producing consumers: a critical textual analysis of post-communist Polish advertising', *European Journal of Cultural Studies*, 15 (6): 753–68.

Sood, S., Shefner-Rogers, C. and Skinner, J. (2014) 'Health communication campaigns in developing countries', *Journal of Creative Communications*, 9 (1): 67–84.

Wilken, R. and Sinclair, J. (2009) '"Waiting for the kiss of life": mobile media and advertising', *Convergence: The International Journal of Research into New Media Technologies*, 15 (4): 427–45.

FURTHER READING

Ariztia, T. (2013) 'Unpacking insight: how consumers are qualified by advertising agencies', *Journal of Consumer Culture*, doi: 1469540513493204 (first published 25 June 2013).

Branchik, B.J. and Chowdhury, T.G. (2013) 'Self-oriented masculinity: advertisements and the changing culture of the male market', *Journal of Macromarketing*, 33 (2): 160–71 (first published 4 November 2012).

Hackley, A.R. and Hackley, C. (2013) 'Television product placement strategy in Thailand and the UK', *Asian Journal of Business Research*, 3 (1): 97–110.

Hackley, C. (2003) 'Account planning: current agency perspectives on an advertising enigma', *Journal of Advertising Research*, 43 (2): 235–46.

Hackley, C. (2003) 'From consumer insight to advertising strategy: the account planner's integrative role in creative advertising development', *Marketing Intelligence and Planning*, 21 (7): 446–52.

Hackley, C. (2003) 'How divergent beliefs cause account team conflict', *International Journal of Advertising*, 22 (3): 313–32 (reprinted in C. Hackley (ed.) (2009) *Advertising*, Vol. 1 *Advertising Management*. London: Sage, pp. 1–17).

Loo, B.K. and Hackley, C. (2013) 'Internationalisation strategy of iconic Malaysian high fashion brands', *Qualitative Market Research: An International Journal*, 16 (4): 406–20.

Mocarski, R. and Billings, A.C. (2014) 'Manufacturing a Messiah: How Nike and LeBron James co-constructed the legend of King James', *Communication & Sport*, 2 (1): 3–23 (first published 11 March 2013).

https://hbr.org/2013/06/creativity-in-advertising-when-it-works-and-when-it-doesnt

NOTES

1 Rebecca Davison, 'Kendall Jenner "devastated" by the controversy surrounding "offensive" Pepsi advert', 6 April 2017, www.dailymail.co.uk/tvshowbiz/article-4385878/Kendall-Jenner-devastated-Pepsi-controversy.html (accessed 30.04.2017).

2 Olivia Pearce, 'Pepsi debuts "Moments" campaign starring Kendall Jenner', 4 April 2017, https://brandingforum.org/branding/pepsi-moments-campaign-kendall-jenner/ (accessed 30 April 2017).

3 'How to write an advertising plan', www.adcracker.com/plan/Advertising_Plan.htm (accessed 20 February 2017).

4 *Communication Strategy: A Best Practice Guide to Developing Communication Campaigns*, www.thegoodpitch.com/wp-content/uploads/2011/09/CommunicationsStrategyGuide.pdf (accessed 17 February 2017).

5 Ibid.

6 'Oreo: a social media powerhouse', http://mwpartners.com/oreo/ (accessed 30 April 2017).

7 Rebecca Borison, 'Click-through rate triples for mobile video ads: report', www.mobilemarketer.com/ex/mobilemarketer/cms/news/research/16373.html (accessed 22 February 2017).

8 Ava Seave, 'What is "creativity" in advertising, and when does it lead to market performance?', 30 November 2013, *Forbes*, www.forbes.com/sites/avaseave/2013/11/30/what-is-creativity-in-advertising-and-when-does-it-lead-to-market-performance/ (accessed 17 February 2017).

9 'State Farm "Like a Good Neighbor" jingle ad', www.youtube.com/watch?v=OB6r2Wi0E98 (accessed 28 March 2017).

10 Gillian West, 'Guardian of creativity or rarefied leader? Is an executive creative director still essential to agency DNA?', 12 February 2015, www.thedrum.com/news/2015/02/12/guardian-creativity-or-rarefied-leader-executive-creative-director-still-essential (accessed 30 April 2017).

11 Paul Suggett, 'Advertising industry profile: Bill Bernbach', 7 April 2017, www.thebalance.com/advertising-industry-profile-bill-bernbach-38613 (accessed 28 March 2017).

12 www.greatvwads.com/ (accessed 20 February 2017).

13 'VW Polo – Lamp Post – TV commercial', www.youtube.com/watch?v=HocWrnbaKik (accessed 29 March 2017).

14 'Example creative brief 2017', www.adcracker.com/brief/Sample_Creative_Brief.htm (accessed 18 February 2017).

15 'C.P. Snow: The Two Cultures', www.age-of-the-sage.org/scientist/snow_two_cultures.html (accessed 20 February 2017).

16 www.ipa.co.uk/effectiveness (accessed 30 April 2017).

17 'Budweiser – The story of WHASSUP?!', 1 September 2011, https://thisisnotadvertising.wordpress.com/2011/09/01/budweiser-the-story-of-whassup/ (accessed 30 April 2017).

18 'Diagonal thinking self-assessment', www.DiagonalThinking.co.uk/ (accessed 20 February 2017).

19 David Cohen, 'Study: global social media ad spend to reach nearly $36B in 2017', 20 April 2015, www.adweek.com/digital/emarketer-global-social-media-ad-spend/ (accessed 17 February 2017).

20 'EPC's 2016 Global Media Trends book tells story of seismic change in newspaper and magazine publishing', 24 February 2016, http://epceurope.eu/epcs-2016-global-media-trends-book-tells-story-of-seismic-change-in-newspaper-and-magazine-publishing/ (accessed 30 April 2017).

21 https://socialblade.com/youtube/user/pewdiepie/realtime (accessed 28 March 2017).

22 Mathan McAlone, 'These are the 18 most popular YouTube stars in the world — and some are making millions', 7 March 2017, http://uk.businessinsider.com/most-popular-youtuber-stars-salaries-2017?r=US&IR=T (accessed 28 March 2017).

23 'Extremists make money off taxpayer funded YouTube ads', 17 March 2017, www.rt.com/uk/381171-taxpayers-extremists-advertising-youtube/ (accessed 28 March 2017).

MEDIA AND AUDIENCE PLANNING

CHAPTER OUTLINE

The media infrastructure for advertising and promotion has changed radically over the last 20 years and continues to do so. Convergence is changing the way marketing communications professionals approach their tasks, as advertising now sits within an integrated media environment. McLuhan's (1964) dictum that the medium is the message seems truer than ever, as media channels and platforms shape the interpretation of messages and the behavioural responses of media audiences. Media strategy for advertising has become a multi-channel, multi-platform, multi-genre discipline more akin to audience planning given that it involves both bought and earned media space. This chapter discusses the implications of convergence for media strategy and planning, using the traditional methods as a point of departure.

KEY CHAPTER CONTENT

- Media, messages and readers
- Media planning – key tasks
- Media planning terms and concepts
- Media strategy
- The media mix – channel characteristics

Want a primer? Go to https://study.sagepub.com/hackley4e and watch...

Gwyn March – Advertising **to learn**
How the key roles match up to the key roles identified

Verica Djurdjevic – Media Planning and Buying **to learn**
What skills are required for the different tasks
What additional tasks and roles these experts have identified
How the different types of media impact on the key tasks of media planning

Verica Djurdjevic – Media Planning and Buying **to learn**
About the media strategies used by this company

... to tackle the video questions at the end of the chapter.

MEDIA, MESSAGES AND READERS

Media buying has always been about audience buying, but a shift of perspective from media channels to audiences is mooted by some senior industry figures as a response to the complexities of the new media environment. This environment demands that agencies combine bought media space with media share (of voice) that is earned through shareable content that people like. Indeed, the content produced for traditional mass media must also be shareable in order to generate the audience reach that clients need. This chapter will revolve mainly around the traditional concerns and craft skills of media planning, since these still structure our understanding of this rapidly evolving field. It is important, though, to bear in mind that relevant as the old skills are, they are becoming more complex and quantitative while, in addition, there are new, strategic ones needed. In 2015, Google, Baidu, Yahoo, Facebook and Microsoft had 19% of all global adspend while global internet advertising expenditure is set to exceed $200 billion in 2017, according to media giant Zenith Optimedia.

In Chapter 2 some of the theoretical issues around media were touched upon. Among them was McLuhan's (1964) idea that a media channel is far from being an empty vessel. The medium is far more than the content (Hirschman and Thompson, 1997). McLuhan (1964) offered the example that a light bulb is a medium, and we only notice this when lights are used to spell out neon advertising messages. But the light is not empty of content – a point McLuhan makes with a quote from Shakespeare's *Romeo and Juliet*: 'But soft! What light through yonder window breaks? It speaks, and yet says nothing'. In recent years we have seen social media platform Twitter attributed with the power to enable revolutions, as in the short-lived 'Arab Spring', while at the time of writing in mid-2017 it looks as if social media may be about to upturn the post-war Western world order as popular sentiment fomented (and also propagandised) on social media seems to have been highly influential in the UK's political exit from the EU and, across the Atlantic, in the election of the first tweeting American President. In both cases, social media stand accused by all sides of facilitating and amplifying polarised political standpoints, being vehicles for 'fake' news, and of being acquiescent in the spread of propaganda. All these things, political ideologies, false stories, propaganda, were in play in politics long before social media. The technology has changed the landscape.

We make this point to suggest that advertising cannot easily be bracketed away from other aspects of communication of which it is an inherent part in the convergence era (Jenkins, 2008). Indeed, advertising is becoming increasingly politicised through social media. For example, as noted in Chapter 1, advertisers who buy programmatic advertising sometimes object to the content that their brand is being associated with by the algorithm. Some terrorist social media channels have large audiences for their posts and therefore attract programmatic advertising, but of course the brands paying for the advertising did not intend to be associated with those sites (see Chapter 5 case study). There is nothing new about brands boycotting a media vehicle because they object to the other advertising in that vehicle, but when they advertised in old media print or broadcast vehicles, they knew exactly who the other advertisers would be. Indeed, most media brands would be highly sensitive towards the advertising they accepted in view of their other advertisers and their audience. The media content that is juxtaposed with programmatic advertising cannot be controlled as precisely, and that is a problem for advertisers. In an era when media brands are constantly accused of political bias, there are clear ideological lines drawn between many news brands, while consumer brands that are associated with values or ideologies to which their consumers object are quickly made aware of this. For example, in mid-2017 Nike announced their first sports hijab, targeted at Middle Eastern women, and according to reports some other Nike fans posted objections to this on social media. Consumers seem to be increasingly sensitive to competing ideologies and, while brands have always tapped into and exploited ideological ruptures that create identity crises, the speed and responsiveness of social media are making this terrain very difficult for brands to negotiate (Holt and Cameron, 2010). The media planning task is inherently complex and under convergence it is becoming more so. Even though artificial intelligence is driving much of the boom in digital advertising on social media, there is still the need for qualitative judgements that machines cannot make.

MEDIA PLANNING – KEY TASKS

Think about media channels and media vehicles – which media channels do you access regularly? TV? Or mainly the internet through your smartphone? Do you ever buy a print newspaper? A magazine? How about listening to the radio in your car, and do you notice the roadside billboards? So, how would a brand target you through the media you engage with? Into which market segments could you be classified? The job of the media planner or strategist is to know this kind of information, and also to know how much it costs to buy the media space to reach people like you.

Advertising media consist of 'any means by which sales messages can be conveyed' to audiences (Jefkins, 2000: 74). Of course, the term 'sales message' does not really capture the genre conventions of much contemporary advertising since there is often no sales pitch, and, indeed, no message as such. Communication is mediated (that is, carried on a medium) when there is some intervening vehicle between the source and the receiver, such as a newspaper, mobile device or billboard site. Advertising messages can be carried on radio waves, static outdoor billboards, paper and ink, ceramic mugs and ballpoint pens, dynamic outdoor sites such as motor vehicles and public transport; even air balloons and loud hailers can carry promotional messages. Media strategy refers to the decisions around media channel, media vehicle, media exposure timing and style in combination with creative execution. Media strategy occupies a more abstract level than media planning, which tends to be focused on the operational task of planning the exposure of the creative execution to the target audience.

SNAPSHOT 6.1

The world's top media agencies

1	Starcom Mediavest
2	OMD
3	Zenith Optimedia
4	Mindshare
5=	Mediacom
5=	Carat
7	MEC Global
8	Havas Media
9	UM Interpublic
10	Initiative
11	PhD
12	Maxus

Source: www.adbrands.net/top_media_agencies.htm (accessed 21 February 2017).

'INTERRUPTION' AND 'ENGAGEMENT' ADVERTISING MEDIA

Media planning and buying today are dominated by media independents, specialist agencies many of which have their origins as in-house ad agency departments. The demands of media planning and buying have grown more complex with the proliferation of new media channels and media vehicles. As Dawson (2009) points out, 'Integration is now so much the norm that the term itself seems almost obsolete, with "new" and "old" media rapidly blurring into a single communications armoury ... Interruption and engagement channels are complementary tools rather than "old" pitted against "new" media' (2009: 28). 'Interruption' refers to advertising that interrupts the audience's enjoyment of media entertainment, such as where the TV shows are broken into segments so that ads can be shown in the commercial breaks. In order to get around the problem of audiences not viewing ads placed in advertising spots (say, by recording shows and fast-forwarding through the ads), advertisers can use methods that weave the promotion seamlessly into the audience media engagement, such as by placing branded products in the set of TV shows, using native advertising on digital media brands, or buying 'idents' and other forms of sponsorship that show the ad after the TV show titles to reduce the chance of viewers avoiding them.

What this means is that now it is incumbent on media planners to think not only in terms of advertising exposure but also in terms of brand contact 'touchpoints', that is, all the points across all media at which the consumer has contact with the brand.

Brand contact is any planned and unplanned form of exposure to and interaction with a product or service. Television commercials, radio ads or internet banners are planned forms of brand contact. Word-of-mouth or social media mentions can be part of a plan, but the outcome is less certain.

'BOUGHT' AND 'EARNED' MEDIA

Further complicating the already complex media planning task is the distinction between bought and earned media. The advantage of bought media, acquired by buying a pre-set advertising 'spot' to be aired at a particular time, on a particular day, and on a particular channel, is that there is certainty about when the ad will be broadcast and some degree of certainty about the numbers of the target group who will see it. The advantage of earned media, such as a piece of branded video content that is shared millions of times on social media, is that it can be far more cost-effective and more engaging than bought media spots. The disadvantage of earned media is that content cannot be made to go viral at the whim of the agency. Earned media space depends on the users liking something enough to share with friends, and what people like can be very quirky.

Exceptionally, the content might be shared on such a huge scale that journalists want to write and blog about it, further leveraging the amount of media space earned. This kind of earned space is what PR, social media marketing and activation agencies hope to achieve, but even with extensive media contacts and a big budget, no agency can earn media on demand. Earned media is often reactive and supplementary to the bought media strategy. Media planning, then, focuses mainly on the craft and science of planning bought media, but with one eye on the possibilities of leveraging the bought media through PR and social media. The main stages of media planning are summarised in Table 6.1.

THE ROLE OF THE MEDIA PLANNER

The media strategy, planning and buying tasks are of key importance in advertising. Media, as they say, are where most of the money goes. The costs of producing broadcast advertising may be very high indeed but the cost of buying mass media

TABLE 6.1 The main stages in media planning

1	Set media strategy and objectives (with reference to advertising/communication strategy)
2	Define target audience
3	Select media channels
4	Schedule media exposures (the media plan)
5	Buy the media space
6	Assess the media effectiveness

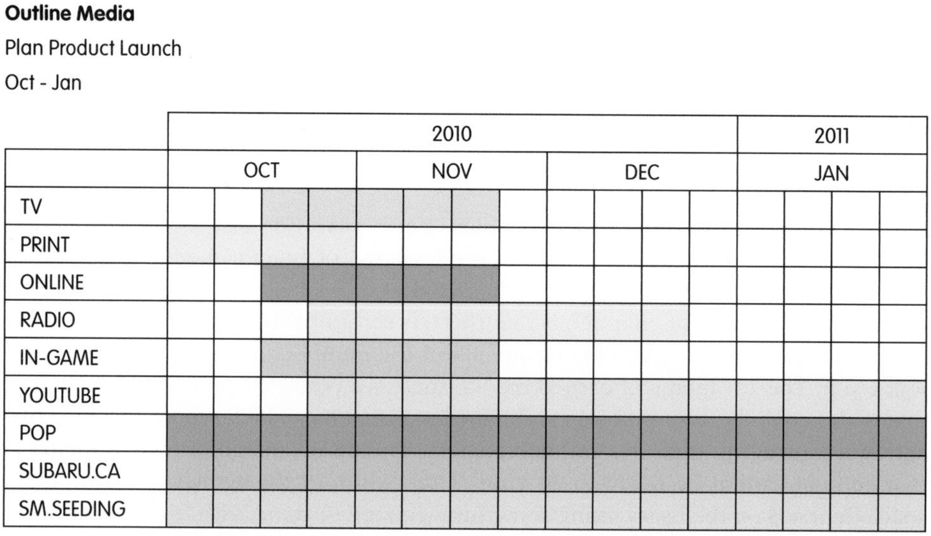

Outline Media
Plan Product Launch
Oct - Jan

	2010												2011			
	OCT				NOV				DEC				JAN			
TV																
PRINT																
ONLINE																
RADIO																
IN-GAME																
YOUTUBE																
POP																
SUBARU.CA																
SM.SEEDING																

FIGURE 6.1 Example of a media plan graphic

time and space to show the ad is usually much higher. The high cost of mass media exposure means that getting the media mix right is every bit as important to the success of a promotional campaign as getting the creativity right. However, according to commentators such as Manning (2009) and Binet (2009), many advertising agencies remain relatively poor at accurately calculating the return on investment of advertising spend on digital media. There is much science in media planning, since there are many data sources detailing consumer media viewing/reading/listening habits, but it also remains something of an art.

The basic media planning task (see Figure 6.1) is to achieve optimum levels of exposure for the campaign, utilising the most cost-effective and appropriate combinations of medium possible. The media planner negotiates the price and buys the space on which the advertisements will be shown, whether TV or radio airtime, OOH sites, billboards, print ads in press publications, click-through or banner ads on internet sites, sponsored tweets or whatever.

The media planner seeks to expose the creative execution(s) to a relevant audience defined by segmentation criteria such as age, sex, demographic, socio-economic or lifestyle/psychographic characteristics. They try to achieve the greatest possible reach and penetration. Reach refers to the proportion of the target audience reached by an exposure. Penetration refers to the accumulated reach over time, including repeated exposures. Timing is important, since the advertisements must be exposed at times when they will achieve the highest impact. Media planners will schedule advertisements according to the campaign objectives, perhaps in a short burst of intensive exposure (called 'blitz'), or alternatively in a stepped exposure of, say, one week on, one week off, over several months (called 'pulsing'). Issues of seasonality of demand also need to be considered. The cost-effectiveness of the exposure is often assessed by the cost-per-thousand (CPT) of the target audience reached.

MEDIA PLANNING TERMS AND CONCEPTS

In an era of integrated marketing communications the terms above-the-line and below-the-line are heard less often in the industry than was once the case. Their rationale, which was based on the largely outdated commission model for agency remuneration, is now redundant as most agencies now charge by labour hour. Nonetheless, the terms still have resonance. Above-the-line refers to mass media advertising, television, cinema, press and commercial radio. Once, ad agencies were paid through the commission they gained from buying spot advertising on these media. Below-the-line refers to everything else, from direct mail and database marketing, sponsorship, product placement and celebrity endorsement to sales promotion and merchandising. The term 'through-the-line' refers to media planning which deploys both mass advertising media and non-advertising promotion in an integrated campaign.

Another term that has become popular in media planning for advertising is **media-neutral planning**. Media-neutral planning refers to the way the agency agenda has been broadened from advertising to a far broader treatment of the media mix. In the past, advertising agencies were notorious for their attitude that mass media advertising was the default solution for any client's communication problem. Today, with a non-commission billing system predominant, there is less need for agencies to push advertising as a solution as opposed to other forms of promotional communication. There is also much more pressure from clients for ad agencies to provide integrated communication solutions. The media-neutral planning attitude holds that the solution to the client's communication problem might lie in any medium, or in any combination of media, even if none of these include mass media advertising.

SNAPSHOT 6.2

Media planning and media buying

Mediacom, one of the world's biggest media agencies, states that their media planning process is underpinned by their advanced research techniques and sophisticated analysis, all informed by their experience in helping clients to find, reach and engage their actual and potential customers. They then work with advertising agencies to identify the media channels that these consumers use most, in order to negotiate and buy the required media space. Global media agencies buy a lot of media, so they have a strong position for negotiating prices with TV channel owners, cinema chains, radio stations, magazine publishers, or website owners.

THE GRP

Other important concepts in media planning include the cost per gross rating point (GRP), which is a measure of the proportion of households who are exposed to the advertisement. GRP can be calculated by multiplying reach times frequency, for example, 100,000 people are potentially exposed to 10 ads and 50,000 people see the ads an average of 5.4 times: 50,000/100,000 × 5.4 = 50 × 5.4 = 270 GRPs.

REACH AND FREQUENCY

Reach refers to unique audience members, while GRP refers to the accumulated figure as a result of repeated airings of the ad. Frequency refers to the number of opportunities a member of the audience has to see the ad (see Figure 6.2). These concepts can be used in setting media objectives. For example, a campaign might be planned to reach 75% of the target audience.

There are different views about the usefulness of repeat exposures. Some commentators feel that many repeated exposures can serve a purpose, while others feel that there is little point to any beyond the first exposure. However, as always, it depends on the nature of the communication problem being addressed, the market, competitive context and target audience characteristics, all of which influence the advertising and the media objectives.

MEDIA PLATFORMS AND VEHICLES

Other important terms in media planning and strategy include media 'platform', which normally refers to a channel format, such as the internet or mobile digital communication. A media vehicle is a specific media brand, a newspaper, TV show, radio show, internet channel, magazine, etc. Each media vehicle is a brand in its own right, and has a carefully researched audience profile that is used to sell their advertising to

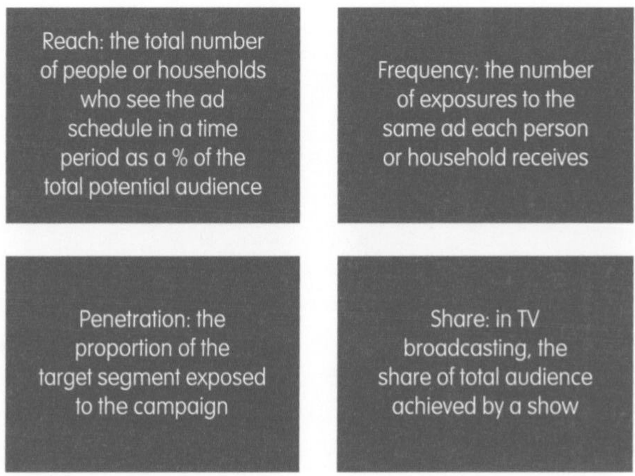

FIGURE 6.2 Reach, frequency, penetration and audience share

brand clients. For example, the TV show *The X Factor* is a media brand that enjoys multiple revenue streams, not from the advertising, although this is lucrative revenue for the broadcasting TV channel, but for other things such as phone voting and music downloads and live show ticket sales from the website (Hackley et al., 2012). The information a media brand holds on its audience is carried on a 'rate card',[1] and this is the information upon which advertisers may base their decision on whether or not to use the media vehicle.

AUDIENCE FRAGMENTATION

Audience 'fragmentation' refers to the reduction in audience/readership/viewers for media vehicles during the past decade as audiences are now fragmented across hundreds more media vehicles, especially digital media. For example, the top TV shows in the UK now attract around 10–12 million viewers, when 30 years ago the figure for the top shows would be nearer 30 million. A similar pattern can be seen all over the world in all media – consumers' media consumption patterns have changed since we now have many more media channels from which to choose.

SNAPSHOT 6.3

Media budgets shifting away from advertising

The shift of media budgets from advertising to digital has been noted for some time, exemplified in Coca-Cola's noted Content 2020 initiative.[2] Coke's experiences with mass media have had some setbacks, one being their controversial Super Bowl TVC in early 2014, in which 'America the Beautiful' was sung in different languages. The ad generated complaints from conservatives.[3] Coke, though, were responding to the fall in perceived ROI from mass media adspend that other companies have also noted. For example, Mondelez, makers of Oreo and Trident, have been candid in announcing that digital and mobile will grow from a quarter of the company's advertising budget to half by 2016, reflecting a loss of faith in traditional advertising to deliver sales. Mondelez's North American President is reported[4] saying that digital generates twice the ROI as traditional spot advertising. Mondelez may have been influenced by the success of their Oreo brand on digital. They claim that Oreo is the number one food brand on Facebook, with 35 million fans, and a tweet from Oreo was the most talked about ad in Super Bowl 2013. These two examples are illustrative of a wider shift in media spend towards engagement media and against the interruptive media of traditional broadcast spot advertising.

COST EFFICIENCY OF MEDIA

The media planning task tends to be quantitatively driven by the CPT or cost-per-gross rating point (CPGRP) and number of exposures, as noted above, but it is a mistake to suppose that it is just all about procurement. Judgement is required to decide which combination of media (known as the media mix) will provide the maximum impact for a given advertisement. Questions such as 'What are the viewing/reading/listening habits of the target audience'? and 'How might they be reached and engaged with'? have to be answered. Also, 'What interval frequency of advertising exposure will best support the campaign objectives?' and 'Can the campaign creative executions be integrated across differing media so that consumers' view of the brand is reinforced from a number of sources?' A significant constraint, of course, is the budget. This might constrain attempts to shout as loud as competitors, leading to a declining share of voice. 'Share of voice' is an important consideration in media effectiveness. This refers to the share of the total audience for that medium at that time. It can also be measured longitudinally, over a period of time.

MEDIA AGENCIES

The advertising case studies on the website of one of the world's biggest media agencies, Zenith Optimedia (ranked number 3 in the top 12, see Snapshot 6.1),[5] illustrate integration well. Zenith focus on creating engagement by leveraging social media, but the seamless links between advertising, digital and activation are well illustrated by these cases, which include BA and the London 2012 Olympics and Toyota's branded content media campaign. As noted earlier, the media buying scene today is dominated by media independents, agencies that specialise in media planning, scheduling and buying. In a sense, the evolution of advertising agencies has turned full circle, since advertising agencies began as media brokers before developing in-house functions of copywriting, artwork, strategy and research to become full-service agencies. Over time, media planning and also market and media research have been farmed out to become independent agencies. Many advertising agencies that formerly bought media through their own in-house operations now buy their media space through independent media brokers.

Lateral mergers and takeovers have increased industrial concentration in the media industry over the last decade, resulting in fewer sellers and fewer buyers. This means that media costs have been driven up, and advertisers usually have to go through the big media buyers to get the best economies of scale. The rise of the independents has partly been a response to the increasing media buying costs, as well as to technological advances including digital media. The rise in the cost of advertising media, partly resulting from the monopoly position of many regional media owners, has not been well received by agencies. Media buyers therefore needed more buying power to generate economies of buying scale. As a consequence there has been increased industrial concentration among media buyers parallel with that among media owners. Media planning decisions should be uppermost at every stage of the creative advertising development process; the increased complexity of market conditions for media planning and buying necessitates specialist agencies with the expertise and buying power to perform this function effectively.

GLOBAL ADSPEND BY MEDIUM

The move towards integration is reflected in global adspend trends.[6] Print media show a continuing decline, with outdoor stable and internet advertising rising fast.

Previously, increases in internet adspend tended to reflect parallel reductions in print spend, but the new figures show how television and social media are intimately linked as advertisers seek to engage consumers and drive social media buzz from TVC platforms. Consequently, internet, and especially mobile, are now independently driving total global adspend growth.[7]

Within internet advertising, banner and display advertising spend is being challenged by 'programmatic' advertising such as data-driven direct promotions on social media, mobile and video advertising. Click-through rates on website banner ads can be low, and advertisers want to use the interactive and multi-media potential of the internet to make advertising more engaging and relevant for consumers. Hybrid forms of advertising, such as native advertising or brand blogging, are, anecdotally, rising fast but the truth is hard to quantify.

Out of home advertising continues to grow but at a varied pace, depending on the country. OOH consists of billboards, street furniture, vehicular advertising and alternative media. Billboards are the largest sector and these are being enhanced with digital displays and even interactive technologies that can personalise a response to individuals using movement-detecting or even face-recognition technology. OOH comprised about 7% of global adspend in 2012.

MEDIA VEHICLE PROLIFERATION

Global trends in adspend are not only shifting because of a change in the priorities of brand advertisers. Integration is also being driven by changes in media consumption patterns. In particular, the reduction in media production costs because of digital technology has resulted in many new media brands coming onto the market, in the form of digital TV channels and radio stations, specialist print publications, new media brand launches such as Huffington Post, and of course countless new blogs and brand websites. As a result, global media audiences are fragmenting across many new media vehicles because they have so many more opportunities to access news, comment and entertainment than ever before, especially online but also through new print media vehicles such as free newspapers. There are more media vehicles than ever before, but each is competing for a small share of audience as audiences fragment across the spectrum of the media mix.

For media planners, the implication of this trend to audience fragmentation is that targeting to specialist interest groups is easier and more precise, but it requires more media vehicles and a wider media mix to achieve the required audience reach.

Conventional wisdom about the strategic importance of a particular medium and also about targeting, audience segmentation and cost-effectiveness is being challenged. Media strategy and advertising strategy increasingly have to be understood as two dimensions of the same thing. Most importantly, account people and media planners can no longer easily categorise their target audience by external indicators like social class, age, income or sex. Instead, they have to think in terms of the lifestyle choices of brand consumption communities and the implications of these choices for media planning.

MEDIA STRATEGY

The term media planning is sometimes used to refer to the entire task of devising media strategy, choosing and buying media, and sometimes it is used more narrowly to refer to the process of media buying and scheduling only. Media strategy uses audience research to ascertain how best to reach the required target consumers in the right way. The media strategy would also consider the communication and the advertising strategies, the creative execution and, of course, the budget. The primary requirement of media strategy is to use relevant information to show that the target audience will be reached in the appropriate time frame and at the appropriate times of day, with the highest possible impact and lowest possible CPT.

The two key components of an effective media strategy are, firstly, accurate knowledge about media audiences and, secondly, a sound advertising strategy. If the advertising strategy is based on an accurate understanding of who the relevant consumers are and the creative execution has assimilated a coherent strategy, then all the media strategy has to do is deliver the required number of those target consumers. The accurate knowledge about media audiences that is needed is not confined only to who is watching/reading/listening to which media channel. It is also necessary to know how consumers consume media, and why.

For example, how do working mothers in the south-east of the UK research holidays? What newspapers do teachers read? How many Baby Boomers listen to the radio for 2 hours per day? Which medium do consumers trust the most for factual information? Which media vehicle do farmers in Ohio use the most for their information and entertainment? Much of this kind of information is available to media planners from syndicated research companies such as Global TGI[8] and Nielsen Media Research. For example, Americans now own an average of four mobile devices and spend an average of 60 hours a week consuming content, according to Nielsen;[9] 84% of American smartphone owners say they use the device as a second screen for watching TV, very often in order to deepen their engagement with what they are watching by looking up cast members or plotlines on the internet, or discussing the show on Twitter. Mobile devices like smartphones and tablets are driving the uptake of social media. TGI generates its continuous panel data from many regions around the world, so media planners can access the information they need for international campaigns as well as domestic campaigns.

The media strategy could be expressed quantitatively, for example, 'Reach 1.5 million ABC1 25–55-year-olds across the UK'. In this case, the ABC1 refers to socio-economic groups, discussed below, but there are many other ways of classifying target groups, some of which are described below. The important issue for advertisers is that the creative execution they think will resonate with their desired audience segment will reach that very segment. This may seem obvious, but as this chapter has noted, the media infrastructure is increasingly complex for advertisers and it is by no means a simple matter to define and reach large audiences.

SNAPSHOT 6.4

TV ad revenue driven by audience figures

It was reported that British broadcaster Piers Morgan's CNN show *Piers Morgan Live* was cancelled in March 2014 because of poor ratings. It was also reported that the prime time evening show was gaining as few as 270,000 viewers, and only 50,000 of these were the group advertisers want to pay to reach the 25–54 year olds. In a country of 300 million people, US TV shows are doing exceptionally well if they reach 20 million viewers. The top ten list for February 2014 had NBC's Sochi Winter Olympics coverage taking the top seven positions, with up to 23 million viewers.[10] News or current affairs based programming struggles to reach high viewing figures. Morgan's rival shows on Fox and MSNBC were reported to be reaching up to 1 million viewers. All the major TV channels in the USA are commercial, so viewing figures are reflected in advertising revenue. In contrast, in the UK, the world's biggest public service broadcaster, the BBC, carries no advertising. The market for UK TV advertising is served mainly by ITV, a group of regional channels, and Channel 4, a commercial broadcaster with a public service remit. The top TV show on UK TV in autumn 2013 was a dancing competition, *Strictly Come Dancing*, but since this was shown on the BBC advertisers could not buy advertising around it. Its main rival, ITV's *The X Factor*, averaged around 10 million viewers, making it one of ITV's top shows for generating advertising revenue. The American *X Factor* show, in contrast, slumped to around 3 million viewers in its 2013 series and was cut from the schedule in early 2014. American TV is regarded as a particularly competitive advertising market and new TV shows are cut from the schedule in mid-series if the figures are not stacking up.

TARGETING AND AUDIENCE SEGMENTATION

It is worth mentioning a little more about targeting and segmentation, given their importance to media strategy. The increase in the number of media channels and vehicles, and the consequent fragmentation of media audiences, mean that target groups of consumers are both easier and more difficult to reach. They are easier to reach in the sense that audiences have fragmented into narrow interest groups that are served by thousands of special interest magazines and TV channels. If an advertiser wants to reach, say, trout fishermen, sports car enthusiasts or TV soap opera fans, there are specialist publications and TV shows that are ideal vehicles for targeting such narrowly defined audiences. But consumer groups are also more difficult to reach because agencies have great difficulty in categorising audiences into target groups that are sufficiently large to be viable for general advertisers. Being able to target trout fishermen is useful if you are selling fishing tackle, but not for general FMCG (fast moving consumer goods) sales that require varied target groups. While trout fishermen probably have other consumer interests too, media vehicles that cater for one hobby are of limited use to most advertisers.

Each commercial medium that is funded by advertising has a research-based reader/listener/viewer profile, which provides an idea of the typical person who consumes their medium. This information (held on a 'rate card') is important for selling advertising space or time to advertisers who need to know the age, sex, income and economic behaviour of the typical consumer. It is not difficult for media owners to construct this kind of profile. Never before have there existed more data sets on consumer habits, behaviour and attitudes. Electronic communications and transactions mean that it is possible to construct and cross-reference massive databases of consumer information. The difficulty brand organisations have is how best to use all these data to focus on the key characteristics of their typical consumer.

SNAPSHOT 6.5

The UK national daily press circulations[11]

The UK has a population of about 64 million, with high literacy rates and relatively high disposable income in the seventh richest economy in the world. Newspaper readership, though declining, remains relatively high compared to that of many other countries. The Audit Bureau of Circulation (ABC) reported in January 2017 that *The Sun* sold the most print copies of any British newspaper, at 1.6 million daily sales. The *Daily Mail* followed with 1.5 million, and the *Daily Mirror* sold about 700,000 copies per day. The UK print newspaper market is thus dominated by a mixture of showbusiness gossip, celebrity scandal and populist political posturing. The *Daily Mail*'s website, *MailOnline*, is the most popular and profitable newspaper website in the world. Long-form, analytical journalism trails a long way behind and most national dailies are making huge losses. The right-leaning *Daily Telegraph* sells around half a million copies a day with *The Times* at about 400,000 and the business specialist daily the *Financial Times* at a quarter of a million. Print newspaper sales in general are facing a long-term sales decline, along with declining advertising revenue. All print publications rely on ABC auditing so that advertisers will trust their circulation figures. The advertising market is dominated by *The Sun* and *Daily Mail* since these deliver the mass of C1C2D readers (see Table 6.2) under 50 years of age, who are in the market for mass selling consumer goods. Newspaper reader profiles differ in terms of age, education level, political orientation, income and geography. *The Times*, for instance, sells more copies in the south of England than in the north, while *The Guardian* is a favourite with teachers and Labour Party voters. Precise costs for newspaper advertising depend on the timing and other circumstances, but can run to between £30,000 and £50,000 for a full colour page in a national UK newspaper.

INTERNATIONAL MEDIA PLANNING

Campaigns that cross international boundaries present more planning and scheduling problems for the media planner, in addition to the creative problems of cross-national advertising (see Chapter 8). The media infrastructure varies enormously region by region and country by country, as do media consumption patterns, literacy rates and disposable income, and this variation accounts for major differences in the character of advertising and promotion in different national and international contexts. The media mix for national and international campaigns may need to be very different.

In general, in the developed north there is a complex communications infrastructure that reaches most of the population through thousands of press publications, radio and TV shows and other media, and there is almost comprehensive access to internet services and mobile phone networks. In the developing south, there is a far less well-developed communications infrastructure, and also lower levels of TV and mobile phone ownership, internet access and adult literacy. This is not to say that there are not still vast potential markets of many millions of people, but audiences are, in general, more difficult to reach where the communications infrastructure is less developed. However, in spite of such variation, the global reach of digital communication is having a striking effect on the tone, type and cost structures of advertising in all its forms, not to mention its effect on audience reach.

The international media agency networks have an advantage in that they are able to administrate the media buying for global campaigns through their various international offices. The media plans for different countries, and also the creative executions, may be different out of necessity, although there will be crossover from cable and satellite TV channels and websites that cross international borders.

DEMOGRAPHIC SEGMENTATION AND CONSUMER HETEROGENEITY

The problem for advertisers is that although they may need to reach large numbers of consumers in order for advertising expenditure to be recovered in increased sales, the media consumption behaviour of these large groups is often heterogeneous. Specialist media, then, facilitate more closely specified targeting than mass media, but they tend to serve audience numbers that are much lower than those formerly served by mass market media. The mass media channels of TV, radio and press were once easy access routes to large, relatively homogeneous, audience groups. Today, mass audiences display far more heterogeneity in their consumption patterns and behaviour than they used to. Increased income levels and social and geographical mobility in many countries mean that a person's social status no longer reliably indicates his or her consumption behaviour or lifestyle.

SOCIO-ECONOMIC CLASSIFICATIONS

Demographic and social changes have rendered the old socio-economic groups of A, B, C1, C2, D and E increasingly redundant (see Table 6.2). Created by the British Civil Service in 1951, the classification of socio-economic groups (SEGs) was extensively revised in 1961, and has been adjusted for various purposes since then. The aim was to create a classification of social class by employment as a basis for social policy analysis. But the original SEGs classification, still extensively used in marketing and media research, carries a number of dated assumptions. For instance, no longer can household members easily be classified and their consumer behaviour

TABLE 6.2 UK socio-economic groups

A Higher managerial, administrative and professional (3% of the UK population)
B Intermediate managerial, administrative and professional (20.4%)
C1 Supervisory or clerical and junior managerial, admin (27.2%)
C2 Skilled manual (21.8%)
D Semi-skilled and unskilled manual (17.4%)
E State pensioners, casual workers or unemployed (10.2%)

predicted on the basis of the occupation of the (male) 'head' of the household. In Western developed economies rising rates of divorce, increasing numbers of females involved in the professions, greater social mobility and increases in the number of single-person households have changed the composition of media audiences. In the past, it was more likely that a person's social status, education level and employment would be the same as their father's; hence, the profile of the father was a more reliable indicator of the status of the rest of the family.

Another problem of SEGs for marketing analysis is that classification of manual or non-manual occupation no longer necessarily indicates income levels in Western developed economies. Many non-manual workers earn less than skilled manual workers. Plumbers or builders might earn more than teachers or junior civil servants, and they may be just as likely to take holidays abroad and drive an expensive car. In spite of their shortcomings, SEGs are still commonly used to classify newspaper readers (*Daily Telegraph* AB; *The Sun* C1C2DE) as a shorthand for helping advertisers target their brands.

ALTERNATIVE SEGMENTATION APPROACHES

There have been some attempts to improve on SEGs for media segmentation and targeting. For example, one attempt has involved commissioning research to delve into consumer lifestyles and behaviour in order to form proprietary classification systems that claim to capture the intangibles that evade systems based on demographic data alone. One example coming out of Madison Avenue in the 1980s was the Values and Lifestyles classification (VALS), another was termed psychographics. These systems used coined terms to classify consumers according to a claimed insight or set of insights about their lifestyle. For example, two lifestyle segments that entered the popular lexicon in the UK in the 1980s were Yuppies (Young, Upwardly Mobile Professionals), and Dinkies (Dual Income, No Kids). There were many other irreverent, acronymic soubriquets. The agencies' objective was to persuade clients that in spite of the breakdown of traditional mass audience characteristics, they still understood the motivations and behaviour of discrete consumer groups. They could, therefore, claim that they had proprietary knowledge and insight that enabled them to reach exactly the kinds of consumer their clients wished to reach.

There have been periodic marketing buzzes around other consumer segments, such as Baby Boomers (born between 1945 and 1964), Generation X, Millennials (also known as Generation Y) and Generation Z. There are no precise definitions for these terms and they are used very loosely to label anyone born between 1980 and the early 2000s. Conventional media wisdom holds that the Baby Boomers have the income, the pensions and own their houses, while the subsequent generations no longer read print newspapers, watch much less TV, and define their identities through consumer lifestyles rather than through their social class and geographical origin.

BRAND COMMUNITIES

Another way to categorise consumers is through their consumption, as a brand community or even as a tribe (Muñiz and O'Guinn, 2001; Cova et al., 2007; Parsons and Maclaran, 2009). The implication of conceiving a consumer group as a community is that there is shared experience that can be exploited through engagement. Brand communities thus fit well with the convergence era in which consumer activism and interaction with brands are facilitated through social media. Academic studies of brand communities have highlighted that the bonds that bind the group can be moral and ritualistic as well as simply consumption-based. To be part of a brand community is to be a member of a sub-cultural group with its own cultural idiom. To Harley Davidson owners, Manchester United fans, VW Camper owners, surfers, snowboarders, die-hard WWF fans and many more, the way they choose to spend their leisure time and money is far more important to them than merely being a purchase decision. The community can be radically heterogeneous but their shared bond is deeply felt. Engaging with these communities in a way that they see as authentic can be highly beneficial for brands.

Increasingly, it is becoming commonplace for brands to refer to their customers as a community, even where there is little basis for regarding it as a sub-cultural group. For many consumers, a fondness for a particular brand may be something they are happy to deepen with various forms of engagement through mobile and social media or other means, but it falls short of an obsession or a lifestyle.

THE MEDIA MIX – CHANNEL CHARACTERISTICS

Sales promotion, TV advertising, press, SMS text messaging, direct mail, radio, outdoor billboards, vehicular advertising, point-of-sale promotion and merchandising, cinema advertising, direct mail and direct response marketing, product placement and sponsorship, trade conference and exhibition stands, public relations, internet and interactive TV, social media, email and content marketing, even product packaging and non-mediated channels such as personal selling and word-of-mouth campaigns can all be understood broadly as advertising via different channels. As we have seen, these channels are increasingly used in combination in integrated or 'through-the-line' campaigns. Media planners and creatives alike need an understanding of channel characteristics in order to fully grasp how consumers will engage with different media channels, and thereby to understand how they might react to different forms of communication strategy on different channels.

The choice of media channel is often based on criteria such as the following:

- coverage of the target audience
- the type of engagement
- the communication context that the medium provides for the brand
- the cost in relation to the promotional budget.

These issues have to be considered in the light of specific campaign objectives. For example, a campaign to support a new brand launch demands a different kind of engagement with the consumer, and possibly a different medium, from a campaign requiring a direct response from consumers. A new brand launch needs to spread the word about the brand and link it with the values that reflect the brand's competitive positioning, so for a major FMCG product a mass media channel such as TV would probably form a necessary part of the campaign. Alternatively, a bank launching a new mortgage might place less emphasis on TV and more on targeting their existing consumers with rational appeals through email and social media.

Consumers engage with media channels in different ways. For example, TV viewing is good for conveying big images and simple ideas, but viewers are not paying detailed attention to it, so detail can be lost. Newspapers are regarded as better for conveying detail, say, for financial services products, since readers often give newspaper articles their undivided close attention. As another example, a radio listener may be preoccupied with other tasks and may use radio as a form of minor distraction. A cinema audience may be supposed to pay greater attention to pre-show ads than, say, a TV audience. So, media channels are often considered by professionals to have particular strengths and weaknesses (see examples in Table 6.3).

TELEVISION

In spite of a decade of predictions of its demise, TV advertising remains the most visible and prestigious form of advertising and the most convenient way to reach an audience of millions. It is especially valuable as a real-time medium – popular sports events are the last media platform delivering real-time audiences of millions (see the Chapter 6 case study below). Many viewers record scheduled programming to watch later and skip through the ads. Many others watch DVDs of their favourite shows and don't bother with broadcast shows at all. Translating TV show viewing figures directly to the spot advertising for pricing has always been a dubious principle, but today it is more questionable than ever because of viewers' changing habits and more flexible scheduling and on-demand programming.

TV is expensive, at least for national, peak-time spots. Figures of up to $4 million for a 30 second spot have been reported for the most expensive advertising on American TV, during the Super Bowl American football final. Depending on time of day, regional coverage and the viewing figures of the TV show, the figure can come down a lot.

TV has such a dramatic impact that it will often dominate a room, demanding attention even if the people present are not particularly interested. Appearing on TV bestows

TABLE 6.3 Media channels: strengths and weaknesses for advertising

Medium	Strengths	Weaknesses
TV	Dramatic audio-visual impact Large audience reach in real time Can demonstrate products Prestige	High production cost Low attention Short exposure Long lead time
Newspapers	Source credibility Immediacy Regular exposure	Cost can be high Short exposure Uneven audience reach
Magazines	Special interest targeting Long life in household	Lower circulations High cost
Radio	Regular, repeated exposure Lifestyle targeting Immediacy, low cost	Low attention Low prestige Short-lived
Out of home (OOH)	Prominent in busy settings High local visibility Repeated exposure for commuters Creative possibilities (electronic, 3D)	High cost Geographically limited
Internet	Engagement Direct response Measurability for ROI	24/7 exposure and monitoring Sensitivity to PR Difficult to build traffic
Direct mail	Personal communication Tailored message Sales trigger	Resistance Database currency Low response rates
Mobile	Immediacy, intimacy Individual targeting	Software issues Consumer resistance
POS and merchandising	Sales trigger Persuasiveness	Limited reach (in-store) Low coverage
Sales promotion	Sales generator Local impact	Low reach Short-term benefit
Exhibitions	Source credibility B2B capability	High cost per event Time- and labour-intensive

prestige on a brand that ripples outward to impress not only consumers but also employees, suppliers and other stakeholders such as shareholders. A TV ad sends a message about the aspirations of the brand and places it in juxtaposition with the most prestigious brands. TV is the media vehicle that most powerfully reflects and projects audience aspirations and fantasies. It is therefore the perfect medium for portraying brands as accessories to these aspirations. In addition to TV channels, there are over 1,500 independent production companies making TV programmes. Most of the new stations are commercial, funded by advertising and sponsorship revenues. Audience fragmentation into consumer communities and lifestyle groupings has made selected audiences more accessible through lifestyle and special interest TV channels. Millions round the world now have access to satellite TV channels that cross international borders, widening exposure to potential new markets.

TV has extraordinary dramatic power to convey values and to communicate norms across cultures, where the ways TV is consumed show striking similarity. TV is viewed in a relaxed mood, often in the home and in the company of other people. It can be a social occasion as well as a leisure pursuit and a source of relaxation. TV gives advertisers intimate access to domestic settings. What is of interest to advertisers is that TV's assimilation into social settings means that people are suggestible when they are watching. TV advertising reaches those who are looking for entertainment, information and ideas about new ways of living and consuming.

TV, then, retains its importance in the media mix because of its potential to create a huge dramatic impact for the brand and to drive large audiences to social media. The creative possibilities are vast for televisual portrayals of the brand in lifestyle settings. The global reach and prestige of TV advertising, then, still surpass that of any other medium. For many brand clients, though, TV advertising is problematic because ROI is difficult to calculate precisely. Get it right and it can create a powerful sales impetus for brands. Get it wrong and a lot of money disappears very quickly. As noted above, production costs for a modest TV ad are often a mere tenth of the cost of airing the ad a few times at prime time. Such ads can take many months from storyboard to airtime exposure. They last only a few seconds, although today the lifecycle of TV ads is extended indefinitely through video sharing websites and compilation TV shows of the best, strangest or funniest ads.

The attentiveness of viewers to TV ads has been problematic for clients. Some studies have suggested that viewers don't really watch the ads. Whether this is a problem for clients depends on whether they feel that conscious attention is necessary for the ad to be effective, or whether they feel that TV ads feature at some level in viewers' unconscious even if they are not paying explicit attention to them (Heath and Feldwick, 2008). For brand clients, a TV campaign represents something of a leap of faith. The potential benefits are great but unpredictable, and difficult or impossible to quantify.

PRINT PUBLICATIONS

Classified and display advertising in print publications is a declining sector of advertising, and many print publications are struggling to find a business model to replace the loss of advertising revenue. Circulations are falling and advertisers are increasingly tempted by the flexibility, reach and ROI of digital media. Adspend on print publications remains substantial, but digital adspend has surged to £10 billion per year in the UK and exceeds adspend on all other media combined.[12]

There are many kinds of print publication, including national and local daily newspapers, local free-of-charge newspapers, local and national general interest magazines and special interest magazines. Digital technology has made it cheaper and easier to launch new print publications. Conventional media wisdom holds that newspaper and magazine readers may be more critically engaged and more attentive than TV viewers when consuming advertising. Classified and display advertising in newspapers and magazines might, therefore, be well advised to use more rational content and offer greater product detail, while TV advertising should rely on the simple message with a big impact.

Press, especially daily newspaper advertising, has a quality of immediacy that TV does not. That is, press advertising can respond to current events in a lead-time of days, whereas TV advertising requires months or even years of production and planning. This topicality can be leveraged further with 'native' advertising, sponsored content that looks like editorial. Newspapers can be useful vehicles for targeting. The readers of particular newspapers, while heterogeneous in their consumer behaviour, often share particular demographic characteristics of age, social status and income. Regional and free newspapers offer opportunities for advertisers to reach local consumers within the context of local news and events. This too is an opportunity to present the brand in a setting that makes it more accessible for potential consumers. In many regions of the world reading the newspaper is a symbolic social ritual, engaged in daily, often at the same time every day, perhaps in the same place, in the same company and accompanied by the same refreshments. Newspapers consumed as intimate parts of social normality are powerful vehicles for promoting other types of consumption, since the context of the advertisement implies that the products and services portrayed are also a normal everyday part of the social fabric.

RADIO

The Radio Advertising Bureau (RAB) of America states that radio is a 'social medium that sparks brand conversation', and also claims that 'heavy' radio listeners who listen for more than 2 hours per day (as many people would in their car on their commute to and from work) generate 329 billion word-of-mouth impressions annually, more than heavy TV, print media or internet users.[13]

In recent years, radio has acquired greater credibility among advertisers for its reach and impact, and has even been used as the main medium for new brand awareness campaigns in countries where radio can give national coverage. Radio can also be highly focused for local campaigns. Radio has the quality of immediacy, since radio ads can be produced in a few hours and broadcast that very day. Unlike TV or print media, radio is seen as a medium that occupies the periphery of people's attention. It is often background music in workplaces, motorcars or households, and listeners are generally doing other things while the radio plays. However, with the radio on for long periods of time there is plenty of opportunity for a listener to hear and recognise a given ad.

Furthermore, radio may play an intimate part in listeners' lives if they forge a relationship with a particular show or announcer that they listen to at the same time each day. Most consumers listen to the radio at some time during the week, so the medium has extensive reach to many kinds of consumer segment. Another advantage is that the relatively low cost to advertisers gives scope for many iterations of a creative execution. For example, in a Capital One radio campaign in the USA, the brand used 135 vignettes of local life across 15 USA radio markets.[14]

OUTDOOR OR OUT OF HOME (OOH) ADVERTISING

Outdoor advertising has a long and distinguished history but is being transformed by new technology. Traditional billboards can yield considerable influence, and in the UK, one in particular is widely regarded as the most successful billboard advertisement of all time. It was produced by Saatchi & Saatchi for the UK Conservative Party's 1979 election bid. The poster featured a queue of people, snaking from a sign saying 'Employment Office'. On the top in huge capital letters were the words 'LABOUR ISN'T WORKING'.[15] In the bottom right corner, in smaller letters, were added the words 'Britain's better off with the Conservatives'. The reader is left to infer the intended meaning by drawing on his or her cultural knowledge. In order to 'get' the ad, the reader has to understand the pun on 'working', which refers both to a general failure of Labour policies, and a literal lengthening of queues of unemployed people outside employment offices. The reader would need to know that people queued up in employment offices to see the clerk, and they would have to infer that Labour policies had caused the queue to lengthen. In fact, the poster apparently failed to elicit much voter attention until the Labour Party discovered that the people photographed in the poster were not unemployed, but were Conservative party activists. This deceit (these were innocent days in British political advertising) was mentioned by Labour in Parliament with the intention of discrediting the Conservatives. The ploy backfired, the poster became famous and was credited with winning the 1979 election for the Conservatives and Margaret Thatcher.[16]

New technology has permitted many developments on the static poster or 36-sheet billboard – some appear to move as the viewer goes by in a car. There are sites with digital LCD displays, sites that are three-dimensional with large items (sometimes motorcars) stuck onto the site for added effect, and laser-beam projected promotional images on the sides of large buildings. OOH advertising includes adverts on street furniture like postboxes, bench seats, lamp posts and bus shelters, ads on moving vehicles especially taxis and buses, and of course street billboards and shop signage. There are more than 80,000[17] static poster sites in the UK, most near or in large centres of population, especially by roads with large traffic volume, and about a third of these are digital billboards that can carry moving images and show many different ads in a loop. Digital OOH is a rapidly growing sector of advertising and

PHOTO 14 Labour isn't working

Image Courtesy of the Advertising Archives

The 1979 billboard is regarded by many as the most effective advertisement ever in UK politics. The poster, designed by agency Saatchi and Saatchi, was initially rejected by the then leader of the Conservative Party, Margaret Thatcher. She didn't get it (unemployment was rising under the then Labour Government), but it was eventually launched to huge publicity. It generated even more publicity when it was discovered that the queue in the photograph was made up not of unemployed people but of paid up Conservative Party members. In spite of the furore, or perhaps because of it, the election was won by the Conservatives.

the possibilities for OOH to feature personalisation and other aspects of internet advertising are increasing as the technology develops.

There are also numerous non-static, outdoor advertising sites. For example, many vehicles such as London taxis and public bus companies sell their advertising space. There are companies specialising in providing advertising space on air balloons or airships for exposure at large, open-air public events or simply in the sky above towns and cities. Digital outdoor has taken off in a big way with video outdoor sites showing a range of ads in strategic sites (see Snapshot 6.6).

SNAPSHOT 6.6

Static, mobile and digital OOH advertising

Outdoor promotion specialists (such as CBS Outdoor) offer packages that include (in the UK) advertising on trams, tube trains and buses: according to the Target Group Index (TGI), 29 million people in the UK see an ad on a bus each week. Entire buses can be painted (wrapped) with the advertisement to maximise impact. Lenticular designs allow advertisers to use moving images, making a 3D effect on bus sides. Bus advertising can be used regionally to coincide with TV campaigns. The London Underground is a fertile site for outdoor advertising since commuters using the underground are predominantly young (49% are between 15 and 34 years old) and in the ABC1 socio-economic category. Outdoor specialists offer custom paint and design services to convert virtually any visible object in the urban environment into an advertising medium. Digital OOH is making new techniques possible. For example, research showed that purchases of Stella Artois cider brand Cidre rose in line with the ambient temperature. OOH outfit Posterscope created 120 digital screens linked with site-specific weather data so that content was triggered when the temperature rose above a certain threshold.[18] The science fiction scenario of billboards and posters that recognise consumers personally is also being realised through face recognition technology.[19] Some poster sites in Tokyo shopping districts use holographic technology to position a sales assistant to welcome shoppers into the store. The holograph reacts to customer body movements and gestures.

Car drivers are supposed to be focusing only on the road, but roadside billboards are difficult not to notice. In some urban areas in some countries the skyline is pitted with billboards as high as tower blocks, such as on Sunset Boulevard in Hollywood. In the UK, many farmers have sites for mobile billboards in their fields if they are adjacent to motorways. OOH agencies can make fine calculations on the footfall or traffic volume on busy roads and they use these data to price static OOH sites. In general, national coverage is difficult to achieve and targeted audiences cannot always be well defined, but outdoor advertising can be a powerful medium for local awareness and sales promotion.

PHOTO 15 Wraparound Bus

Image Courtesy of the Advertising Archives

This bus was turned into a mobile advertisement for the UK National Lottery. Branded vinyl wraps for vehicles have grown in popularity as a form of OOH (Out Of Home) advertising media in recent years. They are visually very striking and can be seen by large numbers of commuters and shoppers in busy cities. OOH in general has had a major revival in the past decade, partially as a result of new technology making it possible to create promotional street furniture, moving billboards, projected images in urban settings, and, indeed, vehicular advertising. But does too much urban advertising pollute the visual environment?

INTERNET

The internet is still seen as a communication channel category but it has developed many branches that are sometimes treated as separate categories for media planning. Mobile, social media, websites, email or SMS campaigns can use video or textual content and can be transmitted through broadcast for mobile or programmed targeting. 'Digital' is a technology rather than a medium, but it is often used to refer to all digital advertising technology including internet, mobile and OOH digital sites. Digital also covers TV and radio (for example, for internet-only TV and radio channels) and even print, since many print publications have a branded website carrying print stories but also facilitating reader comment and links with archived stories. E-marketing is another category sometimes used (as in this book) because it is conveniently broad, but it covers all the above plus email and SMS marketing, and these in turn can be accessed on mobile devices. Indeed, mobile is becoming the most important category simply because the technology is developing to permit most internet functions to be accessed on mobile devices. With the penetration of mobile devices, especially smartphones, approaching that of TV, many promotional techniques covered under the categories internet, e-marketing and digital can be accessed through mobile. Hence, we have a convergent media environment in which most channels can, in principle, be connected and accessed on one device.

The possibilities internet advertising holds for audience reach, target group segmentation, personalisation, interactivity, consumer engagement, retail interface functions, order reconciliation, integration of and interconnection with mass media, customer service and CRM are discussed with examples throughout this book. Programmed advertising that responds through algorithms to target consumers based on their browsing or buying or demographic or social profile has boomed and is helping to push the internet into rapid growth as a channel category. Social media marketing has become a sub-discipline in its own right, although it is strictly not a channel, but a wide variety of techniques that use the internet as a channel. Because of their importance, this chapter will conclude with some points about mobile as a sub-channel category of the internet, focusing mainly on smartphones.

MOBILE ADVERTISING

Mobile devices such as mobile phones, notebooks and iPads, as well as laptops and other devices with mobile connectivity such as in-car satnavs and iPods, are the central space in which media convergence is taking place. According to Sharma et al. (2008), the first mobile advertising was created in Japan in 2001 when the country's largest mobile operator and the advertising agency Dentsu formed the first advertising agency specialising in mobile, calling it D2C. New developments in mobile gaming soon followed. Internet advertising in general is the fastest-growing category of advertising spend, and mobile is the fastest-growing sub-category of internet advertising.

At the time of writing, the Samsung Galaxy S5 smartphone is being launched at the mobile World Congress and, appropriately enough, with a piece of native advertising/editorial in the British *Daily Telegraph* that includes an embedded video clip.[20] Among many technological advancements, including an advanced camera, large touchscreen and fingerprint screening to facilitate rapid mobile financial transactions, the phone doubles as a fitness monitor with heartbeat measurement. It has the capacity for 12 hours of video watching or 10 hours of web browsing before re-charging, making it an ideal vehicle for personalised advertising, engagement promotion and branded content. Smartphones are taking over from desktops and notebooks as advertising media and are driving rapid growth in online video advertising.[21]

Mobile phones are, of course, highly personal devices: people feel that their choice of phone is a statement, and the device occupies an intimate part of their lives. It is often on for 24/7 and never leaves the arm's reach of the user. It contains masses of personal data, memos, contacts, photographs, saved web pages, movies and music. Some apps can access this personal information to facilitate personalised advertising and promotion, although many users are not comfortable with this level of access on privacy grounds. Mobile phones are also fashion accessories, as well as highly practical devices. They can be used to get us home when we are lost, if we use the satellite navigation and GPS facility. A parent who gives a mobile to a child knows that they can always find them, provided the phone is switched on, and advertisers too can always find us if we have the GPS location service switched on. Smartphones can be used for pleasure, for work and for business, and through social media they have been credited with facilitating popular revolutions, as well as being implicated in crime. Smartphones can be used to access your bank account, to switch the lights on and off or to lock the front door in your home, to locate a restaurant, to play games (branded, of course), to show you the way home ... and the number of functions is multiplying.

In sum, mobile digital communication is driving convergence and creating countless new scenarios for advertising and promotion. Some of these are fraught with ethical problems, especially privacy. They also hold out enormous potential for improving quality of life, and advertising techniques are evolving to become integrated into this new, always internet-connected, way of living.

CHAPTER SUMMARY

This chapter has reviewed current issues in media strategy, planning and buying for advertising. The media environment is evolving rapidly under convergence and the media planning and buying functions are becoming more complex. The chapter outlined the media infrastructure for advertising and discussed the characteristics and qualities of the media mix for advertising and promotion. It described the tasks and terminology of advertising media planning and outlined the ongoing changes that are taking place in the global media infrastructure.

PHOTO 16 Wonderbra

Image Courtesy of the Advertising Archives

Czech model Eva Herzigova gained international fame as the Wonderbra model in the 1990s. The Hello Boys billboard is regarded as one of the most iconic ads ever. It became notorious for stopping traffic and causing accidents, and it also earned the brand a mountainous profile. There was criticism of the ad for its focus on the female form, but the controversy around it was, according to Herzigova, puffed up. It was reported that the model felt that it was empowering and stayed within the bounds of good taste.

REVIEW QUESTIONS

1 Devise an IMC media plan to support the launch of a new model of motor car. The creative executions include a 20 second TV ad, national daily press ads and direct-mail shots to current owners of cars in that class. How would you plan your targeting? Which media vehicles might you use? Explain the timings of exposure. What are the main problems and difficulties of this task?

2 Discuss the axiom 'The medium is the message'. What does it imply? Offer examples to support your suggestions.

3 Discuss ways in which media impact might be reconciled with segmentation and targeting issues. Is there an economic trade-off between impact and targeting?

4 What are the key characteristics of mobile phones and how might these be useful to advertisers?

5 Imagine that you are part of an account team devising a campaign for the launch of a new chocolate snack called 'Sleek'. It is to be positioned to a largely female market as a sensuous indulgence. What suggestions would you have for media planning?

VIDEO QUESTIONS

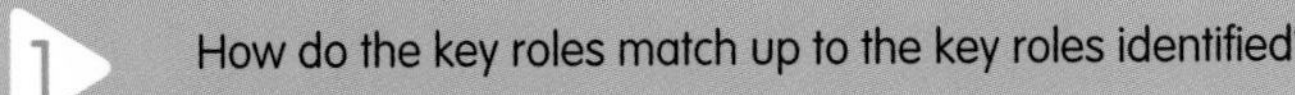

1 How do the key roles match up to the key roles identified?

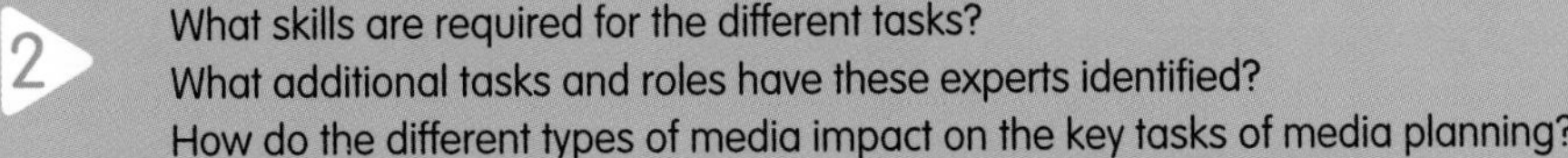

2 What skills are required for the different tasks?
What additional tasks and roles have these experts identified?
How do the different types of media impact on the key tasks of media planning?

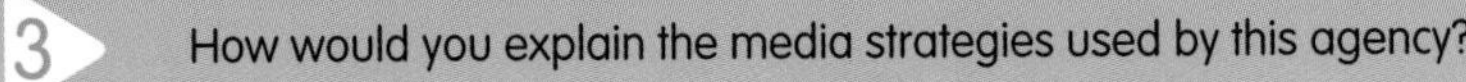

3 How would you explain the media strategies used by this agency?

CASE STUDY

NFL audiences collapse and the future of TV is at stake

TV advertising has continued to grow its volume of global adspend, in spite of predictions that it was outdated as an advertising medium. However, the signs are that its rate of growth is slowing and more adspend migrating to digital and engagement media (see Snapshot 6.3). At the same time, more digital TVs are being produced, so media channels are converging in a pincer movement as more TVs acquire internet connectivity, and more mobile devices acquire the software to play broadcast TV as well as video. One reason why TV has held up so well so far is because it is the only medium that can give advertisers access to large audiences in real time. But a great deal of TV is now watched on demand, on DVD box sets, or recorded for viewing later. Only live sports coverage offers real-time audiences and this is why sports sponsorship has boomed. An advertising hoarding around the perimeter of a sports field used to be viewed only by the spectators physically present at the game. Now, with global coverage on TV and internet, the audience reach for pitch-side advertising is potentially huge, and many of these viewers are watching live.

The importance of a live audience to advertisers is shown by the hype around the Super Bowl, the American football final held each year. Live TV audiences have dipped, but from a considerable height, so while there is concern, the demise of the advertising fest that is Superbowl is still some way off.[22] American football matches last about an hour, but TV coverage is stretched to 4 or 5 hours with TV ad breaks. American audiences are used to this, but the owners of the game, the NFL, want to grow their revenue overseas.

The NFL is the richest sporting franchise in the world. According to a report in *USA Today*, it generates around $10 billion in annual revenue, the largest portion being earned through its monopoly position exploiting TV viewing rights in the USA. The NFL is bent on expansion and part of the plan to double revenue is to export the sport to London. The three NFL games played in London each year quickly sell out.[23]

The NFL knows that sport is the last TV platform that can deliver mass audiences for advertisers in real time. Live viewing figures for TV shows have crashed with the advent of view-on-demand, streaming and recording, and of course the internet. Only sport is still watched live in huge numbers, and the Super Bowl claims to deliver 100 million American viewers, about 1 in 2 American households.

American TV channels, advertisers and the NFL all have a vested interest in boosting the hype over Super Bowl ads. The channels are reported to charge up to $4,000,000 for a 30 second TV slot during the Super Bowl. They have to, to get the money back they paid the NFL to show the game. The advertisers use the spectacle as an informal competition in which they step outside the typical hard-sell American TV ad script to try harder to charm audiences with a little creativity.

All this is designed to generate all-important social media shares. In the 2013 Super Bowl, to the ad agencies' dismay, the most talked about ad was a tweet by biscuit makers Oreo that was shared 14,000 times in a few hours.[24]

Of course, these figures make the Super Bowl look like a school sports day compared to the one billion worldwide audience the BBC reached for the 2012 London Olympics, but then the BBC can't show advertising, so only the Olympic sponsors could benefit. The NFL wants to internationalise, and no doubt it is envious of the worldwide audience British Premiership soccer (or football, to Brits) reaches. The NFL can imagine the riches if Asian sports fans started to care about American football. Or indeed if anyone did, in addition to Americans.

The problem for American TV is that NFL viewing figures are dipping[25] rapidly and the TV executives are worried. NFL has made increased efforts to broaden its market by exploiting interest in other countries, and sell-out NFL matches now played annually in London are treated as if they are precursors to higher profile NFL coverage in the UK.

The quintessentially American character of American football is both part of its appeal and a limit to its worldwide marketing reach. One very American feature that will be difficult to translate overseas is the frequency of cutting to ad breaks during the action. In the UK, even commercial channels are only allowed to show up to 7 minutes of ads per hour. The NFL has the problem of how to earn the kind of advertising revenue it does in the USA without piling on the ad breaks. American viewers may not be thrilled about the amount of advertising foisted on them but they're used to it. In the UK, the BBC, the world's biggest public service broadcaster, carries no advertising yet airs many of the top UK sporting occasions, giving fans an entirely ad-free experience. The NFL knows its game has appeal in the UK. It has to think of ways to monetise this in a very different media infrastructure to that in the USA.

Case questions

1 Why is a live audience platform so valuable for advertisers?
2 What reasons can you give for sport turning out to be the last big live audience platform for broadcast media? Why are NFL audiences falling?
3 List five ways sports coverage might translate into consumer engagement via social media.
4 In what ways might the NFL's media business model have to be adapted for it to succeed commercially in the UK?

USEFUL JOURNAL ARTICLES

(These Sage articles can be accessed on the companion website.)

Bevan, A. (2013) 'Nostalgia for pre-digital media in *Mad Men*', *Television & New Media*, 14 (6): 546–59 (first published August 14, 2012).

Dewe, M., Ogden, J. and Coyle, A. (2013) 'The cigarette box as an advertising vehicle in the United Kingdom: a case for plain packaging', *Journal of Health Psychology*, doi: 1359105313504236 (first published October 22, 2013).

Hackley, C., Brown, S. and Hackley, R.A. (2012) '*The X-Factor* enigma: Simon Cowell and the marketization of existential liminality', *Marketing Theory*, 12 (4): 451–69.

Walden, J. (2012) 'Global advertising, attitudes and audiences', *New Media & Society*, 14 (5): 886–8.

Wu, J., Hu, B. and Yu Zhang, Y. (2013) 'Maximizing the performance of advertisements diffusion: a simulation study of the dynamics of viral advertising in social networks', *SIMULATION*, 89 (8): 921–34.

FURTHER READING

Chalaby, J.K. (2008) 'Advertising in the global age: transnational campaigns and pan-European television channels', *Global Media and Communication*, 4 (2): 139–56.

Croft, R. (1999) 'Audience and environment: measurement and media', in P.J. Kitchen (ed.), *Marketing Communications: Principles and Practice.* London: Thomson Learning, pp. 111–34.

Katz, H. (2006) *The Media Handbook: A Complete Guide to Advertising Media Selection, Planning, Research and Buying.* Mahwah, NJ: Lawrence Erlbaum Associates.

Kawashima, N. (2006) 'Media advertising agencies, media and consumer market: the changing quality of TV advertising in Japan', *Culture & Society*, 28: 393–410.

Kelley, L.D. and Jugenheimer, D.W. (2008) *Advertising Media Planning: A Brand Management Approach*, 2nd edn. Armonk, NY: M.E. Sharpe.

Ridout, Travis N. and Smith, Glen R. (2008) 'Free advertising: how the media amplify campaign messages', *Political Research Quarterly*, 61: 598–608.

NOTES

1 See for example, 'Our audience: Q1 2013', *The Telegraph*, http://i.telegraph.co.uk/multimedia/archive/01863/Digital_Media_Pack_1863797a.pdf (accessed 18 February 2017).

2 Joe Pulizzi, 'Coca-Cola bets the farm on content marketing: Content 2020', 4 January 2012, http://contentmarketinginstitute.com/2012/01/coca-cola-content-marketing-20-20/ (accessed 28 March 2017).

3 Ethan Sacks, 'Coca-Cola Super Bowl ad angers conservatives', 3 February 2014, www.nydailynews.com/entertainment/tv-movies/coca-cola-super-bowl-ad-angers-conservatives-article-1.1600849 (accessed 22 February 2017).

4 E.J. Schultz, 'Mondelez plans big digital ad spending jump', 18 February 2014, http://adage.com/article/digital/mondelez-plans-big-digital-ad-spend-jump/291753/ (accessed 22 February 2017).

5 www. zenithmedia.com (accessed 28 March 2017).

6 Rayana Pandey, 'Global ad spend: trends for 2016 and 2017', 18 March 2016, www.marketing-interactive.com/global-ad-spend-trends-2016-2017/ (accessed 28 March 2017).

7 David Kaplan, '2014 Forecasts: global ad dollars surge, driven by mobile, social', 9 December 2013, www.adexchanger.com/agencies/2014-forecasts-global-ad-dollars-surge-driven-by-mobile-social/ (accessed 22 February 2017).

8 'TGI survey data: identify, target and reach the right consumers', www.kantarmedia.com/uk/our-solutions/consumer-and-audience-targeting/tgi-survey-data (accessed 18 July 2017).

9 'What's empowering the new digital consumer? 10 February 2014, www.nielsen.com/us/en/newswire/2014/whats-empowering-the-new-digital-consumer.html (accessed 24 February 2017).

10 'Top ten lists', www.nielsen.com/us/en/top10s.html (accessed 24 February 2017).

11 Dominic Ponsford, 'National newspaper print ABCs for Jan 2017: Times and Observer both boost print sales year on year', 16 February 2017, www.pressgazette.co.uk/national-newspaper-print-abcs-for-jan-2017-observer-up-year-on-year-the-sun-is-fastest-riser-month-on-month/ (accessed 18 July 2017).

12 See IAB/PwC Digital Adspend Study, https://iabuk.net/research/digital-adspend (accessed 28 July 2017).

13 www.rab.com/ (accessed 24 February 2017).

14 www.coloribus.com/brands/capital-one-134855/ (accessed 28 March 2017).

15 'Labour isn't working', www.citizenarcane.com/index.php/archives/2005/04/18/labour-isnt-working/ (accessed 4 March 2017).

16 For the BBC News account of the story see http://news.bbc.co.uk/1/hi/uk/1222326.stm (accessed 4 March 2017).

17 Liam Ward-Proud, 'Digital advertising on the street: why posters are no longer static', 3 February 2014, www.cityam.com/article/1391399919/digital-advertising-street-why-posters-are-no-longer-static (accessed 25 February 2017).

18 Ibid.

19 Judith Grey, 'Inside the Orwellian world of ad-funded face-recognition technology', 21 May 2013, www.businessinsider.com/advertisers-using-facial-recognition-technology-2013-5? op=1 (accessed 24 February 2017).

20 'Mobile World Congress 2014: Samsung launch Galaxy S5 and Gear Fit smart band', 25 February 2014, www.telegraph.co.uk/technology/news/10659758/Mobile-World-Congress-2014-Samsung-launch-Galaxy-S5-and-Gear-Fit-smart-band.html (accessed 25 February 2017).

21 John Shinal, 'Online video advertising has become "a tale of two markets"', 2 March 2014, www.usatoday.com/story/tech/columnist/shinal/2014/03/02/online-video-advertising-prices-new-tech-economy-john-shinal-usa-today/5870323/ (accessed 4 March 2017).

22 'Super Bowl TV viewership in the US 1990–2017', www.statista.com/statistics/216526/super-bowl-us-tv-viewership/ (accessed 28 March 2017).

23 Tariq Panja, 'NFL games in London sell out every time and still lose money, 29 September 2016, www.bloomberg.com/news/articles/2016-09-29/nfl-games-in-london-sell-out-every-time-and-still-lose-money (accessed 18 July 2017).

24 I discuss this case in detail in Hackley (2013a).

25 Derek Thompson, 'NFL ratings just fell off a cliff: why?', 11 October 2016, www.theatlantic.com/business/archive/2016/10/nfl-ratings-just-fell-off-a-cliff-why/503666/ (accessed 28 March 2017).

NON-ADVERTISING PROMOTION

CHAPTER OUTLINE

Advertising is often conceived narrowly as a 30-second television commercial or radio ad, or a classified or display print ad, with other promotional techniques grouped together as 'below-the-line'. A major theme of this book is that categories of promotional communication are becoming less easy to distinguish under media convergence, but there is, nonetheless, a need for classification, however provisional it may be. Non-advertising promotion is a term used to describe the many techniques that do not conform to traditional definitions of advertising. This chapter reviews a number of the most popular techniques of promotional communication that do not usually fall under the category of traditional advertising, and sets these within the broader context of integration.

KEY CHAPTER CONTENT

Non-advertising promotion in IMC
Product placement
Branded content
Public relations
Sponsorship
Other elements of non-advertising promotion

Want a primer? Go to https://study.sagepub.com/hackley4e and watch...

Sponsorship Development **to learn**
How the objectives of sponsorship align with the objectives of advertising and promotion

Redskins Football Sponsorship **to learn**
How the objectives of sponsorship align with the objectives of advertising and promotion
How sponsorship supports advertising and promotion
How the Redskins Football team use sponsorship to create promotion opportunities

3

Product Placement **and** ***Neil Quick – Analyzing Data*** **to learn**
What advantages there are to using product placement
What challenges there are to product placement
How product placement helps brands achieve their promotional goals

Anthropomorphic Marketing **to learn**
How brands engage in non-advertising promotion
How being on social media promotes brands

... to tackle the video questions at the end of the chapter.

NON-ADVERTISING PROMOTION IN IMC

One of the main themes of this book is that advertising is evolving new forms in concert with developments in digital communications and the thrust for integrated communications planning. These new forms challenge traditional classifications of the promotional mix. As a general category, non-advertising promotion has assumed greater importance in the media mix in the last ten years. Brand clients want to see the brand values portrayed across several platforms simultaneously as part of 'through-the-line' or integrated marketing communication campaigns, and many non-advertising promotional techniques are being absorbed into advertising agency practice as part of the move towards IMC. Non-advertising promotional techniques such as direct mail, events management, public relations, product placement, branded content, sponsorship, native advertising, digital and direct response are being assimilated into and around traditional mass media advertising campaigns. Spot advertising on television, classified or display ads in print media, outdoor/out of home advertising, commercial radio and cinema advertising spots before the main feature, all remain popular with advertisers. But alongside these traditional methods non-advertising approaches, especially digital, are taking an increasing proportion of promotional budgets. Table 7.1 gives some examples of non-advertising promotion.

What, precisely, is advertising as opposed to non-advertising promotion, or non-traditional advertising, can be difficult to define given the rise in hybrid promotional methods. For example, product placement, the practice of putting branded items in shot as scene props, combines elements of advertising, PR, celebrity endorsement and sponsorship (Balasubramanian et al., 2006). As another example, content marketing can include videos made as advertisements but circulated virally on earned media space, while traditional advertising can include a direct response element.

TABLE 7.1 Some examples of non-advertising promotion

Direct mail/direct response
Conferences and exhibitions
Pop-up shops and events
Public relations
Product placement
Branded content
Sponsorship
Native advertising
Ambient
Sales promotion
Merchandising and POS

All these forms of promotion confound easy categorisation. A further difficulty is the question of when a form of promotional communication should be classified according its medium, as in direct mail, or by its genre category, as in branded content. Classification in marketing is invariably provisional, and always tends to be challenged by the next innovation. Because of this definitional difficulty, it is easier to define non-advertising promotion by what it is not, than by what it is. It can be seen as any promotional communication that does not clearly fit into a definition of traditional mass media, above-the-line promotion.

SNAPSHOT 7. 1

Epic Split – branded video content going viral

When videos go viral, it can create a lot of goodwill and profile for the brands that paid for them. One such was called 'Epic Split'. Movie star Jeanne-Claude Van Damme is known for his karate skills, although at over 50 years of age he could be forgiven for spending more time with his slippers and a crossword puzzle. In spite of his age he did the splits with one foot on each of two Volvo trucks as they reversed along a highway. The viral video[1] has been seen some 100 million times on YouTube and other video sharing websites, making it the third most successful viral video of 2013, according to a newspaper report, after Dove 'Real Beauty Sketches', a series of videos that together accumulated more than 135 million views in about six months, and Turkish Airlines's 'selfie shootout',[2] at 130 million views. Commercial content that goes viral cannot be guaranteed, but the most popular branded virals have serious resources and strategy behind them. Some virals made cheaply can also capture the public imagination and become hits. The key is to create compelling content, then devise a well-conceived media plan to push the video out to a receptive audience. After that, it all depends on the public.

The examples of content marketing in Snapshot 7.1 defy easy categorisation. Should they be classified as sponsorship, since the brand has sponsored the making of a piece of entertainment? Are they advertisements, admittedly not sales-oriented but of the brand-building variety, that are simply using digital 'earned' media space instead of traditional 'bought' advertising spots? Could they be seen as public relations, since they are designed to generate publicity, or even as product placement, since the brand is visible in the movie as a scene prop but otherwise not mentioned? They are treated as 'content marketing', since they are created as entertainment that is free to access, but they are clearly branded and intended to be promotional in their effect. They count as non-advertising promotion since they were produced mainly for video sharing websites and not for traditional advertising spots. In addition, they do not conform to the advertising genre category since they do not actively promote the brand, although it has to be said that many spot advertisements are equally as tacit in their appeal.

In 'Epic Split', Van Damme is not scripted to say 'buy Volvo trucks', and if he did, it is doubtful that his fanbase is focused in the truck-buying business. The term 'influencer' has gained currency to refer to a social media celebrity who attracts marketing deals, but influence is not really what is being peddled. What is being sold is audience reach, and that is achieved through novelty and entertainment value. This particular video is clearly demonstrating not only the actor's prodigious flexibility but the precision steering of the trucks, yet there is no apparent targeting strategy here – the video was made to be shared by anyone in order to generate publicity. In an indirect way, the makers intend that the video will contribute to the prestige and profile of the Volvo brand, which is better known among most consumers for cars rather than trucks. Hence, while the video satisfies some of the genre conventions for a TVC, it is also a piece of entertainment that is strategised not as advertising, but as publicity.

Some clients would be very wary of this kind of marketing since they may not be able to see a direct link between exposures and sales. Nonetheless, it cannot be denied that, as publicity, viral videos like 'Epic Split' have been astonishingly successful in their own way since they have reached global audiences far in excess of the numbers they could reach with a traditional advertising exposure, and at a fraction of the cost. Who knows, perhaps many people never knew that Volvo make pretty good trucks as well as cars, and if some of those people work for haulage companies, there might be a trickle-through of influence that gets Volvo into the frame when new truck purchases are being considered. When successful, viral videos can be seen to be far better value than traditional advertising, at least in terms of cost per thousand pairs of 'eyeballs' that see them. Whether or not they represent good value in terms of sales ROI is another question.

Non-advertising promotion, then, can be a difficult area to classify, but it is of such importance in IMC that it cannot be treated as entirely separate from advertising. As we note, it can be defined by exception, as promotional communication that is not a traditional TVC, newspaper or magazine print ad, OOH billboard or radio ad. However, as we have seen in these examples, medium-based definitions fail to capture some of the changes in the way the concept of advertising is being challenged in hybrid promotional forms. One of the most striking changes in non-advertising promotion in recent years has been the rise in importance and variety of sponsorship.

BRANDED CONTENT

Marketing is a set of practices that tend to be recycled with a new gloss (Brown, 1999, 2001). For a time, as TV ownership grew and newspaper circulations boomed in the post-war affluence of the West, mass markets developed that simplified the art and science of reaching large numbers of people with persuasive communications that glamorised buying stuff. There were brands, and then there were media agencies, and media owners (Brown, 2016). The media owners were the people who sold the TV and radio spots, the cinema spots and street advertising hoardings, and the newspaper feature and classified advertising. Finally, and most importantly, there were the creative advertising agencies, and they added the pizzazz, the sparkle, the tease that turned branded products into objects of desire (Brown, 2003; Hackley et al., 2012). The creative agencies were the special intermediaries who added the magic and acted as channels connecting consumers and producers (Cronin, 2004). Today, as we have noted throughout the book, things are very different. There is a miasma of would-be intermediaries offering their services to brand producers, including PR agencies, influencers, tech companies who offer apps, programmatic strategies and other technology-driven interventions, media owners and media agencies who now offer creative services since something of the mystique of commercial creativity has fallen away from advertising agencies, talent agencies that hawk their stars for sponsorship and endorsement deals, digital agencies, sports marketing agencies, mobile agencies, video production companies, SEO agencies, and many more. The variety of marketing and communication services on offer is expanding too quickly, quantitatively and qualitatively to be accommodated by the existing promotional mix categories. What they are doing is not fundamentally new if one looks closely. What is new is the environment in which they are doing it, technologically, demographically and behaviourally.

So, there is a need for a superordinate category that can accommodate these various styles, genres and techniques of advertising and marketing communication. There are various candidates, including entertainment marketing, content marketing and branded content. We will explore something of the latter since it seems to be gaining purchase in the world of practice, even though, as with all labels, it remains much debated and disputed.[3] Ostensibly, content marketing refers to the use of media content of any kind for marketing purposes. But, of course, that definition seems too broad to be analytically useful, even if it does capture the media-neutral character of advertising and promotional practice under convergence. Arguably, all promotional communication is branded content, although we have noted many examples in this book of media content that is produced or paid for by a brand but which is not overtly branded as such. Content can encompass video clips, memes, movies, blogs, spot advertising, sponsored tweets, interviews, PR releases, native advertising features in press and digital formats, idents in TV shows and many other forms of media execution, so pinning down just what it is can be a difficult task.

Kirby and Marsden (2006) and Kirby and Dzamic (2018, in press) have researched a wide range of approaches to branded content/content/viral marketing and provisionally feel that content-based approaches fall broadly within three overlapping categories. Firstly, there are trade discipline approaches. These tend to be exclusive since they define branded content as what they do, and not what other people do. Secondly, there are consumer behaviour approaches that define branded content in terms of the kind of engagement or behavioural response it is designed to elicit in the consumer. Finally, there are narrative-based approaches that refer to branded content as stories that may be iterated through different media executions. It is important here to mark the distinction between the traditional advertising strategy approach to integrated campaigns, which entails a big idea that can be executed in different but thematically connected ways across different media channels, and the transmedia approach, which refers to telling one story using different media channels for each chapter or scene (Jenkins et al., 2013).

There are also what Kirby and Dzamic (2018, in press) call meta-factors that connect the three categories. Content is the meta-discipline because digital media are enabling convergence to take place. This is a new landscape for business and it is already changing the ways businesses and other organisations operate in fundamental ways that we are only just beginning to understand. Consider, for example, the new business models for internet-based models that we have discussed and the ways in which these are changing how advertising of all kinds is commissioned, conceived and consumed. The categories of content marketing/branded content have evolved in order to solve the problems of how to engage conceptually with the issues of organisational communication under convergence. Finally, Kirby and Dzamic (2018, in press) observe that there could be additional vectors based on, for example, the aesthetics or style of the content and theoretical approaches that capture the blurring of the lines between advertising and journalism/editorial.

There are many possible directions that lead from these initial and provisional conceptual foundations. For example, one implication of the consumer behaviour approach is that content might be differentiated for consumers who browse, search or subscribe to digital media. The trade discipline approaches to defining the scope of content seem doomed because they will have to follow the consumer into different content genres. The narrative-based approaches seem to be implicit in, for example, the Coca-Cola 2020 initiative mentioned earlier, and the Dove campaign (see the Chapter 10 case study) along with many others. However, there is a great variety of creative executions and genres within each of these examples. Another framework Kirby and Dzamic refer to is the Hero, Hub and Help approach. The Hero refers to branded entertainment in which the brand is the star – think *The Lego Movie* or the BMW movies discussed earlier. The Hub part refers to brands getting into publishing through SEO, social and direct marketing to try to co-ordinate the consumers' key contact points with the brand through search and browsing. The Help part refers to a focus on the customer experience design (user experience or UX), which attempts to manage the customer through the process of search, purchase and after sales using interactive media and other physical touchpoints. One thing seems clear – advertising agencies and other intermediaries need to become very fluent in different genres and different channels if they want to continue to act as brands' strategic partners across the new content landscape.

SPONSORSHIP

Sponsorship is essentially a mutually beneficial business arrangement with defined outcomes between two or more parties (Head, 1981; Fill, 2002, 2009; Cornwell, 2014). A sponsor makes a contribution in cash or kind – which may or may not include service and expertise – and expects a return in publicity. Sponsorship was originally seen as a part of public relations since it offers a support medium to mainstream advertising and is not necessarily as explicit as advertising. In recent years, the value of sponsorship has come to be understood as less a matter of exposure than an opportunity to activate consumers through social media and/or on-the-ground events and experiences. Television sponsorship has a high profile and it has been common in the USA from the beginning of the television era in the 1950s.

Global sponsorship expenditure has grown at 4–5% between 2010 and 2017, and amounts to around $63 billion at the time of writing, according to estimates. In the USA, about 70% of total sponsorship spend goes on sports-related sponsorship, with 10% on entertainment sponsorship, and the rest on arts, causes and festivals.[4] This proportion is reflected globally, with sports sponsorship dominating the spend. The growth in sponsorship spend has slowed since its breakneck pace of growth between 1980 and 2005, but it is still growing.

Sponsorship grew so quickly for several reasons. In some cases, brand marketing organisations have been forced to move to sponsorship by factors beyond their control. For example, some governments legislated against mass media tobacco and alcohol advertising, forcing brand owners in these industries to seek other promotional methods. After the UK government banned cigarette advertising on TV in 1965, huge tobacco advertising budgets began to shift into sports sponsorship and OOH advertising. Another factor pushing advertisers towards sponsorship is the increase in the cost of mass media advertising relative to other channels. Still another factor has been the growth of affluence, which, for the fortunate, has seen increasing leisure time for sport and TV viewing. Consequently, TV programme makers naturally looked to new spectator events that could provide cheap TV. As we saw in the Super Bowl case study in the previous chapter, many sports events now receive blanket media coverage and constitute a highly attractive promotional vehicle (Meenaghan, 1991; Amis et al., 1999; Meenaghan and Shipley, 1999; Cornwell, 2014).

In the UK, entrepreneurial sports agents have introduced sponsors to unlikely spectator sports such as snooker and darts as their popularity and media profile have grown. In the 1980s, snooker became, for the first time, a televised sport in the UK. A minority sport became a global television phenomenon because of the charisma and publicity generating acumen of stars such as Alex 'Hurricane' Higgins. Cigarette and alcohol companies realised that the sport needed funds for promotion and prize money, and they faced increasing controls on their mainstream advertising. Sponsorship of televised sports offered a new way of getting their brand into mainstream media. Sports sponsorship offered the perfect alignment of need and opportunity. Sport has assumed even greater importance for brands since media audiences fragmented and live TV viewing fell. Live televised sports events now offer the most important real-time audience platform that brands can access.

SNAPSHOT 7.2

The English Premier League parts company with major sponsor

The English Premier League (EPL), the top-tier of English soccer (football), is watched by a cumulative global audience of 4.7 billion people according to consultants Brandwatch,[5] so sponsors from around the world, including brands from China, Thailand, the USA, the United

Arab Emirates, South Korea and South Africa, were encouraged to spend a record £166 million on shirt sponsorships in the 2013/14 season. This figure doesn't include Manchester United's £19 million a year deal for their training kit. North London club Arsenal was reported to receive £30 million a year from Fly Emirates for shirt sponsorship, while Liverpool received £20 million from Standard Chartered bank, and Chelsea £18 million from Samsung. A big rise occurred in 2014/15 when Manchester United's £50 million deal with Chevrolet kicked off. Clubs make additional sums from pitch-side advertising hoardings. Many Premiership grounds have LCD technology on their hoardings so that they can show specific ads when the play goes to a particular area of the ground, followed by the camera. They also earn revenue from sponsors of matchballs, stands, hospitality boxes, and anything else that a brand logo can be printed upon. Finally, TV rights revenue is reported to be £1 billion a year for Premiership clubs. TV channels now use live sport to drive cable and satellite subscription sales and to ramp up audiences to make their spot advertising more attractive to brands. Not all sponsors are convinced of the value for money. Barclays was the headline sponsor for the EPL, paying £40 million a year for the privilege since 2004, but in 2017 both sides decided to end the arrangement[6] because the EPL doesn't need the money, and Barclays decided that it didn't need the profile in the UK. Besides, the EPL makes about £5 billion per year in TV rights, so it should just about manage.[7] Other leagues, such as the German Bundesliga, are beginning to get wider international coverage but don't yet generate the revenue to rival the EPL.

Sponsorship of sport has become the top sponsorship category over the past three decades. Nike, the world's biggest sportswear brand, followed the trail blazed by Adidas (see the Chapter 8 case study) into sports sponsorship. Phil Knight, Nike's co-founder, persuaded the US middle distance athlete Steve Prefontaine to wear his running shoes. Since then Nike has targeted countless sports personalities who gain international fame so that each post-performance TV or press interview is accompanied by an image of the hero of the hour wearing the ubiquitous Nike 'Swoosh' on his or her clothing or cap. Nike's recent deals are reported to include Christiano Ronaldo, Kobe Bryant, Kevin Durant, Maria Sharapova, Roger Federer, LeBron James, Derek Jeter, Rory McIlroy, Raphael Nadal and Michael Jordan, who has been sponsored by Nike for some 30 years.[8] This is celebrity endorsement, but the endorsement is largely implicit, making it sponsorship. The suggestive sub-textual power of sponsorship is telling; no explicit celebrity statement is required. The unspoken message is that Nike is cool by association, because it is the choice of winners. Sponsorship taps into the sub-text of mediated communication by juxtaposing brands with images of success, objects of desire and mythical heroes and heroines. The message is covert and all the more powerful for its subtlety.

TV SHOW SPONSORSHIP

Sponsorship of TV shows, once common (originating in 1950s American TV with the original 'soap operas' sponsored by soap manufacturers such as P&G and Lever

PHOTO 17 Nike

Image Courtesy of the Advertising Archives

The Nike Swoosh is one of the most recognisable symbols on the globe. The Swoosh was created by Carolyn Davidson when she was a design student in Portland, Oregon. It was intended to be as dynamic and economical as the Adidas stripes. Nike paid her $35. Later, when the brand grew more successful, they gave Davidson some stock which is now worth a lot of money. It is interesting to note how many iconic brand names and logos were created spontaneously without any research or strategic intent. The rich cultural meanings associated with these logos became loaded into them over time.

Brothers), has made a comeback in the last decade, although the format differs. In the UK, a brand may sponsor a TV show and place a short film, called an 'ident', after the titles but just before the action begins. The sponsorship deal allows the sponsor to identify with a particular show more closely than it could by buying spot advertising in the commercial break. In addition, the ident means that it is more difficult for viewers to fast-forward recordings to avoid seeing it. Alternatively, the sponsorship deal might simply entail briefly being announced as the sponsor of the show, and being listed as such on the website. For example, sponsors of shows on the UK commercial Channel 4 include Fosters, the Australian lager brand (comedy shows); Honda (documentaries); Rimmel (fashion); Dubai Holdings (horse racing); Anadin (*Deal Or No Deal*); Kia Carens (*The Simpsons*); Old Jamaican Ginger Beer (*Man v. Food*); Halfords Autocentre (motoring shows) and many more.

In some countries, such as the USA, commercial TV channels allow advertisers to broadcast 'paid programming', which is effectively an extended advertisement constructed as a quasi-entertainment, sometimes with a studio audience cheering wildly while an actor demonstrates the product. This kind of 'advertorial' is not permitted on UK TV, but is common on commercial TV in Thailand. Sponsors of UK TV shows are not permitted to show their own products in the same show, but they can purchase advertising around which the show is wrapped. On Thai TV, and on TV in the USA, sponsored shows often use the sponsor's brand in scenes throughout the show. A relatively new development is the **native pod**,[9] which is a commercial arrangement whereby the sponsor buys joint creative control over a segment of a successful TV show. It could be a sketch, a scene, an item, but there are potentially no limits on the way the brand is represented in that scene. It is a radical shift in product placement and generates the leverage of a sponsored show, without the expense or loss of credibility.

SPONSORSHIP OF THE ARTS AND GOOD CAUSES

Sponsors also make use of the arts. A brand name seen in association with a book award, health organisation or theatre production creates goodwill that may resonate with the target group of consumers and pass for community involvement or corporate social responsibility (CSR). Prestigious promotion can also have a positive influence on the perceptions of other interested groups such as shareholders, local government authorities or the press. Arts sponsorship provides funds for traditionally under-funded arts organisations and so there are social benefits that can generate general goodwill towards the brand organisation (Chong, 2009). Gaining publicity for the sponsorship among a wider audience may depend heavily on whether the sponsored organisation can gain media coverage.

Sponsorship links between commercial and non-profit or charitable companies are based on a mutual benefit: goodwill and publicity for the commercial organisation, revenue for the charity, so they are highly sensitive to negative publicity. For nine years, Nike sponsored cyclist Lance Armstrong's Livestrong cancer charity but the deal ended when Armstrong admitted taking performance-enhancing drugs.[10]

Sponsorship relationships are evaluated closely for the advantages they bring to the sponsor. As the fortunes of the sponsored sports star or sports club wax and wane, the sponsors make business decisions that will benefit their brand. As noted in Snapshot 7.2, the English Premiership is a huge commercial success, but its long-time sponsor Barclays dropped out of the frame in 2017 on the grounds that it didn't need the exposure, while the Premier League has the financial clout to manage on its TV rights.

SPONSORSHIP EVALUATION

Sponsorship is an intuitively appealing communications technique because of the potentially high profile it can generate through public relations and press coverage, the targeted audiences it can reach and the positive connotations it can generate around the brand. Its traditional drawback has been that as a promotional technique its precise effectiveness is far from easy to measure. However, it is increasingly seen as a technique that should be used in tandem with digital and experiential forms of activation.

As with advertising, sponsorship evaluation can make use of measures of brand recall, awareness, liking and purchase intention before, during and after a sponsorship arrangement. Sales and inquiry patterns are, of course, also carefully tracked. But, like advertising, the precise ROI of sponsorship is difficult to calculate. Conventional wisdom around sponsorship today is that its value will not be maximised unless its publicity is leveraged with social media buzz, experiential events and consumer engagement.

It is possible for sponsors to gather evidence that can, with careful interpretation, provide insights into the impact of a campaign or a relationship. Measures of audience viewing habits and purchasing behaviour deriving from panel data provide some data-driven insights into the effects of sponsorship. Its effectiveness is invariably contingent on the objectives that were conceived for it. Measures of awareness may be irrelevant in comparison with the way that the meaning of the brand is reinforced and consumers are reassured through the sponsored link. The outcome can only be conclusively assessed in terms of long-term brand market share, share price, sales revenue and profitability.

Sponsorship, like advertising, works to normalise a set of contrived brand values by juxtaposing the sponsoring brand with a separate brand in another field, for example where the Emirates airline engages in sponsorship with Arsenal football club. In this case, a brand that had been relatively unheard of in the UK became a household name, juxtaposed with a quintessentially British brand. This presumably supported the airline's internationalisation strategy. This kind of exposure can be seen to be extremely powerful, since it operates at the sub-textual level of suggestion and renders the sponsor's brand a taken-for-granted part of consumer cultural life. The benefits of sponsorship in such cases might be measured in terms of attitude scales or recall/promoted recall tests.

PRODUCT PLACEMENT

Product placement refers to branded items being placed in the scene or mentioned in the script of movies or TV shows. Product placement is also common in pop songs, novels, radio broadcasts, computer games and stage plays (Lehu, 2007). In movies, in particular, it has become common for brands to feature as part of a commercial arrangement, generating a contribution to production costs or free scene props for the movie production company, and getting valuable exposure in a glamorous setting for the brand. For example, General Motors (GM) provided scores of cars for the movie *Transformers: Revenge of the Fallen* and the sequels, *Dark of the Moon* and *Age of Extinction*. GM did not charge a fee for the cars but enjoyed huge sales of the Camaro model as a result of its role in the movie. Chinese brands such as Lenovo and Shuhua Milk also bought placements in Transformers.[11] *Superman: Man of Steel* was reported to have earned more than £110 million from product placement deals, more than 75% of the movie's production costs.[12] Product placement is also common in TV, although the regulations controlling it are tighter than in movies (Tiwsakul et al., 2005). For example, placements for alcohol, cigarettes and unhealthy foods, and placements targeted at children, are regulated more strictly in most countries for TV than for movies (Hackley et al., 2008).

Product placement can take various forms (d'Astous and Seguin, 1999). Placements can be visual, scripted, peripheral or in tight focus; position on the screen can be varied (and rated and costed differently); brands can be used actively in the scene, or simply passively present as screen props, sometimes described as integrated or non-integrated placements. Musical scores can constitute brand placements where particular artists or musical tracks receive valuable exposure in advertisements. For example, the Dandy Warhols gained valuable exposure by licensing their music for ads. More established artists like Lenny Kravitz have used ads to pre-launch a new single, bypassing the radio playlist route to get exposure to millions for nothing. Variations on product placement are sometimes called brand placement, entertainment marketing (in the sense that brands are inserted into entertainment vehicles) or embedded marketing. In spite of the revenue that can be earned by TV channels and programme makers for brands placed in their shows, it is estimated that only two in five brands seen on TV have been paid for in the USA, and a lower proportion in the UK (Hackley and Hackley née Tiwsakul, 2012). One reason for this is that the pace and volume of TV programme making simply outpaces the ability of marketers to arrange contracts for every brand exposure. Producers, prop managers and set designers need branded items as scene props, and they often need them quickly when they are working to tight production schedules.

Many brands are not worried about how their products are seen in entertainment, they value the exposure regardless of the context. Consequently, they are happy for their goods to be used as scene props. In some countries, such as Thailand, product placement contracts on TV can be very closely specified, with the brand dictating exactly how the brand will be used, seen or spoken about in the show (Hackley and Hackley, 2013). In some other countries, such as the UK, brands are not permitted to influence editorial, while in the USA, for example, brands can dictate content if they buy entire programmes as 'paid for programming'. In the UK, all paid-for placements on commercial TV were banned by the regulator, Ofcom, until February 2011. As a result, there is a thriving industry in free prop supply, which occurs through agencies supplying scene props on demand to programme makers. The agencies earn a retainer from the brand suppliers, and they use sophisticated content analysis methods to track and rate the exposure of their clients' brands.

Since 2011, a small paid-for product placement market has emerged in the UK alongside the free prop supply market. To date, this market has not grown as rapidly as the industry hoped because of the tight restrictions placed on paid-for placements by Ofcom, but it has apparently provided a boost to the UK TV free prop supply market, which seems to be booming.[13] The non-commercial BBC dominates the UK TV scene, with a 30% audience share across its six channels, and it produces about 27,000 hours per year of new domestic programming. That means a lot of scenes that need cars, clothes, breakfast cereals, fully stocked supermarket shelves, street furniture, mobile phones and other scene props. The BBC is not allowed to sell product placements, so it has to rely on the free prop agencies. As a result of these market dynamics, opportunities for paid-for placements on UK TV are somewhat limited.

PRODUCT PLACEMENT PROS AND CONS

There are a number of advantages to product placement as a promotional technique. One is that, as with sponsorship, the link between the entertainment vehicle and the placed brand is implicit rather than explicit. This means that the consumer is left to read the association in the entertainment text. Leaving the consumer to complete the gestalt, as it were, can be powerfully persuasive. What is more, product and brand placement offers brand organisations a way of circumventing consumer resistance to or cynicism towards, conventional 'interruptive' advertising.

The hybrid status of product placement as a form of promotion that combines advertising, celebrity endorsement, sponsorship and PR gives it great flexibility as a tool for generating brand awareness, demonstrating product features, and creating brand positioning in the context of highly aspirational and attractive settings (Balasubramanian, 1994). Product placement can be exceptional value for brands in comparison to traditional spot advertising. The brand owner pays once for a placement but there may be multiple re-runs, DVD sales and internet clips, not to mention the leverage to be gained if a movie or TV show becomes a big hit winning huge audiences. Added value can be gained if the brand owner leverages the appearance in the entertainment vehicle with additional advertising and digital engagement activities, as beer brand Heineken did in their deal with the James Bond movies, *Quantum of Solace* and *Skyfall*. On the other hand, the brand owner paying for the placement takes the risk that the movie might bomb, making the brand placement poor value for money. Generally, while costs of placements vary widely, they compare favourably with the costs of producing a TV advertisement and paying for airtime.

The dilemma for brands is that placements that are not paid for, called serendipitous placements, can be as useful as those that are. For example, brand partners in James Bond movies have included Heineken, Omega, Audi, Sony and Adidas, who paid heavily for the privilege, but Macallan Scotch whisky was scripted in *Skyfall* at no declared cost to the manufacturer, and achieved exposure valued at over $7 million worldwide according to one marketing analytics company.[14] Brands can be very useful for scriptwriters and directors to develop characterisation, and Bond is known for his discernment and fine taste in alcohol. Declaring a fondness for a 50-year-old brand of Scotch whisky is a way to signal that aspect of Bond's character, and the brand merely had to give their permission. Brands are important to entertainment makers, since consumers of movies, video games and TV soaps want to see verisimilitude in scenes, they want the entertainment to look realistic in terms of the urban settings and consumer lifestyles of characters, so there is a huge latent demand for brands that are interested in the exposure.

Some brands worry about the precise context of the exposure, and occasionally veto movie scenes. For example, a case of product 'displacement' was reported in the 2008 movie *Slumdog Millionaire*, when director Danny Boyle claimed that Coca-Cola and Mercedes asked for their brand logos to be obscured after they had seen the rushes and didn't like their brands being seen in the context of Indian slums and gangsters.[15] The movie turned out to be a huge hit. Editorial control can be a sticking point for some brand placement deals.

SNAPSHOT 7.3

Brands star in Hollywood movies

Since exposure in *ET: The Extraterrestrial* sent sales of confectioner Hershey's Rees's Pieces up by 65% according to reports, brands have been keen for parts in major entertainment projects. Product placement in Hollywood films dates from the silent movies, but the practice has become much more widely known about in recent decades. Received wisdom among Hollywood marketing agents is that just 'showing the can' is not enough (Hackley, 2003a). Brand owners want to project the brand personality, so they want creative access to projects, and this can sometimes be arranged if it fits with the director's vision for the project. Movie placements even have their own 'Oscars'. London-based product placement agency NMG[16] won the 2014 'Brand Cameo' award in an Oscar-nominated film for the use of stout beer brand Guinness in the film *Philomena* starring Dame Judi Dench. The award is given by consultants Interbrand and is based on Brand Channel research and online brand recall surveys that measure product placement exposure effectiveness. Of course, product placement can be annoying to audiences when it seems too incongruous or excessive and lacks a good fit with the plot. For example, the *Smurfs* movie franchise has been heavily criticised on social media because of the prevalence of Sony brands throughout the movie. In *Smurfs 2* Gargamel, the villain, makes his evil plans on a Sony Vaio tablet, and all the main characters use Sony Mobiles, among many other prominent Sony products that feature in the movie. On the other hand, the makers of the movies, Sony Pictures, are no doubt happy to receive more revenue in placement deals than it costs them to make the films.[17]

MUSIC AND BRANDS

Music is very important in marketing. It makes advertising and promotion more fun, it gives dramatic force to the visuals, it aids brand recall, and, in the case of licensed popular music used in ads, it pre-segments the audience by making the people who like that track turn their heads to notice the ad when they hear the music. Today, jingles are regarded as corny, and music licensing is the most common method used. Musicians once felt chary about working with brands. It wasn't considered cool. Not anymore. Many rock musicians are happy to have their music featured in an ad.[18] Not only that, but brands have found that sponsoring and supporting popular music is a way of reaching young audiences in a subtle but high profile way. The benefit has sometimes been reciprocal – a new track licensed for an advertisement is gaining exposure for the artist or for the single release, so the music is in effect 'placed' in the advertisement.

Companies such as BMG can license classics from artists from Iggy Pop and Frank Sinatra to Christina Aguilera and Coldplay to provide a musical hook to a broadcast advertisement. The track guarantees the attention of a particular audience segment. The advertiser who wants to use an original track to give the ad extra impact has to buy rights to both the CD master and to the published sheet music, which are often owned by different music-licensing houses. They have to get the agreement of the original artists as well. In some cases, the stars as well as their music become vehicles to gain the attention of the desired target audience: 1960s American rock icon Iggy Pop featured, in person, in a series of 2009 advertisements for an insurance company. A few years ago, that would have been considered the definition of un-cool, but today the artistic barriers between marketing and advertising, and entertainment, seem to have dissolved.

In fact, established performing artists are falling over themselves to win contracts with brands, as celebrity spokespeople, as 'creative directors', or simply as actors featuring in the brand's ads. Sometimes, the endorsement itself appears to be reciprocal, such as where celebrities are appointed to quasi-official positions as creative directors for major brands. Fashion designer Marc Jacobs moved into a successful perfume line before being appointed as creative director by Diet Coke;[19] Stella McCartney was given a similar title to design athletes' outfits for Team GB and Adidas[20] and none other than Lady Gaga took a (no doubt 9–5 with lunch vouchers) post as creative director for some four years before a parting of the ways with Polaroid.[21] These show appointments might be nominal, but they represent a mutual accommodation between the creative ego of the artist and the commercial imperative of the brand. The artist and the brand now work on the same plane, using the same media materials (Schroeder, 2005).

INTERTEXTUALITY AND EMBEDDED MARKETING

Embedded marketing in general, including product placement, music licensing and all forms of entertainment marketing, makes use of intertextuality (see Chapter 2).

When differing media draw on shared symbols and reference points they can instantly convey particular values in association with a brand, as the Bond movie did when they had Bond declare his love of Macallan Scotch. Bond may be a murderer, but he's a cultivated murderer. We listen to music for our own entertainment, if we hear the same track in an entertainment vehicle this provides a bridge between the world of entertainment and our personal cultural experience. Intertextuality, in effect, is what makes advertising and promotion meaningful as cultural products.

Music, in particular, is a deeply personal choice, bound up with our sense of identity (Shankar, 2000). It can reach out with an emotional hook to segmented audiences. Indeed, embedding popular cultural references within advertising and promotion, and embedding brands within popular cultural media, represents the logical development of the 'the entertainment economy', and perhaps of the 'culture industry' (Horkheimer and Adorno, [1944] 2002; Wolf, 2003). Of course, marketing is not all about entertainment; it is also about innovation, materials sourcing, design, organisation, manufacture, logistics and more. But important features of marketing are converging in the entertainment and communications areas. In post-industrial economies, increased affluence and leisure opportunities have created a huge demand for entertainment. Sports coverage on TV now extends to the internet and mobile, while movies, music and news, information and retail shopping can all be accessed digitally, driving the demand for mobile devices. The absence of an explicit sales message in much embedded marketing communication does not impair the promotional effect: humans are interpreting creatures, we seek to impose meaning and coherence by making sense of our experience. We actively make the connections between brands and values that are left implicit in embedded marketing initiatives. Convergence is driving the marketing wedge ever deeper into consumer cultural life. Whether this is a force for ideological domination, or a force for postmodern liberation, is a matter of debate (Firat and Venkatesh, 1995).

SNAPSHOT 7.4

PR, viral, content marketing, or newsjacking?

The difficulty of categorising non-advertising promotion in the convergence era was illustrated by one initiative from tampon brand Bodyform. A Facebook post attributed to aspiring author 'Richard'[22] (who wanted to plug his book) lamented that watching

Bodyform advertising over the years led him to believe that, once a month, his female friends would be the most terrific fun, taking him bike riding, skiing, mountain climbing or horse riding and enjoying life with a verve he would hardly be able to match. The reality, he claimed, was sadly different, reminding him more of a scene from the horror movie *The Exorcist*, in which the main female character gets a little bad tempered, and he blamed the advertising for creating this altogether misleading impression. The post went viral and earned 40,000 likes in a day. Just four days later, Bodyform had a witty video response on YouTube with an actress in the role of Bodyform CEO explaining the true nature of periods to Richard. The video had earned over 5.9 million views[23] at the time of writing (2017). SCR, manufacturers of Bodyform, and their ad agency, Carat, picked up on Richard's Facebook joke and ran with it, supported by astute PR. Much admiring press comment followed, adding to the buzz.[24] Essentially, this rapid response initiative was a piece of PR, since it generated a huge buzz and many column inches of mostly admiring press comment. Getting almost 6 million views of a 1 minute 45 seconds TV ad could cost several million in production, even before the TV spots were paid for. A video for YouTube normally costs tens of thousands, or less. Consider that viewers actively sought out the video to watch it and share it with friends, as opposed to half-listening to it during a TV ad break, and you have the essence of branded content: active consumer engagement. The scriptwriting was astute: the YouTube video parodied sanitary promotion, but it also invoked Bodyform's tradition of advertising in an admiring way that dovetailed nicely with the brand history. The tone of this social media exchange was, perhaps, rather British – the humour of the video seemed offbeat and a little weird or vulgar to some. This unique marketing initiative was founded on an acute sensitivity to the particular context in which the exchange would be received.

PUBLIC RELATIONS

The Institute of Public Relations (IPR), the main professional body for the discipline in the UK, defines public relations as 'the way organisations, companies and individuals communicate with the public and media'. The IPR's website goes on to state that 'A PR specialist communicates with the target audience directly or indirectly through media with an aim to create and maintain a positive image and create a strong relationship with the audience. Examples include press releases, newsletters, public appearances, etc. as well as utilisation of the World Wide Web'.[25] The Public Relations Society of America (PRSA)[26] emphasises PR's task of helping an organisation to interact, communicate with and win the co-operation of its public.

PR is a function where the aim is to create goodwill towards the brand or the corporation, to deflect criticism, or to foster a generally positive view of the corporation or brand among stakeholders and the general public. It encompasses the dark art of 'spinning', much used and criticised in politics. 'Spinning' means putting a positive interpretation on information or news that might be interpreted negatively.

At the turn of the century, PR was very important in selling big business to America. Historian Roland Marchand (1998) showed in his historical studies of corporate America how big business had to manufacture a sense of legitimacy. Ordinary American citizens saw the growth of the big corporations like GM and AT&T as threats to Main Street America. Small operators were being put out of business by these new Leviathans and questions were even being asked at a presidential level about the threat they posed to the American way of life. They had to present a human face to the public and used PR techniques, including well-publicised corporate philanthropy, sponsorship of good causes, educational programmes for workers and for consumers, advertising and direct mail to humanise the corporations. It worked. Today, corporate communications has evolved as a distinct sub-discipline involving PR for big corporations, as opposed to PR for brands, individuals or other kinds of organisation. For many years PR operated in the shadows, little understood and somewhat separated from marketing and advertising. Today, under integration, PR has been brought within the marketing and advertising toolbox.

Edward Bernays is often credited with inventing PR. Bernays, Sigmund Freud's nephew, was a wartime propagandist for the USA who coined the term 'public relations' because he felt that the term 'propaganda' was too closely associated with war (Bernays, 1928). Bernays believed that the best way to influence public opinion was through news media, and one of his early successes illustrated his method well. Charged with a brief to persuade more American women to take up cigarette smoking, Bernays realised that he had to undermine the severe social stigma that surrounded female smoking in the USA at that time. Women could even be arrested for public smoking. He commissioned a psychoanalyst (not his uncle) to explain that cigarettes were symbolic phalluses, and if women were persuaded to smoke, they would have the feeling of male power.

Bernays saw an opportunity at the New York Easter Parade of 1929, which he knew would be heavily covered by press and TV reporters. He hired a group of debutantes to join the parade. At a given signal, they would take out Lucky Strike cigarettes from their garters, and light up. This shocking sight was sure to attract the attention of the camera crews and journalists. Bernays told the women to say they were demanding their rights by lighting up 'torches of freedom'. He thought this term would evince an emotional response because of the metaphoric visual link with the Statue of Liberty. The newsreels duly presented the sight of smoking debutantes as a spontaneous protest on behalf of women's rights to self-determination. The incident was credited with breaking the taboo against female cigarette smoking in public, and the practice was both normalised and valorised. It was normalised because women of high social standing were seen to do it without shame, and it was valorised through the association with feminine freedom and the values of America. Bernays enjoyed similar success with many other corporate clients.

PR practitioners generally keep lines of communication open between their client or organisation and their stakeholders and respond to enquiries and questions clearly and in the light of the client organisation's agenda. They also actively try to influence public opinion through the media by, for example, issuing press releases of stories

PHOTO 18 Lucky Strike

Image Courtesy of the Advertising Archives

This 1934 magazine ad for American cigarette brand Lucky Strike appeared some five years after PR genius Edward Bernays had changed attitudes to female smoking (see page 225). As described in this chapter, Bernays used an ingenious PR stunt to break the taboo around female smoking in America. The use of elegant ladies in the advertising reflected his use of debutantes in the now notorious newsreel footage that put Lucky Strike in the public eye as a bogus symbol of women's emancipation.

they would like to be published as editorial. They also engage in dialogue with journalists and influential people and organisations. Most organisations like to tell 'good news' stories as often and as loudly as possible. PR specialists (often former journalists) solicit stories, write them up as press releases and use their journalist contacts to get coverage for them.

OTHER ELEMENTS OF NON-ADVERTISING PROMOTION

DIRECT MAIL

Direct mail (incorporating many forms of database marketing) continues to be popular for its accountability and cost. The attraction of direct mail advertising over broadcast media is that each mailshot can be directed at a named person who may have a personal interest in the products or services being offered. Of course, email marketing, SMS messaging and algorithm-driven social media advertising also offer digital versions of the same method. As any householder knows, the belief of advertisers that direct mail is good value is highly suspect; much of it ends up unread in the waste bin, and a lot is misdirected because the customer databases driving direct mail campaigns are notoriously difficult to compile and maintain accurately. Databases have to be 'cleaned' regularly otherwise they date rapidly as addresses and phone numbers change for an increasingly mobile population.

The volume of mail in developed countries is reducing as fewer people write letters and use email or SMS instead. Accordingly, direct mail agencies are expanding their remit to reflect the trends of convergence. The UK-based Institute of Direct Marketing (IDM), for example, changed its name to the Institute of Direct and Digital Marketing (IDDM)[27] to reflect the shift towards digitisation, anticipating a time when paper-based marketing might be displaced to an even greater degree by digital forms of direct and database-driven marketing.

SALES PROMOTION, AMBIENT MARKETING, POS AND MERCHANDISING

Sales promotion refers to a vast range of novelty items that can carry promotional messages or a visual representation of the brand. Often these items, such as coffee mugs, pens, bags, T-shirts or other things, are given away, so the element of goodwill is bound up with the brand when they are used by a consumer.

Sales promotion also refers to in-store promotions such as two-for-the-price-of-one, temporary price discounts, free gifts, redeemable coupons, competitions or money back for returning so many bottle-tops or labels (the latter technique is called the self-liquidating premium). Conventional marketing wisdom holds that the major strength of sales promotions is that they can persuade people to try the brand. It can also be argued that some brands use perpetual sales promotions to encourage repeat purchase and brand loyalty. For example, McDonald's hamburgers regularly have a promotional offer of free toys with children's meals, usually thematically tied in with a movie release. Long-term sales promotion encourages not just trial but long-term, repeat purchase.

SNAPSHOT 7.5

Ambush marketing at the London 2012 Olympics

Ambush marketing loosely refers to incidents that are designed to earn publicity for a brand when they didn't pay for it. In one notorious example at the 2010 World Cup in South Africa, a Dutch beer brand block-booked 36 seats in the stand and at a given signal women paid by the company all stood up, wearing the colours of the brand. The incident gained a lot of publicity, along with a lawsuit.[28] Beats by Dre, the headsets brand associated with rap artist Dr Dre, contributed to the distinguished history of ambush marketing[29] at the London 2012 Olympics. The organising committee, called LOGOC, had made clear their intention to block ambush marketers. Brands including McDonald's, Coca-Cola, BMW, Samsung, Omega and P&G were paying up to a reported £65 million each to be top-tier sponsors while supplying products and services too. LOGOC wanted to protect these investments while also staying within the rules of Olympic broadcaster the BBC, which is the biggest non-commercial public service broadcaster in the world and does not carry paid advertising or promotion. LOGOC was, however, outmanoeuvred by Beats, who noticed that the Olympic swimmers liked to wear headsets to block out the noise until the starting pistol fired. The swimmers were given free Beats by Dre headsets, and then wore them as they entered the swimming venue in front of a worldwide TV audience of 1 billion. Top category, 5-star product placement ensued, closely followed by thousands of column inches of trade press comment, most of it admiring. This exposure fitted the youthful, rebellious positioning of the brand perfectly, and the association with cool, young, multinational athletes resonated with the Beats target audience. The stunt was probably premeditated – Beats had reportedly performed a similar ambush at the 2008 Beijing Olympics by giving headsets to American basketball star LeBron James who passed them out to other team members.

Some sales promotional techniques converge with customer relationship management approaches in that they seek to reward, and thereby encourage, brand loyalty. Airlines and credit cards try to reward repeated use with air-miles for free travel and points or cashback. Credit card companies and mortgage providers often offer good rates to new customers for loan servicing in countries where only short-term loans and mortgages are offered. In the UK, for example, most new mortgage offers are for two, three or five years, while in the USA it is common for house buyers to be offered 20- or 30-year fixed rate mortgages. Many credit card customers now switch suppliers readily to take advantage of short-term promotional interest or balance transfer rates.

Some retailers have abandoned the conventional wisdom of sales promotion inducing trial and have opted instead for continuous sales promotion to solicit bargain-conscious consumers. In Europe, Aldi and Netto supermarket brands are just two that are positioned as cheap, no-frills providers. There has been a huge growth in the UK in £1 shops and similar, continuous sales promotion retail positioning. In the airline market there has been a rapid growth in low-cost air travel, with firms such as EasyJet and Ryanair, and many hotel chains have developed low-cost, no-frills rooms, such as the

French chain Formula 1 and the Holiday Inn Express chain of budget hotels. Sales promotion, of course, implies a tactical manoeuvre that is short-term, while low-cost as a marketing strategy is a rather different approach. Nevertheless, low-cost marketing strategies simply extend the logic of sales promotion, because many cost-conscious consumers are not brand-loyal as such but shop around for bargains all the time.

Ambient marketing, the insertion of brands into the consumer's experiential environment, comes in many forms and can cross into other categories such as outdoor, packaging, sales promotion or direct mail (Shankar and Horton, 1999). The key element is how the promotional message has been inserted into the consumer's environment. For example, ambient promotion has a longstanding, in-store tradition in retailing: supermarkets pipe the smell of baking bread into the shop to create a relaxed and pleasing ambience that is conducive to uncritical purchasing. Retailers play lift-music that relaxes shoppers so that they put more goods into their basket than they really came in for. Ambient promotion has become a taken-for-granted aspect of the urban shopping scene. We now expect to see brand promotions, advertisements and logos everywhere, including theatre programmes and car parking tickets, on steps and walls in underground train stations, on petrol pumps, on street furniture, beer mats, and even on dogs' coats, cars (that are 'wrapped' with ads in exchange for a fee) and baseball caps. In recent years brands have become so cool that it is now common to see people wearing clothing with the brand name prominent, effectively turning themselves into a mobile advertising hoarding for the brand. Brands are now common sights in urban settings, on OOH displays or being worn as clothes or accessories by commuters and shoppers.

CELEBRITY MARKETING

Sponsorship of celebrity sportspeople is well established as a marketing ploy. Sometimes they actively wear the brand as part of the deal, and at other times they merely promote it. Beyond sports marketing, the use of celebrities has moved beyond the traditional model in which a celebrity, famous for achievement in some other field, is chosen for the way their personal brand fits ('matches up') with the sponsor's brand, and then acts out scripted ads in which he or she claims to be a keen user (see, for example, McCracken, 1989; Erdogan, 1999; Hackley and Hackley, 2015). The convergence of media channels through the digitisation of communication has connected market segments and provided a powerful space for leveraging brand equity (Powell, 2013). Conventional wisdom in branding holds that extending brand strategies across new markets and new audiences carries risks, principally the risk of confusing consumers by diluting the brand positioning, but these risks seem to be at least partly ameliorated through the connection with celebrities such as David Beckham, whose fanbase cuts across nationalities and socio-demographic groups, allowing his sponsors to reach new markets with their brands (Aaker, 2004). Beckham has had commercial contracts with Sainsbury's, Adidas, Breitling, Armani, H&M, Samsung, Diet Coke[30] and many more (See Photo 12). Beckham's earnings have increased since his retirement from football and were estimated at £45,000,000, in 2016.[31]

In new model celebrity marketing, the celebrity is sometimes given a nominal but official position with the brand. This hints at a strategic relationship that, if believed, is deeper than a typically insincere 'endorsement'. Some, though, seem to have a stronger fit than others. For example, Katy Perry's deal with the makers of *The Sims*, Electronic Arts, might seem more meaningful as a partnership than others, such as Madonna's with Diageo.[32] The artist and the brand now often work in the same premises, using the same media materials (Schroeder, 2005).

In some other cases, the brand appoints a relative unknown, because the publicity generated will not only give the brand exposure but will also make the appointee more famous, hence increasing the brand exposure again.[33] Alternatively, unknowns can become celebrities (or 'celetoids'; Rojek, 2012) in their own right, and then with the help of a good agent they can leverage that into sponsorship deals.[34] Some performers have used YouTube as a platform to generate exposure, earning major press coverage, recording contracts[35] and TV appearances, while some bloggers are now regarded as celebrities within their milieu, whether that be fashion, film criticism or travel writing.[36]

SNAPSHOT 7.6

Japanese girls use their bodies as billboards

According to news reports, some 4,000 young Japanese women have been making an income of up to $100 a day by renting their thighs for 8 hours a day to advertisers and posting photos of themselves online.[37] Non-advertising promotion on the human body has also included brand tattooing and 'sandwich' boards. The human body has been used as an advertising medium since the beginning of modern advertising with 'sandwich board' wearers parading their advertising signs up and down London streets in the days of *Punch* magazine. Their modern day equivalent, the human billboard who stands at a junction in the road twirling a sign for the local pizza parlour, is hardly a technological advance. Using the skin for advertising is a more recent development, but with the rise in the popularity and social acceptance of tattoos, perhaps it is not entirely surprising. Clearly, there are issues of ethics, dignity and cultural norms involved.

NATIVE ADVERTISING/CONTENT MARKETING

Native advertising is a rapidly growing category of promotion for media brands – for example, news and entertainment media brand Huffington Post see native advertising as the leading component of the dominance of digital advertising.[38] Native advertising is regarded by some as just another angle on content marketing or branded content. Content marketing, as discussed at the beginning of the chapter, is the art of creating entertaining media content in the form of news stories, videos, photographs or anything else that might interest media users and can be shared. The content may be informative, entertaining, surprising, shocking or intriguing, but the motive is always the same – to subtly promote a brand's internet presence. Native advertising is a category of content marketing that focuses on digital content, and especially on media brands.

Native is somewhat similar to old style print advertorial, a bought section of a newspaper that looks like editorial, unless the eagle-eyed reader notices the word 'advertisement feature' in tiny letters by the headline. Proponents argue that native advertising entails a wider variety of techniques, although the fact that content is paid for should always be clear to the reader. Sponsors want the source credibility of news media but they don't want to buy their display or classified advertising, so native advertising has been mooted by media owners as the saviour of journalism since it apparently offers a new business model to replace the collapsing advertising model for newspapers. It has been adopted by some serious organs of record, such as the UK *Guardian* and the *New York Times*[39] as well as by the newer show business and sensation-driven media brands. Native advertising raises questions of media and marketing ethics. When marketing techniques are not necessarily immediately apparent for what they really are, it raises questions about ideological influence (Hackley et al., 2008). This has been called implicit or 'masked' marketing. The ethical question is to what extent should consumers be credited with sophistication about such marketing techniques.

TRADE CONFERENCES AND EXHIBITIONS

According to one estimate,[40] $24 billion is spent annually on exhibiting in the USA. Many of these are trade exhibitions for business-to-business promotion but some also include consumers, such as trade exhibitions for motor vehicles, higher education, home furnishings and leisure crafts. The bigger exhibitions charge an entry fee to the public and attract many thousands of visitors to the manufacturers' exhibition stands. Exhibitions can generate a massive throughput of actual and potential consumers while also acting as a presence in the market in general. The advantage of trade exhibitions is that audiences are pre-segmented, and they come direct to the manufacturers. The disadvantages are cost, time and effort, and manufacturers are situated in a hall with all their major rivals. A well-attended conference and a well-organised stall can, however, generate considerable business.

SNAPSHOT 7.7

Illegal guerrilla marketing

In some areas of the UK, spray-painted graffiti appears on the walls of derelict buildings. The graffiti depicts a website address, as if a member of the public has spontaneously committed this act of public vandalism so delighted were they with the website. Of course, the organisation concerned has paid people to spray-paint public property with their web address and take the risk of being caught and prosecuted. The effect is striking: the spray-painted message is antithetical to glossy, mainstream advertising and carries connotations of an underground, people-driven movement. The messages are huge, painted on walls, which thousands of cars pass every day. Illegal fly posting has also long been a common advertising technique in the music business to promote new bands or local performances. Spray-painting the message as if it is graffiti is a neat, attention-grabbing (and usually indelible) twist on this technique.

POINT OF SALE AND MERCHANDISING

Merchandising is normally a term used in a broad sense to refer to the whole retail setting for purchase, including the way the product is displayed and promoted in the retail store. **POS** is sales promotion that takes place at the **point of sale**, by the checkout. POS promotion might entail a sales person offering free samples, or a cardboard model of the product featuring prominently on display to put the brand foremost in consumers' minds at the point of sale. The term can also be used more broadly to refer to any in-store promotion such as liquid crystal TV screens placed in-store showing continuous ads for a brand sold there, or other promotional structures such as 'tubes' – printed with promotional images of brands – which customers have to walk through.

Advertising and promotion at the POS are intended to create a persuasive ambience in the space where the consumer makes a decision and hands over the cash. POS should give a cutting edge to the broader merchandising activities that are common in retail marketing. In the small TCN shops (tobacco, confectionery, newspapers) that are common in much of the UK and Europe, brand marketers know that the position their branded item occupies is crucial to its sales performance – the 'golden arc' consists of an arm's length radiating from the cashier's position on each side. This is where leading brands of tobacco and confectionery prefer to be located in the shop for easy viewing and access. In larger retail stores brand marketers know that the volume of shelf space occupied is a powerful generator of sales and they will use all the bargaining power they can to get retail managers to devote as much of this volume as possible to their brand.

CHAPTER SUMMARY

This chapter has reviewed a number of non-advertising promotional techniques. The difficulties of definition under convergence have been noted, and many examples cited to illustrate some of the ways in which categories of the promotion mix are being split into hybrid forms. Some, like product placement, combine elements of celebrity endorsement, sponsorship, advertising and PR. Others seem to be a digital revision of traditional analogue methods, like native advertising as a digital development of advertorial. Still others, such as content marketing, seem to be contingent for their effect on a combination of genre and medium. Overall, the category non-advertising promotion is becoming more important to advertisers since it is taking an increasing proportion of promotional budgets.

REVIEW QUESTIONS

1 Record an evening's TV viewing on commercial channels. Watch the playback and list the number of sponsorship and product placement events. What do the results tell you about the changing practices of sponsorship and brand placement on broadcast entertainment? What impact do you feel such events have in comparison with conventional TV advertising? Has the character of TV advertising changed to reflect the growth in sponsorship and its variants?
2 How can sponsorship of TV shows generate tangible benefits for brand organisations?
3 Imagine that you are the public relations officer of a soccer club, a university or a retail organisation. Think of six ways in which you could draw on other communications disciplines to promote a positive public perception of your organisation.
4 Find five examples of native advertising. Explain how they benefit sponsors, and discuss what ethical issues they might raise for journalism.

VIDEO QUESTIONS

1 How do the objectives of sponsorship align with the objectives of advertising and promotion?

2 How does sponsorship support advertising and promotions?
How do the Redskins Football team use sponsorship to create promotion opportunities?

3 What are the advantages of using product placement?
What are the challenges to product placement?
How does product placement help brands achieve their promotional goals?

4 How can brands engage in non-advertising promotion?
How does being on social media promote brands?

CASE STUDY

The selfie that 'broke Twitter'[41]

The 2014 Hollywood Academy Awards, the 'Oscars', were sponsored by the world's biggest handset business, Samsung.[42] Host Ellen DeGeneres used a Samsung Galaxy Note 3 smartphone to take a selfie of herself, Bradley Cooper and Meryl Streep. When Kevin Spacey,

PHOTO 19 Samsung Galaxy Note 3

Image Courtesy of the Advertising Archives

The Samsung Galaxy Note 3 + Gear was launched with an integrated campaign that included TV, online videos, print (such as this 2013 example) and a variety of OOH executions such as digital displays projected onto noted landmarks. The TV spot (called Design your Life) featured the then 16-year old singer Lorde's hit song 'Royals'. Samsung's marketing also benefited the following year from the most successful commercial selfie to date – the Hollywood Oscars selfie that 'broke Twitter' (see Case Study in this Chapter).

Julia Roberts, Brad Pitt, Angelina Jolie and Lupita N'Yongo also managed to squeeze into the pic, along with N'Yongo's brother, DeGeneres tweeted it, and the re-tweets caused Twitter to briefly crash. DeGeneres announced that the image 'broke Twitter'. By the next evening, CNN reported that the selfie had been re-tweeted more than 3 million times, making it the world's biggest viral selfie, and achieving more than triple the shares of a selfie taken by US President Barack Obama. During the coverage Samsung products featured in something like 5 minutes of screen time, along with advertisements in the commercial breaks. The selfie, no doubt a planned piece of spontaneity, leveraged this sponsorship through viral social media shares into peak time, global mass media news coverage, trade press and comment.[43] The 2014 Oscars shown live on ABC gained its biggest American TV audience in ten years, some 43 million, with probably many millions more watching around the world. According to research specialists Nielsen,[44] the 3-hour telecast was tweeted about 11.2 million times by 2.8 million people. In this case, sponsorship was combined with advertising, brand placement, celebrity endorsement, content marketing and PR, and achieved a highly leveraged combination of bought and earned media pace.

The Oscars selfie is a good example of how elements of the promotional mix no longer operate independently. Sponsorship was undertaken of a televised event that was certain to achieve a large live TV audience (the event was also streamed live on the internet) and global coverage in news and entertainment media. It was leveraged through in-coverage placing of the sponsor's brands, allowable under US TV sponsorship rules, and the coverage was wrapped around bought spot advertising. The selfie tweet achieved news coverage in its own right and huge earned media space as the most shared selfie ever. Other media stories even piggy-backed on the selfie story, giving it even more earned mentions, with reports that some stars tried to push their way into the selfie group and failed, and that DeGeneres used an iPhone to take another selfie backstage. The incident illustrates that, under convergence, integration is an integral part of the dynamic of advertising and promotion.

Case questions

1 How might you categorise the 2014 Oscars selfie tweet as a form of promotional communication?
2 In what ways might viral content benefit brands? Are there risks?
3 What are the advantages and disadvantages of earned media space over bought media space for brands?
4 In what other ways might sponsorship deals be leveraged through social media? Give five examples.

USEFUL JOURNAL ARTICLES

(These Sage articles can be accessed on the companion website.)

Cronin, A.M. (2011) 'Researching urban space, reflecting on advertising: a photo essay', *Space and Culture*, 14 (4): 356–66.

Jessen, I.B. and Graakjær, N.J. (2013) 'Cross-media communication in advertising: exploring multimodal connections between television commercials and websites', *Visual Communication*, 12 (4): 437–58.

McStay, A. (2013) 'I consent: an analysis of the Cookie Directive and its implications for UK behavioral advertising', *New Media & Society*, 15 (4): 596–611 (first published September 30, 2012).

Morreale, J. (2014) 'From homemade to store bought: *Annoying Orange* and the professionalization of YouTube', *Journal of Consumer Culture*, 14 (1): 113–28 (first published October 15, 2013).

Smith, K. (2006) 'Rhetorical figures and the translation of advertising headlines', *Language and Literature*, 15 (2): 159–82.

FURTHER READING

Bernhardt, J.M., Alber, J. and Gold, R.S. (2014) 'A social media primer for professionals: digital dos and don'ts', *Health Promotion Practice*, 15 (2): 168–72.

Eckhardt, G.M. and Bradshaw, A. (2014) 'The erasure of antagonisms between popular music and advertising', *Marketing Theory*, doi: 1470593114521452 (first published February 12, 2014).

Fan Yang (2014) 'China's 'fake' Apple store: branded space, intellectual property and the global culture industry', *Theory, Culture & Society*, doi: 0263276413504971 (first published March 17, 2014).

Hackley, C. (2003) 'IMC and Hollywood – what brand managers need to know', *Admap*, November: 44–7.

Hackley, C. and Hackley née Tiwsakul, R.A. (2012) 'Unpaid product placement: the elephant in the room in the UK's new paid-for product placement market', *International Journal of Advertising*, 31(4): 703–18.

Lehu, J.-M. and Bressoud, E. (2009) 'Recall of brand placement in movies: interactions between prominence and plot connection in real conditions of exposure', *Recherche et Applications en Marketing (English Edition)*, 24 (1): 7–26.

Taylor, C.R. and Weih Chang (1995) 'The history of outdoor advertising regulation in the United States', *Journal of Macromarketing*, 15: 47–59.

Tiwsakul, R., Hackley, C. and Szmigin, I. (2005) 'Explicit, non-integrated product placement in British television programmes', *International Journal of Advertising*, 24 (1): 95–111.

NOTES

1 'Volvo trucks: the Epic Split', www.youtube.com/watch?v=M7FIvfx5J10 (accessed 25 February 2017).

2 Jessica Twentyman, 'The secret to viral video', 26 February 2014, marketingwww.theguardian.com/technology/2014/feb/26/secret-to-viral-video-marketing (accessed 25 February 2017).

3 Some of the ideas for this section are adapted from seminars of the Branded Content Research Network, www.brandedcontentresearchnetwork.org/ (accessed 29 March 2017).

4 'Sponsorship spending growth slows in North America as marketers eye newer media and marketing options', 7 January 2014, www.sponsorship.com/iegsr/2014/01/07/Sponsorship-Spending-Growth-Slows-In-North-America.aspx#.UxAK4yifPao; see also 'Global sponsorship spending by region from 2009 to 2017', www.statista.com/statistics/196898/global-sponsorship-spending-by-region-since-2009/ (both accessed 26 February 2017).

5 'Sponsorship and social media: a Brandwatch analysis of Barclays Premier League sponsorship', April 2013, www.brandwatch.com/wp-content/uploads/2013/05/Brandwatch-Barclays-Premier-League-Report-May-2013.pdf (accessed 26 February 2017).

6 Charles Sale, 'Premier League to be without a title sponsor from 2016–17 season in bid to mirror major American sports' "clean" branding strategy', 4 June 2015, www.dailymail.co.uk/sport/football/article-3111413/Premier-League-without-title-sponsor-2016-17-season-bid-mirror-major-American-sports-clean-branding-strategy.html (accessed 28 March 2017).

7 Kamal Ahmed, 'Barclays considering exit from Premier League sponsorship deal', 25 January 2014, www.telegraph.co.uk/finance/newsbysector/banksandfinance/10597404/Barclays-considering-exit-from-Premier-League-sponsorship-deal.html; see also Owen Gibson, 'Sky and BT retain Premier League TV rights for record £5.14bn', 10 February 2015, www.theguardian.com/football/2015/feb/10/premier-league-tv-rights-sky-bt (both accessed 26 February 2017).

8 Sarmeer Arshad, 'Nike's top 10 highest paid endorsement deals to sports players', 12 January 2014, www.tsmplug.com/richlist/nike-highest-paid-endorsement-deals/ (accessed 26 February 2017).

9 Ryan Waniata, 'As TV cuts commercials, product placement is worming its way into your shows', 15 June 2016, www.digitaltrends.com/movies/how-ads-are-going-underground-to-invade-your-favorite-tv-shows/ (accessed 28 March 2017).

10 'Nike drops sponsorship of Livestrong', 28 May 2013, http://articles.chicagotribune.com/2013-05-28/business/chi-nike-livestrong-20130528_1_texas-based-livestrong-lance-armstrong-livestrong-spokeswoman (accessed 26 February 2017).

11 Clarissa Sebag-Montefiore and Steven Zeitchik, 'Chinese pay for product placement in Hollywood movies', 11 September 2012, http://articles.latimes.com/2012/sep/11/entertainment/la-et-ct-chinese-pay-for-product-placement-in-hollywood-movies-20120910 (accessed 28 February 2017).

12 Amanda Killelea, 'Superman film Man of Steel rakes in record-breaking £110m in product placement deals', 1 July 2013, www.mirror.co.uk/lifestyle/going-out/film/superman-film-man-steel-rakes-1947071 (accessed 1 March 2017).

13 'UK product placement – NMG product placement's market predictions 2013/14', 25 April 2013, http://newmediagroup.co.uk/uk-product-placement-—-nmg-product-placement's-market-predictions-201314/ (accessed 3 March 2017).

14 Abe Sauer, 'How *Skyfall* screwed Heineken while rewarding Macallan', 20 December 2012, www.brandchannel.com/home/post/2012/12/20/James-Bond-Skyfall-Heineken-Macallan-122012.aspx (accessed 1 March 2017).

15 Claude Brodesser-Akner, 'Coke, Mercedes avoid gritty film cameos', 6 November 2008, http://adage.com/article/madisonvine-news/coke-mercedes-avoid-gritty-film-cameos-slumdog/132301/ (accessed 1 March 2017).

16 'NMG Oscar success Philomena', 23 December 2013, http://newmediagroup.co.uk/nmg-oscar-success-philomena/ (accessed 1 March 2017).

17 'Product placement in pictures: The Smurfs', 26 September 2011, http://brandsandfilms.com/2011/09/product-placement-in-pictures-the-smurfs/ (accessed 1 March 2017).

18 Laura Petrecca, 'Super Bowl marketers play up musical tie-ins', *USA Today*, 17 January 2014, www.usatoday.com/story/money/business/2014/01/17/pepsi-grammy-super-bowl-halftime/4529529/ (accessed 1 March 2017).

19 'Marc Jacobs new creative director for Diet Coke', *Daily News*, 6 February 2013, www.nydailynews.com/life-style/fashion/marc-jacobs-diet-coke-new-creative-director-article-1.1256714 (accessed 28 March 2017).

20 'Stella McCartney appointed creative director for Team GB and Adidas', 11 May 2011, http://styleclone.com/17342/stella-mccartney-appointed-creative-director-for-team-gb-and-adidas/ (accessed 20 January 2017).

21 Diana Bradley, 'Polaroid splits creative director Lady Gaga', *PR Week*, 2 October 2014, www.prweek.com/article/1315548/polaroid-splits-creative-director-lady-gaga (accessed 28 March 2017).

22 www.facebook.com/Bodyform/posts/10151186887359324 (accessed 23 February 2017).

23 Bodyform's video response is here: www.youtube.com/watch?v=Bpy75q2DDow (accessed 23 February 2017).

24 Including this piece in the UK *Daily Mail*: Martha de Lacey, 'Is this the best ever response to a Facebook rant? Bodyform "boss" enlightens confused boyfriend about periods in witty spoof video', 17 October 2012, www.dailymail.co.uk/femail/article-2218920/Bodyform-viral-spoof-YouTube-video-Response-Richard-Neills-Facebook-rant-period-adverts.html (accessed 23 February 2017).

25 www.ipr.org.uk/ (accessed 1 March 2017).

26 www.prsa.org/ (accessed 1 March 2017).

27 www.theidm.com/ (accessed 3 March 2017).

28 Katherine Levy and Daniel Farey-Jones, 'FIFA cracks down after World Cup ambush marketing stunt', *Campaign*, 18 June 2010, www.marketingmagazine.co.uk/article/1010807/fifa-cracks-down-world-cup-ambush-marketing-stunt (accessed 3 March 2017).

29 Charlie Minato, 'Ingenious ambush campaigns from Nike, Samsung and BMW make official sponsorships look like a waste', 14 June 2012, www.businessinsider.com/best-ambush-marketing-campaigns-2012-6?op=1 (accessed 3 March 2017).

30 Sammy Said, 'David Beckham earns $37 million from commercial contracts alone', 30 June 2013, www.therichest.com/sports/david-beckham-earns-37-million-from-commercial-contracts-alone/ (accessed 20 January 2017).

31 Daniel Bates, 'Goldenballs enjoys his golden years,' 31 March, www.dailymail.co.uk/news/article-3516539/David-Beckham-earns-45m-year-retirement-t-ex-sports-stars-rich-list.html (accessed 18 July 2017).

32 Russell Parsons, 'Madonna signs deal with Smirnoff owner Diageo', 18 August 2011, www.marketingweek.com/2011/08/18/madonna-signs-deal-with-smirnoff-owner-diageo/ (accessed 18 July 2017).

33 Melissa Hoyer, 'Jessica Gomes replaces Miranda Kerr as David Jones ambassador', 22 March 2013, www.news.com.au/entertainment/celebrity/jessica-gomes-replaces-miranda-kerr-as-david-jones-ambassador/story-fn907609-1226603425211 (accessed 16 January 2017).

34 Heather Wood Rudulph, 'Get that life: how I became a world-famous blogger', *Cosmopolitan*, 11 May 2015, www.cosmopolitan.com/career/news/a40238/get-that-life-heather-b-armstrong-dooce/ (accessed 29 March 2017).

35 Maria Aragon is one of numerous singers who have used YouTube as platform to gain a recording contract, see CTV News, 24 July 2011, www.ctvnews.ca/youtube-sensation-maria-aragon-inks-recording-contract-1.674417 (accessed 19 January 2017).

36 'Local blogger gains national recognition for travel blog', *Curaçao Chronicle*, 20 August 2013, www.curacaochronicle.com/tourism/local-blogger-gains-national-recognition-for-travel-blog-writes-about-curacao/ (accessed 19 January 2017).

37 Sam Webb, 'Selling their skin: Japanese women paid to put adverts on their THIGHS to catch the attention of men', MailOnline, 24 July 2013, www.dailymail.co.uk/news/article-2375732/Japanese-women-paid-adverts-THIGHS-catch-attention-men.html (accessed 4 March 2017).

38 Tony Muna, 'Here's the native advertising trends 2017 you need to know', 2 January 2017, https://nativeadvertisinginstitute.com/blog/native-advertising-trends-2017/ (accessed 18 July 2017).

39 Emily Bell, 'Native advertising is the new paywall in media economics – but is it here to stay?', *The Guardian*, 15 January 2014, www.theguardian.com/media/media-blog/2014/jan/05/native-advertising-paywall-transparency (accessed 3 March 2017).

40 Rachel Wimberley, 'CEIR releases new version of "How the Exhibit Dollar Is Spent" Report', 6 August 2012, www.tsnn.com/news-blogs/ceir-releases-new-version-how-exhibit-dollar-spent-report (accessed 3 March 2017).

41 Lisa Baertlein, 'Ellen's Oscar "selfie! crashes Twitter, breaks record', 3 March 2014, www.reuters.com/article/2014/03/03/us-oscars-selfie-idUSBREA220C320140303 (accessed 3 March 2017).

42 Beth Snyder Bulik, 'You need to see this: Samsung's Oscars Campaign', 1 March 2014, http://adage.com/article/media/samsung-breaks-samsung-campaign-oscars/291938/ (accessed 3 March 2017).

43 Mat Smith, 'Samsung debuts its first Galaxy S5 ad during the Oscars and turns sponsorship dollars into all-star selfies', 2 March 2014, www.engadget.com/2014/03/02/samsung-galaxy-s5-oscars-selfies/ (accessed 3 March 2017).

44 Ryan Faughnder, 'Oscars 2014 draws 43 million viewers, biggest audience in 10 years', *Los Angeles Times*, 3 March 2014, www.latimes.com/entertainment/envelope/cotown/la-et-ct-oscars-ratings-ellen-degeneres-20140303,0,6631180.story#axzz2uxfDdxy6 (accessed 3 March 2017).

8 GLOBAL ADVERTISING STRATEGY

CHAPTER OUTLINE

Advertising and promotional communication is now conducted in an international space that crosses national and cultural boundaries. Standardising brand marketing communication across the globe is attractive to organisations because of the potential savings and control over the brand image. However, communicating one message to different national cultures raises many difficulties. As a result of this trade-off, there are many nuanced issues to consider in designing global advertising strategies. This chapter discusses some of the managerial opportunities and problems of promoting brands internationally, and explores some of the wider implications of the globalisation of the marketing environment.

KEY CHAPTER CONTENT

Advertising and the global economy

Cross-cultural communication

Standardisation or localisation of advertising and promotion?

Cultural tensions around global brand advertising

Advertising management in non-domestic economies

Want a primer? Go to https://study.sagepub.com/hackley4e and watch...

Watch *Localized Product and Leveraging the Brand* to learn
How global branding impacts on advertising in the global economy
What standardisation and localisation are, and how they impact on advertising and promotion

Watch *Gillette: Stimulating Primary Demand* to learn
What challenges cultural tensions pose for advertising and promotion, and how these challenges can be transformed into opportunities…

… to tackle the video questions at the end of the chapter.

ADVERTISING AND THE GLOBAL ECONOMY

Advertising expenditure is closely linked to growth in economic activity, and the generation of jobs and wealth. It is seen as a reflection and also a driver of GDP growth.[1] Rising expenditure on advertising is seen as a healthy sign of a growing economy, and the opposite is also true – when advertising expenditure contracts, the general economic picture is probably poor. The causal relationship between advertising and GDP growth is difficult to establish one way or the other, but it has been shown that digital advertising, in particular, contributes to company performance.[2] Advertising and economic growth can be said to be two sides of the same coin – they are mutually interconnected. One cannot happen without the other. The case for advertising is made by most of its trade bodies, such as the Advertising Association.[3] Arguments include the case that advertising widens consumer choice of products and services and makes consumers aware of these choices; creates more choices in employment by creating jobs; creates more choices in news and entertainment media by creating revenue to fund those media; and helps to generate revenue for entertainment, the arts and sport.[4]

Advertising is fundamental to the global economy. At the time of writing, global advertising expenditure is projected to rise by more than 5% a year by consultants McKinsey and Zenith Optimedia,[5] while digital advertising is predicted to show double-digit annual percentage growth for the foreseeable future. Digital growth is being led by mobile.[6] Worldwide advertising spend in total has surpassed $500 billion and is forecast to continue its growth.[7] Television, cinema, OOH and radio advertising also show modest growth, but advertising expenditure (known as adspend) on print newspapers and magazines is predicted to continue its relative decline. Digital media extend the reach of businesses across the world and advertising is an essential part of business growth. The global penetration of digital media is increasing as an increasing proportion of the world's population acquires access to internet-enabled smartphones and other devices.[8] It is estimated that some 20% of the world's population owns a PC, and 22–30% own a smartphone.[9] This degree of penetration is making new global markets more easily accessible through digital media.

Advertising's global scope is extended by the shift in the proportion of adspend towards digital media. This includes purely digital formats such as Google Adwords,[10] sponsored content on social media such as Twitter and advertising on Facebook,[11] or native advertising on internet media brands, but it also extends to film, audio and print ads conveyed on digital media channels. For example, Dove's 'Real Beauty Sketches',[12] a viral YouTube ad with more than 160 million views (discussed in Chapter 10) was uploaded to 45 YouTube channels in 25 different languages. The videos were not differentiated for national audiences, just the commentary, reflecting the need to maximise the reach of the video across Dove's international markets. The global audience reach of the internet, especially via mobile, has changed the terms of the debate around international advertising from 'what can work with international audiences' to 'what must work with international audiences'. There is more need than ever before for advertising and promotional agencies to deploy their communication craft skills in ways that translate across cultural, ethnic and linguistic boundaries – indeed, internationalisation, like integration, is becoming a default position for promotional communication. Advertising and promotion will be viewed across the world via mobile, PC and internet cable TV, even if it was not conceived specifically to achieve a global reach. Social media sharing of popular marketing content tends to span the globe – marketing news quickly becomes global.

The topic of international advertising remains fraught with potential difficulties of interpretation and complexities of media and audience planning. There is still a need in traditional mass media for above-the-line executions that will be designed, or at least conceived, by a group in one country, to be consumed by audiences in other countries. The need for cross-national mentalities in advertising remains. In addition to the difficulties presented by differences of cultural and linguistic communication codes, ethical standards and regulations, media agencies have to negotiate radically different media environments in different counties. So, in a sense, the problems of international advertising are not fundamentally different in the convergence era – they are simply extended through all levels of integration because of the reach of digital media.

WHY GLOBALISE MARKETING EFFORT?

Global marketing entails risk, but there remain sound and pressing reasons why brand marketing organisations want to operate on a global scale. In fact, as noted above, given the increase in global access to cable television and the internet via mobile, it can be difficult for brands to remain local. A website, for example, is intrinsically a global presence, at least in the sense that it can, in principle, be accessed by anyone, anywhere. Information and advertising cross cultural boundaries increase consumer choices and raise consumers' lifestyle expectations. The scenes of affluence portrayed in brand advertising or in movies viewed around the world on satellite TV or the internet have a powerful effect. This helps to stimulate latent demand for brands and in so doing helps to wear away cultural and political resistance to controls on the movement of labour, goods, services and capital. This creates potential foreign markets for domestic producers. When domestic demand reaches a point of slow growth because of increased competition or saturated local demand, foreign markets offer a means of continued organic growth. In addition, domestic competition drives up labour costs and foreign countries seeking inward investment can offer global brand corporations cheaper labour and production costs, adding momentum to the cycle of globalisation.

SNAPSHOT 8.1

National stereotypes offer easy solutions for advertisers

Stereotypes of all kinds are frequently exploited in advertising, both intentionally and unintentionally. International bank HSBC was behind a long-running campaign that used national stereotypes to humorous effect by drawing attention to ways in which cultural differences of non-verbal communication can cause embarrassment, offence or misunderstanding, through misread gestures, body language or behaviour. One ad looks at the Chinese tradition of adults presenting envelopes of money to children on special occasions,[13] while another contrasts American and Japanese work rituals for business meetings.[14] Other campaigns have made humorous use of national stereotypes. One that is especially popular with creatives is the German reputation for being passionate about precision engineering, exploited in a series of ads for VW and BMW cars. One particularly popular ad aired during the American Super Bowl showed engineers growing wings every time a VW clocked up 100,000 miles, and generated multiple millions of social media shares and views.[15] In another twist on the theme of national stereotypes, a Heineken TV ad makes fun of British tourists who expect Jamaican locals to conform to a steel-drum-playing, reggae-loving stereotype.[16]

The impetus for global marketing may often derive from competitive activity. If brand X is active in a particular foreign market, then brand Y will want to be there too in case it loses ground against the competition by not having a presence in that market. Another factor in the globalisation of markets is the relative ease of technology transfer. National boundaries no longer hinder the transfer of production capability to low-wage economies. The competitive need for international expansion, the ease of access to new consumer markets and low-wage labour markets, and the cross-cultural communication driving an ideology of brand consumption are, taken together, important drivers of the globalisation of corporate activity. So, while global markets are far from homogeneous there are considerable opportunities for international brand marketing activity given the relative ease of capital transfer and cross-border transportation, the internationalisation of financial payments, and the latent demand for many brands created by the international reach of, and increasing access to, cable television, movies and the internet (see Levitt, 1983).

PROBLEMS AND PITFALLS OF GLOBAL MARKETING

Marketing in non-domestic markets presents a number of managerial problems that may be less acute when dealing with domestic markets alone. For example, the marketing and communications infrastructure may differ widely between regions. In advanced economies well-developed road, rail and air transport links, the presence of wholesale distribution facilities and easy access to local retail or other sales outlets facilitate marketing by domestic or non-domestic firms. In less developed economies, the absence of a well-established communications and marketing infrastructure may present real challenges. Logistics can be a problem: while densely populated cities may have good communication links, vast numbers of people live in areas with poor communications and few retail outlets. Rates of literacy and access to TV, internet and telephones differ widely from region to region. Factors such as these clearly have major implications for the design of marketing initiatives.

In addition to the practical and managerial problems of marketing internationally there is the self-evident difficulty of communication across linguistic, cultural and ethnic boundaries. Advertising and promotion agencies deal in culturally specific linguistic and social practices and this local knowledge is indispensable to coherent and resonant promotional communication. Advertising agency management is subject to much the same kinds of cultural variation as advertising itself. A great many international agencies are organised along similar operational lines with account management, account planning or research, creative and media roles in account teams. There are, nevertheless, differences in management approach that reflect broader cultural differences (West, 1993; Hackley, 2003a; Hackley and Tiwsakul, 2008). For example, the Thai advertising industry has evolved under Western influence, and it has also developed a distinctive style reflecting the particular cultural mores and traditions of Thailand (Punyapiroje et al., 2002). Thai agencies tend to have local management, creative and planning functions, within Westernised corporate structures, reflecting the distinctive media infrastructure, demographic and unique communication culture of Thailand. To plan global campaigns effectively it is necessary to make use of detailed local knowledge of the advertising and consumer cultural environment (Hackley and Hackley, 2013).

A further managerial difficulty of advertising internationally is the fact that codes of advertising practice, media law and consumer marketing regulation can differ greatly from country to country, as noted in Chapter 9. Many ads that are deployed in one country simply cannot be used in other countries if they fall foul of regional regulations. The differences in international advertising regulation present a further problem for standardisation in international advertising campaigns.

There are many differences in the cultural practices of international business that will influence how advertising and marketing are managed regionally. For example, the difficulty of getting distribution agreements for Western brands in East Asian markets is legendary. This is at least partly because the Asian tradition of building mutually advantageous business relationships carefully over long periods of time (within a culture of Guanxi, in China, and similar relationship orientation elsewhere in Asia) is difficult for the Western business mentality, which is based on instant rapport, agreements of convenience and instrumental relationships. A further difficulty is that the language and dialect used in neighbouring regions may have nuances that can only be understood by local people, creating highly locally specific trading and communicating conditions within a single national border.

SNAPSHOT 8.2

The international appeal of the BMW MINI

BMW Mini's launch of the Countryman in 2017 plays on the retro-appeal that has become a hallmark of the brand but updated for the hipster era.[17] In 2016, BMW reported record sales of the Mini in the UK at almost 70,000 units, whereas the much smaller Mini market in the USA dropped by about 18%. BMC (British Motor Corporation), formed from the merger of the UK car brands Austin and Morris, launched the Mini in 1959. The car, then owned by Rover, ceased production in the UK in October 2000 after over 5 million had been manufactured. The revolutionary front-wheel drive design of Sir Alec Issigonis created a car with great appeal, but sales were falling sharply by the late 1950s. BMW bought the brand in 2001 and Frank Stephenson redesigned the car, keeping the sense of fun and style but producing a vehicle that is contemporary in style and performance. The promotions for the new Mini brand positioned it as a pan-global small car and exploited its quirkiness.

Mini has a long tradition of innovative ads in the USA, with early examples including the brand's 2013 'Not Normal' ads[18] from California agency Butler Shine, Stern & Partners and continuing to the 2016 Superbowl ad, 'Defy Labels', before the agency resigned the account ahead of a BMW creative review in 2017. In spite of trading difficulties in the USA, the quirky but cool brand positioning has been regarded as a big success for BMW since the re-launch of Mini in 2001. Traditional Mini advertising made much use of TV,[19] but the new Mini has largely exploited experiential, content, OOH and digital advertising, and also sponsorship of TV shows, brand placement in movies (especially the re-make of *The Italian Job*), numerous publicity stunts, and extensive PR coverage. Its international success reflects a conscious effort on the part of BMW to position the car internationally rather than over-exploiting its British heritage. Many new consumers of the Mini are unaware that it is an icon of 1960s Britain. The swinging sixties connotations of the car, while arguably an important part of its appeal, have been downplayed in the marketing communications for the new BMW Mini in favour of a more powerful global appeal.

Communicating and doing business may be very difficult for foreigners who do not have a deep knowledge of local culture, language and business practices. Systems of business regulation and attitudes to communication can differ widely from culture to culture. For example, what is acceptable in advertising in one country may not be allowed in another. In Muslim countries, for example, the portrayal of females in advertising must adhere to the public standards of dress and conduct expected, while portraying sexuality and nudity in advertising is often regulated more liberally in Scandinavia in Northern Europe than in the USA or the UK. Specific rules about advertising of particular goods can differ as well. For example, in Sweden no TV advertising directed at children under 12 is permitted. Marketing internationally encounters numerous differences in regulation, infrastructure and consumer culture.

To some extent, the advance of digital communication has ameliorated some of these management problems, since communications with a global reach through social media and other digital formats can be managed locally. For example, the Dove campaign 'Real Beauty Sketches' (mentioned above) was created by a Brazilian agency and achieved global impact. The management challenges of localisation are perhaps more intense with regard to 'old' media, but are still relevant to non-advertising promotion and digital.

CROSS-CULTURAL COMMUNICATION

Advertising is inherently a cultural product. The managerial problems of advertising internationally cannot be reduced simply to a matter of accurate translation of the message, and neither can they be addressed by recourse to crude stereotypes of national culture (McSweeney, 2002). Different people interpret advertising communication through quite different systems of value and symbolism that are both cultural, and sub-cultural. Advertising is a curious case in communication because it is at once a universal symbolic language, and a personal appeal. In a general sense, all advertising communicates exactly the same message. It tries to persuade us to buy stuff. Advertising represents a global value system, the value system of capitalism and the consumer lifestyle, from a predominantly Western perspective representing the historical economic dominance of the West. Advertising holds a unique place in contemporary discourse, it permeates global culture, carrying consumer ideology in forms that are framed within local cultural meaning systems (Lash and Lury, 2007). Advertising executions for global brands that cross cultural borders have to achieve a balancing act, so that the sense of the brand is preserved in a persuasive way but articulated through local cultural communication codes.

Global brands' international advertising, then, must achieve two levels of communication. On the one hand, the brand must be instantly recognisable through some commonality of theme that transcends local communication codes. On the other hand, it must also say something in the local idiom, in order to resonate with local consumers. For example, one McDonald's advertisement in Thailand used the same 'I'm Lovin' It' slogan used all over the world but the artist recited a rap song in the Thai language. In a Japanese TV ad, the iconic clown Ronald McDonald was played by a Caucasian woman.[20] McDonald's advertising is localised in many different countries, but it is also always recognisable as McDonald's by anyone from any culture, through the use of the colour scheme, the arches, the strapline, the jingle or the clown. The flexibility of brand symbolism offers scope for adjusting the international market positioning. For example, German sportswear brand Adidas was better known for its association with soccer and track and field athletics in Europe for many years, but moved into rugby with the help of a joint sponsorship deal with national team the All Blacks in rugby-mad New Zealand (see this chapter's case study).

Exacerbating the problem of cross-cultural communication, people will take different meanings from a promotional communication even if they happen to have the same cultural background. Where cultural backgrounds differ, there is even more scope for consumers to take different meanings from the same advertisement. The elements of cultural background that might influence interpretation include ethnicity, language, locality, religion, family, sub-culture, peer group, education and any other influences that have featured in individuals' environment. Of course, as we have noted in Chapter 2, many advertisements are designed to be relatively 'open' texts that can be interpreted in many different ways. The key issue for advertising in the convergence era is to create a sense of cultural resonance around the brand, perhaps generating enough interest among consumers for them to want to share the ad and talk about it on social media. The fact that different consumers will bring different interpretations to an ad is not, then, fatal to a campaign's success. This stands in contrast to the sales-directed logic of AIDA (described in Chapter 2), but nonetheless reflects a truism about advertising that pre-dates the convergence era: that is, an ad that is talked about is a good ad, regardless of whether it is hard sell or soft sell.

Saying that there is a positive value to open advertising texts, though, should not be misconstrued to imply that attention is everything and meaning is nothing. The kinds of discussion around a piece of promotional content are important and they can be cued through artfully designed creative executions. It is important for advertisers to understand the ways in which meanings are cued in different cultures of communication in order to create constructive conversations around brand stories.

It may seem self-evident to draw attention to differences in cultural and meaning systems and the challenges these present for advertisers. Nevertheless, it is important to understand that all of us can fall into conventional, culturally bound ways of seeing the world, which can impede our understanding of otherness. In our everyday communication we constantly interpret visual and linguistic signs whose meanings, as we easily forget, are highly specific to our own idiom, culture and sub-culture. International advertising offers examples of cultural differences in communication that can consistently surprise because local cultures of communication are so easy to stereotype or take for granted.

SNAPSHOT 8.3

Mattel tries again with Barbie in China

In 2013 the biggest toy maker in the world Mattel re-launched their iconic Barbie doll into the Chinese market. Mattel have found the Chinese toy market difficult to crack – in 2011 it closed its $30 million 'House of Barbie' flagship store in Shanghai, China, just two years after it had opened.[21] The store was spread across six floors and featured a fashion runway, Barbie bar and design studio. It held the world's largest collection of 875 Barbie dolls, displayed on a spiral staircase.[22] China is often considered as a challenging market by many toy companies because of the education-focused Chinese culture. Chinese parents see toys as a waste of time. 'Tiger moms' in China would rather have their daughters reading books than accessorising Barbie dolls. Peter Broegger, Mattel's Asia Pacific Senior Vice President, in an interview with the *Wall Street Journal*, was quoted saying, 'Joy and learning are like oil and water in China'. Learning and education are a serious business for Chinese parents, and not to be confused with toys and play.

Mattel has tried to localise its products and advertising strategy. For example, its Fisher Price toys are labelled 'Play IQ', rather than 'Joy of Learning', as they are advertised in

Western markets.[23] The company changed its emphasis on fashion and lifestyle to incorporating learning as a part of Barbie's life. It launched a Violin Soloist Barbie to appeal to the Chinese culture of learning. However, the Barbie store seemed ill fated since it was built without a real attempt to popularise the Barbie concept in China. It may also have been hindered by the lack of an ethnic range of dolls. Barbie is strongly associated with an American ideal of female beauty and glamour, and rivals such as American Girl (Diamond et al., 2009) play up the association with national identity, while also adapting more ethnic variations into the dolls. Barbie has followed this trend and now offers more ethnic and body shape variations in its product range.[24] Barbie is an iconic Western toy that does not translate directly to the Chinese market in its Western form – whether the violin playing cultivated Barbie will do better remains to be seen.

NON-VERBAL COMMUNICATION

The use of national stereotypes in advertising is common (see Snapshot 8.1), often as a lazy source of humour to ingratiate the brand with those for whom the stereotype resonates. It is deeply misleading to overstate the notion of national characteristics, but nonetheless there are cultural conventions of communication that are of great importance in advertising development (see McSweeney, 2002). As a useful exemplar of the quirkiness of communication practices, it may be instructive to look briefly at a few aspects of non-verbal communication. It is axiomatic that 95% of face-to-face communication is non-verbalised or implicit in gesture, tone, intonation, 'body language' and facial expression. This is also true of advertising, as Chapter 2 notes. There are implicit, non-verbal aspects of communication encoded into visual advertising that provide important context for the decoding of meaning. Non-verbal communication is an integral feature of many visual promotions, and this element of communication can be highly sensitive. This is not just an issue for consumer interpretation of advertising. Advances in technology are resulting in outdoor advertising that can recognise and respond to face and gesture, as in examples in Tokyo and also Sydney, Australia.[25] Street billboards can be constructed to recognise whether the person approaching is a male or female, and a tailored message is provided. Other street displays react to the gestures of the viewer.

As Cook (2001) points out, communication always has a context that informs the meaning of a message. Viewing ads in the company of people from countries and cultures other than one's own can be a salutary reminder of this truism. A university class of international students asked to explain a particular ad will usually illustrate this vividly with widely diverging interpretations. They are all viewing the ad from a different cultural **frame of reference**. Advertising is a social text, as we have seen, that has to be learned, and there is much local cultural knowledge that is necessary in order to interpret an ad plausibly. Advertisers therefore need to be especially sensitive to the uses of gestures in a TV commercial script or press ad, in case meanings are construed that are not consistent with the brand values. The international marketing world is awash with stories of brand names, packaging designs or ads that failed because they were interpreted to mean something inappropriate or outrageous in some regions. This generally happens because the brand planners did not think outside their own cultural frame of reference. This is a communications lesson that even domestic advertisers and marketers must learn. It is a fundamental precept of brand planning that the cultural beliefs and practices of the target consumers should be thoroughly understood by creative teams and brand planners. If this level of understanding is achieved, it may be possible to design communications that resonate with meaning for the intended target audience.

STANDARDISATION OR LOCALISATION OF ADVERTISING AND PROMOTION?

An important question facing brand organisations is to what degree they ought to try to standardise their advertising throughout the world. We have already seen that the meaning of advertising narratives is often unstable and open to a variety of interpretations, even within relatively homogeneous consumer communities. How much more difficult must it be to maintain brand coherence through communications that cross international boundaries? As we have noted, the rise of digital communication technology, liberalisation of regulation in many media, financial and product markets and increase in foreign travel for the rising middle classes have created a ready audience for global brands. As brand organisations compete to exploit this tendency by internationalising their brands they face the decision of how best to do this in a way that maximises effectiveness and minimises costs.

The management problem of whether to standardise or localise arose partly because the issue was initially represented as a dichotomy in the 1980s as world markets began to open up. A famous article in the *Harvard Business Review* expressed this oversimplification on the basis that heterogeneous cultures around the globe appeared to be converging in attitudes, aspirations and consumer lifestyles, tastes and beliefs (Levitt, 1983). The logic of the argument was simple. If you can see Nike trainers and McDonald's hamburger joints in practically every capital city in the world then is this not evidence that consumers the world over are essentially the same in their needs and wants? Or, as an alternative interpretation, could it be that global consumer wants were converging under the umbrella of Western style consumerism?

The suggestion that the aspirations and values of differing cultures have united under the ethos of consumerism seems far-fetched more than 30 years after Levitt wrote his article. The values of economic neo-liberalism have swept across the world in some respects but there remain powerful and often strident voices articulating alternative visions of capitalism, along with anti-capitalist ideologies, since the 2008 financial collapse of the Western banking system (Hackley, 2009b). Consumption has become a prime site of contested ideologies around environmentalism and sustainability, consumer rights, gender and economic inequality. For many commentators, economic globalisation is predicated on a need for relentless consumption-driven economic growth that is unsustainable environmentally and socially.

At the very least, we can say that the standardisation thesis understated the robustness and uniqueness of local cultural values and the heterogeneity of global consumers, not to mention the tensions inherent in global capitalism. It remains true that most major global brands are Western in origin, but it is also true that the most successful have mastered a pan-global marketing orientation that assimilates international cultural communication codes, while increasing numbers of non-Western brands are becoming influential in the West (Loo and Hackley, 2013, and see Snapshot 8.4).

In sum, when discussing international advertising campaign planning, it is important to specify just what might converge in differing cultures and what cannot. Indeed, the notion of converging cultures makes little sense since cultures are defined by enduring and powerful differences. In important regards, what is of a particular culture can only be understood in terms of its difference from other cultures. But in the smaller world of advertising it is still worth posing the question to what extent is standardisation feasible because of the evident commonalities between cultures that make global consumer brands possible. One might also view this from a critical perspective in terms of the power of marketing to transcend, or perhaps to suppress, cultural difference. This latter viewpoint is the one that most attracts anti-brand and anti-marketing voices which argue that marketing in particular and economic neo-liberalism in general tend to obliterate local culture. Yet, consumption appears to be a site in which both globalisation and diversity seem represented. Indeed, the allure of cultural difference, the mystique of otherness, seems to be part of the dynamic that gives domestic brands appeal for global consumers.

THE BUSINESS CASE FOR STANDARDISATION OF INTERNATIONAL ADVERTISING

One of the reasons why the arguments for standardisation of international marketing gained credence among the academic and consulting circles of management was the force of the business case. The appeal of standardised international marketing lies in economy and control. As regards cost, it is expensive for a brand organisation to appoint a local advertising agency to create bespoke campaigns for the same brand in each country. Production and media costs increase with the number of different national campaigns that are needed. Creating just one ad to show all over the world, co-ordinated by one advertising and one global media agency, means saving a lot of expense in production and advertising development costs.

Cost minimisation is one issue, control over the way the brand is represented is another. Control results from keeping creative executions under central command rather than having to co-ordinate the work of local agencies, so that brand values and the brand personality are portrayed in exactly the desired way in every region. International brand organisations take a great deal of time and trouble to develop the ideas of their brand's values and personality, and to plan how these values might be portrayed in advertising and promotion. Giving control of advertising away to an agency in another country is seen as a risk for major brand organisations. Local agencies will invariably employ a culturally specific interpretation of the brand values, which may not necessarily be the interpretation that the brand organisation conceived of in its strategic planning. The risk of diluting the brand identity and/or confusing consumers is seen as a major one to be guarded against for fear of damaging long-term brand equity. In practice, the question of whether to standardise or localise advertising and promotion is not a straight choice between alternatives but a question of nuance. Most international organisations reach an accommodation between the need for localised communications strategies driven by culture-specific knowledge, and a need for control over costs and creative executions.

SNAPSHOT 8.4

How Malaysian fashion brands used Western PR

A study by Loo and Hackley (2013) entailed interviews with four of Malaysia's most successful fashion designers: Jimmy Choo, Melinda Looi, Bernard Chandran and Zang Toi. Each has been hugely successful with innovative designs that assimilate Eastern with Western influences. Fashion marketing relies a lot on PR – a stylist has to be noticed in the major fashion shows before fashion journalists write about them, then they might be worn by style leaders at newsworthy events, or even by actors in movies. For example, Jimmy Choo shoes were championed in *Vogue* magazine and mentioned in the script of the movie *The Devil Wears Prada*, while hit TV show *Sex and the City* became a shop window for high fashion brands, often including Jimmy Choos. In order to be successful in the West these Malaysian designers had to learn the fashion business in New York, Paris or London, and they had to combine Western management techniques with their Eastern sense of style.

More Asian brands are establishing in the West – and along with high fashion, the motor car, beer and technology sectors have had some noticeable successes. The love of Western brands in the East remains extremely strong though, and many luxury brands from the USA and Europe see their strongest growth in markets in China and South-East Asia. British clothing, fragrance and accessory brand Burberry, for example, has 71 stores in China and saw rapid sales growth there for a decade before being hit by the economic slowdown in China in 2015.[26] Many Western celebrities are so popular in the East as symbols of glamour and affluence that they can earn a lot of money featuring in advertising. Cameron Diaz, Leonardo DiCaprio, Matt Le Blanc, David and Victoria Beckham, and Jennifer Lopez, are just a few of the stars who endorse both Western and Eastern brands in Asia.

'GLOCALISATION' IN INTERNATIONAL ADVERTISING

Most international brand marketing organisations have found that neither localisation nor global standardisation entirely serves their purpose. What they require instead is a policy that reconciles the need for consistency of presentation of the brand in all communications across the world on the one hand, and the need for advertising to resonate with culturally specific consumer groups on the other. To achieve the specificity required, the brand values and personality have to be portrayed in terms of local language, priorities and practices. The broader marketing mix activities, in addition to the advertising, have to reflect local realities and practices.

The term **glocalisation** refers to the local adaptation of globally oriented marketing. Global brand marketing organisations often seek to impose control over the presentation of their brand at a certain level, allowing local marketing agencies some licence to portray the brand in ways that will cohere with local cultural meaning systems. So, for example, the brand logo and colour scheme might be mandatory inclusions specified in the creative brief, as appears to be the case in McDonald's advertising, mentioned above, and perhaps the strapline, jingle and music, even if the creative execution in other respects is generated by the agency to fit with local consumer interpretive frames. There are many ways this could be done. As we have seen, in some McDonald's print ads in China, the context of the imagery is distinctively Chinese, with Chinese customers in a restaurant or a Chinese sports star pictured, while the image of a burger and the arches is universal.

A glocalisation policy in international advertising is often pragmatically the best course. Local agencies can place the brand in an appropriate localised context while preserving key aspects of a global brand personality. The flexibility of this approach in advertising reflects the extent to which brand symbolism can be semiotically extended. Consider the economy of brand signs such as the Nike 'Swoosh', McDonald's arches, Apple's forbidden fruit logo, and logos for Google, BMW, Adidas, Pepsi, Coca-Cola, Virgin, Polo, Shell and many more.[27] These signs offer instant recognition, but are also relatively open texts in the sense that readers can associate them with a flexible range of stories and meanings. The brands can take on and exploit those stories they wish to, while rejecting those that they don't. Many advertising texts develop a story element and only acknowledge the brand with a logo placed in a discreet location in the visual image. This says both less and more, in the sense that rhetorical understatement can signify confidence that the brand and its values will be widely recognised without the need for over-elaboration. A powerful logo facilitates brand storytelling over a wide range of media formats.

STANDARDISING INTERNATIONAL ADVERTISING

A relatively small number of brands have been able to standardise advertising cross-culturally if their ad agency can find a common denominator of meaning that transcends cultures. They have to exploit this common meaning by devising ingenious creative executions, but no communications solution is effective indefinitely and brands must remain connected to the ebb and flow of consumer cultures if they are to retain vitality and relevance in the marketplace.

One can argue that many globally recognised brands represent something that does not cross cultures at all, but instead transcends culture in some way. Iconic brands can be understood in this way (see Holt, 2002). For example Coca-Cola, Mercedes–Benz and BMW all proudly represent their national origins but also succeed in spanning the globe in spite of their distinctive national history (but see Snapshot 8.5).

SNAPSHOT 8.5

Advertising and national identity

Country-of-origin effect is a feature that can influence the perception of quality in certain markets if a country has a strong reputation in a particular domain. Country myths can also be played out in brand communication, as has been the case with much Coca-Cola advertising over the years. The brand has long been associated with its origin in the USA and many campaigns played on this identification with America, exploiting that cultural resonance in 125 years of Coca-Cola advertising campaigns.[28] During the Second World War, the brand realised that American servicemen stationed abroad were pining for Coke because it reminded them of home, and they also gave it away to win the hearts and minds of local people. Free consignments of Coca-Cola were sent out to military service personnel overseas to exploit this cultural resonance. According to Holt and Cameron (2010), this may be one reason why Coca-Cola is an iconic brand and Pepsi is not. For Coca-Cola, advertising campaigns such as the legendary 1970s ad 'I'd Like to Buy the World a Coke'[29] have helped maintain the brand's iconic status, showing the brand as a symbol of America and also as a worldwide symbol of friendship. However, while iconic brands can help to resolve ideological dilemmas such as the tension around nationhood and identity, they can also expose those tensions (Holt, 2002). A Coke ad aired during the American Super Bowl in 2014[30] celebrated America's multiethnic population and showed people of many ethnicities singing 'America the Beautiful' in different languages. The ad caused a storm on social media, with many supporters lauding its multicultural theme, but many others claiming that it did not reflect their idea of a predominantly white, English-speaking America. Holt and Cameron offer many examples of brands that used advertising astutely to offer a symbolic resolution to dilemmas of national identity, but as political ideologies become more polarised perhaps brands will find it more difficult to resolve identity myths without alienating adherents of one ideology or another.

Many global brands are American in origin because the USA has been the world's foremost economic power during the era of branding. Of the world's top 20 brands by value noted in 2016, only two are Asian – Toyota and Samsung.[31] This is because of 'soft' cultural influence as well as because of manufacturing, marketing and innovation. The worldwide popularity of Hollywood movies and TV shows has popularised American culture, making its brands commonplace anywhere American movies can be seen. In the Western economic boom of the 1950s, US products gained a reputation for representing luxury, affluence and high-quality production standards. American provenance is no longer a guarantee of prestige, and economic times have changed, Asian economies are advancing at speed and Asian brands are slowly gaining a global foothold beyond their strong bases in car manufacturing, electronics and fashion (Loo and Hackley, 2013).

CULTURAL TENSIONS AROUND GLOBAL BRAND ADVERTISING

Foreignness can be a marketing virtue. Country-of-origin effects can bestow a halo of prestige on brands emanating from particular countries. For example, German motorcar design and engineering, Japanese electronics, Swiss watches, Russian vodka, French food and wine, Italian fashion, Colombian coffee, Indian tea, Belgian beer and holidays in Thailand are all thought to have special qualities. In many Asian consumer markets brands with a European connotation are often thought to have special glamour or prestige, while Asian brands of beer and fashion are making inroads alongside the traditional strengths of Asian brands in manufacturing and electronics.

It is very human to feel desire for the unattainable or the unfamiliar, the allure of the 'other'. No doubt, there is something of human nature in the country-of-origin effect.

National or regional reputations, myths and symbols that resonate with consumer aspirations are powerful drivers of consumption. This can be a strong lever for advertising and marketing internationally. And, as we have seen, there can be an adverse effect for brand marketing corporations if they happen to be closely associated with a country that acquires negative press coverage and receives international disapproval for whatever reason.

Not everyone welcomes the globalisation of brands. In many countries, there is a sense that brands from other countries represent an ideological challenge to traditional values and lifestyles. In many South-East Asian countries, for example, Western brands are loved by younger generations, but older generations regard extravagant consumption with suspicion. When Walt Disney wanted to set up Disneyland Paris, and McDonald's were planning to set up in France, there were popular movements and protests against the imposition of American brands on French culture. The McDonald's ethos of fast and simple food is anathema to French cuisine, but the restaurants remain popular in France as elsewhere. McDonald's has also attracted criticism for the effect of its supply chain practices on agriculture. In the USA, the brand has created a supply chain establishment that has apparently changed the structure and culture of the farming and cattle processing industries (Schlosser, 2002). French farmers have been worried that the same thing might happen in France. The protests against the Walt Disney theme parks seemed to be more focused on the resistance to the imposition of American popular culture in the land of Asterix the Gaul.

SNAPSHOT 8.6

De Beers Gem Diamonds' standardised campaign

One interesting example of a creatively standardised campaign was that of De Beers Gem Diamonds. De Beers is a South African diamond producing and cutting organisation. In 1996, in response to competition from West African diamonds and new technology that enabled a brand logo to be stamped on a diamond, De Beers commissioned JWT to create a campaign that would make De Beers known as a prestige diamond brand in a largely unbranded gem market. JWT's consumer research found that one common factor linked the meaning of diamonds across all cultures – diamonds meant love.[32] This theme was adapted into the differing diamond-giving practices in different countries in creative executions designed to resonate with local consumers.[33] The giving of diamonds to convey love was celebrated in national contexts of Continental Europe, the Middle East and the UK. The campaign, filmed in black and white and called 'Shadows', used a (then) new cinematic technique that enabled diamonds to stand out on a TV screen. The ads were made in the same studio and same style, and the script and music were adapted to reflect different diamond-giving rituals in regional variations. For example, the UK version featured a large stone on a wedding ring, a Spanish version featured an anniversary ring and a Middle Eastern version featured extravagant diamond necklaces and tiaras. Significant sales increases were reported and the campaign was reputed to have helped change the cultural meaning of diamonds by encouraging their use in cultures not traditionally predisposed to diamond-giving. In Japan, for example, it was said that there was no word for diamond before the 1960s but the term 'diamondo' became widely understood after the De Beers campaign.

Global brands can also hold a powerful sense of liberation for citizens who want access to the brands of the world. For example, for much of the twentieth century it was unthinkable that an American brand would have a state-approved presence in Russia, but in 1990 what was then the world's biggest McDonald's restaurant opened on Pushkinsklaya Square in Moscow. Customers queued for six hours to taste the first American fast food served in Russia.[34] As Russia has opened up to the world in the post-Soviet era its taste for Western brands is reflected in a demand for luxury marques like German, Swedish, Italian and Japanese cars, French fragrances and fashion, and Swiss watches.[35] Brand globalisation has seeped across borders in spite of the animosities, alliances and human tragedies of the Second World War less than half a century before McDonald's opened in Moscow. As Snapshot 8.5 shows, national identity can be a powerful force in branding, and the Coca-Cola ad that caused such a media storm for its alleged 'un-American' style illustrated the sensitivities than can sometimes obtain around brands and nations. However, in many cases, it seems that brands have more power to unite than national flags.

The resistance to what is sometimes seen as the cultural imperialism of brands is not always in an Eastern–Western direction. In the 1970s, electronics industries from Japan and Taiwan began to undercut indigenous British and European electronics brands, while in the 1980s Asian car brands began to appear in the giant US car market. In both cases, there was some resentment and some anti-brand activism, although that soon faded away as consumers solved the ideological problem by choosing the best, and the best value, products. Now, there seems to be no resistance at all to Asian brands in the West – indeed, an Asian provenance is regarded as a major positive for brands in many sectors, including food, electronics, beers and cars. Some brands make a virtue of their national origin – for example, American clothes brand American Apparel trumpet the fact that their clothes are made in Los Angeles, California, rather

PHOTO 20 De Beers

Image Courtesy of the Advertising Archives

De Beers advertising (see Snapshot 8.6) is credited with changing the cultural meaning of diamonds not only by making them a symbol of love, commitment and value, but also by instilling the idea that they had to be gifted by the man to the woman to seal the deal (using – according to some ads – at least two months' salary). The first major campaign in the 1940s used the strapline A Diamond Is Forever. This slogan has passed into common usage, in an example of advertising giving symbols and meanings to culture, as well as taking them.

than being made in low labour cost countries like Bangladesh and India. Their 2014 ad called 'Made in Bangladesh'[36] featured a Bangladesh-born employee posing topless in a side-swipe at other clothes companies that outsource their manufacturing.

Global supply chains make brands vulnerable to bad press. Brands including Apple and Nike have received criticism because of the labour practices in low wage countries where they manufacture their goods, while budget clothing brand Primark was heavily criticised when a Bangladesh factory where its clothes were made collapsed in 2013, killing more than 1,100 low paid workers.[37] Western brands can make huge profits by manufacturing in Asia. Since the 1980s, many European jobs have effectively been exported to Asia because of the lack of strong unionisation, low labour costs and high skill levels. Ethically, this presents a dilemma. On the one hand, when a global brand comes to Asia bringing thousands of manufacturing jobs, local wages and conditions will improve. On the other, the gap between local pay and conditions and those that obtain in the West is stark. Even global brands that have the will to do so find it difficult to police labour practices and quality control down the supply chain. Resistance to globalisation often rests on issues such as discriminatory or unfair labour practices, and the unsustainable use of raw materials and environmental damage. In a social media age, negative coverage can quickly gain purchase and credence.

From the brands' point of view, global brands make excellent copy for media editors, and hostile stories make even better copy. It is right that global brand corporations should be subject to close scrutiny regarding their social and environmental responsibility. But there can be little doubt that global brands sometimes become symbolic weapons in media circulation and political contests. The activities and consequences of global brand corporations operating in local cultures is an important area of debate and investigation. It is the global profile itself that makes the corporation both more powerful and more vulnerable to criticism. Our concern here is not with the wider issue of the corporate social responsibility and ethics of big corporations. Nevertheless, the general values of the organisation will influence the perceived values of their brands. Global brand corporations have certain resources and media, especially advertising, under their direct control. They have influence rather than control over others, through PR. Global corporations are acutely aware of the importance of public perception. Consumer movements that turn attention away from consumption of the brand and towards the activities of the producer can be powerful influences on corporate behaviour. Given the sensitivities over the activities of (mainly Western) brand corporations, communications assume great importance in managing or responding to consumer and activist attitudes and expectations.

ADVERTISING MANAGEMENT IN NON-DOMESTIC ECONOMIES

Management of advertising in non-domestic economies presents many challenges then, including the establishment and management of staff, the design of creative executions and media strategy. But it is an effort worth making. Liberalisation of currency controls and capital transfer, increases on global travel, rising middle classes, growth in disposable income and the rise of digital and cable technology have made the world, for brands at least, into a kind of global village in which our senses have become extended through electronic media so that we can experience far-away events and objects as if they are at hand (McLuhan, 1964). The internet, above all, has made brands accessible internationally and sparked global demand. Even where an economy is developing, this does not mean that there are not large and sophisticated consumer markets in the urban centres. Indeed, the rising middle classes of the high growth economies in South and South-East Asia and South America are providing the fastest growth areas for many global brands.

SOUTH AND SOUTH-EAST ASIAN MARKETS FOR ADVERTISING

Asian 'Tiger' economies such as China, South Korea, Taiwan, Thailand, Japan, along with Indonesia, Malaysia and South Asian nations such as India and Pakistan and Bangladesh, all represent important advertising and consumer growth markets for certain brands. Many of the world's most valuable 100 luxury brands[38] are seeing record growth driven by sales in Asian markets (Chada and Husband, 2006). Louis Vuitton tops the list of global luxury brands most years (see Table 8.1), worth around $25 billion, with Hermès, Gucci, Chanel, Rolex, Cartier, Prada, Burberry, Michael Kors and Tiffany worth a combined $75 billion according to some estimates. However, only LV and Chanel were on an upward sales trajectory in 2015, as global economic uncertainty took its toll on sales. It is not only luxury brands that have found trading conditions becoming more difficult in Asia in recent years. Hershey's sales dropped by almost half in 2015, and IKEA, Starbucks, Coach and Apple were unusual among Western brands in finding continuing sales growth in China in late 2016.[39] The Chinese market for Western brands is complex and difficult but holds huge potential. Western brands need a deep knowledge of consumers in different regions of Chinese markets to succeed. The practical difficulties and cultural sensitivities, though, cannot be overlooked. In developing countries, the cultural juxtaposition of Western-influenced consumer advertising and local cultural and economic norms can seem particularly discordant. This demands sensitive handling and detailed local engagement. What is more, as Chinese affluence grows, the market preferences are changing and Western brands cannot take for granted that what worked before will continue to do so without careful attention being paid to the evolution of Chinese consumer markets.

In Malaysia, the advertising market is reflecting global trends in that traditional media still represent the largest part of adspend but the digital advertising sector is growing.[40] Advertising standards in Malaysia are very high with advanced production and creativity, as shown in the showcase of the AAAA.[41] In Malaysia, many magazine ads seem to locate Western consumer values in an Islamic cultural context. Malaysia is a culturally complex country, with three main ethnic groups, Indian, Chinese and Malay. Each has a separate language and many differing traditions, but there is also a great deal of commonality. There are also groups of Thais, Filipinos, Taiwanese and Indonesians. Advertising in such a context has to be distinctively Asian and must conform to local sensitivities. There has been some resentment in Malaysia when global brands use advertising produced for Western markets but dubbed into local language. This is always clearly evident and a lazy way for international brands to advertise overseas,

TABLE 8.1 Top global luxury brands by value (excluding car brands) 2015/2016

2015	2016
1 Louis Vuitton	Louis Vuitton
2 Hermès	Gucci
3 Gucci	Hermés
4 Chanel	Cartier
5 Rolex	
6 Cartier	Coach
7 Prada	Chanel
8 Burberry	Prada
9 Michael Kors	Tiffany
10 Tiffany	Burberry

Sources: Estimates from aggregation of several sources including www.forbes.com/powerful-brands/list/#tab:rank (accessed 29 March 2017)

but it usually results in mockery. Approval for ads is often given directly by government officials. There are detailed codes of practice for the advertising of different products and services. Many other Asian countries such as Singapore also have very diverse ethnic and religious demographics that represent major challenges for brand communication. As Asian affluence increases and Western provenance lessens in its attraction there will be no substitute for detailed local knowledge in order for brands to devise effective global advertising strategies.

SNAPSHOT 8.7

Muslim values in Western-style advertising in Malaysia

A Bahasa fashion magazine has many examples of 'glocal' advertising portraying Western products with Western values but in a creative execution that is adapted to be acceptable to Muslim readers. One product, Johnson's pH5.5 cooling body wash, is intended for use in the shower. However, it would not be allowed to show a photograph of a female in the shower, so the ad shows a woman with naked shoulders in a sensuous pose while a graphic, water-like abstract design fills the background. The model's hair is fixed in place so that she might even be wearing a headscarf. The ad's suggestion of a female in the shower is clear, but the advertisers can claim that it does not show a naked female. Other Malaysian print ads portray females in a way that offers a compromise between the traditional values of home-making and husband-nurturing and the less traditional values of female independence. One ad for a 'Pewani' savings account offered by Bank Islam (in a daily newspaper) promotes a savings account for women with the strapline, 'Nurturing success for today's women'. The visual shows a woman in a traditional headscarf with her husband and children and promotes the idea of the account as a gift to her family. Presumably, the ad has become necessary because more Muslim women in Malaysia are going out to earn money independently from their husbands.

The art of adhering to advertising codes and regulations literally while going beyond them is symbolically a mark of advertising under advanced capitalism. Ads such as the Johnson's ad described above illustrate the ideological force of advertising, which promotes the values of consumption while subtly negotiating, or circumventing, other cultural values. Clearly, capitalism and the ideology of consumption tend to exist in a state of tension with religious and traditional values in Western countries as well as Eastern ones. Advertising persists in spite of this tension partly because it is seen as trivial and benign. It is also the case that the imperative for wealth creation means that advertising is usually seen as a lesser evil than poverty.

Thailand, for example, is a developing country with concentrations of urban wealth contrasting with much rural poverty. Unilever's Dove brand of personal care products sells small sachets of its products to rural consumers who cannot afford the full pack sizes, reflecting the need for Western brands to adapt to the uneven distribution of wealth in Asian markets. In urban areas, though, the Thai economy, consumer culture and media infrastructure are sophisticated, with a highly international outlook. Thailand is a country with a long tradition of valuing Western products as a symbol of social status but Western-style commercialism is not pursued at the expense of Thai cultural values (Tirakhunkovit, 1980). Some ads are distinctively Thai, such as one for Sylvania light bulbs that plays humorously on the Thai belief in ghosts and spirits.[42] Many others, though, reflect the cosmopolitanism of Thai consumer culture. An ad for the Japanese snack food Bun Bun carries Thai-language subtitles, while a Japanese green tea brand runs a charming TVC in Thai.[43] Other brands such as Lays seaweed-flavour crisps, Pote snack food and Giffarine facial cream (a local brand) combine Japanese and Thai influences in their advertising. Thais are also very interested in international brands such as L'Oréal, McDonald's (the 'I'm Lovin' It' jingle is sung in Thai) and Scott toilet tissue (showing the same ad as in the UK). Sony, Samsung and Orange all create Thai advertising executions. Chinese culture influences Thai TV ads for Choice soup mix, Mistine powder for oily skin and Pond's facial foam. The leading Thai brand of cooling powder, St Luke's Prickly Heat, was established by a British entrepreneur.

Asian advertising has been known for being racially insensitive, although this is gradually dying out, and occasional controversies, for example in 2013 over a Dunkin' Donuts ad that featured a white woman in black make-up, and another in 2016 about a black man being washed whiter[44], are now regarded as lapses. In contrast, a great deal of Asian advertising is very sentimental and heartwarming, and one Thai 2013 ad called 'Giving Is the Best Communication'[45] for True Move mobile was shared many times on social media by viewers who loved its sentiment.

Managing a communications campaign in Thailand demands a detailed understanding of the local media infrastructure (Hackley and Hackley, 2013). The Thai advertising industry is a mixture of locally owned agencies and branches of global communications conglomerates such as Saatchi & Saatchi, JWT, Publicis, Dentsu and many others (Tiwsakul, 2008). It has a significant adspend and production standards are as high as in any developed country, as are standards of creativity[46] (Punyapiroje et al., 2002). Advertising content tends to be soft-sell and replete with scenes of humour, fun, sensuousness and love,[47] reflecting the easy-going and creative character of Thai consumers (Supharp, 1993). Typical advertising is often very visual, reflecting low literacy rates among the rural population and indicating the subtleties of tone, image and gesture in visual communication to which Asian consumers are attuned. Thai consumers love freedom and novelty and this is reflected in brand-switching behaviour (Sherer, 1995).

SNAPSHOT 8.8

Levi's and the cultural meaning of denim jeans

There are few examples of brands that have successfully adopted a standardised global advertising strategy. One has to go back some years to find the most striking ones, and few can match the Levi's 501 campaign of the mid-1980s. Bartle Bogle Hegarty's legendary TV campaign for Levi's 501 denim jeans linked the brand to a distinctively American sense of youth, freedom and sexiness, and boosted the denim jeans market by a reputed 800%. The original ad (called 'Laundrette'[48] because it was set in one) was produced to show all over the world. There was no copy or voice-over, so there were no language problems to overcome. There were lots of shots of the jeans, along with many images suggesting their American provenance, many of them evocative of the style that actors such as Marlon Brando and James Dean brought to 1950s Hollywood movies. The ad was played to a classic music track ('I Heard It Through the Grapevine' by Marvin Gaye) that was re-released with the Levi's logo on the record sleeve. The campaign targeted male jeans wearers aged 15–19 as an influential style-leading group. In the ad, a young man enters a laundrette, takes his clothes off down to his boxer shorts and washes them in a machine, then puts them back on. The astonished reactions of the other customers are nicely contrasted by his laconic style.

The stunning success of the 'American hero' style of Levi's ads lasted for a decade until the allure of American provenance faded. The jeans market as a whole eventually lost sales and fragmented into niches, each with a somewhat younger profile and different style values. The Levi's 501 campaign was right for its time and its values seemed to transcend the cultural particularities of the countries in which it was shown. But by the early 1990s the cultural meaning of denim jeans had changed. For young people who had never heard of Brando and Dean and had never seen movies like *Rebel Without*

PHOTO 21 Levi's

Image Courtesy of the Advertising Archives

This is a screen grab of one of the most noted TV ads of the last fifty years, 'Laundrette', by BBH of London (see Snapshot 8.8). The ad for Levi's 501s made a (short-lived) star of the insouciant hero, Nick Kamen, and transformed the fortunes of the ailing brand by associating it with a myth of 1950s America. The campaign increased denim jeans sales across all brands by an estimated 800%. The creative brief specified that the ad had to be shown across the world, because Levi's initially could only afford to make one ad. As a result, the ad was wordless, apart from the lyrics to Marvin Gaye's 'I Heard it Through the Grapevine'.

a Cause the American hero ad style meant nothing. Jeans simply meant comfort and informality. They no longer represented rebellion or any distinctively adolescent virtue: how could they when your dad was wearing them?

Japan is a very different economic, religious and ethnic proposition for brand advertising from that of Malaysia or Thailand. It has a technologically and aesthetically sophisticated consumer culture and high if quirky[49] creative standards in advertising.[50] Japan is a very advanced economy with a diverse and sophisticated consumer culture and the advertising can be richly symbolic. Indeed, symbolism, particularly erotic symbolism in advertising, seems to be a mark of the state of development of the consumer markets it serves and reflects. In one pair of examples two ads for a miniature TV set were shown, each of which appeared in the risqué publication *Fookasu* in 1985 (in Tanaka, 1994: 46–51). In one, the TV set was pictured in a scene with two girls and a man in a sensuous setting. The innuendo is supported by the advertising copy which claims that the satisfaction of curiosity is the key to humankind's development. It goes on, 'Can't do this, can't do that ... there are many things forbidden in this world. What's the point of living unless we can at least watch what we want to when we want to ...' The other ad shows the TV in a scene with two girls embracing over a piano. Sexuality is generally not a subject of public discourse in Asian countries. The magazine or ad agency could easily deflect accusations that they were promoting either in a literal sense. But, as we saw in Chapter 2, much of the power of advertising lies in its ability to suggest meanings that are not accessible unless read by the audience, thus imputing the meaning to audience interpretation rather than to the artifice of the advertiser. The ads were in tune with the risqué editorial tone of the publication in which they appeared. They allowed a mundane item to be portrayed in a way that made it seem, perhaps, far more interesting to some readers.

While these ads are not typical of Japanese advertising as a whole,[51] they do illustrate how advertising can be devised that undermines, or at least evades, local cultural taboos and norms. Consumption can therefore be made to appear as an act of symbolic self-realisation that reinforces individual identity because it (symbolically) transgresses social conventions. This individualistic dimension of consumption is often taken for granted in the West, but in the more collective social culture of the East such implicit individualism may promote and also reflect far-reaching cultural change.

CHAPTER SUMMARY

This chapter has reviewed issues of international advertising, focusing mainly on the managerial perspective. The discussion revolved around the dichotomy of standardised versus localised advertising, taking in issues such as differing local advertising regulations and codes of marketing practice, differences in language and culture, and resistance and protest towards brand 'imperialism'. Another issue touched upon was the cultural role of advertising as a carrier of (Western) consumer ideology, and the tensions this can create where it conflicts with traditional values in particular countries. The chapter concluded with some comments about advertising management in South-East Asia.

REVIEW QUESTIONS

1. In groups, decide upon a local brand that you feel has the potential to be marketed internationally. Decide on the core brand values that may be communicated. Devise an outline advertising strategy with creative themes using integrated media channels. How will you ensure that the brand values are interpreted appropriately? What are the major difficulties of promoting this brand internationally?
2. Choose six print or TV advertisements that promote internationally marketed brands. Discuss the need for globally marketed brands to accommodate cultural differences in their advertising. Use specific examples of cultural differences of behaviour, attitude or social practice to inform your discussion.
3. Try to find examples of advertisements for the same brand in different countries. Compare and contrast the respective ads and try to work out the possible differences in local segmentation and positioning and communication issues.
4. What is glocalisation? In what ways is the concept relevant to advertising internationally? Offer examples to illustrate your points.
5. Try to think of potential international co-branding opportunities. To explore the coherence of the respective brands, you will need to list all the possible connotations of each brand and discuss their various merits both singly and in conjunction with the co-brand. What opportunities do you think might arise from such co-branding initiatives?

VIDEO QUESTIONS

How does global branding impact on advertising in the global economy?
What is standardisation? What is localisation? How does this impact on advertising and promotion?

What challenges do cultural tensions pose for advertising and promotion?
How can these challenges be transformed into opportunities?

CASE STUDY

Adidas and the All Blacks extend their partnership

The German sportswear manufacturer Adidas has been well known in Europe for its sports footwear products for many years, and has a long presence in track and field athletics, boxing and football. More recently it has added rugby, general fitness and street style, along with sports accessories and training gear.[52] Erich Stammer, Adidas President and CEO, says

PHOTO 22 Adidas

Image Courtesy of the Advertising Archives

Adi Dassler, one of the brothers who founded the sports shoe company that become Adidas, was sponsoring top athletes some 50 years before Phil Knight of Nike adopted the quintessential sports marketing technique. When Jesse Owens won gold for the USA with Adolf Hitler in the stands at the Berlin Olympics of 1939, Owens was wearing Dassler's footwear. Adidas still endorses some of the world's top athletes, including (in this 2011 ad) Barcelona's football icon Lionel Messi.

that Adidas's strategy has moved into 'content' in the sense that they seek to provide everything a sportsperson might need for training and performance. Sponsorship of leading athletes and teams has been part of their strategy since Adidas founder, Bavarian shoemaker Adolf 'Adi' Dassler, supplied track and field athletes with footwear from the 'Dassler Brothers' for the 1928 Olympics. In 1932, Adi Dassler persuaded sprint star Jesse Owens to wear his running shoes in the Berlin Olympics in what is thought to be the first sponsorship of a black athlete. The 1932 Berlin Olympics is regarded as a PR disaster for the Nazi Party because Owens, a black American, won four gold medals, making Adolf Hitler's ideology of Aryan supremacy look absurd. The Dassler Brothers joined the Nazi party a year later and their factory supplied footwear and other equipment to the Wehrmacht.[53] After the war, Adi re-named the company Adidas and his older brother, Rudolph, left to found rival sportswear brand Puma. In 1949 the distinctive three stripes were added to Adidas shoes to strengthen them, and this was adopted as the official logo in 1967.[54] Today, the Adidas sponsorship roster includes a long-standing partnership with Lionel Messi in a series of ads in which Messi performs his football magic using Adidas kit, as in the 2013 'Speed of Light' ad[55] and the 2014 'Road to the Fifa World Cup' ad.[56] The Messi branding is as prominent as the Adidas branding in these films.

The partnership that pushed Adidas into the New Zealand rugby market is perhaps their most counter-intuitive. In 1999 Adidas won a contract to supply kit to the famous New Zealand All Blacks rugby team. In 2008, they extended the sponsorship deal until 2019.[57] This was always more than a promotional agreement; it was a cross-national, co-branding initiative. The New Zealand Rugby Football Union (NZRFU) is as interested in globalising the All Blacks brand as Adidas is in globalising the Adidas brand.[58] The association of a German sportswear brand and the New Zealand rugby team might seem incongruous on the face of it, and it initially it met with resistance from the New Zealand media. New Zealand people are passionate about the All Blacks and the team represents the national identity in an emotionally powerful way. Many people felt that a local sponsorship deal would have been more appropriate. The incongruence of the respective national cultures (rugby has few followers and little tradition in Germany) seemed overridden in this case by the linked connotations of the respective brands. Saatchi & Saatchi developed creative executions for advertising that played on the reverence New Zealanders feel for All Black players and reflected the proud winning tradition of the team with TVCs like 'Haka'[59] in 1999 and a 2014 clip called 'Alive With Pride'.[60] Adidas and the All Blacks have agreed to extend their partnership until 2019.[61] This is a mutually beneficial partnership as the All Blacks are themselves on a strategy to globalise the All Black brand. The partnership continues with various content initiatives as well as agreements on kit sales and production, such as the Adidas Rugby series of videos featuring All Blacks legends.[62]

Case questions

1 Using internet sources, describe how Adidas's advertising strategy has evolved to fit with and support its expansion of its product lines and movement into new geographical and sporting markets.

2 In what ways do sporting goods brands leverage their sponsorship deals through advertising and promotion?

3 Rugby is a minor sport in Germany, the game is a national obsession in New Zealand. The Second World War saw the two countries on opposing sides. How do co-branding deals such as the All Blacks and Adidas counter cultural incompatibility? Does the success of this partnership say something about the power of brands (and brand stories) to resolve, or perhaps to obliterate, ideological dilemmas?

USEFUL JOURNAL ARTICLES

(These Sage articles can be accessed on the companion website.)

Cody, K. and Jackson, S. (2014) 'The contested terrain of alcohol sponsorship of sport in New Zealand', *International Review for the Sociology of Sport*, doi: 1012690214526399 (first published March 19, 2014).

Enteen, J.B. (2014) 'Transitioning online: cosmetic surgery tourism in Thailand', *Television & New Media*, 15 (3): 238–49 (first published November 14, 2013).

Harmon, B.E., Blake, C.E., Thrasher, J.F. and Hébert, J.R. (2014) 'An evaluation of diet and physical activity messaging in African American churches', *Health Education & Behavior*, 41 (2): 216–24.

Jiang, M. (2014) 'The business and politics of search engines: a comparative study of Baidu and Google's search results of Internet events in China', *New Media & Society*, 16 (2): 212–33 (first published April 22, 2013).

Shaw, P. and Tan, Y. (2014) 'Race and masculinity: a comparison of Asian and Western models in men's lifestyle magazine advertisements', *Journalism & Mass Communication Quarterly*, 91 (1): 118–38.

Shields, P. (2014) 'Borders as information flows and transnational networks', *Global Media and Communication*, 10 (1): 3–33.

FURTHER READING

Banister, L. (1997) 'Global brands, local contexts', *Admap*, October: 28–30.

De Mooij, M. (2013) *Global Marketing and Advertising: Understanding Cultural Paradoxes*, 4th edn. London: Sage.

De Pelsmacker, P., Geuens, M. and Van den Bergh, J. (2010) *Marketing Communications: A European Perspective*, 4th edn. London: Financial Times/Prentice-Hall.

Hsu Jia-Ling (2008) 'Glocalization and English mixing in advertising in Taiwan: its discourse domains, linguistic patterns, cultural constraints, localized creativity, and socio-psychological effects', *Journal of Creative Communications*, 3: 155–83.

Kobayashi, K. (2012) 'Globalization, corporate nationalism and Japanese cultural intermediaries: representation of *bukatsu* through Nike advertising at the global–local nexus', *International Review for the Sociology of Sport*, 47 (6): 724–42 (first published September 12, 2011).

Levitt, T. (1983) 'The globalization of markets', *Harvard Business Review*, April/May: 92–107.

Motion, J., Leitch, S. and Brodie, R.J. (2003) 'Equity in corporate co-branding: the case of Adidas and the All Blacks', *European Journal of Marketing*, 37 (7/8): 1080–94.

Tanaka, K. (1994) *Advertising Language: A Pragmatic Approach to Advertisements in Britain and Japan*. London: Routledge.

Turow, J. and McAllister, M.P. (eds) (2009) *The Advertising and Consumer Culture Reader*. London: Routledge.

Usunier, J.-C. (2009) *Marketing Across Cultures*. London: Financial Times/Prentice-Hall.

White, C., Oliffe, J.L. and Bottorff, J.L. (2012) 'From the physician to the Marlboro man: masculinity, health, and cigarette advertising in America, 1946–1964', *Men and Masculinities*, 15 (5): 526–47.

NOTES

1 Jacques Bughin and Steven Spittaels, 'Advertising as an economic-growth engine: the new power of media in the digital age', McKinsey and Company, March 2012, http://ovalordapublicidade.apan.pt/McKensey_FinalAdvertising_2012.pdf (accessed 17 March 2017).

2 Ibid.

3 'The case for advertising', Advertising Association, www.adassoc.org.uk/the-case-for-advertising/ (accessed 29 March 2017); see also 'IAA launches the case for advertising', press release, 17 February 2014, www.iaaglobal.org/files/Campaign%20for%20Advertising%20launch%20release%202%2011%2014-FINAL.pdf (accessed 17 March 2017).

4 'The case for advertising: your right to choose', www.iaaglobal.org/YourRightToChoose.aspx (accessed 17 March 2017).

5 'Mobiles to drive faster global advertising growth: Publicis unit', 9 December 2013, www.reuters.com/article/2013/12/09/us-advertising-spend-idUSBRE9B800420131209 (accessed 17 March 2017).

6 Ricardo Bilton, 'The state of mobile ad spending in 5 charts', 23 June 2015, http://digiday.com/media/state-mobile-ad-spending-5-charts/ (accessed 18 March 2017).

7 'Global advertising spending from 2014 to 2020', www.statista.com/statistics/273288/advertising-spending-worldwide/ (accessed 17 March 2017).

8 Christina Bonnington, 'Global smartphone adoption approaches 30 percent', 28 November 2011, www.wired.com/gadgetlab/2011/11/smartphones-feature-phones/ (accessed 17 March 2017).

9 John Heggestuen, 'One in every 5 people in the world own a smartphone, one in every 17 own a tablet', 15 December 2013, www.businessinsider.com/smartphone-and-tablet-penetration-2013-10 (accessed 17 March 2017).

10 Google Adwords, www.google.co.uk/adwords/start/?channel=ha&sourceid=awo&subid=uk-en-ha-aw-skmp0~36361006495&gclid=CJanm4Gqn70CFeXLtAodhwEALQ (accessed 17 March 2017).

11 Facebook Business, www.facebook.com/business/ (accessed 17 March 2017).
12 'Dove real beauty sketches', www.dove.com/uk/stories/campaigns/real-beauty-sketches.html (accessed 17 March 2017).
13 HSBC Chinese New Year ad, 28 January 2012, www.youtube.com/watch?v=CLzFuWuQunQ (accessed 17 March 2017).
14 HSBC ads about culture, 16 June 2011, www.youtube.com/watch?v=ALWwK7Vz4gY (accessed 17 March 2017).
15 VW Get Wings Super Bowl ad, 2 February 2014, www.youtube.com/watch?v=sylr-XHKcPg (accessed 17 March 2017).
16 Heineken Jamaica ad, 15 October 2007, www.youtube.com/watch?v=WmUeeurvXgo (accessed 17 March 2017)
17 'BMW Mini – introducing the new Countryman 2017', 9 November 2016, www.adbreakanthems.com/adverts/bmw-mini-introducing-the-new-countryman-2017/ (accessed 29 March 2017).
18 Michael McCarthy, 'Mini Cooper's road map to fending off surging rivals', 15 August 2013, http://adage.com/article/news/bmw-s-mini-fends-rivals-normal-ads/243609/ (accessed 17 March 2017).
19 Sam Adams, 'Launch of new BMW Mini: we take look back at some of the classic Mini adverts from the past', *The Mirror*, 18 November 2013, www.mirror.co.uk/news/bmw-mini-launch-classic-adverts-2793304 (accessed 17 March 2017).
20 Japanese McDonald's ad, 14 May 2006, www.youtube.com/watch?v=_UKLncvGxQ8 (accessed 17 March 2017).
21 Helen H. Wang, 'Why Barbie stumbled in China and how she could re-invent herself', *Forbes*, 24 October 2012, www.forbes.com/sites/helenwang/2012/10/24/why-barbie-stumbled-in-china-and-how-she-could-re-invent-herself/ (accessed 6 March 2017).
22 'Mattel shuts flagship Shanghai Barbie concept store', 7 March 2011, www.bbc.co.uk/news/business-12670950 (accessed 6 March 2017).
23 Laurie Burkitt, 'Mattel gives Barbie a makeover for China', *Wall Street Journal*, 7 November 2013, http://online.wsj.com/news/articles/SB10001424052702304672404579183324082672770 (accessed 6 March 2017).
24 Bauke Schram, 'Barbie: "The Doll Evolves" as Mattel launches figure with different skin tones and body types', www.ibtimes.co.uk/barbie-doll-evolves-mattel-launches-figure-different-skin-tones-body-types-1540652 (accessed 29 March 2017).
25 Parham Aarabi, 'How brands are using facial recognition to transform marketing', 13 April 2013, https://venturebeat.com/2013/04/13/marketing-facial-recognition/ (accessed 17 March 2017).
26 Julia Kollewe and Sarah Butler, 'Burberry sales hit by Chinese slowdown', *The Guardian*, 15 October 2015, www.theguardian.com/business/2015/oct/15/chinese-slowdown-hits-burberry-sales (accessed 18 March 2017).
27 Catalina Nita, '9 stories behind famous brand names', 18 July 2013, http://impressivemagazine.com/2013/07/18/9-stories-behind-famous-brand-names-origins/ (accessed 19 March 2017).
28 'A short history of the Coca-Cola company', http://assets.coca-colacompany.com/a7/5f/95ccf35a41d8adaf82131f36633c/Coca-Cola_125_years_booklet.pdf (accessed 29 March 2017).
29 15 funniest commercials of all time, 22 July 2013, www.youtube.com/watch?v=ib-Qiyklq-Q (accessed 29 March 2017).

30 Patrick Kevin Day, 'Coca-Cola Super Bowl ad stirs controversy', *Los Angeles Times*, 13 February 2014, www.latimes.com/entertainment/tv/showtracker/la-et-st-coca-cola-super-bowl-ad-stirs-controversy-20140203,0,1361331.story#axzz2sbl6JaIo (accessed 6 February 2017).

31 'The world's most valuable brands', 2017, www.forbes.com/powerful-brands/list/#tab:rank (accessed 29 March 2017).

32 1997 De Beers Diamond commercial, 19 November 2010, www.youtube.com/watch?v=fH9bHq9Cvsc (accessed 19 March 2017).

33 De Beers commercial, 25 June 2006, www.youtube.com/watch?v=4vXHm8TzLzE (accessed 19 March 2017).

34 'Moscow McDonalds', http://bridgetomoscow.com/curious-fact-moscow-mcdonalds (accessed 19 March 2017).

35 Sophie Doran, 'The top 50 most-searched for luxury brands in Russia', 24 May 2012, http://luxurysociety.com/articles/2012/05/the-top-50-most-searched-for-luxury-brands-in-russia (accessed 19 March 2017).

36 Lauren Smith, 'American Apparel release controversial Bangladesh ad', *Glamour*, 10 March 2014, www.glamourmagazine.co.uk/news/fashion/2014/03/10/american-apparel-bangladesh-ad-controversy (accessed 3 July 2017).

37 'Rana Plaza collapse: Primark extends payments to victims', 24 October 2013, www.bbc.com/news/business-24646942 (accessed 19 March 2017).

38 Eliza Brooke, 'Louis Vuitton ranked world's most valuable luxury brand', 27 May 2015, http://fashionista.com/2015/05/louis-vuitton-valuation#! (accessed 29 March 2017).

39 Angela Doland, 'Defying tough times, these four foreign brands are successful in China', 29 June 2015, http://adage.com/article/global-news/foreign-brands-successful-china/299242/ (accessed 29 March 2017).

40 'Malaysia sees digital adspend hike', 25 March 2016, www.warc.com/NewsAndOpinion/News/36461 (accessed 18 July 2017).

41 Creative Showcase, 4As Malaysia, www.aaaa.org.my/index.php/showcase (accessed 22 March 2017).

42 Ghost in Thailand, 25 November 2008, www.youtube.com/watch?v=8fgPTN0E6ys (accessed 19 March 2017).

43 Japanese/Thai tea commercial with caterpillars, 2 September 2005, www.youtube.com/watch?v=TgPmaNMReKQ (accessed 19 March 2017 and www.theguardian.com/world/2016/may/28/china-racist-detergent-advert-outrage (accessed 29 March 2017).

44 Jacob Davidson, 'Dunkin' Donuts ad in Thailand causes uproar', *Time*, 31 August 2013, http://newsfeed.time.com/2013/08/31/dunkin-donuts-ad-causes-uproar-in-thailand/ (accessed 22 March 2017).

45 www.youtube.com/watch?v=GLq_Vp5z9D4 (accessed 18 July 2017).

46 Angela Doland, 'Watch These and Weep: Five Great Thai Ads of 2015', 8 January 2016, http://adage.com/article/creativity-news/great-thai-ads-2015-watch-em-weep/301906/ (accessed 18 July 2017).

47 Ads of the World, 'Thailand', http://adsoftheworld.com/taxonomy/country/thailand (accessed 23 March 2017).

48 John Tylee, 'Levi's "Laundrette" by Bartle Bogle Hegarty', *Campaign*, 1 April 2009, www.campaignlive.co.uk/thework/895156/ (accessed 23 March 2017).

49 'Top 20 Japanese commercials', http://hight3ch.com/top-20-japanese-commercials/ (accessed 19 March 2017).

50 'Ads of Japan: advertisiments and popular Japanese advertising campaigns', http://adsofjapan.com/ (accessed 19 March 2017).

51 Ibid.

52 Adidas, 'History', www.adidas-group.com/en/group/history/ (accessed 18 March 2017).

53 Robert Kuhn and Thomas Thiel, 'The prehistory of Adidas and Puma', *Der Spiegel*, 4 March 2009, www.spiegel.de/international/germany/shoes-and-nazi-bazookas-the-prehistory-of-adidas-and-puma-a-611400.html (accessed 22 March 2017).

54 'How the Adidas logo earned its stripes', 3 February 2014, www.creativebloq.com/logo-design/how-adidas-logo-earned-its-stripes-11135390 (accessed 29 March 2017).

55 Leo Messi – The New Speed of Light – Adidas Football, 31 July 2013, www.youtube.com/watch?v=yjjb_Dy7tXg (accessed 22 March 2017).

56 'Adidas launch long version 2014 FIFA World Cup Brazil™ advert', 12 June 2014, http://news.adidas.com/GLOBAL/Latest-News/World-Cup-Adverts/s/9760c83b-60b8-4c83-b81f-443b8692da06 (accessed 29 March 2017).

57 'Adidas extends All Blacks sponsorship until 2019', 28 November 2008, http://news.adidas.com/GB/Latest-News/ALL/adidas-extends-All-Blacks-sponsorship-until-2019/s/cfed5176-9238-45b9-85c4-fd1f864fde1d (accessed 18 March 2017).

58 Ibid.

59 All Blacks Haka, 2 October 2010, www.youtube.com/watch?v=JUiGF4TGI9w (accessed 18 March 2017).

60 Adidas Rugby TV, www.youtube.com/user/adidasrugbytv (accessed 18 March 2017).

61 'Adidas extends All Blacks sponsorship until 2019'.

62 'The Greatest Partnership: Adidas Rugby', 10 December 2015, www.youtube.com/watch?v=lthTdZ8J-Ho (accessed 29 March 2017).

9 BRANDS ON THE DEFENSIVE – ETHICS AND REGULATION FOR ADVERTISING

CHAPTER OUTLINE

The world is beset with critical environmental, economic and social issues and persisting geo-political tensions. Under convergence, every lobby, organisation and consumer has a voice that can be expressed powerfully through digital communication. Brand organisations must expect, anticipate and engage with complaints, boycotts and other expressions of dissent and dismay. In this highly sensitised environment, global advertising strategies must be informed by an acute sensitivity to advertising and promotional ethics and regulation. Advertising communication has the potential to generate a sense of 'giving offence' on a scale and with an intensity that even the most potent works of art, drama or literature would find hard to match. The chapter outlines some of the major issues of advertising ethics and regulation, and introduces some concepts of moral philosophy that can be of assistance in understanding the ethical dimensions of advertising.

KEY CHAPTER CONTENT

Brands and ethics

Ethics and controversy over advertising

International advertising regulation

Advertising to children

Applied ethics and advertising regulation

Want a primer? Go to https://study.sagepub.com/hackley4e and watch...

***Advertising and Ethics* to learn**
If advertising should be ethical
What it means for advertising to be ethical
What ethical challenges advertising faces
How it can be of advantage to the brand to court controversy
How brands can act ethically responsible while still courting controversy
How a brand can successfully manage an ethical controversy

***Guy Parker – Advertising* Regulation to learn**
What advertising regulators do
How this differs in different countries

***Anthropomorphic Marketing* to learn**
How ethics and regulation are applied in branding

***Advertising and Alcohol* to learn**
What the role of policy and regulation is in advertising

... to tackle the video questions at the end of the chapter.

BRANDS AND ETHICS

Brand managers have a problem. Consumers are fussy and fickle, shareholders are demanding, marketing is expensive, and competitors are ruthless. Sales and market share must be maintained otherwise jobs, livelihoods and pensions will be lost. Who has time for ethics? Marketing, in particular, is often accused of being an ethics-free zone, and advertising is often seen as the dark heart of marketing with concerns about the putatively sinister and manipulative uses of research and subliminal advertising techniques (Packard, 1957; Samuel, 2016). Brands have huge potential to generate confusion, controversy, anger and angst (Klein, 2000; Holt, 2002; Ritzer, 2011). How can brand management possibly pay attention to the minefield of ethical sensitivities as well as protecting the brand's market share? A chapter on ethics in an advertising text might be seen as tokenistic, or worse, it might be seen as a manual for ticking the ethical communications box in corporate social responsibility programmes. If the shareholders, regulators, employees and senior officers of the company, along with the trade press, are all happy, then consumers can look after themselves. Right?

But this mis-characterisation oversimplifies the nature of ethics in management, and it ignores the fact that brands are now in a continuous dialogue with the world (Crane and Matten, 2015). Consumers place great trust in brands, and they expect brands to respond to that trust. Brand managers who ignore this truism place their brands' long-term welfare at risk. The purpose of this chapter is not to caricature or to preach, but to try to tease out some of the complexity entailed in considering the ethical status of advertising and promotion and the ways in which brands engage with consumers' concerns about fairness, honesty, the environment and other ethical issues. There are many topic areas in marketing that connect to ethics, including consumer protection, environmental protection and sustainability, financial reporting, privacy, surveillance and use of data, employment practices and community responsibility. Advertising and promotion agencies of all kinds along with brand marketing organisations need to pay heed to all these and more for both commercial and non-commercial reasons. In this chapter, we will focus mainly on the ethical issues that are particular to advertising and promotional communication. The chapter will argue that this is far more complex than a matter of telling truth or untruth, although standards of truth are unquestionably important in maintaining trust in marketing in general.

We have seen over the past few years that as brand marketing techniques have embraced political and social campaigning, brands find themselves in the firing line for their perceived association with one ideology or another. Earlier in the book we have seen how Nike's 2017 announcement of its sports hijab[1] has excited both ideological support and protest on social media. There is clearly a powerful commercial case for the garment, but it is also an illustration of how even innocuous items such as clothing cannot avoid being seen by some through an ideological lens.[2] In the Chapter 10 case study, we discuss the Dove campaign that has attached itself to ethical issues of women's representation in media and society. Of course, some brands have gone the opposite way and thrived on controversy, such as Ryanair, FCUK, Benetton (see Snapshot 8.3 and this chapter's case study), and Brew Dog.[3] The latter, in particular, seems to have tapped into a trend for anti-politically correct sentiment with a series of public controversies that have served only to bring the craft beer brand to even greater public attention.[4] For most brands, though, controversy and giving offence are things they want to avoid. However, consumer activism and lobbying can be very active and, even though many concerns raised about the conduct of brands are matters of deep importance, it is also true that brands can be great opportunities for lobbyists to earn some publicity for their cause. For every promotional campaign there will probably be some claims of being offended or deceived by the advertising, and further critical comment will be levelled at brands' environmental practices, their pricing or supply chain and labour practices, and their policies and practices on race, gender and disability.

Under convergence, PR and ethics/CSR are intimately connected but they are not the same thing (Crane and Matten, 2015). Dealing with complaints at the level of communication is a PR task. Dealing with the underlying issues is a matter of CSR and brand policy. Brands must accept that, for many consumers, their relationship with a brand is deeply personal, and, equally for many consumers, personal choices are political choices. For example, the VW emissions scandal that exploded in the USA in 2015 has major ongoing implications for the company. Many environmentally concerned consumers felt let down. Trust, and sales in the USA and Europe, have been affected. Nonetheless, the brand still became the world's biggest car brand by sales volume in 2016, overtaking Toyota with some 10.3 million sales.[5] Clearly, when a brand is as global as VW, catastrophic problems in one region do not necessarily dent the global sales picture.

But then again, selling cars is rarely seen as an inherently controversial business and exhaust emissions constitute an arcane technical detail to many consumers. What are the issues around more ethically charged products, such as formerly illegal drugs? The newly legalised marijuana market in the USA is booming[6] in spite of stories emerging of rising health problems associated with marijuana use.[7] At the time of writing, marijuana cultivation and sale in the USA is still a controversial business that isn't quite mainstream, but in time (assuming current or future US administrations don't reverse the legalisation of non-medical use and sale of marijuana) the industry will develop trade associations with PR officers to compete with anti-drug lobby groups in the propaganda wars around drug use. There may be calls for tighter regulation that will be met by counter-arguments insisting that use is a matter for individual judgement. So, this chapter will attempt to offer some frameworks for perhaps not resolving but at least for understanding more clearly some of the ethical issues arising from commercial activity that might impact on global and local advertising strategies.

WESTERN ETHICS APPLIED TO ADVERTISING AND MARKETING

In Western philosophical traditions, ethics refers to what is right, good or consistent with virtue. A related concept concerns justice, in the sense that we would all like to be treated justly and fairly by the organisations with which we deal. The study of ethics is often concerned with abstract principles, and the study of morals is seen as an applied field that focuses on personal behaviour in specific situations. However, the terms are also linked and sometimes used interchangeably, as in 'applied ethics'. Marketing in general offers a variety of ethical issues for consideration, many of them mobilised through advertising (Brenkert, 2008; Hackley et al., 2008; Eagle and Dahl, 2015; Shaw et al., 2016). For example, is it ethically correct to advertise to children using the same techniques that are used when advertising to adults (a problem that particularly exercised Packard, 1957)? Is it right to advertise toys that are not necessarily good for children's development, and which might cost their parents or carers a lot of money? Should advertising be permitted to use imagery and words that shock, offend or insult particular groups? Should advertising intrude on such a large number of social spaces such as roadside billboards, posters and even in-school advertising? Indeed, is advertising intrinsically a medium of exaggeration, mendaciousness and illusion? Should it be permitted at all? These and many more questions arise around advertising.

Advertising communications can commit many acts of dubious ethics in their attempts to seduce us into buying. Some are listed in Table 9.1.

Ethical issues in product or service marketing can be relatively clear-cut in the sense that if, say, a car explodes when shunted from the rear because of a rear-mounted petrol tank, this is clearly dangerous manufacturing practice. If a product or service is injurious to health, such as cigarettes or alcohol, again this is subject to public view and can be handled accordingly. We can probably all agree that things that might harm anyone's health are generally bad, even if some may be legal in some countries, although this runs into the problem that we do sometimes willingly choose to consume things that we know are bad for us. The problem with advertising, as we can see straight away, is that ethical judgements in general are predicated on certain

TABLE 9.1 Some examples of unethical advertising practices

Overselling
Exploitation of vulnerable groups
Deception
Misuse of lists
Intruding on privacy
Promoting negative racial, sexual or gender stereotypes
Promoting prejudice against certain vulnerable groups
Promoting socially or personally harmful values or behaviours
Offending public taste
Exploiting base motives of greed and envy

values and interests that are not universally agreed upon. People cannot agree on matters of secular civil governance that are, on the face of it, quite concrete and substantial, such as the correct penalties for particular crimes or the right way to fund education. How much more difficult is it to agree on the ethical status of an advertisement, especially since all too often, as we saw in Chapter 2, it is far from easy to agree on exactly what the ad means?

ADVERTISING'S PUBLICS

For some people, business is business and one should always be sceptical, even cynical, in assessing commercial claims. *Caveat emptor* or 'buyer beware' is a maxim that could apply here. Another way of putting this is to say don't be a taken for a sucker. Advertising is just trying to sell us stuff, so perhaps we should not be surprised if it sometimes crosses into hyperbole. After all, we often read press or books and watch TV news reports that we regard as exaggerated, inaccurate, one-sided, misleading or even in bad taste, so why should we expect advertising to be any different? On the other hand, just because someone wants to sell you something can they be excused from any ethical standards? Is making money more important than other values? It is all very well to say that buyers in a marketplace have a responsibility to look out for themselves, but should they not also be protected from unscrupulous or mendacious sellers? Furthermore, advertising is a profoundly symbolic communication form that operates in a grey area characterised by polemic, puffery and implicit, rather than explicit suggestion. It is often very hard to reduce advertising claims to truth or lies. What about Axe/Lynx advertising and its claims that the deodorant will make men irresistible to women, or bread advertisements that evoke Victorian values when they are, in fact, made by modern production methods (see Snapshot 9.1)? The question is, to what extent should consumers be regarded as sophisticated readers of advertising?

SNAPSHOT 9.1

Allinson bread and Victorian values[8]

The Real Bread Campaign (RBC) is a food lobby group. RBC contacted the author (C.H.) for support in a complaint they made to the UK advertising regulator, the ASA, about an advertisement on the website of breadmaker Allinson. The ad, made up in sepia with Victorian images, juxtaposed a picture of a pair of hands kneading dough with the line 'Allinson Today'. RBC felt that it misleadingly suggested that the bread was made by Victorian methods, when in fact it is made by modern production methods. The ASA ruled that the complaint was without grounds because consumers would be expected to know that the images were merely part of the branding, and did not literally suggest that human hands were involved in kneading dough as part of the manufacturing process. Advertising regulation tends to hinge on debates about the meaning of ads, which often assumes that they carry distinct meanings, as with legal or scientific material. As we have seen, much advertising carries both ostensive and covert communication used in combination. The precise intended meaning of the ad is left open to interpretation. Cook (2001) uses the example of a British TV ad for Cadbury's Flake chocolate bar to illustrate that ads, like any discourse, have connotations that are subtle and personal. The 1960s Flake campaign[9] was open to a Freudian interpretation, since it used an amusing though sexually risqué visual metaphor. The consumer who points this out is risking the accusation that they are relating their interpretation, not the reality. As Cook (2001: 51) states, the 'assumption that meaning resides in the text quite independently of group or individual perceptions, is depressingly common in discussions of advertising'. Of course, the fact that certain individuals, perhaps even large numbers of individuals, might read particular connotations into an ad is well understood and used as a stratagem by the advertiser. Their indeterminacy of meaning makes ads a more intriguing and more compelling communication. Ads are frequently accused of using sexual suggestiveness and symbolism; they are able to do this without risk of official censure by locating sexual connotation within the covert dimension of the ad, where its presence cannot be objectively proven.

Further complicating advertising ethics is the fact that advertising serves many disparate interests: consumers, manufacturers, media owners, government agencies, charities, the economy as a whole, employers, employees, and so on and so forth. Consequently, deciding whether an ad is ethically acceptable by agreed standards, or unacceptable, can be a complex matter because of the different interests advertising must serve. An ad might be very effective in generating sales, and that is good for the company, its employees, its shareholders and its suppliers. If it is deemed to be an unethical ad, then consumers will be protected if it is banned, but what of the potential harm to the employees, shareholders and so on? Most shares are held by large financial institutions such as pension funds and insurance companies. These financial institutions manage savings schemes and pension funds and invest in businesses. People depend upon these funds for their retirement, health insurance, savings and so on. Hence, advertising is not simply a matter of greedy companies trying to get our money – it is part of the connected economic system into which we pay, and from which we hope to get employment, pay, a lifestyle and eventually, if we're very lucky, income for our retirement.

Even consumer protection is not a simple issue. Which groups, exactly, deserve protection, and from what or whom? Should citizens be protected from advertisers? Or should advertisers (and the income and employment they generate) be protected from citizens who are too easily offended by communications that were not aimed at them? Are there groups that deserve extra protection, such as children, the elderly, the less educated, the poor? And what if they don't want to be protected? For example, smokers of cigarettes cannot be unaware that they are potentially shortening their lives, yet in many countries they pay large taxes on each packet. The taxes are sometimes justified as a public health measure to reduce consumption. But those smokers who do not want to give up smoking would, no doubt, prefer not to pay the taxes on each packet.

Ethical issues in advertising are not confined to the matter of economic relationships. Advertising does not merely sell stuff, as we have seen, it is also a form of social communication that can illustrate, reflect and amplify the social norms and conventional values of its time. Advertising, in the broadest sense, is a historical document detailing changing tastes, fashions, norms and attitudes. It reflects current standards of public taste and decency and modes of public discourse. By implication, from an ethical perspective, we get the advertising we (as in the silent majority) want and deserve. Of course, the 'we' in question is a heterogeneous group with the sharply differing views and values of the communities in which we live. Controversies about advertising, then, can serve a social function as a public forum for revealing fundamental differences between social groups. Advertising also impacts on pressing issues of public policy such as alcohol-related social harm and ill-health, obesity, or lung and heart disease through unhealthy food and smoking, and there are ethical issues around guns, drugs or environmentally damaging products. All can elicit protests from lobby groups promoting a particular cause.

ADVERTISING'S ECONOMIC ROLE

All these potentially problematic issues cannot obscure that fact that advertising exists for a very important reason. It creates wealth, for individuals, for companies and for economies (although the economic justifications for advertising and marketing are also disputed, e.g. Davis, 2013). The regulations surrounding advertising must take account not only of ethical issues but also of the economic functions that advertising putatively fulfils. Advertising performs the indispensable economic functions for capitalist economies of communicating offers to consumers, increasing demand, and facilitating competition and choice.

For whole economies, there is a strong correlation between advertising expenditure growth and growth in GDP.[10] Growth in advertising expenditure reflects general economic confidence and feeds through to increased demand. So, advertising is said to be indispensable to economic growth, wealth and job creation. Without it, competition would be blunted since consumers would not be made aware of the rival offers and product features available. Manufacturers could not communicate

TABLE 9.2 Economic arguments in favour of advertising

Through advertising, it is claimed that producers are able to:
Expand their markets, enter new markets, defend market share
Differentiate offers to target heterogeneous consumer groups
Take advantage of economies of scale to reduce unit production costs
Increase revenue, employment, investment funds and returns to shareholders
Make consumers aware of choices, product qualities and offers
Compete with other producers, lowering prices and stimulating innovation
Contribute to GDP growth and aggregate employment

offers and local monopolies would thrive. Companies would have no incentive to be more efficient or to improve their offer. Advertising is said to be the price we pay for wealth creation. There is an argument that poverty is the greatest evil facing the world and if advertising can help reduce poverty by creating demand, jobs and income then it should not be subject to regulation at all. But for others, advertising is too important not to be regulated since uncontrolled advertising could not only discriminate against minorities and offend public decency, it could also undermine public trust in marketing by making exaggerated or untrue claims.

SNAPSHOT 9.2

Advertising regulation – TV ads for drugs

Advertising regulation differs in different countries depending on local laws. In the USA, for example, DTC TV advertising of controlled prescription-only drugs is permitted, when it is not allowed in many other countries, including the UK. TV ads for drugs create a pull-effect when patients ask their doctors about brand named drugs for particular conditions, putting pressure on the medics to supply those drugs, even though the patients typically have no pharmaceutical knowledge. From the drug companies' point of view, why should they be prevented from using advertising for their legal products? TV advertising is also beginning to be seen for drugs that were, until recently, highly illegal. Many states in the USA have legalised marijuana for personal use[11] either for medical use, for leisure use, or both. *USA Today*[12] reported that a major cable TV operator, Comcast, was to air the world's first TV ads for marijuana, in 2014. The ads were for a website that matched doctors who prescribed marijuana with prospective customers. The ads sought to normalise marijuana purchase for leisure use and were greeted with protests from anti-drug legalisation lobbies. The concession from regulators was to forbid the ads from being aired in children's programming or before 10 p.m. The American marijuana market had grown to around $7 billion in 2016[13] and looks to be on a very strong upward trajectory.

The expression 'public trust in marketing' might have brought a smile to some readers' lips but the role of trust in economic growth should not be underestimated. At a basic level, we need to believe that if we pay for something, we will receive the product we saw in the advertisement. Electronic payment systems require a good deal of trust too, to facilitate the electronic commerce that businesses such as Amazon and many others depend upon. It helps too if we can feel pretty confident that the things an advertisement says about a product or service are substantially true. Trust, in this sense, is a fundamental requirement of commercial communication and a very underestimated component of Western business practice (Harris et al., 2014). The element of trust only becomes apparent when one experiences an economy with very low levels of trust, and the extent to which lack of trust inhibits trade becomes starkly apparent. Advertising is no exception to this rule and it spite of its poor public image, much of it does not tell literal untruths because it would not be in the long-term interests of any advertisers to do so. In the age of social media, bad faith on the part of advertisers is rapidly exposed.

ADVERTISING'S IDEOLOGICAL FRAME

In order to understand our reactions to advertising it is important to appreciate that it has always been a contested area. Two hundred years ago there was public concern at advertising's presence as a form of 'social pollution' in London streets (Hackley and Kitchen, 1999; McFall, 2004). Even in the USA, advertising was not always welcomed with enthusiasm. In particular, early advertising was associated with the large corporations. The activities of these corporations were met with great suspicion, even open hostility, in the USA at the turn of the century. These corporations needed some help to create the public acceptance of mass marketing and mass retailing that they required. It was to advertising agencies that they turned for that help.

Historian Roland Marchand (1985, 1998) has described how the rise of big business in the USA was facilitated by advertising and communication. At the turn of the twentieth century, there were many mergers and acquisitions in US business. As a result there were fewer, bigger corporations. Many Americans regretted the demise of the local high street store and the rise of vast, 'soulless' corporations. As corporations grew, many feared that they posed a threat to American values and institutions such as the church, the family and the local community. Serious questions were asked at presidential level about the activities of these leviathans and their influence over American cultural life. The entrepreneurs who created great corporations such as AT&T, GM, GE, Ford Motors and US Steel were acutely aware of the need to legitimise their activities and manufacture a 'soul' for the new corporatism. Over the following decades a profound transformation took place in the public image of corporations.

From being perceived as potential threats to American values, the giant corporations became the very epitome of those values and a legitimate part of American life. Marchand (1998: 2) points out that this new legitimacy flew in the face of classical economic theory that held that the nature of competitive businesses is that they cannot rise above self-interest or the dictates of the market. As these companies attained extraordinary size and power it became clear that they were no mere slaves to market forces but exercised considerable monopolistic power. Not only did they have to persuade the public of their right to play a part in American life, they also had to create an identity to soften their soulless image. The corporations addressed this pressing problem partly through welfare capitalism and patriarchal initiatives to improve the workforce through education and training. Many corporate PR and advertising campaigns personalised communications to give a human face to the faceless corporation. Anthropomorphism in marketing is by no means confined to corporate communications, but is a mainstay of brand strategy (Brown and Ponsonby-McCabe, 2013).

They also used grand architecture to impress their status and power on the skyline, such as the gothic spectacle of the Woolworth building in New York City and the massive factories of manufacturers such as the Jell-O company and Pillsbury's. Retail emporiums quickly took up the challenge to inspire consumers with the imaginative and evocative use of physical space, for example with John Wanamaker's store in Philadelphia, now occupied by Macy's. Paris has possibly the world's first purpose-built department store, Le Bon Marché, and the stunning La Samaritaine, a blend of art nouveau and art deco, the largest department store in Paris and home of the LMVH luxury goods brand. These cathedrals of consumption invited their guests to trade up in social class, by entering the stores, buying the goods and acquiring the symbolic cultural capital to display in their living room, or on their arm. Architecture became a PR tool as the images were reproduced in posters and on company literature. The semiotic force of architecture helped bring lifestyle consumption to the masses. In a sense, the spaces of retail buildings and headquarters were invested with ideology (discussion in Hackley, 2013a). Sociologists have long understood that spaces are not neutral but can be seen as ideologies that inform the way people think and feel.

Corporate advertising, corporate architecture (that often featured in the advertising) and public relations, then, played a significant part in creating a soul for corporate America. Their advertising agencies produced a stream of imagery and copy on postcards, posters, in magazines and press editorial and, later, on radio portraying the corporations in terms of such values as integrity, service to the community, localism, tradition and moral uprightness. This corporate advertising also served a more pragmatic purpose in helping to produce an internal sense of corporate identity (and a sense of collective purpose) for thousands of employees.

In legitimising capitalist corporatism and selling consumption to citizens as a lifestyle, advertising was central to the development of the marketing ideal of consumer orientation. Advertising and branding have a distinctly ideological character and this can be viewed critically or turned to their advantage (Williamson, 1978; Elliott and Ritson, 1997; Holt, 2002; Holt and Cameron, 2010). To adapt Bernays's (1928) notorious phrase, Western consumers' complicity in and consent to a society based on consumption was manufactured by intermediaries working on behalf of big corporations. As consumers we are taught, through advertising, that branded goods and services reflect our discernment, meet our requirements, and express our social identity. Through responses (or non-responses) to advertising, consumers play a part in the market mechanism and cast a vote in favour of our own personal consumer vision. Consumers' collective sense of self-interest is fired by the drama of consumption played out in advertising. Clearly, in affluent economies most categories of consumer need are not fundamental and absolute, but derivative and relative. Consumer goods are not created by advertising, but the symbolic social status attributed to the ownership and display of goods is (Leiss et al., 1997: 299). Advertising teaches us that the social status of brand attributes is scarce and carries a premium cost. In this important historical sense, advertising has been central to the development of the idea of consumer marketing. The consumer orientation preached by marketing management textbooks can be seen as a continuation of the ideology promoted by the early American corporations. In spite of the practical limits to consumer orientation in large manufacturing organisations, marketing texts nevertheless deploy the rhetoric of consumer orientation to promote a sense of connection between you, the little consumer, and your personal friend, the big corporation. The rise of brands as foci for consumer attention and trust rather than the corporations is merely a continuation of the activity described by Marchand (1998).

The rhetorical force and apparent popularity of marketing rhetoric ('satisfying consumer needs', being 'customer-focused' and 'market-oriented' to serve the 'sovereign consumer') might reflect a continuing need for capitalist corporatism to re-assert its legitimacy amidst a contemporary crisis of confidence in the activities and motives of global business corporations, or it could merely be a reflection of the continuous tension between capitalism and society (Hackley, 2003g). Advertising's success in setting the preconditions for a consumer society has been striking even while organised resistance to global capitalism is evident in the form of sporadic but numerous consumer protests and boycotts (see, for example, Klein, 2000). Capitalism seems to be highly creative in re-inventing itself, although there are many claims today that in an age of neo-liberal economics it has finally exhausted its potential (e.g. Streeck, 2016).

ADVERTISING'S COLLECTIVE EFFECT

On a wider scale, it can be argued that advertising and other forms of promotional communication collectively create the cultural preconditions that lead to consumers' acceptance of marketing and the consumer society (Wernick, 1991; Leiss et al., 2005; Davis, 2013). Of course, marketing communications managers and brand managers are interested only in the efficacy of advertising for their particular brands. However, in order to fully understand advertising's specific effects it is necessary to also appreciate its collective influence. It is a form of communication that, as consumers, we have to learn how to read. There is a level of cultural understanding that is a precondition for interpreting ads. Once we are acculturated to reading advertising texts, experiencing new forms of advertising modifies our understanding of subsequent ads. Advertising and promotion within promotional culture constitute a self-generating system of signs that frames our experience as consumers and places our sense of social identity and economic relations within a consumption-based sign system. By being exposed to different kinds of advertising text over time, consumers are educated to understand advertising in all its complexity and variety, which masks the fact that at one level all advertising promotes the same thing – consumption. The ethical status of advertising and promotion has to be understood in the context of its broader ideological frame. In the end, all advertising is selling one thing only – happiness, through consumption.

ETHICS AND CONTROVERSY OVER ADVERTISING

Interest in the ethics of advertising is not new. There are, for example, letters to London magazine *Punch* expressing disquiet over advertising dating back over 200 years (McFall, 2004). Controversy over the quantity of advertising, over its styles of representation and over the ways in which it seems to wield its influence is not confined to the post-war era. Advertising has, though, grown in volume and now reaches us on many new media technologies that extend ever further into our lives.

We now have interactive technology in the home that can listen to us and purchase what we want when we ask, and even internet-enabled 'things' that can, say, re-stock the fridge when stocks run low, without us even asking.

Amidst these astonishing technological developments in consumer culture, the subjectivity of ethical judgements means that questions of ethics in advertising are clouded in a fog of contrasting opinions, which are often held very strongly indeed. Particular ads or campaigns occasionally become topics of controversy, that is, they attract widely diverging opinions that are expressed in public forums such as newspapers' letter pages, editorials, TV documentaries and even in political debates. Of course, not all controversy over advertising is based on questions of ethics. But many disagreements emerge from differing ethical standpoints. Often, the media stories are given their narrative hook by strongly held opinions about whether an ad or campaign should or should not be permitted, broaching issues of free speech and censorship in regulation. In many cases, the brands are grateful for this coverage since, even though it is critical, it publicises the brand to a far greater extent than the advertisement alone could have done. There are even compilation articles in the media of the top ten most controversial ad campaigns, in which ads that were regarded as especially offensive gain additional media coverage.[14]

SNAPSHOT 9.3

Strategic controversy – or 'purposeful polysemy' in Benetton advertising in the 1980s–1990s

Puntoni et al. (2010) use the term 'purposeful polysemy' to refer to advertising that is deliberately left open to a number of different possible interpretations. Some controversial ads have exploited this polysemy to lead to debates that fire up the media and gain valuable exposure for the brand. There are no better examples of this than Benetton's campaigns in the 1980s and 1990s, which elevated the brand from a regional knitwear producer virtually unheard of outside Italy to one of the world's most recognised global brands in a few short years. The story began with the brand's appointment of photographer Oliviero Toscani, one of Italy's top photographers, who was given control over Benetton's advertising by Luciano Benetton in the early 1980s. He decided to change the focus of Benetton advertising from product to lifestyle. From 1984 the creative executions increasingly carried Toscani's personal agenda of social injustice[15] into the commercial world. The 1984 campaign featured teenagers of different races together with the slogan 'All the Colors of the World'. The print and billboard campaign was distributed by JWT in 14 countries and generated complaints from racists in South Africa and also the USA and UK.

Toscani, suitably encouraged, continued with the 'United Colors of Benetton' theme for subsequent campaigns. From 1989 Benetton took all its advertising production in-house to give it complete independence and control. The ads were consciously provocative to

PHOTO 23 Benetton

Image Courtesy of the Advertising Archives

Olivier Toscani's notorious Benetton campaigns in the 1980s and 90s (see Snapshot 9.3) polarised opinion, and generated extraordinary publicity. As a result, the regional Italian knitwear manufacturer was catapulted into the top rank of global consumer brands in just a few short years. This 1989 example is a typically simple yet telling image that deployed elements of intertextuality and polysemy to bring out contrasting interpretations. Some people complained because they thought the ad showed a white police officer with a black prisoner, but in doing so they simply revealed their own assumptions, and sparked more publicity in the ensuing discussions.

racial sensibilities. They outraged many consumers while continuing to give a massive profile to the Benetton brand. One poster, featuring a black woman holding a white baby to her naked breast, generated such protest in the USA that it was withdrawn. For some consumers it evinced an era of slavery. For others, public breast-feeding itself was offensive. The ad also received more praise than any other Benetton visual and won awards in five European countries. Other ads continued the theme of racial juxtaposition. One featured a black hand handcuffed to a white hand. It generated complaints in Britain where it was assumed that the white hand belonged to a police officer. London Transport refused to display the poster. Toscani created a series of iconic images, including copulating horses, a dying AIDS victim, war images, a newborn baby, and a nun and priest kissing, each of which created a PR furore and raised the brand profile even further, until a campaign in 2000 featuring photographs of prisoners condemned to death in American prisons. Benetton retailers suffered a backlash, some business relationships were ended (e.g. with Sears) and some stores were even vandalised by people sympathetic to the victims of the crimes committed by the prisoners and outraged that the men were featuring as poster models. Toscani left Benetton three months later, after 18 years in charge of their advertising. In 2012 Benetton tried to revise the brand's controversial positioning with a series of ads featuring photo-shopped images of statespeople and religious leaders kissing. Called 'Unhate', the campaign won industry awards[16] although many people were unimpressed and the ads were withdrawn, although the Unhate Foundation continued.

CONTROVERSY AS A PUBLIC RELATIONS TOOL

In some cases, controversy over advertising is nothing more than a marketing technique that leverages extended public relations coverage by generating media chatter. As Snapshot 9.3 discusses, brands with a youthful and edgy positioning know that if they can succeed in antagonising groups other than their own target market there are likely to be useful side-effects, such as free editorial publicity and a stronger brand identity. The letters pages of national newspapers, weblogs, comment threads and Twitter comments can act as forums for strongly held feelings about advertising campaigns that are perceived as being offensive, dishonest or irresponsible. If there seems to be a rising tide of popular opinion complaining about an ad, editorial comment starts to appear in the form of feature articles and opinion pieces in the press and on 'magazine' TV shows. Pretty soon, the brand is all over the media, earning sales and brand presence because of all the free publicity, and delighting its market segment if they like the idea that their brand is edgy. These campaigns exploit the provisional status of advertising as a 'parasitic' communication form that continually challenges discourse conventions of what advertising ought to look like.

Of course, there are risks too, and some deliberately 'edgy' advertisements result in a negative market reaction for the brand.[17] The way the campaign will be received by different groups has to be finely judged, and the tone of the ad needs to fit with the brand values. In this chapter's case study below, the ads for Cadillac and

American Apparel, for example, seem to have been well judged in this respect, in spite of, or rather because of, the irate negative reactions they received on social media. More recently, Scottish beer brand Brew Dog has gained many column inches of media with its controversial campaigns, including the launch of the 'world's first transgender beer' in 2015.[18]

It should also be remembered that controversy over advertising cuts both ways, and can sometimes be used as a platform by the complainant to gain publicity for their interests. For example, complaints about ads based around ethnicity and national identity can mask sentiments that may be racist in their motivation, thus gaining a platform for their views. This was a suspicion with a proportion of the complaints about Benetton ads (see Snapshot 9.3). A more recent parallel example could be the Coca-Cola TV ad shown during the 2014 American Super Bowl[19] that generated complaints because it was too multi-racial and not 'American' enough. As it turned out, the Coca-Cola ad was deemed to be one of the more successful Super Bowl ads that year, although company profit growth was slow in 2014.

Advertising is vulnerable to public disapproval because it is a soft target. Advertising is highly visible and it is easier to draw simplistic cause and effect relationships between advertising and social ills than to look at the more complex underlying socio-economic issues. To some extent, the considerable media coverage of advertising in the form of magazine articles and talk on chat shows, dedicated websites and compilation TV shows, reflects advertising's status as a part of the media complex. It is unsurprising that advertising is often discussed in the editorial content of the popular press and TV shows, given the symbiotic relationship between advertising and other media such as the press, movies and TV entertainment. This profile gives advertising media oxygen that allows both brands and lobby groups to breathe the intoxicating vapours of publicity.

ADVERTISING ETHICALLY PROBLEMATIC PRODUCTS

Some controversies over advertising relate to the nature of the product rather than just to the advertising. Advertising for alcohol, drugs, guns and cigarettes tends to attract close critical scrutiny because of the intrinsically difficult ethical problems surrounding the marketing of those products. For example, an American gun company used an image of Michaelangelo's 'David' holding an Armalite sniper rifle in one advertisement, much to the annoyance of the Italian government. As well as guns, drugs can be controversial in advertising. In the UK, for example, DTC advertising of pharmaceutical drugs is not allowed at all, though in the USA and many other countries it is common. On TV in the USA, prescription drugs are often advertised alongside ads for lawyers who will sue the drug companies for you when the drugs go wrong. For example, in 2014 one of the authors watched American TVCs for testosterone supplement treatments that were juxtaposed with ads from lawyers looking for cases to launch against drug companies on behalf of men who had had heart attacks or strokes as a result of being prescribed testosterone. In the UK, TV advertising for cigarettes has been banned since the 1960s as evidence of the damage of cigarette smoking to health mounted, but it is allowed in many other countries, while (as we note above) TV advertising for marijuana can be seen in some American states.

The World Health Organization (WHO) has called for a worldwide ban on all cigarette advertising. In the UK, the medical lobby the BMA (British Medical Association) has called for a ban on all alcohol advertising.

The WHO argues that where partial bans on cigarette advertising have been instituted, the benefits in terms of lower smoking rates and reduced lung cancers and other diseases are significant. The problem for health authorities is that cigarette companies simply shift resources to different media when necessary. So, for example, when cigarette advertising was banned on UK TV, cigarette manufacturers shifted resources to sports sponsorship and OOH advertising. Advertising bans in general have a poor record of reducing harm in the medium term, unless accompanied by other legal measures. For example, the 2010 Ofcom ban on advertising foods that are high in fat, salt and sugar (HFSS) during TV programmes made for children on UK TV has had no impact on rising obesity rates. On the other side of the debate, pro-smoking campaigners argue that tobacco companies are promoting a legal pursuit that mature individuals have the right to indulge in without interference from the state.

ALCOHOL ADVERTISING

In many countries, alcohol advertising is a source of ethical sensitivity. In most predominantly Muslim countries it is forbidden, as is alcohol consumption, while in many other countries there are limits placed on the type and extent of alcohol promotion. Alcohol advertising has become an area of considerable controversy in the UK because of possible links with increases in alcohol-related diseases such as cirrhosis of the liver and connected social harm such as violence, crime and social disorder. The World Health Organization made alcohol advertising control a key priority in its anti-alcohol campaigns (WHO, 1988, in Nelson and Young, 2001). The sexualisation of alcohol advertising and its role in constructions of gender have been linked with increased alcohol consumption among young people and the promotion of a 'binge' drinking mentality (Szmigin et al., 2008; Hackley et al., 2013). The BMA has repeatedly called for an outright ban on alcohol advertising.

Cigarette advertising changed the historical view of femininity and promoted cigarette smoking as a normal social practice of the liberated and independent woman, and alcohol advertising is seen to be playing a similar role in locating alcohol brands as discursive resources for the construction of female (and male) social identity (Williamson, 1978; Lemle and Mishkind, 1989; Young, 1995; Griffin et al., 2009, 2012). Young people are often thought to be particularly vulnerable to marketing that associates drinking alcohol with social and sexual success (Calfee and Scherage, 1994). The extent of official disapproval reached such a pitch that the Advertising Standards Authority and the Broadcast Committee of Advertising Practice (BCAP) were forced to re-write the code of practice on alcohol advertising in 2006, to try to ensure that it did not link alcohol with social or sexual success or overtly promote drinking to young people (Szmigin et al., 2011). TV campaigns such as those for rum, vodka and other drinks have attracted complaints that their scenes of wild partying so glamorise alcohol consumption that they may implicitly promote high-risk sexual behaviour in both sexes. The ASA responded to the increased sensitivity around alcohol advertising by banning a number of ads and insisting that the codes of practice are strictly adhered to. The alcohol industry has representation on the ASA committee and lobbies in favour of the industry. The Portman Group[20] is an alcohol industry funded body that manages the alcohol industry responses to public policy concern around alcohol advertising and marketing.

GENDER AND ALCOHOL

The representation of gender in UK alcohol TV advertising has turned full circle over the last 30 years. In the 1980s, ads for Hofmeister lager featured a man in a bear suit who was the centre of an admiring crowd of young men and women. The ads featuring the lager drinker as a cool, streetwise and charismatic male character allowed females only to be the grateful objects of male attention. These ads, created by legendary advertising man John Webster (see Snapshot 9.4), replaced those that portrayed females only as domestic drudges. In later campaigns for Archer's, Lambrini and other alcoholic drinks targeted at females it is female drinkers who are portrayed as independent, quick-witted and rebellious. The men portrayed are mere accessories. Such advertising would have been unthinkable in 1960s Britain. One might argue that these ads represent a step forward in gender representation, placing women on an equal footing with men, at least when it comes to drinking. Others would take a different view, since gender remains something to be constructed, and women still have to negotiate complex norms and expectations. Heavy drinking is merely a different scenario for women, and not necessarily an equalising one (Griffin et al., 2012).

The UK Hofmeister beer ads were a turning point in alcohol advertising, not only because they contributed to a major shift in UK beer drinking habits from dark to light beer. They also used imagery attractive to children to advertise adult products. The bear in the ads was a character that children enjoyed and understood. Previously, a man dressed in a hairy bear suit would only have been seen at a children's entertainment aimed at pre-schoolers. The ads took a cultural sign that denoted kids' entertainment and placed it in an adult context in connection with an adult pastime, beer consumption. While the product was not targeted at children, the advertising had become very attractive and memorable to children. Advertising agencies know very well that advertising for adult products and services that is visually or thematically appealing to children can be extremely useful in getting a brand name into a household, hence many financial services products are advertised on kids channels on UK TV.

SNAPSHOT 9.4

UK alcohol advertising and infantilism

UK alcohol advertising has been accused of succumbing to infantilism when it portrays scenes that are appealing to children and/or adolescents. This was not always the case. A London agency formerly called DDB London held the Courage beers account for some

25 years. When the account moved elsewhere the agency produced a compilation video that is a revealing document of social history. The tape runs from the 1970s ads with elderly northern English men enacting scenes of conspiratorial male congeniality in ads for John Smith's Yorkshire Bitter. In these ads stereotypes abound, with men portrayed as big children whose main aim in life is to escape the 'nagging' wife so that they can get together with other men to drink beer and giggle. In the 1980s the trend turns to light beers drunk by younger 'Jack the lad' heroes in watershed advertising moments such as John Webster's Hofmeister bear ads. Webster created many iconic campaigns of that time and was particularly fond of dressing actors up in bear suits – he also created the Sugar Puffs Honey Monster character. Subsequent campaigns for Australian lager brands Foster's and Castlemaine XXXX featured post-apocalyptic scenes reminiscent of the Mad Max movie genre, self-deprecation and ironic humour. The adolescent appeal of alcohol branding intensified throughout the 1990s and beyond. The young British drinkers who are displaying strikingly increased rates of liver and other alcohol-related disease today are the first generation who were toddlers when alcohol advertising on TV started to use imagery that was visually appealing to pre-school children (Hackley et al., 2015).

INTERNATIONAL ADVERTISING REGULATION

It is to be expected that attitudes towards advertising vary in different countries, reflecting differing public standards of propriety and levels of tolerance. Consequently, approaches to advertising regulation differ widely.[21] In some countries there are systems of industry regulation that overlap with legal constraints. In others, advertising is part of a censored broadcasting communication system that is directly overseen by state agencies that have to approve every promotional communication. In many countries there are widely differing standards applied to advertising as regards, for example, the veracity and level of proof required for product claims, the timings and placing of advertising on broadcast and print media, and the portrayals of consumption and language used in advertising content.

SNAPSHOT 9.5

Variability in international advertising codes of practice

Advertising regulation can seem highly inconsistent and even quirky when looked at from a cross-national perspective. At various times, the following regulations have been in force:

- TV advertising for marijuana and Viagra is legal in some American states.
- In some countries of Eastern Europe, alcohol advertising is heavily restricted.
- In Sweden, TV advertising for toys targeted at under 12s is banned.

- Tobacco advertising on TV is banned throughout the European Union (EU).
- In Argentina, all advertising was banned on subscription cable TV channels in January 2004.
- In Austria and Finland the use of children in ads is heavily restricted. Italy banned the use of children in advertising in 2003.
- In many predominantly Muslim nations, women in advertising must be fully clothed and wearing headscarves, and advertising of non-halal food products is not allowed.
- Hungary prohibited the 'use of erotic and sexual elements in advertising for purposes not justified by the object and substance of advertising' and no advertisement 'may be such as to reduce the reputation of the advertising profession or undermine public confidence in the advertising activity'.
- In the UK, alcohol advertisements cannot use actors who appear to be under the age of 18 and they cannot show people drinking quickly; they must sip their drinks.
- In Greece, TV advertising of toys to children is banned between 7 p.m. and 10 p.m.
- An EU directive limits the amount of advertising that can be shown each hour on TV across the EU to under 12 minutes.
- The French advertising regulation body, the Bureau de Vérification de la Publicité (BVP), recommended the withdrawal of a Benetton poster showing a kissing priest and nun in the 1990s. The same poster won an award in the UK.

Regulations such as those in Snapshot 9.5 do tend to change as different lobbies win attention for a particular cause, or as media conditions change. Some of the above regulations may no longer be in force, but new ones may have been substituted. Other issues are governed not by regulation but by conventional practice. For example, UK television advertising tends to be quite conservative as regards nudity or sexual references when compared to advertising in some other European countries such as Sweden, Denmark, France and Germany, but the UK is quite liberal in this respect when compared to advertising on American television.

Advertising regulation is sometimes covered by general rules of thumb as well as by specific codes of practice for particular product categories. For example, the UK ASA, an independent, industry-funded body responsible to the government communications regulator Ofcom, applies a rule that advertising must be 'Legal, Decent, Honest and Truthful', while the Hungarian code of advertising ethics uses the principles 'Lawful, fair and true'. In Australia, the Advertising Standards Bureau[22] has a remit to 'ensure that the general standards of advertising are in line with community values'. In the US the AAAA applies its own code of practice that seeks to be a 'constructive force in business' by not producing advertising that makes false claims, is deceptive or offensive.[23]

UK ADVERTISING REGULATION

Advertising agencies and the sellers of advertising space in the UK agree to be bound by the rulings of the ASA,[24] even though there is no legal requirement for them to do so. The ASA is part of Ofcom, the UK media regulator. The ASA applies the codes of advertising practice that are created by the BCAP. Its remit covers press and print advertising, email and SMS text message advertising, broadcast advertising and also internet advertising where this originates from an identifiable UK-based source. The ASA rulings may not have the force of law but they do offer a quicker, more flexible and more efficient regulatory system than the law could provide. Media owners and ad agencies agree to be bound by the ASA rulings, so if the ASA decides an ad is to be banned, it will be promptly withdrawn.

Advertising must be careful about claims regarding the efficacy of products or services, offers of prizes or guarantees. Advertisements cannot make factual claims that they cannot prove. For example, one famous pet food ad strapline claimed that '8 out of 10 owners said their cats prefer Whiskas', and British Airways (BA) ads used the strapline 'The World's Favourite Airline' for many years. After intervention by the ASA the Whiskas line was qualified to those owners 'who expressed a preference'. If the manufacturer is to continue using that line they must be prepared to set up an experiment that representatives from the ASA can watch to verify the claim. The BA claim was mere hyperbole and after some years the ASA eventually ordered the ads to stop making the claim.

Reading ASA judgements, all of which are published on their website,[25] offers a useful insight into how the voluntary regulatory system works. The complaints also reflect current public tastes and trends. What was acceptable in advertising in the 1950 or 1960 may not be considered acceptable today, and of course, the reverse would also be true – much advertising today would seem excessively coarse or sexualised to a 1960s audience. Alcohol advertising is a particularly powerful indicator of changing social norms, especially with regard to gender relations. Ads that are taken for granted today might well have provoked heated complaints 10 or 20 years ago.

ADVERTISING AND CHILDREN

Advertising and children has become an increasingly problematic issue with many debates around the world as to what the correct regulatory approach should be.[26] Children are increasingly treated by marketers as autonomous consumers with their own discretionary purchasing power independent of their parents (Bassiouni and Hackley, 2016). The ASA code of practice today forbids alcohol ads that use imagery attractive to children, but much alcohol advertising seems to be designed to do exactly that. As noted above, the use of imagery in adult advertising that a short time ago one would only associate with children's shows has become commonplace. Many ads on UK TV use animated cartoon characters but are ostensibly directed at adults to sell, for example, branded chocolate, tea and gas central heating. This is no accident – childish advertising might appeal to the child in the adult, but it also conscripts children into brand consciousness.

The trend towards infantilism in advertising reflects the relentless pursuit of novelty in advertising but also springs from the increasing awareness of brand marketers that children are very important to advertisers of adult products. Children enjoy advertising, they remember it and they discuss it. The attention of a child brings a brand into the household and it then becomes a brand that is considered in household buying decisions. Not only do children influence the household budget, they learn about and become conscious of brands at a very early age. Widespread access to video games, the internet and mobile phones has enabled many children to become more active consumers taking part as agents in their own consumption as well as being agitators 'pestering' parents to buy toys and games (Bassiouni and Hackley, 2014). Research has suggested that children under the age of ten are often unaware that when they are watching TV advertising what they are watching is in fact an offer to buy, but access to the internet might be changing the age at which children become commercially aware.

Advertising industry groups lobby to maintain the freedom of advertisers to target children with responsible advertising (for example, in the USA, the Children's Advertising Review Unit).[27] Other groups try to publicise the potentially damaging effects to children of unrestricted advertising. There are now concerns about the effects of advertising for fast food on growing rates of child (and adult) obesity in the UK and USA, and increasingly in other countries too. There is evidence that where fast food outlets have become established in Asian countries, obesity among children is becoming an issue there as well. In the UK, advertising for foods high in fat, salt and sugar (HFSS) was banned during programming watched by a majority of under-16s. This seems to date to have had a sharp negative effect on commercial television advertising revenues but not on rates of childhood obesity, which continue to rise.

Clearly, the existence of codes of practice and voluntary regulatory regimes does not reassure everyone that the brand marketing and advertising industries are exercising proper social responsibility. Debates about advertising's influence on social issues are invariably clouded in supposition, since there is no proven and direct causal link between advertising and behaviour. Yet, while textbooks have regarded this lack of a causal theory of advertising as a problem, the industry itself has managed very well. In this book there are examples of advertising campaigns for which compelling circumstantial evidence has been gathered showing that they did indeed influence consumer thought and behaviour. Even if this point is accepted, the idea of stricter advertising regulation jars with the freedom of choice that advertising represents. Certain individuals and groups have always been quite favourably disposed towards lifestyles that might be regarded by some as unwise or unhealthy. Advertising presents a smorgasbord of options and consumers have the right to exercise their choices as they see fit. Then again, the ability of consumers, and especially children, to exercise truly individual choice may be sharply circumscribed where there is an acutely asymmetrical power between consumers and brand marketing corporations. For all the marketing textbook rhetoric about consumer sovereignty, consumers clearly do not have multi-million dollar budgets to spread their point of view all over the media.

APPLIED ETHICS AND ADVERTISING REGULATION

Advertising regulation needs to consider ethics but its role is not purely ethical. Public policy regulation is political and pragmatic, while ethics in its pure sense is the study of value in itself. Advertising regulation is a political process in that it acts under the influence of complex interests. The values that influence advertising policy are not always based on those of ethical good but on a trade-off between the competing interests of consumer lobbies and other interest groups, the rights of citizens not to be gratuitously offended by commercial communication. Regulators exist as much to protect advertisers from the wrath of the public as to protect the public from the excesses of advertisers. Nevertheless, there is an implicit ethical dimension to advertising codes of practice. However obscured advertising regulation may be beneath complex webs of interest, its rationale at some level is to make life better or more acceptable in some way than it would otherwise be without regulation, and this coheres with the Platonic ethical notion of universal 'justice'.

If we are to analyse the role of ethics in advertising regulation we need to have some ethical concepts to work with. Ethics is broadly concerned with asking questions about the best or most correct way to live, but using terms such as 'better' carries implicit value judgements that complicate ethical debates. The study of ethics entails thinking about which particular acts, thoughts or practices are consistent with living a life of virtue according to given standards. For many followers of formal religious systems, living the good life means living in accordance with particular moral precepts and codes of behaviour that have been set down by religious authorities. The major world religions all place great importance on these codes and compliance is considered compulsory. Observation of the codes is therefore a matter invested with both individual as well as collective significance. But secular ethical systems deny the need for prescribed codes of behaviour or belief and aver that reason and experience, not religious authority, are an appropriate basis for all moral decisions. Humanism, for example, denies the need for either the fixed codes of morality or the eschatology (doctrine of last things) and moral judgement of formal religions.

Moral precepts are, of course, culturally bound and informed by religious traditions. One could make a crude distinction between the Judaeo-Islamic-Christian traditions on the one hand, and the eastern religions such as Hinduism and the versions of Buddhism found in Japan, China and parts of South-East Asia on the other. Both broad groups of religious traditions promote adherence to abstract moral principles such as honesty, compassion, sobriety, piety, non-violence and so on, supplemented by specific rules about clothing, eating and food preparation, sexual conduct and so forth. The cultural, ethnic, national and religious variations in moral codes mean that advertising can be a particularly sensitive area for ethical disagreement. Advertising has to negotiate religious sensibilities in regions where religion is the chief authority. In the West, where secular values predominate, even in countries with strong religious traditions, the religious point of view, while still important, becomes one among many.

ADVERTISING AND WESTERN ETHICS REVISITED

We might seek some clues as to the ethical status of advertising by looking at the works of ancient and modern philosophers. Advertising is far from new – evidence of promotional communication has been found in the ancient civilisations of Greece and Egypt. Modern advertising has been seen since the development of print media in the West some 400 years ago (although printing itself was first developed in China long before). In general, however, advertising, as an aspect of commerce, escaped the specific attention of ancient philosophers. It is probably fair to say that ancient philosophers would look upon advertising with some considerable disapproval, but we can try to apply some concepts of Western philosophy in a way that might take into account the cultural variability of ethical standards. Advertising could be seen as a part of public communication much as oratory, poetry and plays were in the ancient world. It may be a part of commerce, but advertising is also a part of literature because it entails the creation of public texts and could be viewed in the same light as the street-corner storyteller in that it recounts the myths and legends of its time. Of course on another level it is also analogous to the street hawker, and perhaps sometimes to the bar-room comedian. Advertising in its modern forms panders to popular sensibility, is seen on a wide scale and excites and alters the emotional states and values of those to whom it is directed. The poetry of Homer and the plays of Aeschylus were written to produce a similar effect. In *The Republic* Ancient Greek philosopher Plato specifically mentioned Homer's poetry as a candidate for censorship because of what he saw as its morally degrading influence on young people. There are those today who would take a similarly stringent view of the influence of advertising.

One might infer that Plato would not appreciate advertising, though as a member of the elite social class he had no need to respect the imperatives of commerce. But Aristotle, another famous Greek philosopher, eschewed social engineering in his *Nicomachean Ethics*, written for his son Nicomachus. He seemed to have little paternalistic interest in the improvement of the plebeian classes but, rather, adopted the view that individuals should take a balanced approach to personal ethics based on their own predispositions and needs. Aristotle's view of advertising might be liberal, in the sense that advertising would be seen as but one of the challenges individuals must face in the world. By coming to a moderate accommodation with advertising one reaches an ethical standard that is personal to oneself. Aristotle saw the world as a place full of potential deceit, indulgence and temptation that one must learn to live with ethically. He took no account of the need for vulnerable groups to have some degree of protection from the wiles of the powerful.

Another, more contemporary liberal view came from John Stuart Mill, whose book *On Liberty* (originally published in 1859) famously argued that free and unfettered expression and behaviour were necessary prerequisites for a progressive society in which individuals were free to develop according to their needs and imagination, and hence society as a whole progresses through the free and unfettered interplay of the ideas of individuals. Advertising, it is often claimed, is one form of free expression that should not be regulated. But Mill was aware that some popular voices can drown out those of others and he warned against a 'tyranny of the majority'. In other words, free expression that allowed the loudest and most populist voice to dominate public discourse was not consistent with genuine freedom. Perhaps Mill would have regarded advertising as a tyranny of the majority, because it takes the ordinary person's experience of daily life and reflects it back bathed in the warm glow of consumption. The voice of commerce dominates public discourse and makes alternative (not consumption-oriented) ways of thinking, being and behaving difficult to express amid the hectoring insistence of advertising.

ETHICAL CONCEPTS FOR JUDGING ADVERTISEMENTS: DEONTOLOGY, CONSEQUENTIALISM AND VIRTUE ETHICS

It can be useful to apply Western ethical concepts to advertising not because they offer solutions to debates and arguments over advertising but because they can clarify the ethical issues that are involved. Without some theoretical concepts, it is impossible to move beyond the subjective views of individuals that particular ads are OK, or are not OK. **Deontology**, **consequentialism** and virtue ethics offer us three such useful concepts.

Deontology

The ethical status of an act may be judged according to whether it is regarded as ethically good or bad according to a fixed standard. This often applies to religious systems. For example, if an ad promotes condoms, alcohol, beef or pork, such ads might be deemed unethical by Catholics, Muslims, Hindus and Jews respectively, for whom consumption of these items runs counter to religious teaching. **Deontological** judgements, then, rely on moral values that are seen as given and absolute. Clearly, deontological judgements on the ethical status of advertisements have limited use where there is a wide divergence of views on what is intrinsically good or bad. One could argue that most or all world religions would agree that communication ought to be truthful and just, and not coarse or vulgar, and hence there may be cases where an advertisement might be judged unethical on deontological grounds by most religious and secular moral systems. The problems arise when different moral systems apply different standards. A key point about deontological ethics for advertising is that it is the act in itself, in this case, the advertisement, that may be deemed ethical or unethical. There is no need to consider the motive or the consequences, or perhaps even the context. Hence, arguments that 'it is just advertising' or 'people don't have to look at ads that offend them' would be no defence. If the ad is wrong, it is wrong. On the other hand, being offended by an ad in itself would also be irrelevant unless the ad also contravened a given moral code.

Consequentialism

Consequentialist approaches judge the consequences of an act and not the act in itself. Good or bad in this case may be concerned with positive or negative social effects. For example, an ad promoting the use of condoms to prevent the transmission of sexual diseases might be unethical on deontological grounds to someone who feels that the public depiction of sexual relations in any context is indecent and therefore wrong. However, if the consequences of the ad were that fewer people became infected with sexually transmitted diseases then the consequences of the ad might be judged to be good, at least from the public health point of view. A consequentialist approach seems to be taken by the UK regulator in allowing public service and charities ads that would not be appropriate if the motive was commercial. Some ads shown in UK TV have been quite upsetting, such as depictions of car crashes to encourage people to drive more carefully or to wear seatbelts, and depictions of child cruelty to encourage viewers to donate money to child protection charities. Shocking people ('shockvertising') can get attention but has a poor record of success on a commercial level. There is no proof that it is more successful for promoting charities or public safety, but it seems to be more justifiable as a tactic to get attention in those contexts.

Utilitarianism, the doctrine that acts should be judged on the criterion of the greatest good for the greatest number, is a consequentialist doctrine. Advertising that has socially good or benign consequences would be deemed permissible when judged according to a consequentialist ethical approach. Of course, we still have the problem that both deontological and consequentialist approaches entail value judgements about what is a bad act in itself or what is a good or a bad consequence for the individual or for society. Moreover, some people would argue that advertising as a whole promotes wealth generation and that poverty is the greatest evil for humanity to conquer, therefore all advertising is good on consequentialist grounds. However, most would take issue with giving advertising a free pass on ethics. While it may be good for wealth generation, there are questions to be asked about what prices we are prepared to pay and what compromises we are prepared to consider in order to generate that wealth.

Virtue ethics

Virtue ethics considers the motive of the author of an act. As a general ethical principle, people should be considered as ends not as means. If they are being considered merely as means (to make money) then the ethical status of an act such as an advertisement could be regarded as negative and wrong. On the other hand, if an act such as an advertisement is well intentioned, then it might be regarded as ethically satisfactory even if it contravened fixed moral standards and resulted in negative consequences for some. Aristotle's 'golden mean' is sometimes regarded as an axiom of virtue ethics since he regarded ethical behaviour as relative to personal circumstances. For example, one might consider a coffee brand's offer to give more money to coffee growers as a well-intentioned act that helped consumers feel morally better about drinking the coffee, even if it might not make a huge difference to the coffee growers.

These three concepts help us to identify what we feel is unethical about an ad, if we feel that an ad is wrong in some way. It is useful to be able to state clearly why an ad is ethically satisfactory, or not. Unfortunately, many intractable questions remain. Take the example of TV advertising for marijuana, discussed earlier in this chapter. In whose interests should the ethical status of marijuana advertising be judged? Sale of marijuana earns taxes in the US states where it is legal, and much good can be done with those tax revenues since they can be invested in schools, roads and infrastructure. Marijuana or cannabis advertising could, then, be judged ethically appropriate. It would probably also be supported by consumers who feel that the drug has major health and pain control benefits for people with certain medical conditions. On the other hand, promoting the drug might encourage younger people to try it, and research has suggested that maturing brains can be damaged by marijuana use. Of course, the same can be said of alcohol and cigarettes, and although legal, both are indeed the cause of massive social harm for young and also old people. Will legal marijuana use be the cause of as much social harm as alcohol in 20 years' time?

There is, then, a moral compromise to be reached in advertising, as in life in general, between doing what is right, and doing what is best. The kinds of reasoning applied in judgements about advertising combine moral, social and economic arguments. Which will hold sway depends very much on the way that advertising has been constructed, the creative execution. As Chapter 2 pointed out, what is implied but not explicitly stated in advertising can be powerfully suggestive. The implicit dimension of advertising is often the key area for ethical argument, For example, alcohol ads in the UK may not explicitly encourage young people to drink excessively, and they may not explicitly suggest that young people will be more socially successful and confident if they do drink, but do these ads *imply* these things? Advertising regulation often focuses on the explicit, but there is invariably a process of interpretation. Here we get to the nuance and complexity of advertising communication. For an ethical judgement to be made about an ad, a judgement first has to be agreed upon about what the ad means. This ambiguity is the area that advertising often exploits.

Advertising is ostensibly a persuasive text that links images of health, happiness and success with consumption of marketed brands. Images of social reality are normally confined to news media or government-sponsored campaigns. Oliviero Toscani's Benetton advertising (discussed in Snapshot 9.3) created a new form of cultural communication, but one that generated discomfort. Advertising as a whole is a powerfully ideological form of communication (Elliott and Ritson, 1997). It assimilates signs and symbols into a text that promotes consumption above all else. Toscani's work simultaneously revealed and undermined advertising's ideological character and this created a frisson of unease that, perhaps, showed the profound cultural significance of advertising. The tacit agreements and interpretive consensus that surround the public face of advertising were fractured. Ethical judgements applied to advertising were seen in themselves to be based on highly provisional and culturally sensitive notions of value.

CHAPTER SUMMARY

This chapter has explored advertising ethics and discussed its considerable capacity for generating intense controversy. The chapter discussed some regulatory approaches taken in different countries and offered many examples of advertising that has caused offence and generated complaint. Three concepts from Western moral philosophy were offered as principles to apply to advertising in order to clarify the often subjective reasons behind judgements as to the ethical status of particular advertisements.

REVIEW QUESTIONS

1. How is advertising regulated in the UK? Illustrate how it is applied with examples from the ASA website.
2. Discuss the ethical status, as you see it, of three specific print or TV ads. What ethical concepts might you employ to bring some intellectual clarity to the debate? In your view, do these concepts bring clarity to the debate?
3. Using the ASA website, print off five recent adjudications on ads for which you can obtain printed copies. Ask a group of your peers for their views on the ethical status of each of these ads. Discuss the views expressed and compare them with the ASA adjudications. What do the various opinions reveal about the people who hold them?
4. Is advertising ethical? How can ethical principles be applied fairly with integrity in a diverse, market-driven society? Use practical examples and theoretical concepts to discuss your response to this question.
5. Examine the arguments for and against advertising regulation. What might be the result if advertising were not subject to any regulation at all?

VIDEO QUESTIONS

Should advertising be ethical?
What does it mean for advertising to be ethical?
What are the ethical challenges that advertising face?
How can it be of advantage to the brand to court controversy?
How can brands act ethically responsible while still courting controversy?
How can a brand successfully manage an ethical controversy?

What do advertising regulators do?
How does this differ in different countries?

How are ethics and regualtion applied in branding?

What is the role of policy and regualtion in advertising?

CASE STUDY

Controversial and banned ads[28]

As we saw above in Snapshot 9.3, controversial and 'banned' ads are a topic of interest not only for what they tell us about the limits of public toleration of advertising, but also because of how they are sometimes used to strategic effect by brands. 'Banned' is a term sometimes used to generate PR for a viral ad. Video sharing websites carry anthologies of banned ads, many of which are not banned by any regulatory authority at all but created to be 'edgy' viral content and not intended for broadcast on mass media. Setting aside the venality of some PR campaigns, advertising does have a nice way of shining a light on cultural tensions around communication and representation. Some cultural tensions exist around what should or should not be advertised. As noted above, different cultural and religious traditions sometimes dictate the answer to this question. Others change over time. For example, Snapshot 9.2 shows that marijuana and prescription-only drugs are advertised on American TV. More commonly, the tension occurs around the content of advertising, rather than around the commodity that is advertised. The archetype for this type of campaign was set by Benetton in the 1980s and 1990s (see Snapshot 9.3 above), which used photography more typically seen in news and documentary broadcasting. In effect, the campaign challenged the discourse conventions of advertising. Benetton was followed in its controversial advertising campaigns by FCUK, CK and many other fashion and style brands. All these examples were a huge commercial success for a time, before the novelty faded and the brand positioning became tired.

An ad by a UK gambling company exploited a murder trial being conducted at that time (a case of 'newsjacking') and this generated the most complaints ever seen by the UK advertising regulator, the ASA, to that date, for its tastelessness.[29] The ad offered odds on the defendant being found not guilty. The brand, Paddy Power, has made a successful strategy out of controversial and banned ads, with a long record of profits rising in parallel with outrage.[30] Italian knitwear brand Benetton set the standard for this kind of strategy back in the 1990s but Benetton also found that there are limits to public tolerance when they misjudged the line, lost business and changed back to a more anodyne brand positioning. Giving of offence can work well in generating PR provided the target market is not being offended. Being 'edgy' and controversial can give a brand stronger positioning, as fashion brands CK, FCUK and A&F have demonstrated at various times over the past decade. Cultural theorist and brand commentator Grant McCracken[31] noted that an ad for Cadillac that generated much critical comment for its American exceptionalism was a good ad in the sense that being controversial can be a stronger positioning than trying to be inoffensive to everyone and consequently lacking a strong identity. In another example, US clothing brand American Apparel has a record of highly sensual advertising, which, in March 2014, featured a semi-naked employee who originates from Bangladesh, with the strapline 'Made in Bangladesh'. The ad was a side-swipe at other clothing brands that outsource their manufacturing to South Asia. American Apparel make their clothes in Los Angeles. The ad made the news media globally,[32] generating huge additional publicity. However, it is wise to keep a sense of perspective – many ads that earn major mass media and social media publicity for being complained about generate a mere few hundred complaints, suggesting that it doesn't take very much work from an advertising creative team to leverage millions of pounds' worth of free PR. In 2015, one of the most complained about ads in the UK was a street poster for a protein company picturing a slim woman wearing a bikini with the strapline 'Are you beach body ready'? The ad became a negative icon for gender and body stereotyping and received enormous

PHOTO 24 SimplyBe

Image Courtesy of the Advertising Archives

This 2015 ad for www.simplybe.co.uk fashion retailer intertextually references a notorious weight-loss products ad that made waves in the UK. The original poster (for a brand called Protein World) featured a slim model with the caption 'Are You Beach Body Ready?' There were complaints about the ethics of using a slim model (who probably didn't need weight loss products) to make other women feel insecure about their bodies. The SimplyBe brand caters for sizes 12-32. This magazine ad parodies the Protein World ad to reinforce the brand's own ethos of body confidence and position it as the good guy in the media debate.

critical publicity, and a petition was launched to have it banned that generated scores of thousands of signatures, but initially the ASA only received 380 complaints about it.[33] The company was so delighted at the response they subsequently released the same campaign in the USA.[34] After some months of deliberation, the UK regulator decided that the ad did not, after all, breach its code of practice[35] and the company returned to its theme in 2017 with a similar series of ads in the London Tube.[36]

Case questions

1 What are the risks and opportunities of creating a controversial advertising campaign, and how might the risks be assessed and mitigated?
2 How are the discourse conventions of advertising being challenged by digital media?
3 Can the giving of offence for commercial gain ever be justified?
4 What do controversial ad campaigns tell us about culture?
5 Search 'controversial and banned ads' and try to find three examples that could be judged as unsuccessful and ultimately damaging to the brand. In what ways were these campaigns misjudged?

USEFUL JOURNAL ARTICLES

(These Sage articles can be accessed on the companion website.)

Kendrick, A., Fullerton, J.A. and Jung Kim, Y. (2013) 'Social responsibility in advertising: a marketing communications student perspective', *Journal of Marketing Education*, 35 (2): 141–54.

Nairn, A. and Berthon, P. (2005) 'Affecting adolescence: scrutinizing the link between advertising and segmentation', *Business & Society*, 44 (3): 318–45.

O'Neill, C., Houtman, D. and Aupers, S. (2014) 'Advertising real beer: authenticity claims beyond truth and falsity', *European Journal of Cultural Studies*, doi: 1367549413515254 (first published February 3, 2014).

Ostberg, J. (2010) 'Thou shalt sport a banana in thy pocket: gendered body size ideals in advertising and popular culture', *Marketing Theory*, 10 (1): 45–73.

Phillips, B.J. and McQuarrie, E.F. (2011) 'Contesting the social impact of marketing: a re-characterization of women's fashion advertising', *Marketing Theory*, 11 (2): 99–126.

Prieler, M. (2010) 'Othering, racial hierarchies and identity construction in Japanese television advertising', *International Journal of Cultural Studies*, 13 (5): 511–29.

Winneg, K.M., Hardy, B.W., Gottfried, J.A and Hall Jamieson, K. (2014) 'Deception in third party advertising in the 2012 Presidential campaign', *American Behavioral Scientist*, 58 (4): 524–35.

FURTHER READING

Bassiouni, D. and Hackley, C. (2014) 'Generation Z children's adaptation to digital consumer culture: a critical literature: Review', *Journal of Customer Behaviour*, 13(2): 113–33.

Cayla, J. and Elson, M. (2012) 'Indian consumer *Kaun Hai*? The class-based grammar of Indian advertising', *Journal of Macromarketing*, 32 (3): 295–308.

Hackley, C., Tiwsakul, A. and Preuss, L. (2008) 'An ethical evaluation of product placement – a deceptive practice?', *Business Ethics – A European Review*, 17 (2): 109–20.

Lirola, M.M. and Chovanec, J. (2012) 'The dream of a perfect body come true: multimodality in cosmetic surgery advertising', *Discourse & Society*, 23 (5): 487–507.

Measham, F. and Østergaard, J. (2009) 'The public face of binge drinking: British and Danish young women, recent trends in alcohol consumption and the European binge drinking debate', *Probation Journal*, 56 (4): 415–34.

Pollay, R.W. (1986) 'The distorted mirror – reflections on the unintended consequences of advertising', *Journal of Marketing*, 50(April): 18–36.

Solow, J.L. (2001) 'Exorcising the ghost of cigarette advertising past: collusion, regulation, and fear advertising', *Journal of Macromarketing*, 21: 135–45.

Szmigin, I., Bengry-Howell, A., Griffin, C., Hackley, C. and Mistral, W. (2011) 'Social marketing, individual responsibility and the "culture of intoxication"', *European Journal of Marketing*, 45 (5): 759–79.

NOTES

1 Bernard Banks, 'Why Nike's 'Pro Hijab' is more than just politics', *Fortune*, 11 March 2017, http://fortune.com/2017/03/11/nike-sports-hijab/ (accessed 29 March 2017).

2 Rachel Hosie, 'Nike hijab enrages right-wing joggers: "I will never buy another Nike product again"', *The Independent*, 15 March 2017, www.independent.co.uk/life-style/fashion/nike-hijab-muslim-clothes-line-criticism-after-new-launch-advert-right-wing-a7631091.html (accessed 29 March 2017).

3 Jack Torrance, '5 brands that aren't afraid to court controversy', 2 June 2014, http://realbusiness.co.uk/sales-and-marketing/2014/06/12/5-brands-that-arent-afraid-to-court-controversy/ (accessed 29 March 2017).

4 Cameron Clarke, 'BrewDog's greatest hits – a look at the brand that doesn't give a shit', 30 April 2014, www.thedrum.com/news/2014/04/30/brewdogs-greatest-hits-look-brand-doesnt-give-shit (accessed 29 March 2017); see also William Smale, 'How controversial beer firm BrewDog became so popular', 5 January 2015, www.bbc.co.uk/news/business-30376484 (accessed 30 March 2017).

5 Christoph Rauwald and Jie Ma, 'VW takes global sales crown from Toyota despite diesel crisis', 30 January 2017, www.bloomberg.com/news/articles/2017-01-30/toyota-loses-sales-crown-to-vw-as-threat-of-trade-barriers-looms (accessed 29 March 2017).

6 Ana Swanson and Lazaro Gamio, 'How the price of pot differs in 50 states and 8 major cities', *Washington Post*, 22 June 2015, www.washingtonpost.com/news/wonk/wp/2015/06/22/how-the-price-of-pot-differs-in-50-states-and-8-major-cities/?utm_term=.f51598691cdb (accessed 29 March 2017).

7 Jessica Oh, 'Colorado sees spike in illness linked to marijuana use', 3 January 2017, www.coloradoan.com/story/news/local/colorado/2017/01/03/colorado-sees-spike-illness-linked-marijuana-use/96102776/ (accessed 29 March 2017).

8 Ben Bold, 'ASA rejects Real Bread Campaign claims that Allinson misled consumers', 19 September 2012, www.campaignlive.co.uk/news/1150466/asa-rejects-real-bread-campaign-claims-allinson-misled-consumers/ (accessed 4 March 2017).

9 1960s Flake ad, 12 August 2009, www.youtube.com/watch?v=6mYr90nCFZE (accessed 4 March 2017).

10 Jacques Bughin and Steven Spittaels, 'Advertising as an economic-growth engine: the new power of media in the digital age', McKinsey and Company, March 2012, http://ovalordapublicidade.apan.pt/McKensey_FinalAdvertising_2012.pdf (accessed 8 March 2017).

11 'Marijuana legalization makes TV commercials funny', www.bloomberg.com/news/2014-03-04/marijuana-legalization-makes-tv-commercials-funny.html (accessed 6 March 2017).

12 Rick Hampson, 'TV spots pitch medical marijuana', *USA Today*, 3 March 2014, www.usatoday.com/story/news/nation/2014/03/03/marijuana-medical-legalization-pot-advertisement/5982815/ (accessed 4 March 2017); see also 'First marijuana commercial debuts on major network', 26 February 2014, www.youtube.com/watch?v=jyzxs33B6FA (accessed 6 March 2017).

13 Tom Huddleston, 'Legal marijuana sales could hit $6.7 billion in 2016', *Fortune*, 1 February 2016, http://fortune.com/2016/02/01/marijuana-sales-legal/ (accessed 30 March 2017).

14 '20+ most controversial print advertisements', 18 June 2014, https://designbump.com/20-most-controversial-print-advertisements/ (accessed 30 March 2017).

15 Rosie Tompkins, 'Oliviero Toscani: "There are no shocking pictures, only shocking reality"', 19 August 2010, www.cnn.com/2010/WORLD/europe/08/13/oliviero.toscani/index.html (accessed 9 March 2017).

16 'Benetton "Unhate" campaign, featuring world leaders kissing, wins Cannes Ad Festival Award', 2 February 2016, www.huffingtonpost.com/2012/06/20/benetton-unhate-campaign-cannes-ad-festival-award_n_1613757.html (accessed 9 March 2017).

17 '9 controversial ads that overshadowed their product', www.businessinsurance.org/9-controversial-ads-that-overshadowed-their-product/ (accessed 4 March 2017).

18 Michal Addady, 'This craft brewer's "transgender" beer is causing controversy', *Fortune*, 6 November 2015, http://fortune.com/2015/11/06/brewdog-transgender-beer/ (accessed 30 March 2017).

19 Jolie Lee, 'Coca-Cola Super Bowl ad: Can you believe this reaction?', *USA Today*, 4 February 2014, www.usatoday.com/story/news/nation-now/2014/02/03/coca-cola-ad-super-bowl-racism/5177463/ (accessed 9 March 2017).

20 www.portmangroup.org.uk/ (accessed 8 March 2017).

21 National Media Regulation Authorities, www.international-television.org/regulation.html (accessed 4 March 2017).

22 www.adstandards.com.au/ (accessed 5 March 2017).

23 '4A's standards of practice', 14 October 2016, www.aaaa.org/4as-standards-practice/ (accessed 18 July 2017).

24 www.asa.org.uk/ (accessed 5 March 2017).

25 ASA Rulings, www.asa.org.uk/Rulings/Adjudications.aspx (accessed 8 March 2017).

26 'Cookie Monster crumbles', *The Economist*, 23 November 2013, www.economist.com/news/international/21590489-are-children-fair-game-sophisticated-and-relentless-marketing-techniques-many (accessed 7 March 2017).

27 www.asrcreviews.org/ (accessed 8 March 2017).

28 Gemma Aldridge, 'Hard-hitting TV ads: the 10 most controversial commercials – video', *The Mirror*, 26 February 2014, www.mirror.co.uk/tv/tv-news/save-children-advert-10-most-3184308 (accessed 4 March 2017); 'Controversial adverts', www.huffingtonpost.co.uk/news/controversial-adverts/ (accessed 18 July 2017).

29 Mark Sweney, 'Paddy Power's Oscar Pistorius ad to be pulled after record 5,200 complaints', *The Guardian*, 5 March 2014, www.theguardian.com/media/2014/mar/05/paddy-power-oscar-pistorius-ad-withdrawn-immediate-effect (accessed 30 March 2017).

30 Top 5 most controversial Paddy Power adverts, 3 December 2015, www.youtube.com/watch?v=WehTEgyfkzk (accessed 31 March 2017); see also 'Paddy Power's 10 most controversial adverts', *The Telegraph*, 29 August 2012, www.telegraph.co.uk/finance/newsbysector/retailandconsumer/9506027/Paddy-Powers-10-most-controversial-adverts.html (accessed 7 March 2017).

31 Grant McCracken, 'Provocative Cadillac, rescuing the brand from bland', *Harvard Business Review*, 4 March 2014, http://blogs.hbr.org/2014/03/provocative-cadillac-rescuing-the-brand-from-bland/ (accessed 7 March 2017).

32 Misty While Sidell, '"I was fully comfortable with the photo shoot": meet the topless Muslim model from American Apparel's controversial new ad', Mail Online, 10 March 2014, www.dailymail.co.uk/femail/article-2576055/EXCLUSIVE-I-fully-comfortable-photo-shoot-Meet-topless-Muslim-model-American-Apparels-controversial-new-ad.html (accessed 9 March 2017).

33 Adam Sherwin, 'Top ten most controversial adverts revealed', *The Independent*, 23 February 2016, www.independent.co.uk/arts-entertainment/tv/news/top-ten-most-controversial-adverts-revealed-a6889726.html (accessed 30 March 2017).

34 Peter Holley, 'Banned in Britain, ad arrives in N.Y. with a controversial question: "Are you beach body ready?"' *Washington Post*, 30 May 2015, www.washingtonpost.com/news/morning-mix/wp/2015/05/30/banned-in-britain-ad-arrives-in-n-y-with-a-controversial-question-are-you-beach-body-ready/?utm_term=.f0c8b41f9f81 (accessed 30 March 2017).

35 '"Beach body ready" advert not offensive, rules watchdog', 1 July 2015, www.bbc.co.uk/news/uk-33340301 (accessed 30 March 2017).

36 Gordon Hurd, 'Controversial body-shaming brand at it again with new Khloé Kardashian ad', 16 February 2017, www.yahoo.com/style/khloe-kardashian-body-shaming-protein-world-052255039.html (accessed 30 March 2017).

ADVERTISING RESEARCH

CHAPTER OUTLINE

Advertising agencies act as intermediaries between consumers and brand marketing organisations of all kinds. To fulfil this role they need to acquire sophisticated research skills in order to generate actionable insights into brands, markets, consumers and communication. As Chapter 2 indicated, the aims, methods, purpose and relevance of research in marketing are all matters for intense debate, and it is no different in advertising and promotional agencies. This chapter outlines the key research techniques used in the field and sets this within a discussion of the major debates about the methods and the uses of research in advertising and promotional communication.

KEY CHAPTER CONTENT

Research in advertising: role, issues and origins

Types of advertising research

Uses of advertising research

Research ethics

Want a primer? Go to https://study.sagepub.com/hackley4e and watch...

Fran Cassidy – Content in Advertising **to learn**
What the objectives and challenges are in media research
What different ways media research can be conducted

... to tackle the video questions at the end of the chapter.

ROLE AND PURPOSES OF RESEARCH IN ADVERTISING

It is axiomatic that research is the foundation of effective advertising. Advertising communication that is effective is usually grounded in an experiential truth that will resonate with the target audience. Major advertising industry bodies reflect this ethos, for example in the David Ogilvy Awards given by the Advertising Research Foundation (ARF) for the most powerful advertising research and named after an industry pioneer of the role of research in advertising.[1] Effective promotional campaigns of all kinds are based on knowledge of who the target market segment is, where they are, what they do, what they like and dislike, and how they think and behave. Agencies also need a wide and deep understanding of the market in which the brand operates, the competition and the wider economic conditions in order to craft strategically astute and effective communication campaigns.[2] Finally, agencies need methods for pre-testing advertising executions and post-testing campaign effectiveness against agreed objectives in order to reassure their clients.

Advertising is a knowledge business and research is used in advertising to generate the knowledge and insight that agencies need (Okazaki, 2014; Katz, 2017). Knowledge and insight gained through research are treated as if they are more robust and transparent than mere opinion, hearsay or speculation. Knowledge gained through research should be systematic, coherent and evidence-based, and should be communicable. It should be systematic in the sense that there should be a research framework that raises the knowledge thus generated above the level of mere supposition. It should be coherent in that the framework or method should make sense in terms of the kind of knowledge that is to be generated, and it should be evidence-based in that it should be supported by facts about the world. Finally, it should be communicable because the most important role of social research is not to generate new knowledge but to make existing knowledge public. In advertising, it is not enough to have a penetrating insight giving a hook of reality upon which to hang the fantasy of advertising. That hook of reality that underpins the advertising strategy must be clearly understood by the client team as well as the agency team, so that the reasoning behind the campaign can be articulated, discussed and justified.

SNAPSHOT 10.1

Syndicated panel data and store data

Advertising agencies do not always commission or carry out their own research. They also buy the use of secondary data that are produced by commercial research organisations. Major research companies such as Nielsen[3] and TNS Global[4] publish syndicated panel data based on continuous surveys of consumers. Studies may investigate trends in, for example, household brand shopping and usage, TV viewing, radio listening or internet usage. The information contained in these surveys can be useful for advertising professionals to understand the underlying trends and behaviours that are typical in a given product or service category to help brand clients on decisions such as advertising strategy and targeting.

It is important to distinguish panel data from store data. Store data are gathered from retailers and show exactly what customers are buying day-by-day, pack sizes, brands, categories and so on. If the customer has a loyalty card these scanner data can be cross-matched with customer profiles to break down into demographic segments, depending on the detail of the customer profile. Store data can track volume sales in different stores, which can be particularly useful for measuring the effects of regional retail price and sales promotions.

Panel data, in contrast, are based not on store sales but on households. This means that households who sign up to a panel will be giving daily information through diaries or other means on what they buy, who buys it and how frequently. The detailed demographic information means that deeper insights can be generated than from store data. On the other hand, panels are necessarily limited in size and self-selecting, limiting the extent to which the results can be generalised. Panel data analysis focuses on four elements: penetration (the percentage of total households that have bought an item), buying rate (the average amount bought by households over a time period), purchase frequency (the number of an item bought by a household over a year) and purchase size (the amount of an item bought on each buying occasion).

Research in advertising is undertaken to improve the effectiveness of communication by, for example, generating ideas and inspiration for strategy and creativity, for keeping abreast of consumer trends, for filling in gaps in knowledge outside the immediate field of expertise, for enhancing creative development by generating ideas, for testing creative executions, and for monitoring campaign effectiveness. Advertising research includes the use of secondary sources such as panel data and market reports, and also primary research methods such as focus groups, depth interviews, ethnographies and video ethnography, projective studies, discourse analysis and content analysis of internet sources such as chat, comment threads and Twitter trends, observation research, street or online surveys and consumer panel 'link' tests, prompted and unprompted recall tests, ethnographies, eye-tracking and psycho-galvanometer tests, neuro-psychological MRI scans and other laboratory methods, and many more.

Research in advertising uses broadly the same methods as market research but the conditions under which it is used and the objectives are somewhat different. Typically, research in advertising is pragmatic, time-constrained and a means to an end rather than an end in itself. Consequently, it may not conform to the usual sequence of research in marketing (see Table 10.1). Research in advertising has to be less formal and more flexible than commissioned market research projects because it has to be undertaken within a condensed timescale and, sometimes, without a formal budget – it is a cost to the agency because the client is paying for advertising and promotion, not for consumer insights. If the client wants research, they will usually go to a specialist research provider. The agency needs the insights from research, though, to inform

TABLE 10.1 The five main stages for research in marketing

1	Defining the research problem
2	Setting research objectives
3	Deciding on the research method
4	Collecting data and analysing results
5	Presenting findings

its creative execution and enhance the effectiveness of its campaigns. In advertising, the research problem definition and research objectives will often be very broad and exploratory, particularly in the early stages of the advertising development process. The research method will often be a default method given the budget and time constraints – for example, secondary sources such as panel data and discussion/focus groups for initial brand and market research with target consumers. Data collection and analysis will often be done rapidly and informally by the account planner in discussion with the rest of the team – for example, focus groups might be videoed and the videos replayed to the group. The findings, similarly, will not necessarily be formally presented within the account team, but the key insights that underpin the communication strategy may eventually be presented more formally to the client at one of the client meetings.

Another reason why research in advertising can be less formal than traditional market research is that research in advertising agencies is contested and political. The different disciplines involved in making advertising have very different perspectives on what constitutes a valid insight (Hackley, 2008). To make matters even more complex, there is an inherent tension between formal research as part of bureaucratic business processes, and creativity. Advertising and promotion agencies are ideas factories and the ideas can come from anywhere, or indeed, ideas can come out of nowhere, but clients need to see accountability, process and evidence. This tension in advertising as a creative and cultural industry can be productive, and it can also be destructive.

There are widely diverging opinions about the role and methods of research in advertising. In agencies, knowledge – about the market and the consumer, about communication, and about the brand – is a hotly contested area. The winners are the people who get their ideas put into action in a campaign. As we noted in Chapter 4, different agency disciplines often carry quite different implicit assumptions into their work. Advertising agencies are not known as places where a meeting of minds is the daily norm. More often, the relevance and implications of research findings are matters of passionate debate. There is a view among some practitioners that research in advertising is often used in the same way that a drunk uses a lamp post, i.e. for support rather than illumination. Clarity about the aims, purpose and also the limitations of research can help to focus the illumination it can offer.

Research in advertising is important for client–agency relationships because clients are more likely to accept the agency's strategic advice if it is backed up with evidence from research findings. In this chapter we will try to negotiate a route through this complex area to outline the most commonly used research approaches in advertising and promotional communication. We will also examine the key areas of contest and debate around the uses of research in the field.

ORIGINS OF ADVERTISING RESEARCH

Advertising research has a long history (Fox, 1984; McDonald and Scott, 2007; Schwarzkopf, 2011). Advertising agencies established their own research departments as they grew the services they offered to clients, and the distinct fields of audience, attitude, opinion, market, media and consumer research evolved. In time, many advertising agency research departments grew to become independent and successful businesses in their own right. Many of today's leading market and consumer research agencies were originally advertising agency research departments. Agencies need to know as much as possible about the client's business, the market sector and the relevant consumers before devising an advertising strategy. The advertising legend David Ogilvy points this out when he refers to the need for advertisers to 'do their homework', in other words, to find out as much about the consumer as they can before trying to devise solutions for the client (Ogilvy, 1983).

According to Richards et al. (2000: 20), US agency group JWT began to commission research in 1916 to acquire greater understanding of the social and demographic trends and structures that formed consumer groups. Universities were sometimes called upon to add methodological sophistication. For example, the behavioural psychologist John B. Watson was diverted from his university career to become an advertising man for JWT. Behavioural psychology aspired to provide a unified theory of human learning and behaviour. If the behaviourists were right, then ads could be conceived in terms of behavioural control, changing human behaviour through **operant conditioning** and behavioural reinforcement without the need for the added complication of consumers who think. Many other academic social science research methods from disciplines including cognitive psychology, sociology, anthropology, neuropsychology and literary studies have been adapted for use in advertising. Examples include attitude measurement, ethnography, surveys, MRI scanning and discourse analysis, respectively.

TYPES OF ADVERTISING RESEARCH

'Research showed that' is a phrase often invoked in debates as a rhetorical device intended to end the argument. Research carries great authority to justify courses of action, but the truth about research is that it is based on a lot of opinions. That is not to dismiss its value – indeed, it is essential in advertising, as it is in countless other areas of science, public policy, health and social work, and commerce. But it is important that anyone who uses research understands some underlying principles, because without that understanding it is impossible to make informed judgements about how much weight to give to research findings in strategy decisions.

While this is not the place for a section on philosophy of science, it is worth noting one particular source of tension in advertising research. Creative professionals often feel that formal research fails to capture the essence of consumer experience. As a result, they feel that it measures things that are not relevant. Of course, for creatives, 'research' is just a word used when they're being told their idea is no good, as in 'research showed that' a panel of consumers didn't like their creative execution (Hackley and Kover, 2007). Many feel that their informal and personal engagement with consumer culture, aided by their creative intuition, is enough. They watch the movies, they engage with popular media, they avidly follow consumer cultural trends and they bring their eclectic intellectual and aesthetic interests to bear on their work. The intuitive understanding of top creative people is built on wide and eclectic interests. It is also based on characteristics such as a capacity for hard work, an acute sense of observation, high intelligence, intellectual flexibility and the ability to work under pressure (Ogilvy, 1963; McKeil, 1985; Wilmshurst and Mackay, 1999). Research, for many creatives, represents the bureaucratisation of a cultural and creative industry, it is a means of imposing managerial control (Lears, 1994). Research is necessary for business people to justify broad budget decisions, but many creatives feel that it doesn't necessarily help to improve the work. Indeed, many feel that research acts as an impediment to risk-taking and creativity. They see it as a futile attempt to explain myths with science.

Of course, to many clients, both risk-taking and creativity are anathema, and the idea that they are propagating myths would astound them. They want certainty. For many on the account management and the client side, research is a tool to keep creatives under control, so that they do work for the client rather than for themselves. A more balanced perspective is that research is necessary but should be treated with care. It can tell creatives things they need to know, such as to whom they need to speak, and it broadens their range by enabling them to communicate with cultural milieu outside their personal experience. Research gives clients something to work with other than blind faith, and it enables them to justify promotional budgets to main board members, shareholders and other stakeholders. For clients, research cannot guarantee success in marketing initiatives, but it does provide a means of managing risk by helping to eliminate really bad work.

The question for advertising agencies, then, is not whether they should use research, but how to use it. This is why it is important that agencies have a good understanding of the details of social scientific methods of data gathering and data interpretation. The following section will not develop detailed methods but, rather, will outline some important principles in research for advertising.

PRIMARY AND SECONDARY RESEARCH

There is an important role for secondary research in advertising. Secondary research entails using information sources that are already published, and there are many to choose from for advertising that deals with market data, continuous consumer panels, opinion surveys, media and audience research and demographic studies, from companies like Nielsen, YouGov, WARC, ARF, BRAD (formerly British Rate and Data) and

BARB, from government statistical sources, and many others. For example, BARB will tell media planners what shows UK TV viewers are watching, how long they watch, and what audience share each show achieves[5] week-by-week, while Mintel carries market reports and panel surveys, and provides competitive intelligence.[6]

Secondary research such as continuous consumer panel data can be expensive. However, it is usually cheaper, and certainly much quicker to access, than commissioning primary research studies. Secondary sources are very useful for building an initial platform of understanding about a brand, its competitive market situation, and general issues of the buying patterns of target consumers.

SNAPSHOT 10.2

VW advertising strategy driven by focus group insights

Volkswagen has earned fame for the groundbreaking creativity of its advertising from Bill Bernbach's iconic VW ads in the 1960s to its Game Day American Superbowl ads.[7] The brand is now the biggest car seller in the world in spite of the 2015 exhaust emission scandal in the USA.[8] In a multi award-winning European campaign, focus groups conducted with car consumers by the ad agency BMP DDB revealed two related insights that drove the advertising for the VW Polo and Golf ranges for two decades. Firstly, the research found that consumers thought they were quite knowledgeable about car prices, but in fact they had very little knowledge about actual pricing structures. Secondly, the research found that consumers had an impression that VW cars were more expensive than other cars in their class. In the case of the (then) new VW small car range, this was incorrect. However, the perception clearly held advantages, since it carried an implication of superior quality. The creative problem was compounded because consumers in Europe and the UK were resistant to advertising that emphasised a price benefit. Not only that, but creative staff in ad agencies are usually bored by a brief that asked them to merely say that 'this price is lower than the others' (called 'a prices brief') because of the perception that little creatively interesting can be done with a prices brief. As a solution the agency produced a creative brief that described a need to make ads that were telling but off-beat in their quirky humour. With humour, the campaign could convey the message about price without alienating or boring consumers. The brief resulted in a campaign that ran for over ten years, based on funny ways to tell consumers that they were wrong about VW pricing. Awards were won and VW increased its market share substantially. The research insight that drove the creative work was derived from qualitative data, interpreted creatively by the agency account planner. A 2014 UK ad for VW called 'Shark Cage' turned the prices brief on its head, not claiming that VWs are less expensive than one expects, but pointing out the risks of going for the cheaper alternative.[9]

Primary research studies (see Snapshot 10.2 above) produce new data for specific purposes. They can be useful since they generate proprietary data – no competitors have access to these data, so primary studies can generate a competitive advantage.

They are also useful because they can focus on a specific set of questions and a specific sample that are directly relevant for a particular brief. They are, though, time-consuming and they require specialist expertise. Primary studies can be flexible. For example, many advertising agencies use 'focus' or discussion groups as a default method of primary data gathering during creative development, not because they offer generalisable or even robust findings, but because they provide stimulation for ideas. Discussion groups can be organised and executed rapidly using agencies that keep a roster of participants from various demographic groups. The agency can use them either to explore consumption practices among a small but representative group, or to get consumer feedback on ideas in development.

QUALITATIVE AND QUANTITATIVE DATA

Advertising and promotional agencies make use of both quantitative and qualitative data in their research. Quantitative data consist of numbers and can be analysed with statistical methods and broken down into bar charts and line graphs. Qualitative data consist of words, pictures, videos, audio recordings, typed interview transcripts and so on, and therefore cannot easily be analysed statistically (although some forms of content analysis can enable a quantitative analysis of qualitative data sets). In the era of convergence, the rise of digital media is creating a vast new area for numerical analysis given the big data sources that now exist for analysing online consumer behaviour.

SNAPSHOT 10.3

Qualitative vs quantitative research

One leading London agency has stated in its own literature that the quantitative approach to creative research often 'looks at aggregated data instead of understanding individuals, and judges advertisements against artificial and often irrelevant criteria … we prefer the flexibility of qualitative research'. This position on advertising research, well established and formalised in the role of the account planner, is not universally shared in the advertising industry. Many agencies prefer quantitative data as the research basis for planning decisions. Qualitative research may involve focus or discussion groups, observation studies or in-depth interviews. Sometimes, qualitative advertising research explicitly draws on anthropology for its theoretical foundation. A major US agency in New York has a 'discovery' team of anthropologists who conduct consumer research studies; it has conducted **deprivation studies** drawing on anthropological techniques to determine the value and meaning attached to the possession of particular types of consumer goods (Hackley, 2000). Agencies have used techniques of ethnography to give their qualitative research greater theoretically driven insight and hence, they hope, greater intellectual weight with clients. However, what agencies claim as ethnography tends to be based on studies of weeks or months rather than the years typically required of ethnography (Elliott and Jankel-Elliott, 2002). Some agencies have a relatively informal approach to their qualitative research. They regard qualitative research as 'talking to' consumers and treat the data of videos, transcripts and audio recordings as stimuli for ideas rather than as empirical evidence to support or reject hypotheses (Hackley, 2000). One major agency in Bangkok, Thailand, assimilates a common sense understanding of consumers they call 'street smarts' throughout the advertising development process (Hackley and Tiwsakul, 2008). Other agencies will have a more explicit, theoretically informed approach to qualitative data interpretation, but most do not. The research skills and sensitivity to nuances of data of experienced planners are relied upon to a great degree, although the interpretations of qualitative research are often hotly debated in the agency account team.

There can be many advantages to quantitative approaches. For example, advertising effectiveness is sometimes tracked using sales figures in relation to the number of target TV spots that the advertisement hits. Clearly, quantitative measurements such as this are essential in fully understanding the impact of a campaign. Statistical techniques such as multivariate analysis can be useful in separating out possible causal variables that might intervene between an advertisement and consumer purchase. Results from experiments can be collated and cross-tabulated, and survey questionnaire results can be statistically analysed for significance. Of course, much of the initial research into the brand category and competitive situation will draw on numerical data to establish items such as brand usage frequency, consumer segment demographics, competitive structure, relative sales volume of the market and so on.

Quantitative data-gathering approaches include surveys, experiments including **biometrics**, and many digital measurement tools. There is a tendency to use the term 'qualitative research' as if it refers to a commonsense interpretation of naturally occurring social data such as audio recordings of talk or video recordings of behaviour. However, such approaches are more accurately labelled 'interpretative research' because the interpretation of qualitative data is not self-evident: qualitative data are invariably open to a range of interpretations.

Qualitative data-gathering methods are largely drawn from traditions of anthropology (especially ethnography) and cultural sociology and include participant observation, in-depth interviewing and questionnaire surveys, consumer diaries, 'focus' or discussion groups, ethnographies (or more accurately, quasi-ethnographies) and other observational methods (Hackley, 2003e). Advertising agencies also make use of psychological research methods, such as **projective tests** (asking the respondent to interpret an image or to complete an incomplete story) and other psychodynamic approaches, and 'depth' interviews (see Packard, 1957, for a famous critique of the use of depth psychology in advertising). Methods derived from literary interpretation include semiotics and discourse analysis.

Much qualitative research focuses on the meaning of consumption, in the hope of generating a resonant insight that can be incorporated into the creative execution to make the consumer emotionally nod with recognition when they see the ad. It does this by seeking methods to understand the lived experience of the group in question. Studies such as Levy (1959), Sherry (1983, 1987, 1991) and Holbrook (1995) have shown how consumers seek and find meaning in their lives from their consumption experiences in ways that are non-trivial and far-reaching. Consumption is carried out not just to solve practical problems but to indulge fantasies and feelings, and for fun (Holbrook and Hirschman, 1982). Qualitative research methods allow consumers to share reflections on their experience of consumption in a non-judgemental setting. The aim is not to elicit rationalisations, which are all too common in consumer research, but sincere insights into the meanings consumption brings to peoples' lives.

Quantitative data sets give the appearance of scientific objectivity and therefore carry a powerful rhetorical force. Findings from qualitative data-gathering methods can be seen as more dependent on subjective interpretation, and hence lack the same pseudo-scientific resonance on a PowerPoint display. In practice, day-to-day marketing relies heavily on qualitative research for its flexibility, ease of use, and ability to generate insights as well as facts.

EXPERIMENTAL RESEARCH

Advertising has a long tradition of scientific experimental research. For example, in campaign pre-testing experiments a selected audience might be gathered to watch an advertisement in a theatre. The audience presses buttons on their seat arms to indicate whether they like or dislike particular parts of the ad. The results are presented in graphical and statistical form. In less technologically enhanced conditions the audience may be given questionnaires to fill out after they have watched the ad, to determine how much or how little they liked it and how well they recalled various components.

Research that tests audience reaction to creative executions is often called copy-testing. There are many variations on the technique for copy-testing. For example, the theatre test described above is often executed today through what is called a link test. Consumers on the panel view the ad on computer and give their response via online questionnaire. A further development of the technique involves magnetic resonance imaging (MRI) scanning. Participants are shown an ad, or elements of it, while in an MRI scanner, and their brain response is monitored. This kind of neuro-psychological research method is becoming increasingly popular in marketing because it avoids the problem of the inaccuracy of self-reports by going straight to the consumer's unconscious physiological response. Self-report methods such as questionnaire surveys are notorious for being inaccurate. The source of this inaccuracy is sometimes our inability to accurately assess and articulate our inner emotional states. Inaccuracy also often occurs because of poorly designed questions, or because of the incapacity of survey methods to capture the nuances of emotional response. If I like a certain brand, then according to a survey I have to like it somewhere on a **Likert scale** from 'not at all' to 'very much'. I cannot qualify my answer with contingencies, exceptions or contradictions.

Other examples of experimental research in advertising include using psycho-galvanometer equipment to measure consumers' central nervous system response to stimuli, and heart monitoring. Biometric tests such as these show our emotional responses through our physiological levels of excitement throughout engagement with a stimulus such as an advertisement. It is axiomatic that humans are primarily emotional rather than rational, and biometrics (including neuroscience) have become fashionable because they offer clear and indisputable data. If my heart rate doubles and my hippocampus lights up while I'm viewing an ad, I cannot deny that I was excited by it. It is taken as a measure of emotional engagement.[10] Ultimately, of course, biometrics and neuroscience suffer exactly the same weakness as surveys – they cannot capture the nuance of human meaning-making.

Many creative staff, incidentally, feel that experimental and quasi-experimental copy-testing techniques are based on mistaken assumptions about how audiences engage with advertising and therefore miss the point. Experimental research designs lack ecological validity because they do not accurately replicate the conditions under which consumers typically engage with advertising. As many researchers have pointed out consumers view advertising in social situations, not in experimental viewing booths (for example, Ritson and Elliott, 1999). Our responses to advertising are similarly socially mediated. Naturalistic experiments try to accommodate the consumer ecology to some extent by attempting to re-create the consumer-advertising environment in the hope of getting more relevant results, for example by setting up a specially created advertisement for consumers to watch in a group. However, even these situations cannot get around the fact that they are contrived experimental conditions. For many account managers and clients, though, experimental designs for copy-testing offer a succinct and measurable means of assessing creative executions before incurring the expense and risk of a full campaign launch.

SNAPSHOT 10.4

Qualitative research informs advertising strategies

There are many examples of products and advertising strategies being developed through qualitative research insights. A successful re-design and re-launch of the (now discontinued) Huggies brand of disposable nappies (or diapers) in the 1990s was developed with the aid of ethnographic observation of parents changing their babies in a dedicated room in the ad agency. A Thai ad agency used a technique they called 'street smarts' and observed how consumers used Nestlé Coffee Mate, a very popular brand in Thailand, in the social context of coffee shops, so that their creative work was informed by an intimate understanding of how consumers use the product within a social setting. In another example, Hovis, a 125-year-old brown-bread brand famous in the UK for its evocative advertising,[11] was suffering declining revenue in the 2000s because of intense downward pressure on price from competition and discounting. Volume was growing but profit declining. DDB London conducted primary research in the form of questionnaire surveys in order to fully understand why brand equity was diminishing. The brand was seen as out-of-date and spontaneous brand awareness was in decline. Qualitative research using projective methods had previously found that people described a 'Hovis room' as a warm and inviting kitchen. By 2001 participants were describing people standing outside the room looking in: people no longer identified with the traditional, old-fashioned positioning of the brand. The new TVC was drawn in a cartoon style[12] reminiscent of animated TV shows like *The Simpsons* to distance it from the old advertising filmed on the cobbled streets of northern England. The relaunch also used new packaging, PR and a supporting website. The brand increased sales while also raising price. The combination of a radical new advertising approach, new packaging and below-the-line support in the form of PR and a website succeeded in repositioning the brand in a contemporary new light. The brand, refreshed, later reached a compromise positioning with a stunning television ad that crossed a century of the brand's history, positioning it in a way that retained a sense of nostalgia but also reinforced its place as a feature of British life in the contemporary age. By 2014, though, the Hovis brand was again in decline.[13]

SURVEY RESEARCH

Survey research has traditionally been a part of advertising research, although its use tends to be confined to wide-scale opinion and attitude surveys. Surveys (as noted above) are often designed with semantic scales such as Likert scales that invite a response on a five-point scale to a question or statement. This enables survey questionnaires to be analysed using statistical tests of significance. Survey results can be analysed and presented in a wide variety of ways according to the needs of the users. They can be foundational to advertising development. If 78% of survey respondents aged 18–30 report that they never buy a paper publication, access all their news and information from the mobile internet and watch less than two hours TV a week, then advertisers will need to seek digital campaigns to reach this group. The above 'finding' is invented, but there have been surveys that suggested a movement in this direction, hence the radical shift in promotional budgets from traditional mass media to digital and mobile.

Surveys can be useful for extending findings from qualitative research to larger samples. For example, if a consumer discussion group revealed that people felt that their music buying was more important to them than their daily newspaper purchase, this could then be tested on a wider scale with a questionnaire survey. Surveys offer a flexible data-gathering tool since they can be administered in person, by telephone or online, and sample sizes can be large. However, sampling is problematic. It is difficult to verify a respondent's characteristics (did the CEO really fill out the survey, or the intern?) and response rates tend to be low, making the generation of truly random samples very difficult. Consequently, regardless of the sample size, surveys can lack generalisability of findings.

The survey industry is a big business: political polls, opinion polls and questionnaire-based market research studies are commissioned daily at great cost. Many people want to know what large numbers of the population think about brands and about politics. Survey companies such as Ipsos-Mori carry out numerous opinion surveys on a wide variety of topics connected to politics, policy and commerce.[14] As with all research, questionnaire surveys can only be useful if they are designed well to achieve carefully thought-through objectives. The interpretation of findings can be complex and must be done in full knowledge of the limitations of the method.

SNAPSHOT 10.5

Self-reports as behavioural data

Self-reports of feelings and emotions may be sincere although hard to quantify, but self-reports of actual behaviour can be wildly inaccurate. This was well illustrated in one retail research study in which security cameras were used to monitor shoppers' in-store browsing behaviour. The research aim was to generate insights that might help improve in-store retail design or merchandising techniques. A sign had been erected at the store entrance warning customers that their behaviour might be filmed for research purposes. On exiting from the store researchers approached the consumers to ask them to explain their behaviour. But the exit interviews proved less than informative. When asked why they lingered for so long at one display, or why they moved from display X to display Y, most consumers had little recollection of their movements and some insisted that they had not behaved in the way described, even when confronted with the film evidence. We are not very good, as consumers, at remembering our behaviour.

There are some famous examples of the flaws of self-report research. The Sony Walkman, the first personal music system, is said to have met with adverse market research results, presumably because the consumers questioned could not grasp the concept of walking around with a hi-fi playing in their ears. The company launched the product nonetheless, to great success. Truly innovative marketing ideas require creative entrepreneurship and teach consumers new consumption concepts. They are beyond the scope of conventional, market research techniques because consumers have nothing with which they can compare a truly innovative concept.

ETHNOGRAPHY AND OBSERVATION

Advertising agencies like to employ anthropologists, for their skills in observing how people derive meaning from their lived experience. To make great advertising, agencies need to understand consumers from an insider perspective – they have to see the world through the consumers' eyes. Indeed, this reflects the classic marketing concept. Anthropologists understand that for humankind the search for meaning is paramount, and ritual and symbolism are central to meaning-making. Brand communications often imply that owning or displaying the brand can transform the consumer's experience or confer upon them a new identity or social status. This experience of liminality, even in forms that are transient and perhaps illusory, is a fundamental need for humans (Hackley et al., 2012). Anthropological methods can capture elements of consumer experience that translate well to advertising with its ability to confer symbolic significance on objects and practices.

Advertising agencies make considerable use of cut-down versions of research methods derived from anthropology, including ethnography and observation. Ethnographers traditionally spent two years or more living with an indigenous tribe, learning their language and rituals, then they would write a book about the experience. Classic anthropological methods are too time-consuming for the business of advertising, but it does make use of 'quasi-ethnography', that is, small slices of ethnographic participation or observation (Elliott and Jankel-Elliott, 2002). Just as cultural sociologists of the 1960s might become members of a biker gang or football hooligans for a time in order to understand and write about the inner motivations of members, so advertising people sometimes try to become a member of a consumer group for a short time in order to experience the world through the eyes of those people and thus generate deep cultural insights that can be translated into advertising and marketing strategies. If that is not possible, they might use ethnographic observation as the next best thing, via video, internet (sometimes called netnography; Kozinets, 2009) or direct observation.

Ethnographic methods can also involve asking consumers to keep diaries or take photographs or video clips of events or situations, for analysis by the agency. The aim is to understand how the consumer makes sense of their subjective experience. Typically, ethnographic studies make use of a variety of data-gathering approaches, including observation, researcher field notes and interviews. The whole data set is then studied carefully for clues as to the symbolic meaning of the participants' actions, talk and behaviours. Ethnographic principles may be applied very loosely in marketing, such as when Toyota established a design centre in Newport Beach, California, to help their development of the Lexus. Newport Beach is an area packed with wealthy people driving prestigious cars, so it is a good place to be in order to understand luxury car consumption. Being physically present in a centre in which certain kinds of consumption are heavily concentrated assists in understanding the cultural milieu of those consumers, their motivations and behaviours. As noted earlier, ethnographic observation can be effective when conducted at arm's length, through the careful analysis of field data.

USES OF ADVERTISING RESEARCH

The advertising industry is both similar and different across the world. It is similar in that it does pretty much the same thing everywhere, and in superficially much the same way. It is different in that each agency has an individual style and difference of emphasis, which manifests in its working practices and style of work (Hackley and Tiwsakul, 2008). So there is room in a creative industry such as advertising for a range of different approaches. Nonetheless, the role of research has been and continues to be a major factor in influencing the kinds of advertising we see.

Different advertising agencies place different degrees of emphasis on applying research at various stages in the creative advertising development process. In this section we will look at both methods and uses of research, since the choice of method is often informed by the purpose for which research is needed.

Among the relatively little published academic research there is on how advertising agencies develop campaigns, Punyapiroje et al. (2002) offer an account of advertising development in Thai advertising agencies and McCracken (1986: 74–6) describes the creative advertising development process in US agencies. Scott's work (1994a: 468) focuses on the ways agency creatives tap into the symbolic consumer consciousness and refers to the 'shared social milieu' upon which advertising professionals depend for the 'learned cultural/textual conventions' (1994a: 463) that will mobilise meaning in their ads. This is the key to great advertising – consumers have to see a kind of truth in the ad, a cultural nod of recognition. Scott and McCracken both refer to the cultural knowledge underlying advertising interpretation that binds both ad maker and ad watcher in a mutually connected communication. 'Research' is part of the industry's attempt to routinise this effect by reaching out into consumer culture to translate its idiom into commercial signs. Hackley and Kover (2007) discuss the tension within which the creative team have to operate as agencies try to reconcile the informal cultural understanding that informs creativity with the formal cultural understanding, derived through research, which reflects the advertising agency's nature as a bureaucratic organisation. Advertising is constructed mainly through talk and texts, in the form of meetings, debates, arguments, presentations, reports, plans and charts, punctuated by material objects such as visuals or video ethnographies (Kelly et al., 2005; Svensson, 2007). Research is an important resource in this process and it is invoked to give force to the argument, in a kind of discourse power game (Hackley, 2000).

The stages of the creative advertising development process at which research can be useful are listed in Table 10.2

TABLE 10.2 Research in the creative advertising development process

Stage in the process	Types of research that can be undertaken
Client brief	Secondary research into market, business, brand, competitors
Strategy development	Primary studies into relevant consumer groups
Creative brief	Anthropological and/or focus group studies of target consumers
Creative development	Focus and/or observational consumer studies
Media planning	Media/audience research using published sources
Pre-launch	Copy-testing, attitude scaling with finished creative executions
Post-launch	Tracking studies, awareness studies, sales response tracking

RESEARCH IN THE ADVERTISING DEVELOPMENT PROCESS

The creative advertising development process begins with the client brief, which the agency account team needs to investigate thoroughly in order to set the terms of reference for the campaign. Initial research will often be undertaken as soon as the client's brief is received. This will establish basic parameters of knowledge about the brand, its market, its consumers and competitors, and the way that the brand fits in with the client's business. All of this work will inform the communications brief, which is the agency's interpretation of the client brief and forms the basis for the advertising strategy, the statement of the purpose for advertising.

Much of this initial research is likely to rely on secondary data sets, that is, data sets already recorded as part of other studies, such as commercial market reports or syndicated surveys, panel data and **household data** (see Snapshot 10.1). Key questions to be asked and answered through secondary research at this stage might include what is the brand history and who is the target consumer of this brand? What is the brand marketing strategy and what does the client want to achieve with communication? What are the target consumers like, where do they live, how old are they, what kinds of lifestyle do they live, what is their typical income? How many items do they buy per year, where do they buy them from? There will also be questions about the market, the competitors and their strategies. Brand positioning is relative to competitors – so where is this brand in relation to competitors? Agencies will need to have some knowledge of these issues in order to suitably address the client brief and to develop it into a communications brief. In some cases, agencies may commission some primary research as well at this stage.

Once the client brief is translated into a communications brief, research might be useful in some cases to refine the advertising strategy. The ad needs to connect with consumers and the best way for it to do that is to reflect some aspect of the consumers' experience that is important or significant to the target audience. There's little point in an ad trumpeting the virtues of paper towels that are made of six layers if the relevant consumers don't care how many layers of paper there are in their kitchen towels. This is where advertising has to reflect the marketing concept and not the product concept – the appeal must be relevant to the consumer, regardless of what the manufacturer feels is important about the product. Research is the way that advertising and promotion agencies get to understand the consumer milieu from the perspective of the consumer. The advertising strategy must reflect what is important to the consumer.

When the brand and the market are fully understood, and the advertising strategy agreed, the creative brief may need additional research into consumer motivations and behaviours. If the strategy is to make the target consumers believe that a particular fashion brand is essential for style leaders, just what kind of appeal might convince them? What kinds of persuasion are most effective with this group? Aesthetically appealing visuals? Ironic humour? A transgressive, anti-authority positioning? Diesel, for example, seems to have used all of these kinds of appeal in their advertising over the past decade, exemplified in their award winning 'Be Stupid' campaign.[15]

PHOTO 25 Diesel

Image Courtesy of the Advertising Archives

Diesel's long running Be Stupid campaign has won creative awards for its agency, Anomaly. The campaign features polysemous images (such as this 2010 example) that associate maverick creativity with its brand, and with its consumers. If you have to ask what the ads mean, then you're not cool enough to be in the target group. It is the kind of enigmatic creative campaign that demands a leap of faith from the client, but this tends to be the case with the most powerful campaigns.

Very often, studies conducted earlier in the process will be engaged with once again, perhaps with more carefully selected participants, or with more focused questions. For example, discussion groups held at the client brief stage might have established broad truths about the consumer group in terms of their attitudes and motivations, but there may be a need at the creative brief stage to dig deeper and perhaps to tweak the sample of respondents.

SNAPSHOT 10.6

The limits of pre-launch testing

Arthur J. Kover, former editor of the *Journal of Advertising Research* and Emeritus Professor of Marketing at the Fordham University Graduate Business School, New York, kindly offers this vignette on the limits of advertising copy-testing:

> Valentine Appel, a revered figure in advertising research, once claimed that research of finished commercials could do two things well. One was to eliminate advertising that is really bad. The other was to select advertising that is really good. Often, however, really innovative advertising does not test well because it cannot be captured by the rational measures of much advertising research. Given the limitations of advertising research to pre-test commercials, one wonders why it is required. The answer is partly political: advertisers need to gain budget approval from many individuals. They therefore need statistical evidence, even if it merely supports the obvious. The other, related reason is that advertisers are highly risk-averse. Advertising research can provide reassurance. It is close to a truism that much advertising is neither good nor bad, just mediocre. Research can test three executions, for example, and show if one is preferred to the others. The advertising manager has the basis for a decision based on concrete numbers, on science, even though the chosen commercial is not really different from the rejected ones. It makes little difference what he or she selects. Cynical? Yes. Reality? Yes. Advertising testing may not be important for decisions but it is necessary for careers.

Creative research is a source of tension in advertising, as suggested in Snapshot 10.7. Some agencies prefer the solid-looking nature of quantitative research, although this can lack flexibility of interpretation. Others feel that qualitative research provides that flexibility when ideas are provisional and iterative. Qualitative studies can provide feedback on ideas in development, or stimulation for idea generation, because of their relatively unstructured character. Consumer research participants in discussion groups or during ethnographic observation can come up with original insights that capture some element of the brand, when the research approach allows them that latitude of expression. A rigid approach to creative research might fail to capture whether a creative execution is emotionally engaging, but it might serve to measure consumer attitudes towards an element of the creative content. This might generate a clear steer for the team, but it would not allow for any nuance to come through. Consumer experience is often contingent, provisional and nuanced, rather than black and white. We don't really know for sure if we like or dislike something, but we are open to suggestions. Creative research should facilitate creativity, rather than close it down.

Media buying is usually carried out by external media specialists, and they will often be involved in devising the media strategy, but media strategy and planning will also be considerations in the creative advertising development process since so many creative issues cannot be dealt with in a media vacuum – account teams, and especially creatives, need to know which media channels they can use. Many creative craft skills are media-specific. Media research entails finding out who reads, views, listens to or uses what media channels, when, how and how much. This is often done through specialist suppliers of media research such as BRAD[16] and Kantar Media.[17]

Once the agency team and client are happy with a creative execution they might wish to reassure themselves about the response of target consumers to specific aspects, such as the script (or copy), the action, scene and actors (if it is a TV ad) or the combination of colours and copy for a print ad. Ads may be adjusted or even abandoned altogether because of results from a pre-launch copy-test. Many a creative execution has been abandoned at pre-launch because of the wishes of the client representative, often to the frustration of the account manager. Copy-testing, as discussed above, often takes place through 'link' tests in which a creative execution is shown to a panel of consumers, possibly in a form such as animatronics rather than a finished production, and they respond to an online questionnaire. If the consumers don't like the idea enough, it may be adjusted or even cancelled and the creative team is told to come up with a new idea. Research agency Millward Brown provide 'Link' tests and also a shorter version called Express Link.[18] As mentioned above, some advertisers make use of biometric measures such as neuropsychological scanning to assess the response of consumers to advertising stimuli, although the Link or other online versions of the theatre advertising test can be used on larger samples of participants.

After the campaign launch, there is a need to evaluate the effectiveness of the campaign against its objectives, so **tracking studies** can be undertaken using a combination of research methods. If, for example, the campaign objective was to change attitudes to a brand in a particular location, then a simple street survey before and after launch could measure the extent to which this has been successful, or not. If the campaign was supporting a new product or brand launch, prompted and unprompted recall tests could be used. More complex statistical tests such as multivariate analysis could be deployed for a long-term assessment of advertising effects.

Evaluation continues throughout the campaign but the most information is available to make the judgement on its success after the campaign has finished. The agency will need to provide a detailed assessment of how effective it was. Tracking studies are very important for agencies since they constitute a record of the campaign's evolution and its marketing results. They can provide evidence for clients that the campaign accomplished the objectives set for it. Case histories that are written up from successful campaigns provide a learning resource and, if they are submitted to awards competitions, can be useful PR for the agency itself. Most ad agencies carry case histories of their successful campaigns on their websites as advertisements for their skills.

TENSION AND CONFLICT AROUND RESEARCH IN ADVERTISING

Much misunderstanding about research in advertising occurs because it is not one entity but many. As we have seen, research is conducted for a number of different purposes. First, it is what is done to initially investigate a brand's market category, its role in the client's business and the consumer segments that are relevant. Second, it is what account planning staff do to try to generate facts about consumer reality that can give communication a particular resonance with the target group. Third, research is what is often done to draft creative work before the campaign is launched, in an effort to predict the likely consumer response. Fourth, research is the process of trying to track the response of consumers to the campaign. Debates around research method in advertising, then, revolve not only around fundamental questions of research philosophy but also around the usefulness of particular methods in given situations. As Kover (1995) and Hackley (2003c) suggest, advertising agencies comprise professionals with very different intellectual backgrounds and equally different implicit theories of practice. These differences are caused by different assumptions about the nature of advertising and consumers, and they give rise to impassioned debates about what a given research finding implies for a particular campaign.

SNAPSHOT 10.7

Creatives and research

Research is an essential part of the advertising and marketing industries, but creatives feel that it can be damaging to the standards of creativity in advertising. Indeed, many creative professionals in advertising would put it much more strongly than this: many are openly hostile to formal research. They see research as a power tool wielded by those who have little understanding of how or why consumers engage with advertising. The following quote is from a copywriter complaining about research in the New York newsletter of the American Marketing Association: 'Don't tell me that … [your] little questions and statistics can pinpoint the complexity and richness of how people respond to my work' (Kover, 1996: RC9). This quote neatly illustrates the conflicts that can arise when research is conceived as a formalised and method-driven technique that offers definitive findings, while creatives see their craft as one of motivating consumers through aesthetically inspiring imagery (Hackley and Kover, 2007).

The debates in advertising practice are reflected in academic research. For example, much research in the field has its basis in the transmission model of communication (deriving from, for example, Schramm's mass communications research, 1948) described in Chapter 2. The linear model of communication conceives of advertising as something that acts on individual consumers in social isolation and this assumption has framed much of the research in the field. Academic researchers (e.g. Mick and Buhl, 1992) have argued that this preoccupation with advertising exposure isolated from its social context risks misconstruing the fundamentally social nature of the interaction between consumers and advertising (but also see Scott, 1994a, for comments on Mick and Buhl, 1992). Consumers usually engage with advertising in a social context and not alone in a viewing booth. Ritson and Elliott (1999, citing Holbrook, 1995: 93; McCracken, 1987: 123, in support) have suggested that advertising cannot properly be understood as if it operates in a social vacuum. Advertising, they argue, is actively consumed, re-interpreted and used for purposes of social positioning and identity formation (Buttle, 1994; O'Donohoe, 1994).

The linear information processing tradition of advertising theory also emphasises conscious and rational information processing. Academic researchers have drawn attention to the symbolic character of advertising communication, suggesting that consumer motivations are not invariably dominated by conscious reasoning. For example, McCracken (1986) has alluded to the deeply symbolic character of consumption and argues that this feature has been marginalised in favour of a rational model of how advertising works. For this researcher cultural meaning has a 'mobile quality' (1986: 71) and advertising is an 'instrument of meaning transfer' (1986: 74). Mick and Buhl (1992: 314) draw critical attention to the tendency for some advertising research to regard ads as 'relatively fixed stimuli' and consumers as 'solitary subjects, without identities, who react to ads through linear stages or limited persuasion routes, for the principal purpose of judging brands'. Holbrook and O'Shaughnessy (1988: 400) maintain that humans live 'embedded within a shared system of signs based on public language and other symbolic objects'. Advertising can be seen as a major site of signification, taking consumer cultural meanings, placing them in the context of brand marketing and reflecting them back so that consumers can perform cultural practices symbolically through the consumption of marketed brands. The particular signs that carry meaning in a given context for a given consumer community are difficult for brand advertisers to ascertain unless they can understand the world in the same way as the group of interest. For Thompson et al. (1989: 433) 'personal understandings are always situated within a network of culturally-shared knowledge, shared beliefs, ideals and taken-for-granted assumptions about the nature of social life'. The implication is that social research cannot fully appreciate personal understandings without also understanding how they interface with the social context in which they are formed. This squares with the creatives' complaint that copy testing fails to capture the true character of consumers' engagement with advertising, but fails to acknowledge the political role of advertising research in agencies.

Advertising is an area in which art and business collide, often with aesthetically striking and commercially fruitful results. Understandably, there are conflicts resulting from the differing values and mindsets associated with each community.

RESEARCH ETHICS

Given the heightened sensitivity over ethical issues in advertising and marketing in general, it is worth briefly discussing some issues of research ethics that might impact in advertising contexts. Conducting research with consumers involves prying into their and our attitudes and lifestyles. In some cultures, consumers tend to be very open about this and happy to tell a researcher whom they have never met before intimate details of their consumer behaviour. In others, it is much more likely that a cold-calling researcher would be given short shrift. Where consumers are willing to give of their time to discuss aspects of their consumer experience, it is incumbent on the researcher to treat information as highly confidential and to respect the wishes, feelings and wellbeing of the research participant.

The emergence of big data under convergence has changed the game and now as consumers we are subject to constant surveillance as we browse social media, buy online, or even go for a walk with our smartphone in our pocket, and our browsing behaviour, location and purchases are all recorded electronically and the data used to infer a great deal about us. These data sets power the algorithms that drive personalised ads to our social media timelines. For some consumers, all this is fine – for many others, it is out of awareness. For still others, the degree and detail of electronic surveillance to which we are subject in contemporary society are a deeply troubling issue of social ethics (Greenwald, 2015; Reeves, 2017). Advertising and marketing drive much of this data gathering, but what concerns critics is not only the potential other uses to which these data could be put, but also the inherently political nature of surveillance in itself (Hackley, 2002).

The leading professional bodies have their own ethical standards to which they require professionals to adhere. There are, also, various ethical conventions that are widely accepted as good practice, such as confidentiality and respect for the individual's wellbeing. Many psychological experiments that are regarded as 'classic' studies would not be permitted by a university ethics committee today. Research studies should not cross legal or ethical boundaries in any way. Some research studies might wish to use minors (children), in which case detailed procedures of vetting and ethical approval would have to be sought. Research participants in focus groups who are being videoed would need to be reassured that the film would be used only for the precise purpose for which it was being undertaken, and only by officials of the relevant companies involved in the research study. They would also need to be reassured of the integrity and trustworthiness of the researcher.

It is important that participants in advertising research studies take part freely and willingly, and that their rights are explained to them at the very start of the session. The uses to which the research will be put should be clearly explained. They should be assured that they can stop and withdraw from the study at any time, that they do not have to make any responses that they feel uncomfortable making, that their opinions and experiences will be treated with respect, and, most importantly, that their contribution will remain completely confidential.

CHAPTER SUMMARY

Chapter 10 has outlined types and uses of research in advertising. Rather than focusing on the execution of methods, it has discussed some of the conceptual foundations of research and the ways in which these can be put to rhetorical use on advertising agency politics. The chapter outlined some key methodological distinctions in advertising research, including qualitative/quantitative and primary/secondary, and it discussed a number of methods. The chapter went on to discuss the role of research in each stage of the creative advertising development process. Finally, some points regarding research ethics were briefly outlined.

REVIEW QUESTIONS

1 Place yourself in the position of an account planner trying to understand a new brief from a manufacturer of branded disposable nappies (diapers). What sources and kinds of information will be required? What primary research methods could be useful? Explain your choices.

2 Why is research a source of potential conflict in advertising agencies?

3 Pick three print ads and conduct copy-test experiments with an audience. Devise scaled questionnaires to assess the strength of feeling subjects have towards various components of the ad. What issues arise? How useful are the findings?

4 Convene a discussion group to explore the issue of ethics in advertising. Use a selection of ethically controversial ads as stimulus material. Write up the main findings. Now write a brief assessment of the main problems and uses of this research technique.

5 Outline how a new brief for a brand of fruit-flavoured alcoholic drink might be better understood through informal and qualitative research.

VIDEO QUESTIONS

What are the objectives of media research?
What challenges are there in media research?
What are different ways that media research can be conducted?

CASE STUDY

Consumer insight and the Dove CfRB[19]

The Dove 'Campaign for Real Beauty' (CfRB), which became the 'Self Esteem Project', reportedly raised the brand's UK market share by 30% in the first few years following its launch in 2004 (Robinson et al., 2009). The brand wished to improve its consumer engagement and a global research study revealed a key consumer insight – specifically, conventional, aspirational ('Revlon don't sell cosmetics, we sell hope'[20]) cosmetics advertising played on women's low self-esteem by making them feel insecure about their appearance. Traditional cosmetics and fashion branding present ideals of beauty that are unattainable,

let's face it, firming the thighs of a size 8 supermodel is no challenge.

There's not much point in testing a new firming lotion on size-eight supermodel thighs, is there? That's why Dove's Firming range was tested on ordinary women with real lives to live – and real, curvy thighs to firm. After using Dove's nourishing and effective combination of moisturisers and seaweed extracts, we asked if they'd go in front of the camera. What better way to show the unretouched, unairbrushed results?

new Dove Firming Range

PHOTO 26 Dove

Image Courtesy of the Advertising Archives

One of Dove's key brand themes since 2004 has been that it appeals to 'real women' so uses 'real women' (i.e. not stereotypical models) in its advertising. The Campaign for Real Women is highly successful in many countries, but not all. The appeal is to create a sense that the brand is not trying to exploit insecurity but, instead, is affirming female confidence. To cynics, it is just a clever way of selling even more deodorant and shampoo.

even for the models themselves, since every asymmetry and blemish is photoshopped away. The team had garnered from interviews that some women resented conventional cosmetics advertising because it didn't represent women 'like them'. The team wanted to feed this insight into a campaign featuring 'real' (i.e. not photoshopped or size zero) women. Legend has it that the predominantly male, middle-aged Unilever board resisted this radical move until presented with videos of their own wives and daughters explaining how insecure typical cosmetics ads made them feel about their bodies. The idea was sold, and Dove CfRB was born. Dove positioned their brand as giving (or to be accurate, selling) women's self-esteem back to them. The theme was expanded across different media platforms with clever PR, tons of media coverage and initiatives including the Dove self-esteem website, charitable donations to Dove's Self-Esteem Fund for disadvantaged women, and some striking viral videos, including one called 'Evolution' of a model being photoshopped, made by Ogilvy Toronto[21] (and a follow up called 'Onslaught' focusing on the influence advertising might exert on young girls' self-image). The positioning was controversial, at least for cynics, who pointed out that Unilever also operate a stable of brands that hardly demur from exploiting beauty stereotypes. Unilever's men's deodorant brands Lynx and Axe are notorious for their ads sexualising women, while the skin whitener Fair And Lovely exploits beauty myths about light skin in the African subcontinent and South, as well as South-East, Asia. What is more, Dove's social marketing strategy seems to play out differently in international markets that don't buy into the media criticism of conventional model shoots – for example, Dove billboards look very conventionally aspirational in Hong Kong.[22] The Dove CfRB campaign insight required an appreciation of the wider context of the issue (beauty myths and the visual representation of women in media), including the way this topic was playing out as a media debate in Western fashion circles. For example, there was much media criticism of 'size zero' fashion models and the role an ideology of super thin-ness was playing in the rise of eating disorders such as anorexia. This issue was expanded further by Dove to take in wider cultural issues of female children's psychological development and women's education and social role. This seems to be an example of consumer insight that was generated by sensitively using qualitative interviews in a way that was flexible enough to accommodate contextual insights. The resulting campaign radically challenged the Western discourse of cosmetics advertising. Dove's 2013 viral campaign called 'Thought Before Action' (on YouTube[23]) offered a piece of software that secretly reverted photographs back to their un-photoshopped state. A number of commentators (for example a brand consultancy called Quo Vadis[24]) pointed out that, while female body image is unquestionably manipulated by marketers, Dove is not exactly above the fray with its enhanced photography of the products (a bar of used soap never really looked this good), its chemical masking of the way the products really look and smell, and its alleged double-standard in exploiting ideologies of female beauty by claiming to take a stand against them. In spite of criticism, the campaign theme has continued to gather pace over a decade and Dove's multiple award-winning 2013 YouTube campaign 'Real Beauty Sketches' became the most watched online ad ever at that time, according to Unilever, with 163 million views[25] and over a million likes on Dove's Facebook page. The films, made by Ogilvy & Mather Brazil, feature a trained artist sketching women according to their own description, and again according to others' description of them. The sketches drawn from self-description show less attractive women than those from third party description, suggesting that women downplay their own beauty. They could also be an illustration that some nice people are naturally self-deprecating, while being generous in describing the physical appearance of others. The campaign continues to resonate powerfully with huge audiences and has evolved through 2017 into a series of emotionally resonant personal stories.[26]

Case questions

1. In what ways does the Dove CfRB advertising illustrate the advantages of qualitative research insights in creative advertising development?
2. Why has Dove CfRB achieved the success that it has?
3. Look at the Dove CfRB material available on the internet. Are there any other initiatives you feel Dove could deploy to leverage the deep sense of engagement its consumers have with the brand?
4. How might a small, regional cosmetics brand without the resources to fund a global research study generate a powerful insight from its research that could ignite social media and engage new consumers?

USEFUL JOURNAL ARTICLES

(These Sage articles can be accessed on the companion website.)

Barry, A.E. and Goodson, P. (2010) 'Use (and misuse) of the responsible drinking message in public health and alcohol advertising: a review', *Health Education & Behavior*, 37 (2): 288–303 (first published August 10, 2009).

Hornikx, J., van Meurs, F. and de Boer, A. (2010) 'English or a local language in advertising? The appreciation of easy and difficult English slogans in the Netherlands', *Journal of Business Communication*, 47 (2): 169–88.

Loda, M.D., Coleman, B.C. and Backman, K.F. (2010) 'Walking in Memphis: testing one DMO's marketing strategy to Millennials', *Journal of Travel Research*, 49 (1): 46–55 (first published May 19, 2009).

Miles, C. (2004) 'The prospect and schizogenesis: a Batesonian perspective on the implications of the double-bind in advertising messages', *Marketing Theory*, 4 (4): 267–86.

Smith, R.E. and Yang, X. (2004) 'Toward a general theory of creativity in advertising: examining the role of divergence', *Marketing Theory*, 4 (1–2): 31–58.

Wentzel, D., Henkel, S. and Tomczak, T. (2010) 'Can I live up to that ad? Impact of implicit theories of ability on service employees' responses to advertising', *Journal of Service Research*, 13 (2): 137–52.

FURTHER READING

Alozie, E.C. (2010) 'Advertising and culture: semiotic analysis of dominant symbols found in Nigerian mass media advertising', *Journal of Creative Communications*, 5 (1): 1–22.

Basadur, M., Gelade, G. and Basadur, T. (2014) 'Creative problem-solving process styles, cognitive work demands, and organizational adaptability', *Journal of Applied Behavioral Science*, 50 (1): 80–115 (first published December 3, 2013).

Chávez, C.A. (2014) 'Linguistic capital and the currency of Spanish in Hispanic advertising production', *Journal of Communication Inquiry*, 38 (1): 25–43.

De Pelsmacker, P. and Dens, N. (2009) *Advertising Research: Message, Medium and Context.* Antwerp: Garant.

Ehrenberg, A. and Barnard, N. (1997) 'Advertising and product demand', Admap, May: 14–18.

Gidlöf, K., Holmberg, N. and Sandberg, H. (2012) 'The use of eye-tracking and retrospective interviews to study teenagers' exposure to online advertising', *Visual Communication*, 11 (3): 329–45.

Jiang Wu, Bin Hu and Yu Zhang (2013) 'Maximizing the performance of advertisements diffusion: a simulation study of the dynamics of viral advertising in social networks', *SIMULATION*, 89 (8): 921–34.

Jones, J.P. (1990) 'Advertising: strong force or weak force? Two views an ocean apart', *International Journal of Advertising*, 9: 233–46.

Rajabi, M., Dens, N. and De Pelsmacker, P. (2014) 'Attention and memory effects of advertising in an international context', in H. Cheng (ed.), *The Handbook of International Advertising Research.* Oxford: Wiley–Blackwell, pp. 313–37.

Wells, W.D. (ed.) (1997) *Measuring Advertising Effectiveness.* Hillsdale, NJ: Lawrence Erlbaum Associates.

NOTES

1 http://thearf.org/ (accessed 15 March 2017).
2 www.warc.com/ (accessed 15 March 2017).
3 www.nielsen.com/content/corporate/uk/en.html (accessed 15 March 2017)
4 www.tnsglobal.com/ (accessed 15 March 2017).
5 www.barb.co.uk/ (accessed 30 March 2017).
6 www.mintel.com/ (accessed 16 March 2017).
7 Eliza Williams, 'Happy Birthday Bill Bernbach', 12 August 2011, www.creativereview.co.uk/cr-blog/2011/august/happy-birthday-bill-bernbach (accessed 17 March 2017); see also Todd Wasserman, 'VW's Super Bowl ad is here and it's wacky', 28 January 2014, http://mashable.com/2014/01/28/vw-super-bowl-2014/ (accessed 17 March 2017).
8 'Volkswagen overtakes Toyota as world's best-selling car maker', *Autocar*, 31 January 2017, www.autocar.co.uk/car-news/industry/volkswagen-overtakes-toyota-worlds-best-selling-car-maker (accessed 30 March 2017).

9 Volkswagen UK, www.youtube.com/user/UKVolkswagen (accessed 17 March 2017).
10 Justin Pearse, 'Are biometrics the next frontier for advertising?', 2 July 2015, www.thedrum.com/news/2015/07/02/are-biometrics-next-frontier-advertising (accessed 18 July 2017).
11 Loulla-Mae Eleftheriou-Smith, 'Do you remember these classic Hovis TV ads?', *Campaign*, 28 January 2014, www.brandrepublic.com/news/1228764/remember-classic-Hovis-TV-ads/?HAYILC=RELATED (accessed 16 March 2017).
12 Hovis ad, 21 November 2010, www.youtube.com/watch?v=48aHtegMo88 (accessed 17 March 2017).
13 Alex Brownsell, 'Premier Foods sells controlling stake in Hovis', *Campaign*, 27 January 2014, www.brandrepublic.com/news/1228649/ (accessed 17 March 2017).
14 www.ipsos-mori.com/ (accessed 17 March 2017).
15 'Diesel: Be Stupid advertising campaign', www.creativeadawards.com/diesel-be-stupid-advertising-campaign/ (accessed 17 March 2017).
16 http://bradinsight.com/ (accessed 18 July 2017).
17 www.kantarmedia.co.uk/ (accessed 17 March 2017).
18 www.millwardbrown.com/mb-global/what-we-do/advertising/ad-testing/express-testing (accessed 18 July 2017).
19 'The Dove Self-Esteem Project: Our Mission in Action', www.dove.com/uk/dove-self-esteem-project/our-mission.html (accessed 17 March 2017).
20 This is a comment often attributed to a Revlon executive and used in textbooks as an illustration of the way the marketing concept focuses on end-user benefit. Other similar illustrations include the alleged comment of a power tools executive that 'We don't sell drills, we sell holes'.
21 Dove 'Evolution', 6 October 2006, www.youtube.com/watch?v=iYhCn0jf46U (accessed 22 February 2017).
22 This comment is based on nothing more scientific than my discussion with students while teaching in Hong Kong, and my observation of the poster advertising for the brand.
23 Dove 'Thought Before Action', 3 March 2013, www.youtube.com/watch?v=m0JF4QxPpvM (accessed 7 March 2017).
24 Rick Julian, 'Dove rant', Quo Vadis blog, 6 March 2013, www.qvbrands.com/dove-rant/ (accessed 7 March 2017).
25 'Real Beauty Shines Through: Dove wins Titanium Grand Prix, 163 million views on YouTube', June 2013, www.thinkwithgoogle.com/case-studies/dove-real-beauty-sketches.html (accessed 17 March 2017).
26 Ibid.

ABBREVIATIONS

AAAA	American Association of Advertising Agencies
AI	artificial intelligence
AIDA	Attention–Interest–Desire–Action
ASA	Advertising Standards Authority (UK)
ATL	above-the-line
B2B	business-to-business
BTL	below-the-line
CPGRP	cost-per-gross rating point
CPT	cost-per-thousand
CRM	customer relationship management
CSR	corporate social responsibility
DOC	director of creativity
DOP	director of planning
DTC	direct-to-consumer
FMCG	fast moving consumer goods
GDP	gross domestic product
GRP	gross rating point
IMC	integrated marketing communication
IPA	Institute for Practitioners in Advertising (UK)
MRI	magnetic resonance imaging
OOH	out of home
PR	public relations
ROI	return on investment
SEGs	socio-economic groups
SEO	search engine optimisation
SWOT	Strengths, Weaknesses, Opportunities, Threats

TTL	through-the-line
TVC	television commercial
UGC	user-generated content
USP	unique selling proposition
VALS	Values and Lifestyles classification
WHO	World Health Organization
WOM	word-of-mouth

GLOSSARY

Above-the-line, below-the-line, through-the-line Terms that originate from the UK system of ad agency remuneration (now largely defunct). If a medium generated commission payment to the agency, it was regarded as above-the-line. Above-the-line media included mainstream advertising on press, cinema, commercial radio and TV. Below-the-line media generated no agency commission and included sales promotion, public relations and direct mail. Through-the-line campaigns utilised combinations of above- and below-the-line media.

Account manager The role responsible for client liaison and the general business management of an account.

Account planner The account team role responsible for research and strategy.

ACORN A Classification of Residential Neighbourhoods: a form of geodemographic segmentation that categorises consumers on the basis of the residential neighbourhood where they live.

Adspend The monetary expenditure on advertising and promotion.

Advergaming The use of interactive games via the internet or mobile as an advertising device.

Advertainment Advertisements that entertain by relating a dramatic narrative or by engaging consumers in an interactive process such as a game.

Affiliate marketing Co-operative ventures, often e-based, with, for example, host websites carrying other brands' material for click-through business.

AIDA Acronym for Attention–Interest–Desire–Action, a sequence of states through which a direct salesperson should take the prospect, popularised by Strong in *The Psychology of Selling and Advertising* (1929). AIDA was designed to model personal selling but is often used to model the alleged effects of mass media advertising.

Ambient marketing Promotional messages inserted into traditionally non-promotional spaces in the consumer environment, such as the back of car parking tickets, farmers' fields, the sides of buildings and printed on toilet tissue.

Appeal the creative content of advertisements can be categorised by the kind of appeal, e.g. humour, sexuality, fear, peer approval, social status, etc.

Audience The number of people or households exposed to a given communication in a specified time period.

Awareness The extent to which consumers have heard of or seen and recall a brand or a particular promotion, often measured by surveys.

Big data sometimes referring (in advertising) to the vast quantities of behavioural data stored electronically and used to target and segment media audiences for programmatic advertising

Biometrics A consumer research approach that entails measuring the central nervous system response to external marketing stimuli via heart rate, brain activation, or sweat.

Brand engagement No agreed definition but the concept revolves around the volitional and active attention of consumers, elicited by making promotions more interesting and, especially, by making them interactive.

Buzz marketing Aims to generate WOM (word of mouth) and/or media coverage through an event, viral or pop-up event.

Buzz word Briefly popular term.

Client The brand manager or brand marketing director who works with the advertising agency in the development of the campaign.

Client brief/advertising strategy/creative brief Internal agency documentation charting and guiding the development of communication.

Connote, connotation A term referring to the secondary meanings that may subsist in a given text. For example, a car advertisement might highlight the car, but the imagery might connote happiness, attractiveness and an exciting lifestyle.

Consequentialist, consequentialism The doctrine that the ethical status of acts should be judged according to the actual or possible consequences. In other words, if an advertisement may have good consequences, it is judged ethically acceptable. Many charities and public-service campaigns that try to shock people into driving more safely, drinking less alcohol and so on, are allowed to do so based on these implicit grounds.

Consumer communities Consumer groups whose only commonality is their mutual interest in a particular set of consumption values or practices. Some advertising agencies use the phrase 'brand communities' to indicate that heterogeneous social groups who share only a mutual interest in a particular brand can be defined as a group on this basis. The 'values' that are integral to the brand are, implicitly, shared by the group. An example might be the Manchester United Supporters' Club, a widely diverse group in terms of age, sex, ethnicity, nationality and social status, which are united only in their interest in the soccer club (and its merchandise).

Content A term for any and all media content. Content marketing entails movies, games, blog pieces or anything else that can be viewed for entertainment or information, shared on social media, and branded.

Convergence A term (often linked with author and eminent media academic Henry Jenkins, 2008) referring broadly to the distillation of all media channels into the internet as access point.

Copy-testing A quasi-experimental group of research approaches usually conducted to test creative executions before a campaign launch. Copy-testing measures attitudes towards an advertisement and its different visual or other components.

Cost-per-thousand A media planning term denoting the cost per thousand consumers reached through a given medium, e.g. website banner ad, direct mail shot, TV ad.

Covert communication Covert communication in advertising occurs where the absence of a clearly designated communication source facilitates meanings that are implicit. For example, the promotional motive of content marketing is usually covert.

Creative Used as a noun to designate one member of the creative team, as in 'a creative'.

Creative advertising development process The term used in some advertising agencies for the process of developing advertising.

Creative execution The finished advertisement.

Creative hot shops/boutiques It is common in the marketing communications field for successful professionals to break away from their employing agency to form new partnerships known as creative hot shops or boutiques. They are normally small partnerships of experienced professionals who seek a more responsive and rewarding environment than a large agency can offer.

Creative team Since the 1960s it has been the convention for advertising agency creative work to be done in teams of two.

Database mining software Data mining entails using large databases of customer information to generate new segments to target with direct marketing initiatives. Software packages can be useful in allowing marketing analysts to create contact lists of consumers from larger customer databases grouped according to any given criterion.

Deontological, deontology The doctrine that acts should be judged on their intrinsic rightness or wrongness regardless of the consequences. For example, consumers sometimes object to particular advertisements on the grounds that they are offensive: this is implicitly a deontological, ethical position.

Deprivation studies A technique used in anthropological studies that requires research participants to forego an item for a period of time and to record their feelings about its absence in a diary. The feelings of deprivation endured (and expressed) can be a measure of the importance and role of the item in the person's life. One such study conducted for a global audio equipment manufacturer examined the role of audio equipment in people's lives by getting a panel of consumers to do without their audio equipment for a month.

Discourse Anything that can be described in words: a category of social text that entails accepted or conventional communicative practices.

DRTV Direct response television.

Earned media Contrasted with paid media, earned media refers to social media shares and other unsolicited likes, saves and uses of a piece of content.

Embedded marketing Marketing initiatives presented in the context of entertainment vehicles such as movies, TV shows or sponsored media events. The key element of embedded marketing is that the audience is not necessarily explicitly aware that the brand exposure is a paid-for promotion.

Ethics The study of the good life, including the exploration of questions of what good conduct is conducive to living the good life.

Eye tachistoscope test A technique of advertising research in which a camera device tracks the movement of a viewer's eye over a creative execution.

Focus group Generic name for informal discussion groups often used by agencies for exploratory research.

Fragmentation of media audiences Mass media audiences have fragmented as the number of media vehicles has multiplied.

Frame of reference The norms and assumptions through which we interpret the world.

Full-service agency An advertising agency that offers the full range of communications services to clients. In practice most agencies rely to a greater or lesser degree on the sub-contracting of specialist services.

Generalisation A truth or fact that holds under any circumstances in any culture.

Geodemographics A technique of consumer segmentation that combines demographic with geographical information.

Glocalisation Casting global advertising campaigns in terms of the local consumer cultural and linguistic idiom.

Guerrilla marketing Marketing that does not use conventional media and may have its true intent deliberately obscured.

Hierarchy-of-effects theories Theories of persuasive communication that conceive of a passive and indifferent consumer who must be persuaded to buy the brand by the accumulated effect of a number of ad exposures.

High involvement A purchase of such importance that it requires a high order of processing, including, for example, an information search and evaluation of alternatives. Purchases such as a house, car or family holiday might be characterised thus. Many purchases that take a lower proportion of disposable income are thought to be more spontaneous and subject to a lower order of rational processing (i.e. low involvement). This binary construct loses its explanatory effectiveness when purchases have a powerful, symbolic value for consumers, e.g. spending months evaluating alternatives for the purchase of a new pair of shoes.

Household data Market research focusing on the household unit, contrasts with panel data, which often focuses on the store or region.

Integrated marketing communications (IMC) A management initiative to link and coordinate brand communications through all media channels. IMC is often only partially achieved because of functional divisions within organisations between different communications disciplines.

Integrated solutions Advertising and promotional campaigns that use co-ordinated creative executions through different media channels.

Interpretive community A group that shares certain cultural reference points and therefore a sense of meaning in some situations. For example, intertextual references in ads to scenes from Hollywood movies or to sports events will be most quickly understood by, respectively, movie buffs and sports fans.

Intertextuality A characteristic of discourses whereby they adapt, copy or refer to other discourses, for example where ads refer to movies, or movies refer to brands.

Likert scales The original form of attitude measurement scale; usually in the form of a statement and a five-item response scale ranging from 'strongly negative' to 'strongly positive'.

Linear information processing (theories of communication) Theories (or models) that draw an analogy between human and machine information processing. Also known as consumer information processing (CIP).

Magnetic resonance imaging (MRI) A medical technique for scanning the brain also used in neurological consumer research (neuromarketing).

Managerial, managerialist The genre of business writing and research devoted to solving the problems of managers without reference to wider social scientific or ethical issues and values.

Marketing mix The four Ps of marketing management: Price, Product, Promotion and Physical distribution. Subsequent versions have added People and Processes.

Media channel Any means by which a message can be communicated, such as TV, radio, OOH (out of home), print, digital, mobile (see also *media vehicle*).

Media planner A specialist whose responsibility it is to see that a given campaign reaches the largest number of targeted consumers possible within the allocated budget.

Media-neutral planning Campaign planning that is not biased towards mass media.

Media vehicle A specific outlet within a given media channel: for example print is a media channel, the *Daily Telegraph* is a media vehicle; TV is a media channel, *The X Factor* is a media vehicle.

Native advertising Advertising that is 'native' to the consumer's environment, especially in digital and print in which sponsored content is included in editorial. Native advertising has been called 'a new name for advertorial', and another name for 'content marketing'. Print publications like the *Guardian* and news websites like the *Huffington Post* have invested much effort in developing revenue streams from native advertising.

Native pods These are a relatively recent development in TV product placement in which the sponsor buys joint creative control over a section of a popular show.

Neuromarketing A biometric consumer research method based on magnetic resonance imaging (MRI) of brain activity under stimulation, to test emotional engagement. For example, some advertising straplines or creative executions will be tested using volunteers in MRI conditions to measure emotional engagement. The rationale for neuromarketing is twofold: (1) consumer responses to marketing stimuli are primarily emotional, driven by physiological responses; (2) research methods based on self-reporting, such as questionnaire surveys, are unreliable instruments.

Operant conditioning In behavioural psychology, operant conditioning changes behaviour in response to repeated stimuli administered by an operator.

Ostensive communication Communication that is explicit and has an identifiable source, usually contrasted with communication that is covert or implicit.

Panel data Continuous data that are collected from a panel of consumers to monitor regular household purchases.

Peer group People like us in age and outlook with whom we associate.

Penetration The percentage of a market that is reached by a given medium or an individual promotional communication.

Pitching The pitching or pitch process is the traditional method by which advertising agencies get new business. They 'pitch' their ideas to a prospective client in response to the client's brief, in competition with other agencies.

Polysemy The capacity of a social text such as an ad to have multiple meanings. The meanings inferred will depend on such things as the cultural context and the interpretive strategy of the reader.

POS Point of sale can refer to sales promotions at the cash till of a store or to any in-store promotion, such as free sample stalls and LCD screen advertising.

Positioning A marketing concept indicating the values or ideas that are associated with a given brand and which differentiate the brand from competition. For example, the Nestlé KitKat chocolate confection is positioned (in the UK) as an excuse to have a break (that is, a rest) from work; the Marlboro cigarette brand is associated (through the image of the Marlboro cowboy) with individualism and toughness.

Positivistic A term borrowed from the philosophy of logical positivism (Ayer, 1936) but referring in management and business research to approaches that model their methods and assumptions on those of natural science.

Primary research The generation of new data. Contrasts with secondary research, which refers to the use of data sets already in existence.

Product placement The practice of placing branded products or services in TV, radio, movie or other forms of entertainment.

Projective tests A psychological technique used in qualitative consumer research. It can take the form of a story-completion or picture-completion task. It originated in the psychiatric technique of asking a respondent to interpret Rorschach ink blots.

Promotional mix The various promotional techniques. The term 'communications mix' is often used to indicate the differing communication channels that are deployed to reach the targeted audience.

Prompted and un-prompted recall Brand recall can be measured with prompted and un-prompted tests: e.g. unprompted – 'Which brands do you recall seeing in TV advertising this week?'; prompted – 'Do you recall seeing brand X in TV advertising this week?'

Psycho-galvanometer tests Tests carried out by a machine that measures the stimulation of the central nervous system by measuring the activity of sweat glands, thereby indicating the degree of interest a viewer has in a creative execution.

Psychographics A lifestyles and attitudes-based approach to consumer segmentation.

Qualitative research Non-numerical research to seek insight into the quality of a group's or person's experience of a given phenomenon.

Quantitative research Research that generates numerical data.

Reach The number of individuals or households within a target audience reached by a given promotional communication over a certain time period. Often expressed as a percentage.

Representative A sample of people that, for research purposes, are assumed to have the same characteristics as the whole population of interest.

Segmentation Aiming marketing interventions at a defined group of consumers who share certain demographic or lifestyle characteristics.

Semiology The study of linguistic signs. Associated with the work of Ferdinand de Saussure.

Semiotics The science of all signs and their meaning in communication, associated with Charles Sanders Pierce.

SEO Search engine optimisation – the techniques of maximising the pre-eminence of results in online searches

Social practices Also consumer practices or cultural practices: things consumers do, that may entail elements of ritual and make use of symbolism.

Socio-economic group An approach to classifying groups of individuals based on the occupation of the main household wage earner. Devised by the UK civil service in the late 1940s and still used in audience analysis.

Split-run studies A technique of measuring advertising effect by comparing two differing creative executions in two different but demographically similar regions.

Sub-culture A non-mainstream group characterised by shared attitudes, lifestyles, symbols and ritual.

Sub-text Texts that subsist beneath the main text, in other words, implied meanings, additional or subordinate to the primary meaning of a text.

Synergy A coined word indicating the mutually reinforcing promotional effect of portraying a brand in a similar style on two or more media channels.

Targeting The task of reaching the chosen segment of consumers by placing creative executions on carefully chosen media channels.

Tracking studies Research studies that monitor the effect of a campaign after its launch against the objectives set for it.

Traffic controller An administrative role within agencies responsible for keeping track of the progress of different accounts. Today, the traffic controller may be called project management.

UX User experience (design)

Viral marketing Originally the establishment of Hotmail was the model for viral marketing since word spread via email. Viral is now used to describe any content that is shared rapidly and widely on social media.

WOM Word-of-mouth (promotion) is the spontaneous exchange of ideas within peer groups about a brand or advertisement.

REFERENCES

Aaker, D.A. (1991) *Managing Brand Equity*. New York: Free Press.

Aaker, D.A. (1995) *Building Strong Brands*. New York: Free Press.

Aaker, D.A (2004) *Brand Portfolio Strategy: Creating Relevance, Differentiation, Energy, Leverage and Clarity*. New York: Free Press.

Ajzen, I. (2002) 'Perceived behavioural control, self-efficacy, locus of control, and the theory of planned behavior', *Journal of Applied Social Psychology*, 32: 665–83.

Al-Siyami, A. (2016) 'Intertextuality in newspaper advertising', *Journal of Modern Languages*, 23 (1): 41–55.

Alvesson, M. (1998) 'Gender relations and identity at work: a case study of masculinities and femininities in an advertising agency', *Human Relations*, 51: 969–1005.

Amis, J., Slack, T. and Berrett, T. (1999) 'Sport sponsorship as distinctive competence', *European Journal of Marketing*, 33 (3/4): 250–72.

Anderson, P.F. (1983) 'Marketing, scientific progress and scientific method', *Journal of Marketing*, 4: 18–31.

Ardley, B. (2008) 'A case of mistaken identity: theory, practice and the marketing textbook', *European Business Review*, 20 (6): 533–46.

Ardley, B. and Quinn, L. (2014) 'Practitioner accounts and knowledge production; an analysis of three marketing discourses, *Marketing Theory*, 14 (1): 97–118.

Armstrong, C.G., Delia, E.B. and Giardina, M.D. (2016) 'Embracing the social in social media', *Communication and Sport*, 4 (2): 145–65.

Arndt, J. (1985) 'The tyranny of paradigms: the case for paradigmatic pluralism in marketing', in N. Dholakia and J. Arndt (eds), *Changing the Course of Marketing: Alternative Paradigms for Widening Marketing Theory*, Research in Marketing, Supplement 2, Greenwich, CT: JAI Press, pp. 1–25.

Arnould, E.J. and Thompson, C.J. (2005) 'Consumer Culture Theory (CCT): twenty years of research', *Journal of Consumer Research*, 31 (4): 868–82.

Ashley, C. and Tuten, T. (2015) 'Creative strategies in social media marketing: an exploratory study of branded social content and consumer engagement', *Psychology & Marketing*, 32 (1): 15–27.

Ayer, A.J. (1936) *Language, Truth and Logic*. London: Victor Gollancz. (Reprinted by Penguin Books, 1990.)

Bagozzi, R., Tybout, A.M., Craig, C.S. and Sternthal, B. (1979) 'The construct validity of the tripartite classification of attitudes', *Journal of Marketing Research*, 16 (February): 88–95.

Baker, M.J. (ed.) (2000) *Marketing Theory: A Student Text*. London: Thomson Learning Business Press.

Bakhtin, M. (1989) 'Discourse in life and discourse in art (concerning sociological poetics)', in R. Davis and R. Schleifler (eds), *Contemporary Literary Criticism*. New York: Longman, pp. 392–410.

Balasubramanian, S.K. (1994) 'Beyond advertising and publicity: hybrid messages and public policy issues', *Journal of Advertising*, 23 (4): 29–47.

Balasubramanian, S.K., Karrh, J.A. and Patwardhan, H. (2006) 'Audience response to product placements: an integrative framework and future', *Journal of Advertising* 35 (3): 115–41. http://class.classmatandread.net/pp1/out-2.pdf (accessed 26 June 2017).

Barnard, N. and Ehrenberg, A. (1997) 'Advertising: strongly persuasive or nudging?', *Journal of Advertising Research*, 37 (1): 21–31.

Barry, T.E. and Howard, D.J. (1990) 'A review and critique of the hierarchy of effects in advertising', *International Journal of Advertising*, 9: 121–35.

Bartels, R. (1988) *The History of Marketing Thought*. Columbus, OH: Publishing Horizons Inc.

Barthes, R. (2000) *Mythologies*. London: Vintage.

Bassiouni, D. and Hackley, C. (2014) 'Generation Z children's adaptation to digital consumer culture: a critical literature review', *Journal of Customer Behaviour*, 13 (2): 113–33.

Bassiouni, D. and Hackley, C. (2016) 'Video games and young children's evolving sense of identity: a qualitative study', *Young Consumers*, 17 (2): 127–42.

Belk, R. (1986) 'Art versus science as ways of generating knowledge about materialism', in D. Brinberg and R.J. Lutz (eds), *Perspectives on Methodology in Consumer Research*. New York: Springer-Verlag, pp. 3–36.

Belk, R.W. (1988) 'Possessions and the extended self', *Journal of Consumer Research*, 15 (2): 139–68.

Belk, RW. and Pollay, R. (1985a) 'Images of ourselves: the good life in twentieth century advertising', *Journal of Consumer Research*, 11: 887–96.

Bengsston, A. (2002) *Consumers and Mixed-Brands: On the Polysemy of Brand Meaning*. Lund, Sweden: Lund University Press.

Berger, P.L. and Luckman, T. (1966) *The Social Construction of Reality*. London: Penguin.

Bernays, E. (1928: this edition, 2005 with introduction by M.C. Miller) *Propaganda*. Brooklyn, NY: IG Publishing.

Berthon, P., Pitt, L. and Campbell, C. (2008) 'Ad lib: when customers create the ad', *California Management Review*, 50 (4): 6–30.

Billig, M. (1996) *Arguing and Thinking: A Rhetorical Approach to Social Psychology*. Cambridge: Cambridge University Press.

Binet, L. (2009) 'Payback calculations: how to make sure you get your sums right', in N. Dawson (ed.), *Advertising Works 17: Proving the Return on Marketing Investment*. Henley-on-Thames: World Advertising Research Centre, pp. 19–22.

Blake, A., MacRury, I., Nava, M. and Richards, B. (eds) (1996) *Buy This Book: Studies in Advertising and Consumption*. London: Routledge.

Brenkert, G.G. (2008) *Marketing Ethics* (Foundations of Business Ethics). London: John Wiley & Sons.

Brodie, R.J., Ilic, A., Juric, B. and Hollebeek, L. (2013) 'Consumer engagement in a virtual brand community: an exploratory analysis', *Journal of Business Research*, 66 (1): 105–14.

Brown, S. (1995) *Postmodern Marketing*. London: Cengage Learning, EMEA.

Brown, S. (1996) 'Art or science? Fifty years of marketing debate', *Journal of Marketing Management*, 12 (4): 243–67.

Brown, S. (1997) 'Marketing science in a postmodern world: introduction to the special issue', *European Journal of Marketing*, 31 (3–4): 167–82.

Brown, S. (1999) 'Retro-marketing: yesterday's tomorrows, today!', *Marketing Intelligence & Planning*, 17 (7): 363–76.

Brown, S. (2001) *Marketing: The Retro Revolution*. London: Sage.

Brown, S. (2003) *Free Gift Inside! Forget the Customer-Develop Marketease*! London: John Wiley.

Brown, S. (2005) *Writing Marketing*. London: Sage.

Brown, S. (2016) *Brands and Branding*. London: Sage.

Brown, S. and Hackley, C. (2012) 'The Greatest Showman on Earth: is Simon Cowell P.T. Barnum reborn?', *Journal of Historical Research in Marketing*, 4 (2): 290–308.

Brown, S. and Jensen-Schau, H.J. (2008) 'Writing Russell Belk: excess all areas', *Marketing Theory*, 8 (2): 143–65.

Brown, S. and Ponsonby-McCabe, S. (2013) 'They're great!' Introduction to the Special Issue, *Journal of Marketing Management*, 29 (1–2). doi: 10.1080/0267257X.2012.762184.

Brown, S. Stevens, L. and Maclaran, P. (1999) 'I Can't Believe It's Not Bakhtin!: literary theory, postmodern advertising, and the gender agenda', *Journal of Advertising*, 28 (1): 11–24.

Brownlie, D., Saren, M., Wensley, R. and Whittington, D. (eds) (1999) *Rethinking Marketing: Towards Critical Marketing Accountings*. London: Sage.

Burr, V. (1995) *An Introduction to Social Constructionism*. London: Routledge.

Buttle, F. (1994) 'Marketing communications theory: what do the texts teach our students?', *International Journal of Advertising*, 14: 297–313.

Calfee, J.E. and Scherage, C. (1994) 'The influence of advertising on alcohol consumption: a literature review and an econometric analysis of four European nations', *International Journal of Advertising*, 13 (4): 287–310.

Campbell, N. (2013) 'Signs and semiotics of advertising', in J. Schroeder, S. Warren and E. Bell (eds), *The Routledge Companion to Visual Organisation*. London: Routledge, pp. 258–79.

Case, P. (1999) 'Remember re-engineering? The rhetorical appeal of a managerial salvation device', *Journal of Management Studies*, 4: 419–41.

Chada, R. and Husband, P. (2006) *The Cult of the Luxury Brand: Inside Asia's Love Affair with Luxury*. London and Boston: Nicholas Brearley.

Chong, D. (2009) *Arts Management*. London: Routledge.

Cogburn, D.L. and Espinoza-Vasquez, F.K. (2011) 'From networked nominee to networked nation: examining the impact of Web 2.0 and social media on political participation and civic engagement in the 2008 Obama campaign', *Journal of Political Marketing*, 10 (1–2): 189–213.

Cook, G. (2001) *The Discourse of Advertising*. London: Routledge.

Cook, W.A. and Kover, A.J. (1998) 'Research and the meaning of advertising effectiveness: mutual misunderstandings', in W.D. Wells (ed.), *Measuring Advertising Effectiveness*. Hillsdale, NJ: Lawrence Erlbaum Associates, pp. 13–20.

Cornelissen, J.P. and Lock, A.R. (2002) 'Advertising research and its influence upon managerial practice: a review of perspectives and approaches', *Journal of Advertising Research*, 42 (3): 50–5.

Cornwell, B.T. (2014) *Sponsorship in Marketing*. London: Routledge.

Cova, B., Kozinets, R. and Shankar, A. (2007) *Consumer Tribes*. London: Butterworth–Heinemann.

Crane, A. and Matten, D. (2015) *Business Ethics: Managing Corporate Citizenship and Sustainability in the Age of Globalization*. Oxford: Oxford University Press.

Cronin, A.M. (2004) 'Regimes of mediation: advertising agencies as cultural intermediaries', *Consumption, Markets and Culture*, 7 (4): 349–69.

Cronin, A.M. (2008) 'Gender in the making of commercial worlds: creativity, vitalism and the practices of marketing', *Feminist Theory*, 9 (3): 293–312.

Danesi, M. (1994) *Messages and Meanings: An Introduction to Semiotics*. Toronto: Canadian Scholar's Press.

Danesi, M. (2006) *Brands*. London: Routledge.

d'Astous, A. and Seguin, N. (1999) 'Consumer reactions to product placement strategies in television sponsorship', *European Journal of Marketing*, 33 (9/10): 896–910.

Davis, A. (2013) *Promotional Culture: The Rise and Spread of Advertising, Public Relations, Marketing and Branding*. Cambridge: Polity.

Dawson, N. (2009) 'The evolution of commercially effective communication', in N. Dawson (ed.), *Advertising Works 17: Proving the Return on Marketing Investment*. Henley-on-Thames: World Advertising Research Centre, pp. 27–34.

De Chernatony, L., McDonald, M. and Wallace, E. (2010) *Creating Powerful Brands*. London: Routledge.

Dermody, J. (1999) 'CPM/HEM models of information processing', in P.J. Kitchen (ed.), *Marketing Communications: Principles and Practice*. London: Thomson Learning, pp. 156–71.

De Saussure, F. (1974) *Course in General Linguistics*. London: Collins.

Deuze, M. (2007) *Media Work*. Cambridge: Polity Press.

deWaal Malefyt, T. and Moeran, B. (2003) *Advertising Cultures*. London: Berg.

Diamond, N., Sherry, J.F., Muniz, M.A., McGrath, M.A., Kozinets, R. and Borghini, S. (2009) 'American girl and the brand gestalt: closing the loop on socioculture branding research', *Journal of Marketing*, 73: 118–34, and at www3.nd.edu/~jsherry/pdf/2009/American%20Girl.pdf (accessed 26 June 2017).

Dichter, E. (1949) 'A psychological view of advertising effectiveness', *Journal of Marketing*, 14 (1): 61–7.

Dichter, E. (1966) 'How word-of-mouth advertising works', *Harvard Business Review*, 44 (6): 147–57.

Eagle, L. and Dahl, S. (2015) *Marketing Ethics & Society*. London: Sage.

Eagle, L., Kitchen, P.J. and Bulmer, S. (2007) 'Insights into interpreting integrated marketing communications: a two-nation qualitative comparison', *European Journal of Marketing*, 41 (7/8): 956–70.

Eagleton, T. (1991) *Ideology*. London: Verso.

Ehrenberg, A., Barnard, N., Kennedy, R. and Bloom, H. (2002) 'Brand advertising and creative publicity', *Journal of Advertising Research*, 42 (4): 7–18.

Elliott, R. (1997) 'Existential consumption and irrational desire', *European Journal of Marketing*, 34 (4): 285–96.

Elliott, R. (1998) 'A model of emotion-driven choice', *Journal of Marketing Management*, 14: 95–108.

Elliott, R. and Jankel-Elliott, N. (2002) 'Using ethnography in strategic consumer research', *Qualitative Market Research: An International Journal*, 6 (4): 215–23.

Elliott, R. and Ritson, M. (1997) 'Post-structuralism and the dialectics of advertising: discourse, ideology, resistance', in S. Brown and D. Turley (eds), *Consumer Research: Postcards From the Edge*. London: Routledge, pp. 190–248.

Elliott, R. and Wattanasuwan, K. (1998) 'Brands as symbolic resources for the construction of identity', *International Journal of Advertising*, 17 (2): 131–44.

Erdogan, B.Z. (1999) 'Celebrity endorsement: a literature review', *Journal of Marketing Management*, 15 (4): 291–314.

Ewing, M.T. and Jones, J.P. (1990) 'Agency beliefs in the power of advertising', *International Journal of Advertising*, 19 (3): 335–48.

Feldwick, P. (2002) *What Is Brand Equity Anyway?* Henley-on-Thames: World Advertising Research Centre.

Feldwick, P. (2007) 'Account planning: its history and significance for ad agencies', in G. Tellis and T. Ambler (eds), *The Sage Handbook of Advertising*. London: Sage, pp. 184–98.

Feldwick, P. (2015) *The Anatomy of Humbug: How to Think Differently About Advertising*. London: Matador.

Feng, D. and Wignell, P. (2011) 'Intertextual voices and engagement in TV advertisements', *Visual Communication*, 10 (4): 565–88.

Fill, C. (2002) *Marketing Communications: Contexts, Strategies and Applications*, 3rd edn. Harlow: Prentice Hall.

Fill, C. (2009) *Marketing Communications: Interactivity, Communities and Content*. London: FT/Prentice Hall.

Firat, Fuat A. and Venkatesh, A. (1995) 'Liberatory postmodernism and the re-enchantment of consumption', *Journal of Consumer Research*, 22 (3): 239–67.

Fletcher, W. (2008) *Powers of Persuasion: The Inside Story of British Advertising 1951–2000*. Oxford: Oxford University Press.

Forceville, C. (1996) *Pictorial Metaphor in Advertising*. London: Routledge.

Fowles, J. (1996) *Advertising and Popular Culture*. London: Sage.

Fox, S. (1984) *The Mirror Makers: A History of American Advertising and Its Creators*. New York: William Morrow.

Foxall, G.R. (2000) 'The psychological basis of marketing', in M.J. Baker (ed.), *Marketing Theory: A Student Text*. London: Thomson Learning, pp. 86–101.

Gabriel, Y. and Lang, T. (2008) 'New faces and new masks of today's consumer', *Journal of Consumer Culture*, 8 (3): 321–40

Gardner, B. and Levy, S. (1955) 'The product and the brand', *Harvard Business Review*, March–April: 33–9.

Gensler, S., Völkner, F., Liu-Thompkins, Y. and Wiertz, C. (2013) 'Managing brands in the social media environment', *Journal of Interactive Marketing*, 27: 242–56. www.socialmediathinklab.com/wp-content/uploads/2014/02/3-Gensler_V%C3%B6lckner_Liu-Thompkins_Wiertz_2013_JIM_Managing-Brands-in-the-Social-Media-Environment.pdf (accessed 26 June 2017).

Gilmore, C., O'Donohoe, S. and Townley, B. (2009) 'The elephant in the room? Class and creative collaboration in British advertising agencies', *Human Relations*, 62 (7): 1011–39.

Gilmore, C., O'Donohoe, S. and Townley, B. (2011) 'Pot Noodles, placements and peer regard: creative career trajectories and communities of practice in the British advertising industry', *British Journal of Management*, 22 (1): 114–31.

Gilmore, J.H. and Pine, B.J. (2011) *The Experience Economy*. Boston, MA: Harvard Business Review Press.

Goffman, E. (1959) *The Presentation of Self in Everyday Life*. New York: Anchor Books.

Goffman, E. (1979) *Gender Advertisements*. New York: Harper&Row.

Goldman, R. and Papson, S. (1994) 'Advertising in the age of hypersignification', *Theory, Culture & Society*, 11 (3): 23–53.

Grainge, P. and Thompson, C. (2015) *Promotional Screen Industries*. London: Routledge.

Greenwald, G. (2015) *No Place to Hide: Edward Snowden, the NSA and the Surveillance State*. New York: Penguin Books.

Griffin, C., Bengry-Howell, A., Hackley, C., Mistral, W. and Szmigin, I. (2009) 'Every time I do it I absolutely annihilate myself: loss of (self)-consciousness and loss of memory in young people's drinking narratives', *Sociology*, 43 (3): 457–77.

Griffin, C., Szmigin, I., Bengry-Howell, A., Hackley, C. and Mistral, W. (2012) 'Inhabiting the contradictions: hypersexual femininity and the culture of intoxication among young women in the UK', *Feminism and Psychology*, 23 (2): 184–206.

Griffiths, J. and Follows, T. (2016) *98% Pure Potato: The Origins of Advertising Account Planning as Told to Us by Its Pioneers*. London: Unbound.

Gronhaug, K. and Kleppe, I.A. (2010) 'The sociological basis of marketing', in M.J. Baker (ed.), *Marketing Theory: A Student Text*. London: Sage, pp. 147–64.

Hackley, C. (1999a) 'Tacit knowledge and the epistemology of expertise in strategic marketing management', *European Journal of Marketing*, Special Edition: Marketing Pedagogy, 33 (7–8): 720–35.

Hackley, C. (1999b) 'The communications process and the semiotic boundary', in P.J. Kitchen (ed.), *Marketing Communications: Principles and Practice*. London: Thomson Learning, pp. 135–55.

Hackley, C. (2000) 'Silent running: tacit, discursive and psychological aspects of management in a top UK advertising agency', *British Journal of Management*, 11 (3): 239–54.

Hackley, C. (2002) 'The panoptic role of advertising agencies in the production of consumer culture', *Consumption, Markets and Culture*, 5 (3): 211–29.

Hackley, C. (2003a) 'IMC and Hollywood: what brand managers need to know', *Admap*, November: 44–7.

Hackley, C. (2003b) 'How divergent beliefs cause account team conflict', *International Journal of Advertising*, 22 (3): 313–32.

Hackley, C. (2003c) '"We are all customers now": rhetorical strategy and ideological control in marketing management texts', *Journal of Management Studies*, 40 (5): 1325–52.

Hackley, C. (2003d) 'Divergent representational practices in advertising and consumer research: some thoughts on integration', Special Issue on representation in consumer research, *Qualitative Market Research: An International Journal*, 6 (3): 175–84.

Hackley, C. (2003e) *Doing Research Projects in Marketing, Management and Consumer Research*. London: Routledge.

Hackley, C. (2003f) 'Account planning: current agency perspectives on an advertising enigma', *Journal of Advertising Research*, 43 (2): 235–45.

Hackley, C. (2003g) 'From consumer insight to advertising strategy: the account planner's integrative role in creative advertising development', *Marketing Intelligence and Planning*, 21 (7): 446–52.

Hackley, C. (2007) 'Marketing psychology and the hidden persuaders', *The Psychologist*, 20 (8): 488–90. www.thepsychologist.org.uk/archive/archive_home.cfm?volumeID=20&editionID=150&ArticleID=1228 (accessed 26 June 2017).

Hackley, C. (2008) 'UK alcohol policy and market research: media debates and methodological differences', *International Journal of Market Research*, 50 (4): 429–31.

Hackley, C. (2009a) *Marketing: A Critical Introduction*. London: Sage.

Hackley, C. (2009b) 'Parallel universes and disciplinary space: the bifurcation of managerialism and social science in marketing studies', *Journal of Marketing Management*, 25 (7–8): 643–59.

Hackley, C. (ed.) (2009c) *Advertising*. Sage 'Library in Marketing'. London: Sage. 3 volumes: Volume 1: *Advertising Management*; Volume 2: *Advertising Culture*; Volume 3: *Advertising Science*.

Hackley, C. (2010) 'Theorizing advertising: managerial, scientific and cultural approaches', in P. MacLaran, M. Saren, B. Stern and M. Tadajewski (eds), *The Sage Handbook of Marketing Theory*. London: Sage, pp. 89–107.

Hackley, C. (2013a) *Marketing in Context: Setting the Scene*. London: Palgrave Macmillan.

Hackley, C. (2013b) 'Marketing psychology', in R. Bayne and G. Jinks (eds), *Applied Psychology: Training, Practice and New Directions*, 2nd edn. London: Sage, pp. 108–24.

Hackley, C. (2014) 'Why product placement on YouTube can't be regulated like television', The Conversation, 27 November 2014. http://theconversation.com/why-product-placement-on-youtube-cant-be-regulated-like-television-34732 (accessed 26 June 2017) .

Hackley, C. and Hackley, R.A. (2013) 'Television product placement strategy in Thailand and the UK', *Asian Journal of Business Research*, 3 (1): 97–110.

Hackley, C. and Hackley née Tiwsakul, R.A. (2012) 'Unpaid product placement: the elephant in the room in the UK's new paid-for product placement market', *International Journal of Advertising*, 31 (4): 703–18.

Hackley, C. and Hackley, R.A. (2015) 'Marketing and the cultural production of celebrity in the convergent media era', *Journal of Marketing Management*, 31 (5/6): 461–77.

Hackley, C. and Kitchen, P. (1997) 'Creative problem solving as a technology of expert behaviour within marketing management', *Creativity and Innovation Management*, 6 (1): 45–59.

Hackley, C. and Kitchen, P.J. (1999) 'Ethical perspectives on the postmodern communications Leviathan', *Journal of Business Ethics*, 20 (1): 15–26.

Hackley, C. and Kover, A. (2007) 'The trouble with creatives: negotiating creative identity in advertising agencies', *International Journal of Advertising*, 26 (1): 63–78.

Hackley, C. and Tiwsakul, A. (2006) 'Entertainment marketing and experiential consumption', *Journal of Marketing Communications*, 12 (1): 63–75.

Hackley, C. and Tiwsakul, R. (2008) 'Comparative management practices in international advertising agencies in the UK, Thailand and the USA', in C. Smith, B. McSweeney and R. Fitzgerland, (eds), *Remaking Management: Between Global and Local*. Cambridge: Cambridge University Press, pp. 586–626.

Hackley, C., Brown, S. and Hackley, R.A. (2012) 'The X Factor enigma: Simon Cowell and the marketization of existential liminality', *Marketing Theory*, 12 (4): 451–69.

Hackley, C., Tiwsakul, R. and Preuss, R. (2008) 'An ethical evaluation of product placement – a deceptive practice?', *Business Ethics – A European Review*, 17 (April): 109–20.

Hackley, C., Bengry-Howell, A., Griffin, C., Szmigin, I., Mistral, W. and Hackley, R.A. (2015) 'Transgressive drinking practices and the limitations of proscriptive alcohol policy messages', *Journal of Business Research*, 68 (10): 2125–31. https://doi.org/10.1016/j.jbusres.2015.03.011.

Hackley, C., Bengry-Howell, A., Griffin, C., Mistral, W., Szmigin, I. and Hackley née Tiwsakul, R.A. (2013) 'Young adults and "binge" drinking: a Bakhtinian analysis', *Journal of Marketing Management*, 29 (7–8): 933–49.

Harbor, C. (2007) 'Pervasive and persuasive: advertisements for concerts in London 1672–1750', conference paper: Marketing Theory into Practice, Academy of Marketing Conference, Kingston Business School at Royal Holloway University of London, 3–6 July.

Harris, J.D., Moriarty, B. and Wicks, A.C. (eds) (2014) *Public Trust in Business*. Cambridge: Cambridge University Press.

Head, V. (1981) *Sponsorship: The Newest Marketing Skill*. Cambridge: Woodhead–Faulkner, in association with the Chartered Institute of Marketing.

Heath, R. (2012) *Seducing the Subconscious: The Psychology of Emotional Influence in Advertising*. Chichester: Wiley–Blackwell.

Heath, R. and Feldwick, P. (2008) 'Fifty years using the wrong model of advertising', *International Journal of Advertising*, 50 (1): 29–59. http://paulfeldwick.com/wp-content/uploads/2017/04/Feldwick-and-Heath.pdf (accessed 26 June 2017).

Hesmondhalgh, D. (2005) 'Producing celebrity', in J. Evans and D. Hesmondhalgh, (eds), *Understanding Media: Inside Celebrity*. Milton Keynes: Open University Press, pp. 97–134.

Hirschman, E.C. (1986) 'Humanistic inquiry in marketing research: research, philosophy, method and criteria', *Journal of Marketing Research*, 23 (August): 237–49.

Hirschman, E.C. and Thompson, C.J. (1997) 'Why media matter: toward a richer understanding of consumers' relationships with advertising and mass media', *Journal of Advertising*, 26 (1): 43–60.

Holbrook, M. (1995) *Consumer Research: Introspective Essays on the Study of Consumption*. London: Sage.

Holbrook, M. and Hirschman, E. (1982) 'The experiential aspects of consumption: consumer feelings, fantasies and fun', *Journal of Consumer Research*, 9 (September): 132–40.

Holbrook, M.B. and O'Shaughnessy, J. (1984) 'The role of emotion in advertising', *Psychology and Marketing*, 1 (2): 45–64. http://onlinelibrary.wiley.com/doi/10.1002/mar.4220010206/abstract (accessed 26 June 2017).

Holbrook, M.B. and O'Shaughnessy, J. (1988) 'On the scientific status of consumer research and the need for an interpretive approach to studying consumption behaviour', *Journal of Consumer Research*, 15: 398–403.

Holt, D. (2002) 'Why do brands cause trouble?', *Journal of Consumer Research*, 29 (June): 70–90.

Holt, D. (2004) *How Brands Become Icons*. Boston, MA: Harvard Business School Press.

Holt, D. and Cameron, D. (2010) *Cultural Strategy: Using Innovative Ideologies to Build Breakthrough Brands*. Oxford: Oxford University Press.

Horkheimer, M. and Adorno, T.W. ([1944] 2002) *Dialectic of Enlightenment* (trans. Edmund Jephcott). Stanford, CA: Stanford University Press.

Hunt, S.D. (1991) *Modern Marketing Theory: Critical Issues in the Philosophy of Marketing Science*. Cincinnati, OH: Southwestern Publishing Co.

Hunt, S.D. (1992) 'For reason and realism in marketing', *Journal of Marketing*, 56 (April): 89–102.

Iser, W. (1978) *The Act of Reading*. Baltimore, MD: Johns Hopkins University Press.

Jefkins, F. (2000) *Advertising*. Harlow: Pearson Education.

Jenkins, H. (2008) *Convergence Culture: Where Old and New Media Collide*. New York: New York University Press.

Jenkins, H., Ford, S. and Green J. (2013) *Spreadable Media: Creating Value and Meaning in a Networked Culture*. New York: New York University Press.

Jones, D.G.B. and Tadajewski, M. (2015) 'Origins of marketing thought in Britain, *European Journal of Marketing*, 49 (7/8): 1016–39.

Jones, J.P. (1990) 'Advertising: strong force or weak force? Two views an ocean apart', *International Journal of Advertising*, 9: 233–46.

Katz, B. (2016) 'Digital ad spending will surpass TV spending for the first time in U.S. History, *Forbes*, 14 September.

Katz, E. and Lazarsfeld, P.F. (1955) *Personal Influence*. Glencoe, IL: Free Press.

Katz, H. (2017) *The Media Handbook: A Complete Guide to Advertising Media Selection, Planning, Research and Buying* (Routledge Communication Series). New York: Routledge.

Keller, K.L. (2012) *Strategic Brand Management: Building, Measuring and Managing Brand Equity*. New York: Pearson.

Kelly, A., Lawlor, K. and O'Donohoe, S. (2005) 'Encoding advertisements: the creative perspective', *Journal of Marketing Management*, 21: 505–28.

Kelly, L., Kerr, G. and Drennan, J. (2010) 'Avoidance of advertising in social networking sites: the teenage perspective', *Journal of Interactive Advertising*, 10 (2): 16–27.

Kennedy, John E. (1924) *Reason Why Advertising Plus Intensive Advertising*. Terre Haute, IN: TWI Press, Inc.

Kirby, J. and Dzamic, L. (2018, in press) *Content Marketing*. London: Kogan Page.

Kirby, J. and Marsden, P. (2006) *Connected Marketing: The Viral, Buzz and Word of Mouth Revolution*. Oxford: Elsevier.

Kitson, H.D. (1921) *The Mind of the Buyer*. New York: Macmillan.

Klein, N. (2000) *No Logo*. London: Flamingo.

Kotler, P. and Keller, K. (2015) *Marketing Management*, 15th edn. New York: Pearson.

Kotler, P. and Roberto, E.L. (1989) *Social Marketing: Strategies for Changing Public Behaviour*. New York: The Free Press.

Kotler, P. and Zaltman, G. (1971) 'Social marketing: an approach to planned social change', *Journal of Marketing*, 35: 3–12.

Kover, A.J. (1995) 'Copywriters' implicit theories of communication: an exploration', *Journal of Consumer Research*, 21 (March): 598–611.

Kover, A.J. (1996) 'Why copywriters don't like research – and what kind of research might they accept', *Journal of Advertising Research*, 36 (2): RC8–12.

Kover, A.J. and Goldberg, S.M. (1995) 'The games copywriters play: conflict, quasi-control, a new proposal', *Journal of Advertising Research*, 35 (4): 52–68.

Kozinets, R.V. (2002) 'Can consumers escape the market? Emancipatory illuminations from Burning Man', *Journal of Consumer Research*, 29 (1): 2038

Kozinets, R.V. (2009) *Netnography: Doing Ethnographic Research Online*. Thousand Oaks, CA: Sage.

Lash, S. and Lury, C. (2007) *Global Culture Industry: The Mediation of Things*. London: Polity.

Lasswell, H.D. (1948) 'The structure and function of communication in society', in L. Bryson (ed.), *The Communication of Ideas*. New York: Harper, pp. 117–29.

Lavidge, R.J. and Steiner, G.A. (1961) 'A model for predictive measurements of advertising effectiveness', *Journal of Marketing*, 24 (October): 59–62.

Lazarsfeld, P.F. (1941) 'Remarks on administrative and critical communications research', *Studies in Philosophy and Science*, 9: 3–16.

Lears, J. (1994) *Fables of Abundance: A Cultural History of Advertising in America*. New York: Basic Books.

Lee, N. and Lings, I. (2008) *Doing Business Research: A Guide to Theory and Practice*. London: Sage.

Lee, N., Senior, C. and Butler, M.J.R. (2012) 'The domain of organizational cognitive neuroscience: theoretical and empirical challenges', *Journal of Management*, 38 (4): 921–31.

Lehu, J.M. (2007) *Branded Entertainment: Product Placement and Brand Strategy in the Entertainment Business*. London: Kogan Page.

Leiss, W., Kline, S. and Jhally, S. (1997) *Social Communication in Advertising: Persons, Products and Images of Well-Being*. London: Routledge.

Leiss, W., Kline, S., Jhally, S. and Botterill, J. (2005) *Social Communication in Advertising: Consumption in the Mediated Marketplace*. London: Routledge.

Lemle, R. and Mishkind, M. (1989) 'Alcohol and masculinity', *Journal of Substance Abuse Treatment*, 6: 213–22.

Levitt, T. (1983) 'The globalisation of markets', *Harvard Business Review*, April/May: 92–107.

Levy, S. (1959) 'Symbols for sale', *Harvard Business Review*, 37 (July): 117–24.

Loo, B.K. and Hackley, C. (2013) 'Internationalisation strategy of iconic Malaysian high fashion brands', *Qualitative Market Research: An International Journal*, 16 (4): 406–20.

Lu, P.X. (2008) *Elite China: Luxury Consumer Behaviour in China*. Singapore: Wiley.

Lury, C. (2011) *Consumer Culture*. Cambridge: Polity.

Lutz, R.J. (1977) 'An experimental investigation of causal relations among cognitions: affect and behavioural intention', *Journal of Consumer Research*, 3 (March): 197–208.

Manning, N. (2009) 'The new media communications model: a progress report', in N. Dawson (ed.), *Advertising Works 17: Proving the Return on Marketing Investment*. Henley-on-Thames: World Advertising Centre, pp. 7–14.

Marchand, R. (1985) *Advertising and the American Dream: Making Way for Modernity, 1920–1940*. Berkeley, CA: University of California Press.

Marchand, R. (1998) *Creating the Corporate Soul: The Rise of Public Relations and Corporate Imagery in American Big Business*. Berkeley, CA: University of California Press.

Matson, O. (2017) Why your B2B Strategy Needs Slideshare. http://info.marketscale.com/blog/why-your-b2b-strategy-needs-slideshare (accessed 24 March 2017).

McCracken, G. (1986) 'Culture and consumption: a theoretical account of the structure and movement of the cultural meaning of consumer goods', *Journal of Consumer Research*, 13 (1): 71–84.

McCracken, G. (1987) 'Advertising – meaning or information?', in M. Wallendorf and P. Anderson (eds), *Advances in Consumer Research*, Vol. 14. Provo, UT: Association for Consumer Research, pp. 121–4. www.acrwebsite.org/search/view-conference-proceedings.aspx?Id=6667 (accessed 26 June 2017).

McCracken, G. (1989) 'Who is the celebrity endorser? Cultural foundation of the endorsement process', *Journal of Consumer Research*, 16 (3): 310–21.

McCracken, G. (1990) *Culture and Consumption: New Approaches to the Symbolic Character of Consumer Goods and Activities*. Bloomington, IN; Indiana University Press.

McCracken, G. (2005) *Culture and Consumption 11: Markets, Meaning and Brand Management*. Bloomington, IN: Indiana University Press.

McDonald, C. and Scott, J. (2007) 'A brief history of advertising', in G. Tellis and T. Ambler (eds), *The Sage Handbook of Advertising*. London: Sage, pp. 17–34.

McFall, L. (2004) *Advertising: A Cultural Economy*. London: Sage.

McKeil, J. (1985) *The Creative Mystique*. London: John Wiley and Sons.

McLeod, C., O'Donohoe, S. and Townley, B. (2009) 'The elephant in the room? Class and creative careers in British advertising agencies', *Human Relations*, 62 (7): 1011–39.

McLuhan, M. (1964) 'Keeping upset with the Joneses', in *Understanding Media: The Extensions of Man*. London: Routledge and Kegan Paul, pp. 226–33.

McQuarrie, E.F. and Phillips, B.J. (2005) 'Indirect persuasion in advertising: how consumers process metaphors presented in pictures and words', *Journal of Advertising*, 34 (2): 7–21.

McSweeney, B. (2002) 'Hofstede's model of national cultural differences and their consequences: a triumph of faith – a failure of analysis', *Human Relations*, 55 (1): 89–118.

Meenaghan, T. (1991) 'Sponsorship: legitimising the medium', *European Journal of Marketing*, 25 (11): 5–10.

Meenaghan, T. and Shipley, D. (1999) 'Media affecting sponsorship', *European Journal of Marketing*, 33 (3/4): 328–47.

Meikle, G. and Young, S. (2011) *Media Convergence: Networked Digital Media in Everyday Life*. London: Palgrave MacMillan.

Melewar, T.C. and Wooldridge, A. (2001) 'The dynamics of corporate identity: a review of a process model', *Journal of Communication Management*, 5 (4): 327–40.

Mick, D.G. (1986) 'Consumer research and semiotics: exploring the morphology of signs, symbols and significance', *Journal of Consumer Research*, 13: 196–213.

Mick, D.G. and Buhl, K. (1992) 'A meaning based model of advertising', *Journal of Consumer Research*, 19 (December): 317–38.

Miles, C. (2013) 'Persuasion, marketing communication and the metaphor of magic', *European Journal of Marketing*, 47 (11/12): 2002–19.

Miles, C. (2014) 'The rhetoric of managed contagion: metaphor and agency in the discourse of viral marketing', *Marketing Theory*, 14 (1): 3–18.

Miles, C. (2015) 'Ericksonian Therapy as a grounding for a theory of persuasive marketing dialogue', *Marketing Theory*, 15 (1): 95–111.

Moeran, B. (1996) *A Japanese Advertising Agency: An Anthropology of Media and Markets*. London: Curzon.

Muñiz, A.M. Jr and O'Guinn, T.C. (2001) 'Brand community', *Journal of Consumer Research*, 27: 412–32.

Nelson, J.P. and Young, D.J. (2001) 'Do advertising bans work? An international comparison', *International Journal of Advertising*, 20: 273–96.

Nightingale, D.J. and Cromby, J. (eds) (1999) *Social Constructionist Psychology: A Critical Analysis of Theory and Practice*. Buckingham: Open University Press.

Nilsson, T. (2015) *Rhetorical Business*. Lund, Sweden: Lund University Press.

Nixon, S. (2003) 'Re-imagining the advertising agency: the cultural connotations of economic forms', in P. DuGay and M. Pryke (eds), *Cultural Economy*. London: Sage, pp. 132–47.

O'Donohoe, S. (1994) 'Advertising uses and gratifications', *European Journal of Marketing*, 28 (8/9): 52–75.

O'Donohoe, S. (1997) 'Raiding the postmodern pantry – advertising intertextuality and the young adult audience', *European Journal of Marketing*, 31 (34): 234–53.

Oetting, J. (2015) The Biggest Threats to the Agency Model, Hubspot Blog https://blog.hubspot.com/agency/threats-agency-model#sm.00000t4d5d6g1tfbjr2bbazi9irx7 (accessed 26 March 2017).

Ogilvy, D. (1963) *Confessions of an Advertising Man*. New York: Atheneum.

Ogilvy, D. (1983) *Ogilvy on Advertising*, 2nd edn. London: Multimedia Books.

Okazaki, S. (ed.) (2014) *Handbook of Research on International Advertising*. Cheltenham: Edward Elgar Publishing.

Olsen, B. (2016) 'Liminality in advertising from the *Mad Men* era', *Journal of Business Anthropology*, 2: 77–104.

Ormrod, R., Henneberg, S. and O'Shaughnessy, N. (2013) *Political Marketing: Theory and Concepts*. London: Sage.

O'Shaughnessy, J. (1997) 'Temerarious directions for marketing', *European Journal of Marketing*, 31 (9/10): 677–705.

O'Shaughnessy, N. (2001) 'The marketing of political marketing', *European Journal of Marketing*, 35 (9/10): 1047–57.

O'Shaughnessy, N. and O'Shaughnessy, J. (2004) *Persuasion in Advertising*. London: Routledge.

Packard, V. (1957) *The Hidden Persuaders*. New York: McKay.

Pantano, E., Nguyen, B., Dennis, C., Merrilees, B. and Gerlach, S. (2016) *Internet Retailing and Future Perspectives*. London: Routledge.

Parsons, E. and Maclaran, P. (2009) *Contemporary Issues in Marketing and Consumer Behaviour*. London: Elsevier.

Pateman, T. (1983) 'How is understanding an advertisement possible?', in H. Davis and P. Walton (eds), *Language, Image, Media*. Oxford: Blackwell, pp. 187–204.

Peirce, C.S. (1958) *Collected Papers*. Cambridge, MA: Harvard University Press.

Peng, N. and Hackley, C. (2007) 'Political marketing communications planning in the UK and Taiwan – comparative insights from leading practitioners', *Marketing Intelligence and Planning*, 25 (5): 483–98.

Peng, N. and Hackley, C. (2009) 'Are voters, consumers? A qualitative exploration of the voter–consumer analogy in political marketing', *Qualitative Market Research: An International Journal*, 12 (2): 171–86.

Percy, L. and Elliott, R. (2009) *Strategic Advertising Management*, 3rd edn. Oxford: Oxford University Press.

Percy, L., Rossiter, J.R. and Elliott, R. (2001) *Strategic Advertising Management*. Oxford: Oxford University Press.

Pickton, D. and Crosier, K. (2003) 'Marketing intelligence and planning', *Account Planning*, special issue, 21 (7): 410–15.

Pollitt, S. (1979) 'How I started account planning in agencies', *Campaign*, 20 (April): 29–30.

Pongsakornrungsilp, S. and Schroeder, J.E. (2011) 'Understanding value co-creation in a co-consuming brand community', *Marketing Theory*, 11 (3): 303–24.

Powell, H. (ed.) (2013) *Promotional Culture in an Era of Convergence*. Abingdon: Taylor and Francis.

Pratt, A. (2006) 'Advertising and creativity, a governance approach: a case study of creative agencies in London', *Environment and Planning A*, 38 (10): 1883–99.

Pratten, R. (2015). *Getting Started in Transmedia Storytelling: A Practical Guide for Beginners*. CreateSpace Independent Publishing Platform.

Puntoni, S., Schroeder, J. and Ritson, M. (2010) 'Meaning matters', *Journal of Advertising*, 39 (2): 51–64.

Punyapiroje, C., Morrison, M. and Hoy, M. (2002) 'A nation under the influence: the creative strategy process for advertising in Thailand', *Journal of Current Issues and Research in Advertising*, 24 (2): 51–65.

Quickenden, K. and Kover, A.J. (2007) 'Did Boulton sell silver plate to the middle class? A quantitative study of luxury marketing in late eighteenth-century Britain', *Journal of Macromarketing*, 27 (March): 51–64.

Reeves, J. (2017) *Citizen Spies: The Long Rise of America's Surveillance Society*. New York: New York University Press.

Richards, B., MacRury, I. and Botterill, J. (2000) *The Dynamics of Advertising*. London: Routledge.

Ritson, M. and Elliott, R. (1999) 'The social uses of advertising: an ethnographic study of adolescent advertising audiences', *Journal of Consumer Research*, 26 (3): 260–77.

Ritzer, G. (2011) *The MacDonaldization of Society*. Newbury Park, CA: Pine Forge Press.

Robinson, N., McWilliams, H., Bullinger, F. and Schouest, C. (2009) 'Dove's big ideal: from real curves to growth curves', in N. Dawson (ed.), *Advertising Works 17: Proving the Payback on Marketing Investment*. Henley-on-Thames: World Advertising Research Centre, pp. 335–70.

Rojek, C. (2012) *Fame Attack: The Inflation of Celebrity and its Consequences*. London: Bloomsbury Academic.

Rosch, E. (1977) 'Human categorization', in N. Warren (ed.), *Advances in Cross Cultural Psychology*, Vol. 1. New York: Academic Press, pp. 1–49.

Rosenbaum-Elliott, R., Percy, L. and Pervan, S. (2015) *Strategic Brand Management*. Oxford: Oxford University Press.

Rossiter, J.R., Percy, L. and Donovan, R.J. (1991) 'A better advertising planning grid', *Journal of Advertising Research*, October–November: 11–12.

Said, S. (2013) 'David Beckham earns $37 million from commercial contracts alone'. www.therichest.com/sports/david-beckham-earns-37-million-from-commercial-contracts-alone/ (accessed 2 May 2014).

Samuel, L.R. (2016) 'Distinctly un-American: subliminal advertising and the Cold War', *Journal of Historical Research in Marketing*, 8 (1): 99–119.

Sawchuck, K. (1995) 'Semiotics, cybernetics and the ecstasy of marketing communication', in D. Kellner (ed.), *Baudrillard: A Critical Reader*. Oxford: Blackwell, pp. 89–116.

Sayre, S. (2007) *Entertainment Marketing and Communication: Selling Branded Performance, People, and Places*. Upper Saddle River, NJ: Prentice Hall.

Schlosser, E. (2002) *Fast Food Nation*. New York: Penguin Books.

Schor, J. (1998) *The Overspent American: Upscaling, Downshifting and the New Consumer*. New York: Basic Books

Schouten, J.W. and McAlexander, J.H. (1995) 'Subcultures of consumption: an ethnography of the New Bikers', *Journal of Consumer Research*, 22 (1): 43–61.

Schramm, W. (1948) *Mass Communication*. Urbana, IL: University of Illinois Press.

Schroeder, J.E. (2002) *Visual Consumption*. London: Routledge.

Schroeder, J.E. (2005) 'The artist and the brand', *European Journal of Marketing*, 39 (11/12): 1291–305.

Schroeder, J.E. and Salzer-Morling, M. (eds) (2005) *Brand Culture*. London: Routledge.

Schultz, D.E., Tannenbaum, S.I. and Lauterborn, R.F. (1993) *Integrated Marketing Communications*. Lincolnwood, IL: NTC Business Books.

Schultz, D.E., Tannenbaum, S.I. and Lauterborn, R.F. (1996) *The New Marketing Paradigm: Integrated Marketing Communications*. Lincolnwood, IL: NTC Business Books.

Schwarzkopf, S. (2011) 'The subsiding sizzle of advertising history: methodological and theoretical challenges in the post advertising age', *Journal of Historical Research in Marketing*, 3 (4): 528–48.

Scott, L. (1990) 'Understanding jingles and needledrop: a rhetorical approach to music in advertising', *Journal of Consumer Research*, 17 (September): 223–36.

Scott, L. (1994a) 'The bridge from text to mind: adapting reader–response theory to consumer research', *Journal of Consumer Research*, 21: 461–80.

Scott, L. (1994b) 'Images in advertising: the need for a theory of visual rhetoric', *Journal of Consumer Research*, 21: 252–73.

Scott, L.M. (2012) 'Polysemy in advertising', *Advertising and Society Review*, 13 (2): 1–2.

Seregina, A. and Weijo, H. (2017) 'Play at any cost: how cosplayers produce and sustain their ludic communal consumption experiences', *Journal of Consumer Research*, 44 (1): 139–59. https://doi.org/10.1093/jcr/ucw077.

Shankar, A. (2000) 'Lost in music? Subjective personal introspection and popular music consumption', *Research: An International Journal*, 3 (1): 27–37.

Shankar, A. and Horton, B. (1999) 'Ambient media – advertising's new media opportunity?', *International Journal of Advertising*, 18 (3): 305–21.

Shannon, C.E. (1948) 'A mathematical theory of communication', *Bell System Technical Journal*, 27 (3): 379–423.

Sharma, C., Herzog, J. and Melfi, V. (2008) *Mobile Advertising – Supercharge Your Brand in the Exploding Wireless Market*. Hoboken, NJ: Wiley.

Sharp, B. (2010) *How Brands Grow: What Marketers Don't Know*. Oxford: Oxford University Press.

Shaw, D., Carrington, M. and Chatzidikas, A. (eds) (2016) *Ethics and Morality in Consumption: Interdisciplinary Perspectives* (Routledge Studies in Business Ethics). London: Routledge.

Sherer, P.M. (1995) 'Selling the sizzle: Thai advertising crackles with creativity as industry continues to grow', *The Asian Wall Street Journal Weekly*, 1: 6–7.

Sherry, J.F. (1983) 'Gift giving in anthropological perspective', *Journal of Consumer Research*, 10 (September): 157–68.

Sherry, J.F. (1987) 'Advertising as cultural system', in J. Umiker-Sebeok (ed.), *Marketing and Semiotics*. Berlin: Mouton, pp. 441–62.

Sherry, J.F. (1991) 'Postmodern alternatives – the interpretive turn in consumer research', in T.S. Robertson and H.H. Kasserjian (eds), *Handbook of Consumer Behaviour*. Englewood Cliffs, NJ: Prentice-Hall, pp. 548–91.

Shimp, T.A. (2009) *Integrated Marketing Communications in Advertising and Promotion*, international edition. Cincinnati, OH: South Western College.

Smith, R.E. and Yang, X. (2004) 'Toward a general theory of creativity in advertising: examining the role of divergence', *Marketing Theory*, 4 (1/2): 41–58. www.alexandujar.4t.com/generaltheoryofcreativeadvertising.pdf (accessed 26 June 2017).

Srinivasan, S., Rutz, O.J. and Pauwels, K. (2016) 'Paths to and off purchase: quantifying the impact of traditional marketing and online consumer activity', *Journal of the Academy of Marketing Science*, 44 (4): 440–53.

Steel, J. (1998) *Truth, Lies and Advertising: The Art of Account Planning*. New York: John Wiley and Sons.

Stern, B.B.(1993a) 'A revised communication model for advertising: multiple dimensions of the source, the message and the recipient', *Journal of Advertising*, 23: 25–16.

Stern, B.B. (1993b) 'Feminist literary criticism and the deconstruction of ads: a postmodern view of advertising and consumer responses', *Journal of Consumer Research*, 19: 556–66.

Stevens, R. (1996) 'Ten ways of distinguishing between theories in social psychology' and 'Trimodal theory as a model for interrelating perspectives in psychology', in R. Sapsford (ed.), *Issues for Social Psychology.* Milton Keynes: Open University, pp. 45–66, 77–84.

Streeck, W. (2016) *How Will Capitalism End? Essays on a Failing System.* London: Verso Books.

Strong, E.K. (1929) *The Psychology of Selling and Advertising.* Chicago, IL: American Library Association.

Supharp, S. (1993) *Thai Culture and Society: Values, Family, Religion and Tradition*, 8th edn. Bangkok: Thai Watanapanich [in Thai].

Svensson, S. (2007) 'Producing marketing: towards a social-phenomenology of marketing work', *Marketing Theory*, 7: 271–90.

Szmigin, I. (2003) *Understanding the Consumer.* London: Sage.

Szmigin, I., Bengry-Howell, A., Griffin, C., Hackley, C. and Mistral, W. (2011) 'Social marketing, individual responsibility and the "culture of intoxication"', *European Journal of Marketing*, 45 (5): 759–79.

Szmigin, I., Griffin, C., Mistral, W., Bengry-Howell, A., Weale, L. and Hackley, C. (2008) 'Re-framing "binge drinking" as calculated hedonism: empirical evidence from the UK', *International Journal of Drug Policy*, 19 (5): 359–66.

Tadajewski, M. and Jones, D.G.B. (2016) *Historical Research in Marketing Management.* London: Routledge.

Tadajewski, M. and Saren, M. (2008) 'The past is a foreign country: amnesia and marketing theory', *Marketing Theory*, 8 (4): 323–38.

Tanaka, K. (1994) *Advertising Language: A Pragmatic Approach to Advertisements in Britain and Japan.* London: Routledge.

Thielman, S. (2014) 'It's getting harder to separate advertising from entertainment', *Adweek.* www.adweek.com/news/advertising-branding/it-s-getting-harder-separate-advertising-entertainment-156323 (accessed 26 December 2016).

Thompson, C.J. and Coskuner-Balli, G. (2007) 'Countervailing market responses to corporate co-optation and the ideological recruitment of consumer communities', *Journal of Consumer Research*, 34 (2): 135–52.

Thompson, C.J. Locander, W. and Pollio, H. (1989) 'Putting consumer experience back into consumer research: the philosophy and method of existential phenomenology', *Journal of Consumer Research*, 17: 133–47.

Thompson, C.J., Pollio, H. and Locander, W. (1994) 'The spoken and the unspoken: a hermeneutic approach to the understanding the cultural viewpoints that underlie consumers expressed meanings', *Journal of Consumer Research*, 21: 431–53.

Tirakhunkovit, V. (1980) 'Why Thais do not like Thai products', *Monthly Business Journal*, February: 22–9.

Tiwsakul, R. (2008) 'The meaning of Kod-sa-na-faeng: an interpretive exploration of consumers' experiences of television product placement in the United Kingdom and Thailand', PhD Thesis, University of London, Royal Holloway and Bedford New College.

Tiwsakul, R., Hackley, C. and Szmigin, I. (2005) 'Explicit, non-integrated product placement in British television programmes', *International Journal of Advertising*, 24 (1): 95–111.

Toffler, A. (1980) *The Third Wave*. New York: William Morrow & Co.

Tonks, D. (2002) 'Marketing as cooking: the return of the Sophists', *Journal of Marketing Management*, 18 (7–8): 803–22.

Torres, E.C. (2015) 'The intertextuality of works of art in advertising', *Advertising & Society Review*, 16 (3): 4–12.

Towner, T.L and Dulio, D.A. (2012) 'New media and political marketing in the United States: 2012 and beyond', *Journal of Political Marketing*, 11 (1–2): 95–119.

Umiker-Sebeok, J. (ed.) (1987) *Marketing and Semiotics: New Directions in the Study of Signs for Sale*. Amsterdam: Mouton de Gruyter.

Vakratsas, D. and Ambler, T. (1999) 'How advertising works: what do we really know?', *Journal of Marketing*, 63 (January): 26–43.

Vargo, S.L. and Lusch, R.F. (2004) 'Evolving to a new dominant logic for marketing', *Journal of Marketing*, 68: 1–17.

Vaughn, R. (1986) 'How advertising works – a planning model revisited', *Journal of Advertising Research*, February–March: 57–66.

Veblen, T. ([1899] 1970) *The Theory of the Leisure Class*. London: Unwin Books.

Wang, J. (2008) *Brand New China: Advertising, Media and Commercial Culture*. Cambridge, MA: Harvard University Press.

Watson, J. (1924) *Behaviorism*. Chicago, IL: University of Chicago Press.

Weaver, W. and Shannon, C.E. (1963) *The Mathematical Theory of Communication*. Champaign, IL: University of Illinois Press.

Wells, W.D. (1975) 'Psychographics: a critical review', *Journal of Marketing Research*, 12 (May): 196–213.

Wernick, A. (1991) *Promotional Culture – Advertising, Ideology and Symbolic Expression*. London: Sage.

West, D. (1993) 'Cross-national creative personalities, processes and agency philosophies', *Journal of Advertising Research*, 33 (5): 53–62.

West, D.C. and Paliwoda, S.J. (1996) 'Advertising client–agency relationships: the decision-making structure of clients', *European Journal of Marketing*, 30 (8): 22–39.

Wharton, C. (2015) *Advertising: Critical Approaches*. London: Routledge.

Wilkie, W.S. and Moore, E.S. (2003) 'Scholarly research in marketing: exploring the four eras of thought development', *Journal of Public Policy and Marketing*, 22 (autumn): 116–46.

Williams, C. (2016) 'Traditional TV viewing is over: YouTube habit is permanent, warn researchers', *Daily Telegraph*, London, 12 January.

Williamson, J. (1978) *The Semiotics of Advertising*. London: Sage.

Wilmshurst, J. and Mackay, A. (1999) *The Fundamentals of Advertising*, 2nd edn. Oxford: Butterworth-Heinemann.

Wolf, M. (2003) *The Entertainment Economy: How Mega-Media Forces Are Shaping Our Lives*. New York: Crown Business Books.

World Health Organization (WHO) (1988) *Alcohol and the Mass Media*. Copenhagen: WHO.

Xie, C., Bagozzi, R.P. and Troye, S.V. (2008) 'Trying to prosume: toward a theory of consumers as co-creators of value', *Journal of the Academy of Marketing Science*, 36 (1): 109–22.

Yannopoulou, N. and Elliott, R. (2013) 'Open versus closed advertising texts and interpretive communities', *International Journal of Advertising*, 27 (1): 9–36.

Yglesias, M. (2013) 'Sweet Sorrow: Coke won the cola wars because great taste takes more than a single sip', Slate.com. www.slate.com/articles/business/rivalries/2013/08/pepsi_paradox_why_people_prefer_coke_even_though_pepsi_wins_in_taste_tests.html (accessed 25 March 2017).

Young, M. (1995) 'Getting legless, falling down pissy-arsed drunk', *Journal of Gender Studies*, 4 (1): 47–61.

Zwick, D., Bonsu, S.K. and Darmody, A. (2008) 'Putting consumers to work: "co-creation" and new marketing govern-mentality', *Journal of Consumer Culture*, 8 (2): 163–96.

INDEX